Hazik Mohamed and Hassnian Ali
Blockchain, Fintech, and Islamic Finance

Hazik Mohamed and Hassnian Ali

Blockchain, Fintech, and Islamic Finance

Building the Future in the New Islamic Digital Economy

2nd edition

DE GRUYTER

ISBN 978-3-11-074489-7
e-ISBN (PDF) 978-3-11-074501-6
e-ISBN (EPUB) 978-3-11-074514-6

Library of Congress Control Number: 2021951188

Bibliographic information published by the Deutsche Nationalbibliothek
The Deutsche Nationalbibliothek lists this publication in the Deutsche Nationalbibliografie;
detailed bibliographic data are available on the internet at http://dnb.dnb.de.

© 2022 Walter de Gruyter GmbH, Berlin/Boston
Cover image: Infografik: miakievy/DigitalVision Vectors/Getty Images
    Ornamente: Creative-Touch/DigitalVision Vectors/Getty Images
Typesetting: Integra Software Services Pvt. Ltd.
Printing and binding: CPI books GmbH, Leck

www.degruyter.com

Dr. Hazik Mohamed:
> I dedicate this book to my daughters, Aliya and Nadrahuda. and to all their cousins, young and old.
>
> This book contains the shifting trends of the world that you're growing up in. Prepare your contributions for the world to come . . . and the Hereafter that awaits.

Hassnian Ali:
> First, to the most devoted and conscientious person in my life, no one else, my late father Ghulam Hussain.

Advance Praise for *Blockchain, Fintech, and Islamic Finance*

The authors are to be congratulated for this book. It is an important pioneering effort. The work is on the frontier of knowledge in the new area of Fintech. As is well known, the financial sector is suffering from low levels of trust in a trust-intensive industry. Islamic finance too is facing a low-trust environment that has denied it the use of the strongest of its characteristics: risk-sharing. As a result, it has resorted to debt-based financing. Blockchain/smart contracts provide potentially powerful tools to address the low-trust challenge. The authors have done a great service to Islamic and conventional finance by producing a book that should be read by anyone interested in finance and economics.
– Prof. Dr. Abbas Mirakhor, former Holder of the First Chair of Islamic Finance at INCEIF; former Executive Director of the International Monetary Fund (IMF), Washington D.C.

This is an important contribution by the authors to two emerging fields – Islamic finance and Fintech. In this respect, it touches two frontiers as this research could pave the way for the development of both fields. Fintech offers great potential for reaping the benefits of Islamic finance and this book provides an excellent overview of the issues and applications. I am confident that researchers, policymakers, and practitioners would benefit from this important work.
– Dr. Zamir Iqbal, VP Finance and Chief Financial Officer (CFO) of Islamic Development Bank (IsDB), Jeddah; former Head of World Bank Global Islamic Finance Development Center, Istanbul

In this digital era, new technology has proven to bring agility, scalability, innovation, and efficiency in operations and means of doing our work. This book argues, persuasively, that the Fintech and Blockchain applications are not only the channels of fusing technology with Islamic finance; it also lays the foundation for new Islamic digital economy, while keeping in view the Maqasid Al-Shariah. This book is a first-of-its-kind contribution to the literature on constructing the Islamic digital economy.
– Dr. Hussain Mohi-ud-Din Qadri, Patron, International Centre of Research in Islamic Economics (ICRIE) Minhaj University, Lahore

While the growth of fintech firms has already become a game changer in the conventional financial sector, its application in Islamic economy is still in an incipient stage. The authors of this pioneering work deserve appreciation to not only offer a historical perspective on these exciting developments but also suggest ways to building Islamic digital economy with the use of these tools, especially distributed ledger technology. I would recommend this book to all those who are interested in building a trusted, just, and efficient Islamic digital economy.

– Zahid ur Rehman Khokher, Islamic Bnaking Expert
Central Bank of Oman, Muscat

The authors have accurately determined that technology needs to become part and parcel of economics, finance, and policy across Muslim-majority countries. It is critical for the ecosystem to understand what blockchain is and its potential application. The authors lay the groundwork in this book, and it is a must-read for the broad audience whose desire is to focus on a next generation technology, its adoption, and implications.

– Ahmad Magad, former Chairman, MDIS, Singapore

As a pioneering effort, this book continues to be a popular read for many researchers and industry practitioners. This second edition is further illuminated by two new chapters that are often talked about or researched but not satisfactorily addressed. One focuses on the unified Islamic currency which has various implications on trade and cooperation, while the other demonstrates risk management applications for Islamic financial institutions through advanced technologies.

– Dr. Ashraful Mobin, Founder and Managing Director, iFINTELL, Malaysia

The real beneficiary of the COVID-19 pandemic is technology in general and Fintech in particular. In the post-COVID world, Islamic Finance will remain relevant to the needs of the Muslim communities around the world, if it not only adopts modern technologies, like the blockchain, but rather excels in it. The authors have covered a wide range of topics under the broader theme of Islamic Financial Technology. This edition includes some new areas that were excluded in the first one, namely Decentralized Finance (DeFi), Securitized Token Offerings (STOs) and Quantum Computing, etc. There is a completely new chapter on Data Risk Management for Advanced Islamic Financial Institutions. All the changes and additions make this edition an improved resource for those interested in understanding the role of Islamic finance in a futuristic context.

– Dr. Humayon Dar, Chairman,
Director General, Cambridge Institute of Islamic Finance

Acknowledgments

All praises to Allah, the All-Compassionate, the Most Merciful, without Whom nothing is possible. Blessings upon our beloved Prophet Muhammad ﷺ and upon his family and companions.

We acknowledge the advice and recommendation extended by Professor Abbas Mirakhor, Nick Wallwork in the first edition, and Steven Hardman in the present second edition.

We also want to express our appreciation to Jaya Dalal and her team again, who have been very supportive and responsive in making this second edition meet our expectations after a highly successful first manuscript.

Hassnian would like to express his profound gratitude to his mother, Muniran Bibi, and his late father. Their forbearance, guidance and support has been exceptional, and he would not be who he is today without them. Hassnian also acknowledges his wife, Hadia Hassnian, dear sister, Rakhshinda Parveen, his elder brother, Arfan Ali, and especially his twin brother, Muhammad Saqlain, who understands and encourages him to achieve great things.

Dr Hazik recognizes his family for being the heart of inspirational support, especially his wife, Anisa Hassan; his siblings, their spouses, and his in-laws for their generosity and prayers; and his beloved parents (deceased) who laid the foundation of belief, endeavor, fairness, and justice.

Foreword to the First Edition

If you have yet to delve into the world of blockchain and fintech and how they are connected to Islamic finance recently, this book is the most comprehensive and practical book ever written on the topic. It looks deep inside the working protocols of both blockchain and fintech. Interestingly, this book covers all the relevant and interconnected topics, making it a must-read book on the subject of blockchain and fintech.

When I was asked to write a few words reflecting on my thoughts about this book that was sent to me, I immediately felt the vibrancy of this book, even by merely looking at the table of contents. The content coverage and selected issues and subtopics reflect well the intensity of the authors' knowledge and exposure, as well as their intuition. As everyone has been looking for a master key for this most timely knowledge, I am confident this book will prove to be useful and timely.

It may surprise you to know that this book's algorithm fits perfectly well with the issues presented in it. This makes this book special, as everything and anything mentioned in this book is essentially framed by cutting-edge knowledge of blockchain, fintech and, to a considerable extent, the digital economy. This is not an easy task to accomplish, unless the authors are exceptionally articulate in explaining these concepts. They have proven themselves to be masters in this field of knowledge and practice.

This book is equally informative with regard to Islamic finance, covering aspects of the Islamic capital markets, Islamic investment, retail banking, takaful, trade financing, and *sukuk*. I would like to believe that this is the most striking contribution of this book toward the further development of Islamic finance via smart technology. It appears to me that Islamic finance has no other option but to embrace this up-and-coming way of doing banking, insurance, investment, and fundraising. If Islamic finance does not choose to be agile and scalable, as well as innovative, Islamic finance is obviously destined to face constraints and obsolescence, due to stiff competition on many fronts. As the saying goes, life is not the art of avoiding, but is the art of adapting and improving.

The era of digitalization and platform has finally arrived. Nevertheless, this brings less benefits and credence to Islamic finance if Islamic finance refuses to embark on further refinement, enhancement, and perfection via blockchain and fintech. This is one of many insights that the authors of this book are trying to impress upon the readers. You will find all these aspects of this books both challenging and yet promising.

How will your knowledge be transformed after reading this book? I have taken the liberty to pose this question in your early journey embarked upon with this book. I have a gut feeling that any reader – of course with an inquisitive mind – will unlock not only the real potential of Islamic finance in the fourth Industrial Revolution era, but also, more importantly, discover the logic and power of smart technology to accomplish more things smarter, quicker, and safer than an average man is capable of, given the same time allocation and complexity of the tasks at hand.

For all intents and purposes, we can't compete with technology, more so smart technology. We must come to terms to these new technologies. It is reasonable and logical for humankind to embrace these developments and use all sorts of technologies to increase production and efficiency. At some point in time, we need to believe in technology as the savior for some of the complex, compelling problems and crises faced by humanity, even in the space of human sciences. In all honesty, I could be a bit biased in my outlook about smart technology, and that includes blockchain, fintech and artificial intelligence – given the fact that I am also a hardcore practitioner of smart technology in some of my initiatives – but of course, I did not conjure up this sentiment out of thin air. The world has long been moving toward perfection and precision – at least in some areas of life. Any and every evolution in this world started from humble beginnings but it will strike hard when it is the right time. The only problem is that we don't know when the best time for everything is. A quote from Martin Luther King may shed some hope. He once said, "There is always the right time to do what is right."

Obviously, I am not in a position to say for sure when is the right time for this new and smart technology. However, I am confident that this book has emerged at the right time for the readers to be enlightened with comprehensive, trendy, and impactful insights about almost everything that is connected with the themes of blockchain, fintech, digital economy, and Islamic finance.

Finally, I am extremely pleased and delighted to introduce this book to you and I hope you will enjoy reading it as I did.

– Datuk Dr. Mohd Daud Bakar
Chairman of the Shariah Advisory Council at the Central Bank of Malaysia
and the Securities Commission of Malaysia

Preface

The demand for fintech solutions is underscored by the rapid adoption of technology, high-levels of mobile usage and rising rates of internet penetration, an increasingly urban, literate, and young population, as well as a segment of consumers and micro, small, and medium-sized enterprises (MSMEs) underserved by traditional banking solutions. These factors and the economic potential of ASEAN have also attracted large numbers of investors to the sector.

To realize the potential benefits fintech innovation can bring will require commitment and collaboration. Banks, industry leaders, fintech companies, and regulators should continue to collaborate to create an ecosystem to drive greater access to financial services in the Islamic economy. Building the Islamic fintech ecosystem is complicated and it involves various market participants and stakeholders coming together and working toward shared goals of a unified Islamic economic community, increased financial inclusion for the unbanked and the seamless cross-border flow of goods, services, and payments.

The Islamic world is ripe for technology transformation across sectors such as e-commerce, travel, and hospitality, and, of course, financial services. Technology unicorns Lazada, Go-Jek, SEA (formerly Garena) and Grab are just the beginning of a bigger push of tech companies enabling connectivity, consumption, and economic growth. Where 2010 saw the rise of Chinese tech giants and 2015 the re-awakening of the Indian subcontinent, the next five years will be marked by the tremendous opportunities in ASEAN.[1] It was imperative that this book covered the developments of fintech in every region of the world, beyond the traditional markets of North America and Western Europe.

When this project was conceived, there were rapid developments in the Initial Coin Offering (ICO) world due to the rapid rise of bitcoin value, which drove up the prices for other cryptocurrencies as well. Suddenly the attention shifted to the ease of raising capital via a decentralized platform where regulations were non-existent. During this time, there were many ICO projects that were launched and were able to raise large amounts of money within a short period of time. Financial opportunists saw this as a great new way of raising capital for businesses at an early stage (or even at the idea stage) while others saw it as highly risky, being in unchartered territory and unregulated by financial regulators. The problem for regulators was multi-fold and one clear issue was its categorization. The tokens issued at ICOs were used differently and due to their nature, would be needed to be categorized differently. This is also the view from the Shariah perspective.

---

1 https://www.forbes.com/sites/outofasia/2017/08/22/the-5-driving-factors-behind-aseans-im-minent-FinTech-boom/#301d2b845cf3.

As this contentious area continues to generate deeper discussions and attract more attention, the greater opportunities actually lie in the applications of the underlying technology. These opportunities involve the construction of a new digital ecosystem and innovation ecology that is able to disrupt and shift all existing ways of doing commerce, right down to its administration and governance. The applicability of such technologies is now only limited by our imagination, having been transformed by the start-up ecosystems sprouting all over the world and investment capital that chase them. No longer are "unicorn" companies built in certain "Valleys" or the limited geographies of traditionally tech-leading nations; they are now being built, and launched from non-traditional countries like Estonia, Kenya, and Indonesia.

Islamic finance and its digital economy offer opportunities for Muslims and non-Muslims as both populations now seek a convergent solution to their pressing issues – rebuilding trust and confidence in a financial system that had lost them. Some technologists imagine this world without intermediaries, while others just want a faster and more efficient way of transacting. Either way, the challenge comes from accountability, and embedding that sense of accountability within the new systems that are being built, based on the sharing of risks and profits that anchor the nature of our economies, including the sharing economy of underutilized assets.

The history of Muslim innovation dates back to the Golden Age when the Muslim world produced great thinkers who shaped the way we looked at the world, and in particular mathematics. The first mathematical step from the Greek conception of a static universe was made by Al-Khwarizmi (780–850), the founder of modern Algebra. Al-Khwarizmi wanted to go from the specific problems considered by the Indians and Chinese to a more general way of analyzing problems, and in doing so he created an abstract mathematical language which is used across the world today. He enhanced the purely arithmetical character of numbers as finite magnitudes by demonstrating their possibilities as elements of infinite manipulations and investigations of properties and relations. Al-Khwarizmi is also credited for the development of the lattice (or sieve) multiplication method of multiplying large numbers, which was later introduced into Europe by Fibonacci. Al-Khwarizmi carefully laid down analytical solutions of the various forms of the quadratic equation and illustrated his method of solution by practical examples – being the basis of what algorithms do in problem-solving. Since algorithms make up many computational as well as AI solutions today, it is apt to recognize these important contributions by him.

Since there are rotten apples and black sheep even in the virtual world, cybersecurity has become an important component in protecting digital rights and associated digital assets. This will be an important area of development which is constantly evolving because of the creativity of hackers and cyber-criminals. That challenge has been prevalent for the police in the physical world, and it continues to be a challenge in the virtual world.

One of the key takeaways from this book is that it helps the reader craft a strategy to embrace digital disruptions so that any agency, corporation, organization, or entity can respond to them in ways that benefit their stakeholders and people whom they serve. Our sincerest hope is for the readers, especially the youth and industry leaders, to be able to use our work as a companion to their digital journey, in traversing the imperceptible terrain of the unknown and providing sound arguments against change inertia and legacy systems stagnation.

In this second edition, we include three new chapters to this important and necessary journey – new technological risks, a modernized tool to combat charity fatigue and a proposal for a Digital Dinar. Chapter 7 will raise the awareness that with new technologies like AI and blockchain being utilized, we need to be aware of new risks that come with them, particularly those that did not exist before, such as AI data sources risks and blockchain governance protocol risks, amongst others. Chapter 10 will further extend practical applications in Islamic Finance through the conceptualization of a traditional socio-economic tool (the waqf system) to fight charity fatigue (or the weariness of constant giving) via the cash waqf concept, administered by the blockchain to prevent leakages and see through the perpetuity condition. Lastly, Chapter 11 deliberates on the proposal for a Digital Dinar – a unified Islamic currency in digital form to achieve the goal of a unified Islamic economy to improve trade between Islamic nations as well as improve the rights and sovereignty of its citizens.

Contents

Acknowledgments —— IX

Foreword to the First Edition —— XI

Preface —— XIII

Chapter 1
Introduction —— 1
    The Rationale for Financial Disruption —— 1
    Ethics and Technology —— 2
    Digital Transformation and Development —— 3
    Shifts in Customer Behavior —— 6
        Changes in Engagement and Purchasing Behaviors —— 7
    Structure of the Book —— 8
    References —— 10

Chapter 2
Fintech – Definition, History, and Global Landscape —— 11
    Introduction —— 11
    Definition and Concept of Fintech —— 11
    Evolution of Fintech —— 13
        Fintech 1.0 (1866–1987) —— 14
        Fintech 2.0 (1987–2008) —— 16
        Fintech 3.0 —— 18
        Decentralized Finance (DeFi) —— 19
    Global Landscape of Fintech —— 20
        Fintech Investment —— 20
        Fintech in Major Regions —— 20
    Cryptocurrencies, Initial Coin Offerings (ICOs) and Securitized Token Offerings (STOs) —— 25
        Cryptoexchanges —— 32
        e-Wallets —— 33
        ICOs versus STOs —— 37
        Fiqh View on Coins and Tokens —— 39
    Stablecoins and Central Bank-Issued Digital Currencies —— 41
    Critical Importance of CyberSecurity —— 43
    References —— 44

Chapter 3
Importance of Fintech and its Applications —— 47
Introduction —— 47
Financial Innovation within the Financial Services Industry
Perspective —— 48
    Payments Industry —— 48
    Crowdfunding and P2P Lending —— 50
    Neo-Banking —— 52
    Asset under Management —— 53
    InsurTech —— 53
Fintech Within the Technological Perspective —— 54
    Blockchain and Its Applications —— 55
    Cloud Computing —— 56
    Big Data Analysis —— 57
    Internet of Things —— 57
    Robo-Advisors —— 59
    Artificial Intelligence —— 60
    Machine Learning and Deep Learning —— 61
    Quantum Computing —— 63
References —— 64

Chapter 4
Emergence of Islamic Fintech and its Developments —— 67
Introduction —— 67
    What Is Islamic Fintech? —— 68
    Alignment between Islamic Finance and Fintech —— 68
    Islam and Fintech in History —— 70
Islamic Fintech Developments Around the Globe —— 71
    Global Islamic Fintech Landscape and Index —— 72
Islamic Countries' Initiatives for Islamic Fintech —— 75
    Islamic Republic of Pakistan (Islamabad, Lahore) —— 76
    Kingdom of Bahrain (Manama) —— 77
    Kingdom of Saudi Arabia (Jeddah, Riyadh) —— 80
    People's Republic of Bangladesh —— 81
    Malaysia (Kuala Lumpur) —— 82
    Republic of Indonesia (Bandung, Jakarta, Surabaya, and Yogyakarta) —— 87
    Republic of Kazakhstan —— 89
    Republic of Turkey (Istanbul) —— 90
    Sultanate of Brunei (Brunei Darussalam) —— 92
    United Arab Emirates (Dubai) —— 93
    United Kingdom (London) —— 95

Obstacles for Islamic Fintech —— 96
Overcoming the Digital Divide in the Islamic Digital Economy —— 97
Implications for Islamic Digital Economy —— 98
Recommendations —— 100
References —— 104

Chapter 5
Blockchain and the Digital Economy —— 108
Introduction —— 108
    Investments in Blockchain —— 108
    Trends of the Sharing Economy and the Internet of Things Era —— 110
    Open Platforms —— 111
    Web and Mobile (Internet of Things Devices) —— 111
    Cloud-Based (Internet of Things Infrastructure) —— 112
    Clearing Trades and Settlement Transactions —— 112
    Widespread Use of Artificial Intelligence —— 113
    Regulatory Controls —— 114
    Institutional Investment —— 115
    Diversity and Choices —— 115
    User Defined and User Experience —— 116
Trust in the New Sharing Economy —— 116
    Trust and Reciprocity in the Economy —— 118
    Trust and Trustworthiness (Reciprocity) in Islam —— 119
What is Blockchain? —— 120
    Blockchain as Currency and Payments —— 121
    Blockchains as Databases and Public Registries —— 123
    Blockchain as Smart Contracts —— 124
    Blockchain as Clearing and Settlement of Securities Transactions —— 125
    Reduction of Fraud —— 125
    Know Your Customer —— 126
Blockchain Infrastructure —— 128
    Storage —— 129
    Processing —— 130
    Communications —— 132
References —— 133

Chapter 6
Expanded Use Cases of Blockchain —— 134
Smart Contracts in Islamic Transactions —— 134
    How Does a Smart Contract Work? —— 134
    Automation and Enforceability —— 136
    Benefits and Evolution of Blockchain-Based Smart Contracts —— 137

Applications of Smart Contracts —— 137
Capital Markets and Investment Banking —— 138
Commercial and Retail Banking —— 138
Takaful —— 138
Islamic Trade Financing —— 139
Blockchain-Based Trade Finance —— 140
Enablers to Blockchain-Based Trade Financing —— 141
Blockchain-Based Smart Contracts —— 141
Instant Payment Structures —— 142
Current Challenges —— 142
Takaful (Islamic Insurance) on the Blocks —— 143
A Model for a Blockchain-Based Takaful —— 145
Fraud Detection and Risk Mitigation —— 145
Blockchain-Based Islamic Capital Markets —— 148
Payments and Settlements —— 150
Sukuk on the Blockchain —— 151
Distributed Ledger Technology and the Over-the-Counter Market —— 152
Media Rights, Intellectual Property, and Trademark Protection —— 153
Generating Advertising Revenues —— 154
Collections and Copyright Tracking —— 155
LegalTech and the Evolution of Legal Services —— 156
Legal Research —— 157
Contract Management —— 157
Intellectual Property Management —— 158
Automation and Analytics —— 158
eDiscovery —— 158
References —— 159

Chapter 7
Data Risk Management For Advanced Islamic Financial Institutions —— 161
Introduction —— 161
Consumer-Related Risks —— 162
Drivers for AI-Driven Risk Management —— 163
Risks in Data Sources and Big Data Processes —— 165
Risk Management in Various Financial Processes —— 167
Conclusion —— 177
References —— 178

Chapter 8
Evolution of Blockchain —— 180
Introduction —— 180
Transnational Justice Applications for the Economy —— 181

      Coordination and Efficiency in Markets Through
      Consensus-Building —— 182
      Pragmatic Approach to Technology Implementation —— 183
      Get it Going First —— 184
  Overcoming Limitations of Technology —— 186
      Technical Challenges —— 187
      Business Challenges —— 187
      Government Regulatory Challenges —— 188
      Privacy Challenges —— 189
  References —— 190

Chapter 9
Response of Islamic Financial Institutions —— 191

  Introduction —— 191
  Important Success Factors in this Era of Digitization —— 191
      Better Customer Experience with Customer Centricity —— 191
      Agility and Scalability —— 192
      Cybersecurity Management —— 193
  Challenges for Islamic Financial institutions —— 195
      Regulatory Issues —— 195
      Comfort Zones and Stagnation in Management —— 196
      Lack of Talent —— 197
      Role of Academia and Islamic Fintech Education —— 198
  Collaboration Models for Islamic Financial Institutions —— 200
      Islamic Fintech Is Opportunity for Islamic Financial Institutions —— 202
      Collaboration Is Better than Competition —— 203
      Open Platforms —— 204
      Open Banking or Financial Platforms —— 204
      The Financial Institution Owns the Platform —— 205
      Other Ownership of the Platform —— 205
  Conclusion —— 206
  References —— 207

Chapter 10
Cash Waqf (Endowments) Management Through the Blockchain —— 211

  Introduction —— 211
  The Different Use Cases for Blockchain to Enhance Governance —— 212
  The Essentials to Understanding Waqf —— 213
  Historical Examples of Waqf Institutions and Their Contributions —— 215
  Waqf Institutions and Modernization —— 216
  The Distinction of Cash Waqf from Other Waqf Models —— 217
  The Blockchain Cash Waqf Model Development —— 218

What the Cash Waqf System Seeks to Solve —— 221
Benefits of a Blockchainized Waqf System —— 221
Conclusion —— 222
References —— 222

Chapter 11
A Unified Islamic Digital Currency – The Digital Dinar —— 224
Introduction —— 224
Why a Unified Currency is Important for the Muslim World —— 224
Considerations for a Unified Currency for Islamic Countries —— 226
Evolution of Digital Currencies —— 228
The Central Bank-issued Digital Currency (CBDC) —— 230
Proposed Constructs For The Unified Islamic Digital Currency (DIGITAL DINAR) —— 233
    The Aggregated Sovereign Currencies Construct —— 234
    The Islamic Central Bank (ICB) —— 235
    The Basket of Commodities Construct —— 237
    Commodity Reserve Division (CRD) —— 238
    The Fixed Price Schedule —— 239
    Parameters of the Price Schedule —— 239
Benefits to the Digital Dinar Implementation —— 240
Conclusion —— 240
References —— 241

Index —— 243

Chapter 1
Introduction

The Rationale for Financial Disruption

The global financial and economic crisis has done a lot of harm to public trust and confidence in governing and financial institutions, as well as the principles and the concept itself of the market economy. It has also eroded a lot of public trust in corporations. The climate of global financial uneasiness can partly be attributed to the global meltdown of 2008 where governments and other regulatory agents failed in their responsibility to monitor and steer unrestrained speculative and damaging financial activities. Outside of the instrumental complexities of collaterized debt obligations and credit default swaps, the repeal of the Glass-Steagall Act,[1] or macroanalysis of global imbalances (in levels of savings and investment), prominent voices have echoed in unison on the erosion of trust and confidence in the global financial system. The main theme of financial reform in the aftermath of 2008 was basically to encourage greater responsibility after (ex post) and accountability for risks taken prior (ex ante), in the form of not bailing out the bankruptcies, and limiting the increasing complexity of financial instruments, transparency, and answerability for derivative trading to prevent investment managers from making enormous bets with other peoples' money, among other improvements.

In response to the deteriorating fiscal and banking conditions in some countries, and increased financial fragmentation, major governments like the European Union (EU) and the United States had supplied liquidity at very long maturity and at low rates to counter the impending risks for their banks. As the monetary policies struggled to deliver their intended outcomes, credit and economic growth were falling, leading to rising unemployment and reduced consumption and investment. The public grew more restless, with increased resentment and decreased confidence in the ability of their governments to tackle the depressed markets.

This frustration worsened with the bailouts of "too big to fail" entities, and have resulted in very smart individuals creating ways to invent their own trust mechanisms through technology. If you look at bitcoin, for example, its blockchain technology was born out of the need to keep people honest in the absence of a central authority and designed to be public and allow anyone to participate. The design sacrificed efficiency in order to ensure that theft would not pay because rewriting the ledger would require so much computational power. Subsequently, with verifications coming in

---

[1] The Glass-Steagall Act of 1933 was enacted in response to the stock market crash of 1929. This bill was repealed in 1999 by the Gramm-Leach-Bliley Act during the Clinton administration because it was seen as being too restrictive for local banks and businesses to compete with foreign banks.

https://doi.org/10.1515/9783110745016-001

from various nodes all over the world, a system like the blockchain has developed a mechanism of trust where two people who have not met and do not know each other are able to make a transaction through a technology that has done the checks and instilled a level of trust that is required in such transactions, by eliminating fraud and margins for fraudulent activities. This is one of the major reasons that disruptions, especially in the financial industry, are occurring and at a massive scale. Creating a system that is harder to tamper with and easier to audit will lead to great benefits in an industry that is being increasingly regulated by central authorities. Beyond such rationale, other additional benefits lie in operational advantages like cost reductions, improved efficiencies, transparency, and productivity.

Ethics and Technology

Two fundamental concepts in the Islamic worldview that would have significant implications on economic (including financial) behaviors are the concept of man as *khalifah* (vicegerent) and *'abd* (servant/slave). The Qur'an (Surah al-Baqarah, Qur'an 2:30[2]) mentions that the human being has been created to be a *khalifah*, a vicegerent on earth to establish God's commandments,[3] a unique position (with a mission) not granted to other creations. To be a *khalifah*, the human being is endowed with a delegation of authority from God to fulfill "consciously" (not by force) the divine patterns on earth. He is granted free will to either implement or annihilate these divine patterns through his actions. He is the only being that can act contrary to his nature (i.e., not fulfilling God's primordial command), while no other creations be it animals, plants, or angels can do so. Human beings are free to use the bounties and blessings conferred upon them (*taskhir*), but at the same time, they must carry out their duty toward God mainly as an *'abd* (who serve and worship Him) and *khalifah* (who holds *amanah* as God's representative on the earth) to *isti'mar*, that is, to prosper the earth and to create a moral social order on earth. All man's actions, including his economic activities, should be viewed in this complete commitment to God by obeying the prescribed framework.

Another example that shapes the relationship of the ethical concepts that make up the ethical foundation of Islam is the belief of the connection of *dunya* (the present world) and *akhirah* (the hereafter). Muslims are advised to be very conscious of this correlation in every action they take and choices they make. When all economic goals

---

[2] "And [mention, O Muhammad], when your Lord said to the angels, 'Indeed, I will make upon the earth a successive authority.' They said, 'Will You place upon it one who causes corruption therein and sheds blood, while we declare Your praise and sanctify You?' Allah said, 'Indeed, I know that which you do not know.'".
[3] Allah's s.w.t. commandments include establishing justice, fairness, equality, and to fight corruption, evil, and fraud.

are *only* directed to the happiness of human beings in this world, institutions are likely to suffer from immoral sentiments that are opposed to upholding divine laws meant to benefit human beings. In conventional economics, a rational individual is free to maximize his utility as much as possible without any moral, social, or religious commitment. Consideration for a "hereafter" reward and punishment of the consequences of economic choices and decisions made are not included in such a theory. Instead, an Islamic or more enlightened or universal concept of justice and responsible viceregency would constrain an individual maximization of utility in view of the greater good.

The presence of *al-jannah* (Heaven) and *al-jahannam* (Hell) provides "the form of the moral conscience" whenever a man chooses to do anything in this world. It is the very source of moral values. Man, as long as he lives as a member of the Muslim community, is morally required to always make choices that are connected with good and to avoid those that are connected with harm. In fact, these universal principles also apply to all other religions and value systems.

However, behavioral economics informs us that our choices are also governed by our emotions as well as situational factors and the environment. Even with deep moral precepts, our actions are highly influenced by our moods, feelings, and peer pressure, which may be irrational to moral decision making. As such, if the prescribed behaviors of the Economic Man can be mechanized in a system that uses technology to overcome our irrationality, those behaviors that harm the integrity of the financial system in the long run can be prevented. Technological advancement may have the ability to limit[4] poor decisions and detect and prevent fraud and deception early before a collapse in trust and confidence occurs again.

Digital Transformation and Development

The computing power of digital systems is becoming stronger, faster, and cheaper at an exponential rate and it is in line with one of the most famous laws, Moore's Law,[5] that predicted it. Digital Islamic revolution, digitalization, and digital transformation have become the most frequently used words in this last decade, but especially in the last few years. This term of digital transformation has no universal definition due to its diversity and it encompasses many dimensions like digital supply chain, digitalization of services and products, and so on. There is a plethora of definitions of this

---

4 While we encourage the limits to bad decisions, it does not equate to limiting choices. There is a difference in removing opportunities for fraudulent activities and leaving room for possible productive ones like innovation.

5 Moore's Law is named after Intel cofounder Gordon Moore. He observed in 1965 that transistors were shrinking so fast that every year twice as many could fit onto a chip while its costs halved. In 1975 the pace adjusted to a doubling every two years.

term, used to describe the offline-to-online migration of commercial operations and businesses, including those found in many published research works. Solis, Li, and Szymanski (2014, p. 7) defined this term in a concise way in these words: "the realignment of, or new investment in, advanced technology and business models to more effectively engage digital customers at every touchpoint in the customer experience lifecycle." There are also different terms used in different countries with the same concept like "smart industry" and "industrial value chain initiative" in Japan, "industrial internet" in North America and "Industrie 4.0" in Germany and so on (Matzner et al., 2018, pp. 3–21).

What started as a digital transformation has not been restricted or limited to a specific industry but has spread to a number of industries, seeking similar improvements and benefits. This has influence and clout in each and every industry like the health care industry (Belliger & Krieger, 2018), manufacturing industry (Liere-Netheler, Packmohr, & Vogelsang, 2018; Rüßmann et al., 2015), engineering, construction, and architecture industries (Boland Jr., Lyytinen, & Yoo, 2007) and at the top of the list, the banking and financial industry (Kenser, 2018).

The agenda of digitalization has not only received considerable attention from different industries and businesses, but governments and regulatory authorities have also had to keep up with the disruption and changed business environment and markets. They have begun to give importance to and keep abreast with the new era of digitalization in order to be able to remain relevant in their fiduciary and "watchdog" duties. The most recent and latest example of this is the newly formed German government, which emphasized it in their list of most dedicated items (Liere-Netheler et al., 2018). Unsurprisingly, other governments are following suit as studies have shown that the use and adoption of information communication technologies (ICTs) by the large number of population has a very positive relationship with the gross domestic product (GDP) of the respective countries (Mićić, 2017).[6]

Digital transformation is imperative for the financial services industry to remain competitive and achieve longevity in the market. The survival of financial institutions is connected with the adoption of innovation, and in embracing digital transformation, to radically improve efficiency and performance within the organization (Scardovi, 2017). Digital transformation and new technology adoption have changed the way of doing business and channels that offer banking and financial products and services are more intuitive and trustworthy. These new ways may be very different from the past and have resulted in reshaping the existing models of businesses and the creation of new innovative ones. In doing so, the transformations have created new industry and market leaders.

---

6 Mićić (2017) cites different empirical and nonempirical studies that explain the link between digitalization, ICTs, and the national GDP. This study is based on evidence from European countries and concludes that digital transformation has positive impact on the GDP of these countries in terms of growth in productivity, and employment.

According to Forbes (2018) ranking of the top 100 brands, the top five brands are from the area of technology. These five top brands are valued at US$585.5 billion. Table 1.1 provides the Forbes ranking and growth of these five giants.

Table 1.1: Forbes Ranking (2018), Top 100 Brands.

Rank	Brand	Brand Value (US$B)	1-Year Change
1	Apple	$182.80	+8%
2	Google	$132.10	+30%
3	Microsoft	$104.90	+21%
4	Facebook	$94.80	+29%
5	Amazon	$70.90	+31%

In a wider trend, the anecdotal evidence shows that the technological conglomerates have been surpassing other industries from the last decade and also in Forbes rankings in terms of number of brands and value. The most recent report also shows that the number of technology brands (20%) and their value (US$872.6 billion, 40%) are much greater than other industries (see Figure 1.1). The value of the financial services industry is only US$160.2 billion with thirteen brands. This difference of number and value of brands in the tech and financial industries is due to the difference in strategy toward innovation and digitalization.

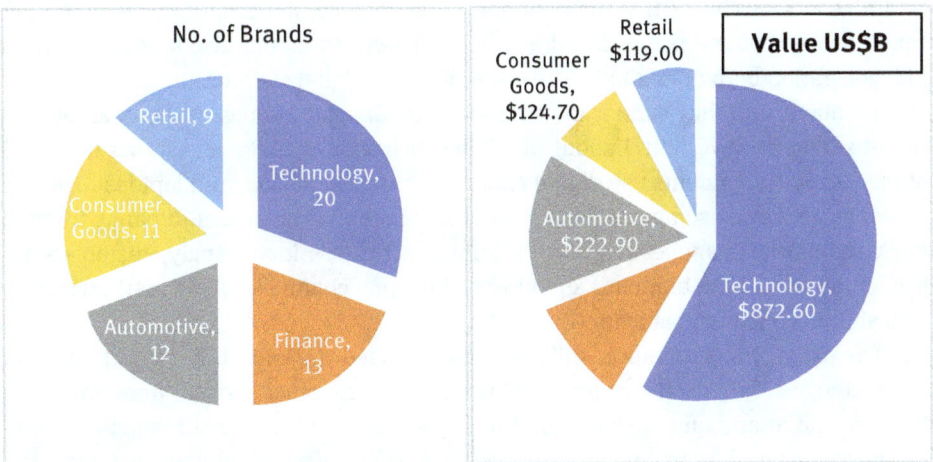

Figure 1.1: Forbes (2018) 100 Most Valuable Brands List.

It was inevitable that technology would meet finance and spawn fintech. The use of technologies like algorithmic machine learning, collecting massive amounts of data and interpreting them for decision-making or "crystal-ball" predictions (predictive analytics), and distributed ledgers (blockchain) in financial industry will give rise to innovative business models with increased levels of efficiency, productivity, cost-effectiveness while also improving on customer-centricity. The most important thing and also a great challenge for both fintech platforms and financial institutions is to adopt and implement a very pertinent, practical, and transparent strategy for digital transformation within the organization as well as in external engagements. This is not only essential to harness the opportunities afforded by such advancements in technologies, but it communicates the vision of the organization moving forward into the new digital economy.

Shifts in Customer Behavior

A customers' journey is the way the customers choose to satisfy their wants and needs and will typically encompass many different processes (Buckley & Webster, 2016). Digital transformation is changing the customers' behaviors in unimaginable ways, and this changing and influence of digitalization in the lives and psychology of customers is very significant for all industries, in particular for the financial services industry.

The new generation's ways of acting and reacting to situations have also changed. The younger generation lives in a different world than their parents lived through. The millennials who are born between 1980 and 2000 encompass more than half of the world's population. They are projected to hold US$7 trillion as liquid assets in 2020 (Aldridge & Krawciw, 2017). The adoption of technology, like smartphones and other smart devices is more popular in the millennial generation and also in digital natives (the generation born after 2000). These youth prefer digital channels to access services and products, and they cannot imagine life without smartphones or the internet. The recent survey by PwC (2017) about the digital behavior of customers shows that 46% of the survey respondents use digital channels, mobiles, tablets, and laptops to access banking services as compared to 27% in 2012. Similarly, the access to banks through brick-and-mortar branches has shrunk from 15% to 10%. Increasingly, customers are leaving physical bank branches and moving to digital channels, which marks a significant shift in consumer behavior (PwC, 2017).

The digital transformation shift has also changed the expectations and wants of the customers. Today, customers want banking (or any other service) from anywhere they are and at any time, regardless of if they are in the office, or at home in the evenings, or at a beach or in a park at the weekend. This digital behavior of customers has set a new bar for different services industries. The industry is trying to fulfill the needs of these digital mindsets by using omni channels and advanced technologies. The competition among financial institutions and fintech platforms to provide more customer-centric services is increasing (Dharmesh, 2016).

In addition, McKinsey[7] notes that fintech startups are moving beyond addressing a customer's financial needs to offering a wider range of services, blurring the industry's boundaries. For example, Social Finance (also known as SoFi), began offering financial products to students and young professionals but has since expanded to provide career coaching and networking services. Another prominent example is Holvi Payment Services, a Finnish start-up acquired by Spanish financial group Banco Bilbao Vizcaya Argentaria (BBVA) in 2016, that began by offering banking services to micro, small, and medium-sized enterprises (MSMEs) and expanded to provide other paired offerings, such as an online sales platform, bookkeeping services, expense-claims systems, and a cash-flow tracker. The scope of products and services offered by fintech companies is expanding rapidly, from being focused on payment applications, lending, and money transfers, their reach now extends into areas that include a broad engagement throughout the value chain. The new offerings cut across a wide range of financial services: corporate and investment banking, insurance, MSMEs, retail, and wealth management.

Changes in Engagement and Purchasing Behaviors

Fintech has also introduced a different way to speak to customers – to understand them, reach out to them through social media channels or any channel the customer prefers, and even accept payments through the means of social media. Businesses can now speak to customers wherever they are at any moment – all thanks to the rate of mobile technology adoption, omnipresent connectivity, and the growing socially enabled apps.

Having a better understanding of how customers behave in their channels of preference also allows businesses to identify the right moment to intervene and develop a comprehensive strategy that works holistically across channels such as search, video, social, and display. This leads to the next important change that happens across industries enabled by their respective fintech solutions – the context and messaging.

Nowadays, the context of conversation between customers and brands is as important as ever. The relevance of the message is arguably the most significant factor predicting the success of the "operation." Companies need to look at how people are searching – the questions they ask, the terms they use – and create ads and content that provide helpful answers.

The ways fintech has contributed to the opportunity to be relevant to every customer without the need for a million customized solutions are with chatbots and chat commerce. Built into messaging apps, chatbots come as close to the customer as possible by being a personal assistant in any endeavor. They provide a relevant answer

---

7 https://www.mckinsey.com/industries/financial-services/our-insights/bracing-for-seven-critical-changes-as-fintech-matures.

and allow them to complete a purchase in an instant. Messenger is an example of a solution that has grown into a platform for chatbots to connect brands with customers, find the exact product customers are looking for and provide an opportunity to buy that product in moments.

Structure of the Book

This book looks at the main building blocks to enable trust in impersonal financial transactions within a highly globalized society. These innovations like artificial intelligence (AI), big data, blockchain, machine learning, internet of things (IoT) devices, are the disruptive tools that will play a crucial role in boosting the financial sector (banking, *takaful* [insurance], investment, etc.) including the Islamic finance sector. Addressing the digital revolution that is happening right now will foster competitive advantage for the Islamic finance industry.

Fintech is a rapidly growing sector of the financial market, which has evolved into a very dynamic area through the rise of smartphone penetration and operational cost reduction. Digital disruption has created a *sharing economy* having the potential to share resources via utilization of underused assets by previously disconnected potential users, and a decentralized scaling power to reach remote and underbanked populations across the world for the enhancement of financial access and inclusion. The blockchain industry is one of the first identifiable large-scale implementations of decentralization models, conceived and executed to scale the complex levels of human activity, possibly even those who have yet to be imagined, which could further establish the sharing economy in the Islamic digital economy.

While this chapter lays down the rationale for financial disruption and explores the emergence of fintech, Chapter 2 examines the different categories of technologies that may have been inaccurately lumped under fintech, which primarily is meant to deal with only the financial industry. In that chapter, we explore its historical beginnings and expand across its movement and scale through the global landscape. In doing so, the chapter sets the foundation and structure, while providing the key concepts needed as a foundation for the understanding of the elements discussed in the remaining chapters.

Chapter 3 iterates the significance of fintech within the current financial services industry from its popular applications like crowdfunding and peer-to-peer (P2P) lending to the trends that will shape it like AI, big data, cloud computing and IoT. Chapter 4 explores the current developments within the Islamic fintech fraternity globally, and tracks the different initiatives being driven by several Islamic countries in the Gulf Cooperation Council (GCC) and the Association of Southeast Asian Nations (ASEAN). It also discusses the challenges faced and impediments to Islamic fintech. Chapter 5 begins by relating the increasing investments into fintech, including the blockchain space, to emphasize the interest in technology that has caused positive disruptions over the last few years. It discusses the potency of fintech and the blockchain for the Islamic economy, along with its potential applications when its capability and strengths are unleashed, very much like what happened for the internet in the late 1990s.

In Chapter 6, the use cases for blockchain are expanded into several key areas that are necessary for the Islamic economy. A key application of the blockchain is the smart contract technology which, along with other enablers like payment, transaction settlement, registries, and document storage systems, will be essential for building more efficient and cost-effective blockchain-based versions of takaful, Islamic capital markets, media rights, property rights, land and title deeds registries, intellectual property, and trademark protection.

Chapter 7 discusses the additional data risk management required when artificial intelligence coupled with blockchain technology are utilized within the Islamic financial management and services industry. Some of the techniques covered on data risk management are those that encompass asset and liability management (ALM) risk, credit risk, liquidity risk, market risk, operational risk, regulatory and Shariah risk compliance within the financial industry, and across all financial sectors. AI can combat financial crime such as monitoring trader recklessness, anti-fraud, and anti-money laundering but the capacity of machine learning (ML) to examine huge amounts of data allows for greater granular and profound analyses in various financial products and services. In utilizing technology in risk management, it is intuitive that using AI itself adds another dimension of risk in the financial risk management framework.

Chapter 8 continues the case studies of the applications into the evolution of the next phase of blockchain where transnational and intergovernmental organizations, like the ASEAN, GCC, International Monetary Fund (IMF), UN, and World Bank are concerned. There is a scale and jurisdiction consideration that certain transnational operations can be more effectively administered, coordinated, monitored, and reviewed at a higher organizational level through a unified blockchain-based system.

Having laid out the relevance, significance, and developments of the global fintech community, Chapter 9 provides recommendations for Islamic institutions to respond in this era of digitization, shifting behaviors of consumers as well as the new challenges that come with it, such as collaboration models to spur innovation, agility, and scalability along with circumventing cybersecurity issues.

Finally, we end this second edition to the widely popular first edition with a chapter that describes a socio-economic tool that may be the key to alleviating lack of provisions, enhancing social services and reducing inequality through active participation by Muslims. Waqf itself does not only refer to non-movable assets but can also include cash endowments but these funds need to be managed sustainably to produce perpetual income. This is only possible if they are properly developed, managed and utilized with accountability, efficiency and transparency. In this applied research, we discuss the use of the blockchain technology to operationalize the specific intents of the Shariah in order to overcome the issues and challenges of traditional waqf administration, collection and disbursement.

References

Aldridge, I., & Krawciw, S. (2017). *Real-Time Risk: What Investors Should Know about FinTech, High-Frequency Trading, and Flash Crashes*. United States: Wiley. Retrieved from http://gen.lib.rus.ec/book/index.php?md5=41c5b796f15ea0e66015278bdac66000

Belliger A., Krieger D.J. (2018) The Digital Transformation of Healthcare. In: North K., Maier R., Haas O. (eds) *Knowledge Management in Digital Change*. Progress in IS. Springer, Cham. https://doi.org/10.1007/978-3-319-73546-7_19

Boland Jr., R. J., Lyytinen, K., & Yoo, Y. (2007). Wakes of Innovation in Project Networks: The Case of Digital 3-D Representations in Architecture, Engineering, and Construction. *Organization Science, 18*(4), 631–647.

Buckley, R. P., & Webster, S. (2016). *FinTech in Developing Countries: Charting New Customer Journeys* (SSRN Scholarly Paper No. ID 2850091). Rochester, NY: Social Science Research Network. https://papers.ssrn.com/abstract=2850091

Dharmesh, M. (2016). Racing from Digital Engagement to Customer Intimacy. https://www.temenos.com/en/market-insight/2016/racing-from-digital-engagement-to-customer-intimacy/

Forbes. (2018). The World's Most Valuable Brands: 2018 Ranking. Forbes Media LLC. https://www.forbes.com/powerful-brands/list/3/#tab:rank

Kenser, K. (2018, March 1). Digital Transformation in Banking and Financial Services. Retrieved June 30, 2018, https://www.tatacommunications.com/blog/2018/03/digital-transformation-banking-financial-services/

Liere-Netheler, K., Packmohr, S., & Vogelsang, K. (2018). Drivers of Digital Transformation in Manufacturing. In *Proceedings of the 51st Hawaii International Conference on System Sciences*.

Matzner, M., Büttgen, M., Demirkan, H., Spohrer, J., Alter, S., Fritzsche, A., . . . Möslein, K.M. (2018). Digital Transformation in Service Management. *SMR-Journal of Service Management Research, 2*(2), 3–21.

Mićić, L. (2017). Digital Transformation and Its Influence on GDP. *Economics, 5*(2), 135–147.

PwC. (2017). Digital Transformation in Financial Services. Retrieved June 30, 2018, https://www.pwc.com/us/en/industries/financial-services/research-institute/top-issues/digital-transformation.html

Rüßmann, M., Lorenz, M., Gerbert, P., Waldner, M., Justus, J., Engel, P., & Harnisch, M. (2015). Industry 4.0: The Future of Productivity and Growth in Manufacturing Industries. *Boston Consulting Group, 9*, 1–20.

Scardovi, C. (2017). *Digital Transformation in Financial Services*. Switzerland: Springer International Publishing Access date: March 04, 2018. www.springer.com/gp/book/9783319669441

Solis, B., Li, C., & Szymanski, J. (2014). The 2014 State of Digital Transformation. *Altimeter Group*, 1–38.

Chapter 2
Fintech – Definition, History, and Global Landscape

Introduction

In the past, fintech was dismissed by traditional financial industry professionals as new skin on old rails. In actuality, Fintech sets new performance standards and has the potential to raise traditional banking and financial industry by offering customer-centric services and upgrading financial products and services designs. It also promotes greater financial inclusion through better means for customers to access the financial products and services. This chapter details the definition and concept of fintech, followed by the evolution and history of its existence. It also attempts to paint the global landscape of fintech, which includes fintech investments in major regions including Europe, the United States, Asia, and Africa, to provide a broad understanding of the changing financial landscape.

Definition and Concept of Fintech

Fintech in the etymological and general perspective is the portmanteau of financial technology, refers to an emerging financial services sector that is fast becoming indispensable to financial institutions, and is constantly impacting the way technologies support or enable banking and financial services. Freedman (2006, p. 1) in his book *Introduction to Financial Technology* describes financial technology as being concerned with building systems that model, value, and process financial products such as stocks, bonds, money, and contracts. Schueffel (2016) defined fintech as "a new financial industry that applies technology to improve financial activities" after making an analysis of more than 200 scholarly studies over the last forty years. We believe that this newly minted term can be associated with start-ups and companies that are providing highly innovative and pioneering financial services or products with the combination of information technology (IT) enabling ventures or by using the latest available technology.

Waupsh (2016) explained the three groups of fintech products as white label, direct, and gold label. "White label" is the type of product that is delivered to end users of financial institutions through the financial institutions. These products are not developed by the financial institutions themselves but are purchased from a fintech vendor who developed them. Examples of these products include Moven's work with TD bank and Westpac in Canada and Bill Pay from Check-Free. The second, "direct (to consumers or to business)" is directly delivered from fintech platforms to consumers and to business. Examples of this type are Stripe, Venmo, Square, and Wealthfront. The third type, in between the above two, is "gold label" and has features of both types of products. Like direct, gold label fintech products are branded solutions to reduce user problems and also have unique features. But these are also designed for financial institutions to help them compete like white-labeled products and services. These are also distributed by the financial institutions. Examples of this type are ApplePay, Dwolla, and Kasasa.

One of the basic differences between fintech and the bulk of the traditional financial institutions, is the use of advanced, innovative, and digital technologies. The traditional financial industry has large built-in IT infrastructures, and the industry is spending a big part of revenues on IT and its infrastructure like servers. But the emerging fintech companies are the ones creating products using more advanced technologies such as internet of things (IoT) devices, mobile phones, blockchain-based innovations, big data analytics, and machine learning. By using these technologies fintech companies are providing cheap and easy-to-access services, from transfers and trading to crowdfunding, while operating largely outside of the banking regulations.

The "fintech" term was coined by Bettinger in 1972 in his "FINTECH: A Series of 40 Time Shared Models Used at Manufacturers Hanover Trust Company." Fintech's popularity began in the early 1990s and was initially used as a reference to the "Financial Services Technology Consortium" – a project started by Citigroup in order to assist technological cooperation efforts. Santarelli (1995) cited many studies on technological innovation and economic advancement, which were conducted during the 1980s and 1990s and showed that economic development can be enhanced and reinforced through the fusion of new technologies. However, as Figure 2.1 shows, it was only after 2014 that the sector took off and attracted the attention of the masses, which included everyone from technologists and researchers to industry participants, regulators, and consumers alike. Forward-looking nations started accelerators, incubators, and designed fintech ecosystems for their industry to thrive and to remain competitive in the increasingly globalized financial environment.

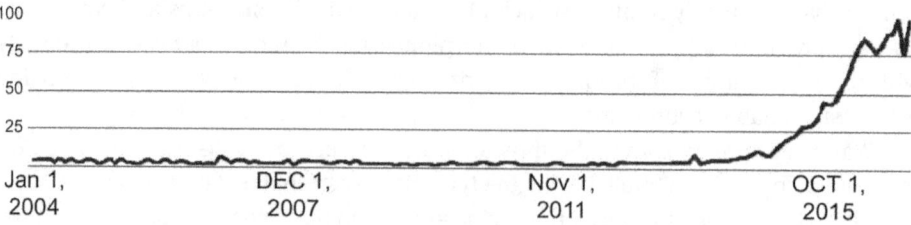

Figure 2.1: Group Trends.

As such, new and ultra-modern models of business are being introduced in the market continuously. Fintech has become one of the most dynamic, engaging, and energetic segments of the financial services marketplace. The most active areas of fintech are data analytics, artificial intelligence (AI), digital payments, digital currencies, crowdfunding, and other forms of peer-to-peer (P2P) financing. Table 2.1 shows the top sectors and investment in those sectors in 2017.

Table 2.1: Investment by Sectors (2017).

Sector	Investment (Year 2017)
Mobile Payments	US$450 billion
P2P Lending	US$9 billion
InsurTech	US$2.1 billion
Blockchain	US$512 million

Source: Compiled from KPMG, 2018 and Statista, 2018.

Evolution of Fintech

There have been four stages (Table 2.2) of industrial revolution, in which the first Industrial Revolution used steam power and water to mechanize and increase production. The second Industrial Revolution used electric power to create the bulk production. The third used advanced electronics and information technology to make the production autonomous. Now we are in the fourth Industrial Revolution that features the digital revolution that started and has been occurring since the middle of the last century. It is typified by a fusion of technologies and cyber-physical systems that are blurring the lines between the economic, physical, biological, and digital spheres.

Table 2.2: Stages of Industrial Revolution.

First Stage	Second Stage	Third Stage	Fourth Stage
1780s–end of eighteenth century	1870–start of twentieth century	1960–1970	1970–present
Start from mechanics, introduction of first water- and steam-powered mechanical manufacturing facilities	Introduction of electrically-powered mass production based on the division of labor	The usage of electronics and IT to achieve further automation of manufacturing	Introduction of cyber physical systems

Source: Modified from Henning (2013).

It is important to discuss three major eras of the fintech evolution. The first era, known as fintech 1.0, was from 1866 to 1987 where the financial industry, while progressively became interconnected with technology, was widely still an analog industry. The next era started in 1987, during which the financial services industry in developed countries were not only becoming significantly globalized but also innovative and leveraging on digital technologies. This period was characterized as fintech 2.0 and this era continued until 2008. During this period, fintech was largely controlled by the traditional regulated financial industry that used technology to deliver financial products and services. Since 2008, we saw the emergence of fintech 3.0 where a large number of new entrants (start-ups) and innovative technology companies have started to provide financial services and products directly to several businesses and the general public. In the following sections, each fintech era is discussed in detail. Table 2.3 summarizes the fintech evolution.

Table 2.3: Summary of Fintech Evolution.

Date	1866–1987	1987–2008		2009–present
Era	Fintech 1.0	Fintech 2.0	Fintech 3.0	Fintech 3.5
Geography	Global/developed	Global	Developed	Emerging/developing
Key Elements	Infrastructure	Banks	Start-ups/New entrants/innovators	
Shift Origin	Analogue linkages	Digitalization	2008 financial crisis	

Source: Modified from Arner, Barberis, & Buckley (2015).

Fintech 1.0 (1866–1987)

In the late nineteenth century, the merger of technology and finance created and established the foundation of the first period of financialization that continued until the start of World War I. During this period, new technologies such as the telegraph, transatlantic cable, steamships, and railroads built financial interlinkages across the borders, permitting speedy transmission of financial transactions, transfers, and payments around the globe. Meanwhile, the technological advancements together with essential resources enabled deeper research and development of new innovations and other existing technologies.

The pantelegraph was invented by Giovanni Caselli in 1865, which was most commonly used to verify signatures in banking transactions. The very first telegraph was introduced in 1838, which was followed by the laying down of the first transatlantic cable in 1866. It provided the fundamental infrastructure for the first cross-border financial transaction in the late nineteenth century. In 1900, consumers and merchants exchanged their goods using credit for the first time in the shape of charge plates and credit coins. The Fedwire Funds Service was established in 1918 by the Federal Reserve Banks to transfer funds and connect all twelve Reserve Banks by telegraph using the Morse code system. It was the first code system used in the banking industry. J. M. Keynes, the renowned economist wrote *The Economic Consequences of the Peace* in 1920 and gave a clear description of the correlation between finance and technology in the first phase of the modern economic exchange: "The inhabitants of London could order by telephone, sipping his morning tea in bed, the various products of the whole earth in such quantity as he might see fit, and reasonably expect their early delivery upon his door-step" (Keynes, 1920, pp. 10–12).

The first modern-day credit card was created in 1950 by Ralph Schneider and Frank McNamara who founded Diners Club. The broad acceptance of credit cards was later boosted by massive payment networks of Visa and Mastercard who worked out agreements with merchants. Quotron Systems introduced the Quotron in 1960, the first electronic system to provide selected stock market quotations to brokers through desktop terminals. The global telex network was put in place in 1966, which played a crucial role in providing the communications necessary for the next stage of financial technology development. Code-breaking tools were developed commercially into early computers by firms such as International Business Machines (IBM), and the handheld financial calculator was first produced by Texas Instruments in 1967. Barclays Bank introduced the first automated teller machine (ATM) in 1967, calling it a "robot cashier," which allowed customers to get cash around the clock. The ensuing decades between 1967 and 1987 was the time when financial services moved from analog to digital.

The Clearing House Interbank Payments System, or CHIPS, was established in 1970 to transmit and settle payment orders in American dollars for some of the largest and most active banks in the world. The NASDAQ – National Association of Securities Dealers Automated Quotations – was established in 1971 in the United States, which signaled the end of fixed securities commissions. The Society for Worldwide Interbank Financial Telecommunications, or SWIFT, was established in 1973 to solve the problem of communicating cross-border payments. The first online brokerage, E-Trade, was founded in 1982, when it executed the first electronic trade by an individual investor. It is also worth mentioning that the first online banking platform was introduced in Britain in 1983 by the Bank of Scotland for the Nottingham Building Society (NBS) customers. It was called "Homelink" and became the first internet banking system by connecting via a television set and the telephone to send transfers and pay bills. The world's first online shopper, Jane Snowball, in 1984 used a Gateshead SIS/Tesco system to buy food from Tesco (Zimmerman, 2016).

Throughout this period, financial services providers enhanced their IT budget and its use in their financial operations, steadily replacing different types of paper-based methods and procedures by the 1980s, as computing power developed and risk management technology proceeded to manage different internal risks. Among the noteworthy examples of fintech innovations that are widely recognized by financial experts and professionals would be the Bloomberg terminals. Michael Bloomberg began Innovation Market Solutions (IMS), later to be known as Bloomberg LP, in 1981 when he left Solomon Brothers, where he used to design in-house computer systems. IMS called its product Market Master at first, and the twenty original units operated at Merrill Lynch at the end of 1982. In the 1980s, stock exchanges from New York to Tokyo were going electronic, a prerequisite for a truly sophisticated online service for traders. And fortuitously, Bloomberg terminals were in ever-increasing use among financial services providers (Arner et al., 2015) along with other forward-looking devices such as the over-the-air (wireless) portable pocket receiver QuoTrek, which gave instant stock market quotes to traders. The Bloomberg Terminal of today provides more than 325,000 subscribers (as of October 2016) with everything from an array of information on financial matters to a chat system to the ability to actually execute trades. It processes 60 billion pieces of information from the market a day.

Fintech 2.0 (1987–2008)

The year 1987 is considered historic because the risks regarding cross-border financial connections and their link with digitalization and technology attracted the attention of regulators. One of the most powerful images from this period is that of the investment banker wielding an early mobile telephone, which was first introduced in the United States in 1983 and completely illustrated in Oliver Stone's film Wall Street in 1987. That same year also witnessed the "Black Monday" stock market crashes whose impact on markets around the world clearly depicted they were interconnected through technology in a manner not seen since the 1929 crash. Almost thirty years later and there is still no clear consensus on the causes of the crash, at the time much focus was placed on the use of computerized trading and finance systems by financial services providers, which bought and sold automatically based on preset price levels. The reaction led to the introduction of a variety of mechanisms, particularly in electronic markets, to control the speed of price changes ("circuit breakers"). It also led securities regulators around the world to begin working on mechanisms to support cooperation, in the way that the 1974 Herstatt Bank crisis and the 1982 developing country debt crisis triggered greater cooperation between bank regulators in respect to cross-border issues (Traxpay Team, 2016).

The heavily digitalized financial services industry in the late 1980s was established on e-transactions between financial industry participants, financial services providers, and customers around the globe, by using the fax, having augmented the telex. In 1998 financial products and services had developed for all practical objectives into the first digital industry. The collapse[1] of Long-Term Capital Management

---

[1] Due to the small spread in arbitrage opportunities, LTCM had to leverage itself highly to make money. At the fund's height in 1998, LTCM had approximately US$5 billion in assets, controlled over US$100 billion, and had positions, whose total worth was over US$1 trillion. At the time, LTCM also

(LTCM) coincided with the Asian and Russian financial crises of 1997–1998 showed the initial risks and limits enabled by complex computerized risk management systems. However, it is important to be aware that the highly leveraged nature of LTCM's business, coupled with a financial crisis in Russia (i.e., the default of government bonds), caused massive losses and made it difficult for LTCM to cut its losses in its huge positions, totaling roughly 5% of the total global fixed-income market, and had borrowed massive amounts of money to finance these leveraged trades.

However, it was the emergence of the internet that set the stage for the next level of development, beginning in 1995 when Wells Fargo used the World Wide Web (WWW) to provide online account checking. By 2001, eight banks in the United States had one million customers online, with other main jurisdictions around the world rapidly developing the same systems and related regulatory frameworks to address risk. By 2005 the first direct digital banks having no physical branches emerged (e.g., ING Direct, HSBC Direct) in the UK.

In the 2000s, advancements in internet connectivity paved the way for a host of new fintech companies to introduce consumer-facing solutions. PayPal was launched in 1998 and it was among the early fintech companies that started transforming the way people managed their money through payments. eBay was also one of the first e-commerce empowerment websites that permitted consumers to create the market and establish prices for auction items. And it all began to snowball from there (Desai, 2015). Crowdfunding was started by a Boston musician and computer programmer (Brian Camelio from the United States) when he first launched a project based on the website with the name of ArtistShare in 2003 (Freedman & Nutting, 2015).

By the start of the twenty-first century, financial institutions' internal operations, cross border interactions and an ever-growing number of their connections with retail customers had shifted to digital mechanisms. Moreover, financial regulators were becoming habitual of technology usage, particularly when it came to securities exchanges, which in 1987 was the most reliable source of information related to market manipulation because their trading systems and records were computerized.

During this era, it was expected that the e-banking solutions' providers would be dominated and supervised by financial institutions, but this is no longer necessarily the case. Although the use of the term "bank" in many jurisdictions is limited to companies duly regulated as financial institutions, there were many new entrants, start-ups, and firms called fintech companies providing different financial services. The fintech companies of that decade were providing services for transfer, payments, investment management, and lending. Envestnet and Yodlee were founded in 1999, Mint in 2006, and Credit Karma in 2007 providing services for personal finance and investment management. Xoom was founded in 2001, and Payoneer in 2005 providing

---

had borrowed greater than US$120 billion in assets. https://www.investopedia.com/terms/l/longterm capital.asp.

services for money transfer and currency. Prosper was founded in 2005, Lending Club in 2006, and OnDeck in 2007 providing lending services. Klarna was founded in 2005, Adyen in 2006, and Braintree in 2007 providing services for payments. Trading and data analysis provider fintech companies are MarketAxess, which was founded in 2000, Market in 2003 and BATS Global in 2005 (FinTech Switzerland, 2016a).

In other words, in developing markets there may be a lack of "behavioral legacies" whereby the public expects that only banks can provide financial services. For this populace, as it was rightly stated by Bill Gates in 1994, "banking is essential, banks are not." Services will be essential to financial transactions, but bank branches will shrink as such services can now be provided on any mobile phone.

Fintech 3.0

The third era of fintech demonstrated that financial services providers may not merely rest with regulated financial services industry. The provision of financial products and services by the institutions called nonbanks may also mean there is no reliable home financial regulators to act on the concerns of host financial regulators, and so whether the provider is authorized or not may make a little difference. It is possible to say that the 2008 Global Financial Crisis was a turning point and has increased the growth in the fintech 3.0 era.

The post-2008 situation was an alignment of market conditions, which laid the groundwork for the emergence of innovative market players in the financial services industry. The rise of Fintech 3.0 is deeply rooted in the financial crisis, where the erosion of trust occurred. People's resentment toward the banking system was the perfect breeding ground for financial innovation. This is considered as good timing, because digital natives (millennials) were becoming old enough to be potential customers and their preferences pointed to the mobile services they understood and mastered, instead of bankers they could not relate to. In this favorable landscape, fintech providers were able to offer new and fresh services at lower costs, through well-designed products or services via mobile apps.

The first-version cryptocurrency bitcoin emerged and was introduced in 2009, providing an equivalent type of transaction and also exchange of digital assets. It was a new type of asset, a new kind of investment. It opened up a cashless way for people to transact conveniently. In 2011, Google released the Google Wallet. In 2016, mobile phone giants Apple and Samsung released their e-Wallet — Samsung Pay and Apple Pay. Before the emergence of this payment solution, PayPal was offering an electronic payment gateway to connect buyers and merchants, which enabled online payments to be used widely. Since then, many other fintech companies have emerged in payments business.

Fintech 3.0 started and emerged as a reaction to the financial crisis along with the JOBs Act in the West, but in Asia and Africa recent and latest fintech developments have been primarily provoked by the pursuit of economic development. Some experts characterize the era as fintech 3.5. In Asia, Hong Kong, and Singapore have seen the formation of three fintech accelerators in less than a year, providing them one of the greatest concentrations of fintech accelerators in the world. Korea also has set up an expanded version of Level 39 (London's prominent FinTech coworking space).[2] On the regulatory side, Asian regulators have initiated a Fintech strategy and met in 2013 in Kuala Lumpur to discuss this agenda alongside the World Capital Market Symposium (Arner et al., 2015).

Eventually, a new sharing economy has emerged, steadily shifting consumers into producers. Robo-advisors are using algorithmic programming so they can provide automated investment advice and produce personalized investment portfolios at a fraction of the cost of human advisors. Online lenders have begun to germinate, providing credit to a widely underserved market of businesses and consumers largely ignored by the traditional banks. Crowdfunding sites are also opening digital channels of financing for new entrepreneurs, many of whom are launching their own fintech start-ups, thus creating a continuous stream of innovative products and services.

Decentralized Finance (DeFi)

DeFi is short for "decentralized finance" for a variety of financial applications in frontier technologies geared toward disrupting financial intermediaries. It removes the traditional central authority from the transactional equation and ensures direct exchange between counterparties.

We are witnessing two fast-growing trends merge and complement each other: The first one is tokenization, where all illiquid assets in the world, from private equity to real estate and luxury goods, become liquid and all liquid assets can be traded more efficiently—either through the exchange of tokens directly between counterparties or traded indirectly though crypto-exchanges or token exchange platforms. The second is the rise of a new tokenized economy where these tokenized assets are accepted as new asset classes, and cryptocurrencies (including stablecoins and tokens) are currency for goods and services. Inevitably, new transactional rules will be established within the digital economy that will guide economic behaviors that are productive, efficient, and just. By unlocking the economic potential of the blockchain, these two complementary and correlated trends will complete the decentralization of finance and the way financial services of smart cities of the future will be implemented. There is a huge opportunity for Islamic economics and finance to participate in determining and implementing its prescribed rules of risk-sharing and

---

[2] British fintech investor to set up S. Korean unit, KOREA TIMES (Oct. 22, 2015), http://www.koreatimes.co.kr/www/news/nation/2015/10/116_189263.html.

social justice in decentralized financial transactions. One of the key factors that will make DeFi work and gain wide acceptance is being able to uphold the principle of self-governance. If trust was eroded due to flaws and incompetence's of the conventional financial system, and the decentralization movement was born out of this, then DeFi needs to show how the economy can function without central authorities and regulations.

Global Landscape of Fintech

Fintech has revolutionized the entire financial services industry by using innovative and advanced technologies such as blockchain, big data and analytics, cloud computing, AI, IoT, and robo-advisors. By deploying these technologies, fintech promises to reshape finance by improving efficiency and quality of financial services, cutting costs, providing agility, and eventually creating a new global financial landscape powered by fintech.

Fintech Investment

From payments to wealth management, from P2P lending to crowdfunding, a new generation of small firms, entrants, and start-ups are emerging, with fintech firms attracting US$19 billion in investment in 2015 (up from US$12 billion in 2013) (Figure 2.2). While 2015 was a record year in terms of deals and dollars invested in venture capital (VC)-backed companies, 2016 continues to see a noticeable pullback in activity. At the current run-rates, both deal count and total global funding are expected to fall significantly under last year's figures (Su, 2016). In 2017, global fintech financing hit a new record of US$16.6 billion as compared to 2016 (it was US$13.3 billion) (CB Insights, 2018).

The segments of fintech that attracted the most investments were InsurTech, with US$2.2 billion, followed by Direct Lending with US$1.9 billion and P2P lending (US$1.1 billion). In the infrastructure and enabling technologies category, main investments went into business tools (US$697 million) – a strong sign of the digital transformation of enterprises – and cryptocurrencies (US$374 million) (Su, 2016).

Fintech in Major Regions

Europe
Investment in fintech has witnessed a decline in Europe particularly in VC investment during Q3′16 due to Brexit vote and market uncertainty. The total number of fintech deals declined to thirty-eight and investment dropped by half, from US$400 million in Q2′16 to US$200 million in Q3.

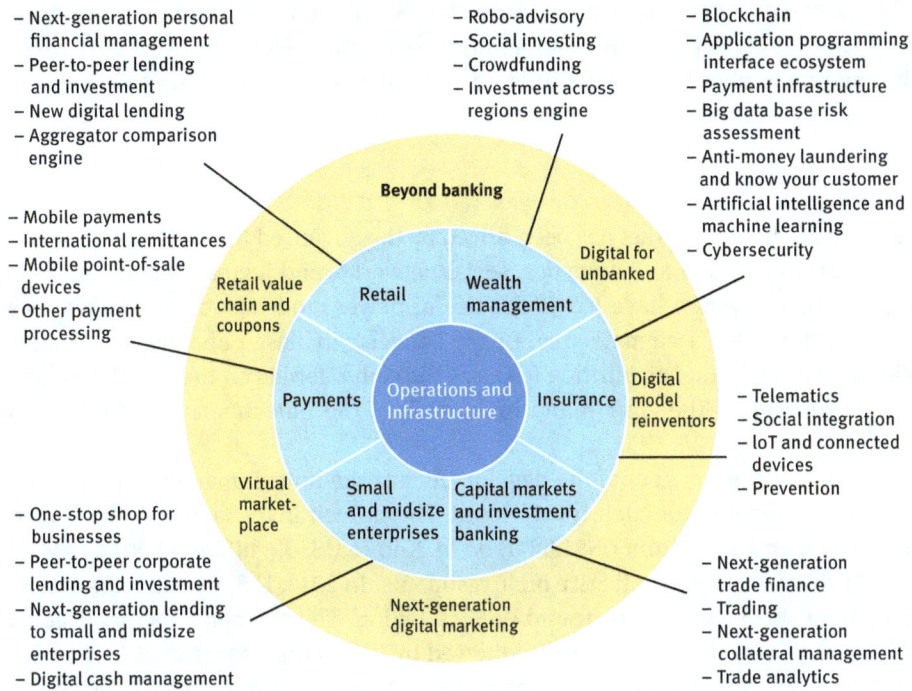

Figure 2.2: Emerging Fintech Trends.
Source: https://www.mckinsey.com/industries/financial-services/our-insights/bracing-for-seven-critical-changes-as-fintech-matures

Despite this, in the UK and Ireland especially, the collaborations between banks and fintech companies continued to increase, such as the Bank of England's fintech accelerator, banks are beginning to take space in incubation hubs to allow direct and ongoing interface with fintech startups. Large financial institutions are seeking fintech companies as more than an investment. Through these fintech collaborations, banks want to create and adopt solutions that can reduce risk and improve customer engagement.

In 2016, in the fintech market of this region, robo-advisory gained traction in the personal and retail banking sectors, especially for front-line customer response or as a tool in an advisor's toolbox. Now, fintech companies are also looking to combine artificial intelligence with robo-advisory solutions to offer personalized customer recommendations more efficiently. This type of development will attract investors to the European fintech market. Germany also showed continued strong performance among the European fintech companies and Switzerland made deals with Singapore for future deals (KPMG & H2, 2016b).

In Q3'17, investment in fintech companies in Europe hit US$1.66 billion across seventy-three deals (KPMG & H2, 2017) Statista forecasted that the transaction value in the European fintech market amounted to US$640.46 billion in 2017. This transaction value is expected to show an annual growth rate of 14.5% (CAGR 2017–2021) resulting in a total of US$1.1015 trillion in 2021. It is also estimated that the number of potential users is expected to amount to 523.4 million by 2021 (Statista, 2016).

United States
The American fintech market has been driven by the advanced technological developments such as big data and analytics, social networks, and increased penetration of the smartphone, which have led to the rise of newer models such as marketplace funding and people-based marketing. Digital connectivity, faster and instant payment options, lower customer acquisition fee costs through referrals on the social networks have contributed to the growth and innovation of the fintech space in the United States.

One of the main factors of the development of the fintech market in the United States is the appetite for such investments. The fintech investments in the United States had seen a peak from US$1.6 billion in 2010 to US$3.4 billion in 2013. In 2014 and 2015 there was a dramatic rise on investments. In 2014, U.S. investments almost tripled from US$3.4 billion to around US$ 9.9 billion. The payments sector attracted the highest proportion of investment followed by the lending space in 2015. The fintech market increased in terms of the transactional value from 2010 to 2015 at a CAGR of over 20% during 2010–2015 (Ken Research, 2016). During Q3'17, fintech investment in the United States continued to be dominated by deals being conducted in the United States. Of the US$5.35 billion invested across the Americas, the United States accounted for over US$5 billion (KPMG & H2, 2017).

Statista forecasted that transaction value in the fintech market amounted to US $1.026 trillion in 2017. And it is also expected to show an annual growth rate CAGR of 17.9% during 2017–2021 resulting in the total amount of US$1.983 trillion in 2021 and the number of potential users is expected to amount to 288.0 million by 2021. The expected market's largest segment is the segment of digital payments, which will attain a total transaction value of US$738.34 billion in 2017 (Statista, 2016).

We observed that the fintech market in North America witnessed peaks and valleys in deal activity and investments. In Q1'16, there were 130 deals, which declined and decreased to 97 deals in Q2'16. Despite this decline in deals, corporate involvement and participation in North American fintech company deals were reasonable, with California taking the lead in Q2'16 for fintech funding, beating contender New York by 200% that quarter.

The overall investment in North American fintech dropped under US$1 billion during Q3'16 showing a trend toward smaller deals not a lack of deal activity. The deal activity in the region was positive during Q3'16. North America saw 96 fintech deals in Q3'16, which was 50% more than in Asia.

The drop-in investment or lack of mega deals in the region during Q3'2016 was due to uncertainties related to the outcome of the U.S. presidential election and the timing of the rate hikes in United States. But in Q4'16 there was the change in the behavior of investors toward fintech markets in the region (KPMG & H2, 2016b). In Q3'17, investment in the United States hit US$5.35 billion across 158 deals (KPMG & H2, 2017).

Asia

Fintech investment in Asia-Pacific quadrupled in 2015 to US$4.3 billion. Now, it is the second-biggest region for fintech investment after North America, accounting for 19% of global financing activity, which is up from just 6% in 2010.

Among the Asian countries, China has the lion's share of investment, 45% in 2015, but India makes up 38% and is growing fast. Bangalore, Mumbai, Tokyo, and Beijing are the main fintech hubs in the region by the number of deals. Looking at deal volumes, 78% went to fintech companies targeting the banking industry, 9% to wealth management and asset management companies and 1% to the insurance sector. Payments are the most popular segment for fintech deals in Asia-Pacific, accounting for 38% of the total (Sparklabs, 2016).

Fintech in Asia faced fluctuated values in 2016, such as a decrease in Q2'16, but Q3'16 saw growth in fintech funding despite a decline in deal activity. Among the other regions of the globe, Asia was the only main region that witnessed an increase in funding between the Q2'16 and Q3'16, with total funding more than North America. It appears that investors will fix their focus in Asia if the fintech funding continues to exceed that of North America for extended periods.

The fintech VC investment in Asia with its peaks and valleys revolves around the worth of US$1 billion plus a large number of deals. For example, lu.com and JD Finance accounted for approximately half of the overall fintech funding in Asia in mega deals in Q1'16. Q2'16 witnessed a rapid drop in mega deals. But, Q3'16 recorded a comeback and attained a high growth in fintech investment; the two major deals of this quarter were US$449 million to Qufengi and US$310 million to 51xinyongka (also known as U51.com).

The fintech market in Asia observed investor focus in areas such as blockchain, data analysis, and RegTech. RegTech is mainly to focus on assisting the regulatory financial institutions in managing their regulatory duties more diligently and effectively. RegTech is gaining attention in the jurisdictions of Hong Kong, Australia, Singapore, and Malaysia; these jurisdictions have started in this area due to initiatives by Sand Box. In Asia, India-based investments have seen a decline because investors focus on higher-quality deals. Singapore aspires to become a fintech hub of the future.

The VC-backed fintech companies in Asia raised US$1.2 billion in funding across 35 deals in Q3'16. On a year-over-year basis, Asia fintech funding is on pace to top 2015's total by 30% at the current run rate (KPMG & H2, 2016b).

Statista reported that the transaction value in the fintech market in Asia was US $1.404 trillion in 2017. The transaction value is estimated to show an annual growth rate (CAGR 2017–2021) of 25.1% resulting in a total amount of US$3.436 trillion in 2021. Statista reported that the transaction value in the fintech market in Asia was US$1.404 trillion in 2017. Moreover, from a global comparison perspective, it has also been shown that the highest transaction value worldwide was reached in China at US$1.086 trillion in 2017 (Statista, 2016).

Africa
Fintech also has immense potential in Africa and the Middle East. Magnitt, a networking business for Middle Eastern start-ups, lists fifty-four new fintech companies across the Middle East and North Africa region, twenty in the UAE alone (Shubber, 2016). The fintech innovators of these regions are M-pesa, Liwwa, Zoomal, Finerd, PayFort, MadfooatCom, Fawry, and Democrance, etc. These platforms are providing services include payments, P2P lending, insurance and wealth management, etc. The payment sector in the Middle East has the highest potential among fintech innovators (Haley, 2016).

Kenya is the best-known fintech hub in Africa. The technical talent pool is maturing with improvements in developments and skills. Regionally, Kenya has a quite stable political environment and attracts fintech companies from other parts of Africa, especially in the sub-Saharan region. The main fintech companies are Innova, Pesa Pal, KAPS LTD, Craft Silicon, and big investors are Savannah Fund, NEST, Centum Investment, Novastar Ventures. M-PESA through its mobile money transfer system has revolutionized the way Kenya does business. It was launched in 2007 and within a short time period more than 17 million Kenyans used M-PESA, which is also accessible on even the simplest mobile phone. MODE was founded in 2010 and provides instant nano-credit for prepaid mobile phone users across Africa. It now has operations in thirty-one countries with a customer base of over 250 million (Deloitte, 2016). Statista forecasts that the transaction value in the fintech market in Africa Middle East (MEA) amounts to US$59.776 billion in 2017 and it is expected to show an annual growth rate (CAGR 2017–2021) of 17.3% resulting in a total amount of US$113.269 billion in 2021 (Statista, 2016).

Fintech is a rapidly growing sector of the financial market. It has witnessed different eras of development along with the different phases of industrial revolution. During fintech 1.0 this sector has gained infrastructural development, which includes the introduction of technologies such as the first trans-Atlantic cable and ATM. FinTech 1.0 was limited to analog technologies and due to this, it remained nonglobalized. Fintech 2.0 was the shifting from analogue to digital and obviously, it was era that pushed fintech toward becoming more globalized. New entrants and start-ups emerged and started working in this era, but still, regulatory financial institutions dominate the financial services industry. Fintech 3.0 emerged after the financial crisis of 2008, which had a catalyzing effect on the growth of fintech due to growing distrust of formal regulatory financial institutions; the public welcomed new entrants, such as the massive use of smartphones and reduction in operational costs. On a global level, fintech investments in various regions like the United States, Europe, Asia, and Africa are continuously growing. Fintech has also played a significant role in creating the sharing economy,[3] which has the potential to maximize the utilization of possessions and transform idle assets so they become productive.

Cryptocurrencies, Initial Coin Offerings (ICOs) and Securitized Token Offerings (STOs)

Cryptocurrencies are virtual digital currencies and named as such because cryptographic techniques lie at the heart of their implementation (He et al., 2016). In modern times the advent of cryptocurrencies is traced to the emergence of the first cryptocurrency, that is, bitcoin in 2009. Historically, the idea and concept of storing important information by using cryptographic techniques is considered older, as the term crypto is taken from an ancient Greek word Kryptos, which means "hidden." Some of the records show that ancient Egyptians also used cryptography as it is evidenced by the use of ciphers by Julius Caesar in 100 BC to 40 BC. This means cryptography has historical roots and has passed through different civilizations (Fry, 2018).

After the emergence of bitcoin in 2009, the experiments in cryptocurrencies started happening in 2011 with the release of SolidCoin, iXcoin, Namecoin, and others. As of August 1, 2018, there are more than 1,737 different cryptocurrencies in the market. This number of cryptocurrencies breaks down into 819 coins and 918 tokens. According to CoinMarketCap data, the combined market of overall cryptocurrencies to date is valued at US$269 billion. Table 2.4 shows the increase in number of cryptocurrencies from June 2013 to the August 2018.

It is very important to distinguish between cryptocurrencies and "tokens" and also "cryptosecurities," as these all are considered cryptoassets. The cryptotokens and cryptosecurities are a very different type of cryptoasset and far beyond the purpose of medium of exchange as in the attribute of cryptocurrencies.

Cryptotokens are also recorded on distributed ledgers and secured by cryptography. There are different types of tokens on the distributed ledger network. These cryptotokens have some sort of claims attached to them, and some tokens resemble

---

3 The Sharing Economy matches underutilized assets with potential users. Grab/Go-Jek/Lyft/ Uber and Airbnb have transformed idle assets into economic value – by drastically changing social behavior and replacing transaction costs in order to match users with assets. In the Sharing Economy, people must become comfortable enough to trust others so they will forego the expense of insurance contracts, lawyers, security systems, and even private ownership enforcement, to enjoy the benefits of sharing assets.

Table 2.4: Number of Cryptocurrencies Available Since June 2013.

Jun 02, 2013	14	Jun 05, 2016	593 (+2%)
Dec 01, 2013	40 (+186%)	Dec 04, 2016	645 (+9%)
Jun 01, 2014	298 (+646%)	Jun 04, 2017	809 (+25%)
Dec 07, 2014	529 (+78%)	Dec 03, 2017	1273 (+57%)
Jun 07, 2015	542 (+2%)	Mar 21, 2018	1568 (+23%)
Dec 06, 2015	580 (+7%)	Aug 1, 2018	1737 (+10%)

Source: Modified from HiveEx, 2018, *lobal Cryptocurrency Exchange Trends, Report & Statistics March 2018 and CoinMarketCap.com*

traditional shares and bonds. They are referred to as "security tokens" or "investment tokens" or "equity tokens." These tokens are the digital presentation of a share in a company or a cooperation that have the most features of traditional shares and bonds but represent a very small fraction of worldwide token issuance (ICO). The more popular ones are those that provide their holders access to future services and goods. These tokens are referred to as "utility tokens." Other types of tokens include "asset-backed token" – tokens that represent some physical asset like gold or real estate, "vote tokens," tokens that confer their holder a right to be involved in a project development and "hybrid tokens," tokens that are the amalgamation and combination of two or more types of tokens.

Cryptosecurities are a concept to securitize assets, just like other securities, but on the blockchain. According to Burniske and Tatar (2017), until March 2017, there were more than 800 cryptoassets in the market. The international policymakers including World Bank, IMF and others also taking an interest in cryptocurrencies. Table 2.5 depicts the perception of policy makers regarding cryptocurrencies.

From the different points that are mentioned above by different policymakers, it appears that there are different perspectives on its definition. The definition and perspective of World Bank and FATF provides an understanding of cryptocurrencies that they are a medium of exchange having a unit of account and a store of value but not a legal tender status as there is no central authority that guarantees them. It is also noteworthy that the different definitions indicate that the structure and use case of each token is also constantly evolving, making it, at times, very difficult to categorize them effectively. This is discussed further in the section "*Fiqh* View on Coins and Tokens."

Currently, there are a slew of cryptocurrencies that have been introduced, and their legality varies across different jurisdictions. Figure 2.3 shows the status of the cryptocurrencies in thirty selected countries.

Due to the advent of cryptocurrencies and also blockchain technology the central banks of major economies started to think and work on their own Central Bank's Digital Currency (CBDC). The central banks of different countries are at different stages regarding CBDC framework (see Figure 2.4).

Table 2.5: Definitions of Cryptocurrencies.

European Central Bank (ECB)	"Cryptocurrencies that are bilaterally linked to the real economy: there are conversion rates both for purchasing virtual currency as for selling such currency; the purchased currency can be used to buy both virtual as real goods and services."
International Monetary Fund (IMF)	"The cryptocurrencies are the subset of virtual currencies as the digital presentation of a value. The concept of virtual currencies covers a wider array of 'currencies,' ranging from simple IOUs ('Informal certificates of debt' or 'I owe you's') by issuers (such as Internet or mobile coupons and airline miles), virtual currencies backed by assets such as gold, and crypto-currencies such as Bitcoin."
The Committee on Payments and Market Infrastructures (CPMI), a body of the Bank for International Settlements (BIS)	They mentioned cryptocurrencies as *digital currencies* or *digital currency schemes*. *These schemes have the following features:* – They are assets, the value of which is determined by supply and demand, similar in concept to commodities such as gold, yet with zero intrinsic value – They make use of distributed ledgers to allow remote P2P exchanges of electronic value in the absence of trust between parties and without the need for intermediaries – They are not operated by any specific individual or institution
The European Banking Authority (EBA)	The digital representations of value that are neither issued by a central bank or public authority nor necessarily attached to a fiat currency but are used by natural or legal persons as a means of exchange and can be transferred, stored, or traded electronically.
The European Securities and Markets Authority (ESMA)	The virtual currencies are defined as "digital representations of value that are neither issued nor guaranteed by a central bank or public authority and do not have the legal status of currency or money."

Table 2.5 (continued)

World Bank	WB classified cryptocurrencies as a subset of *digital currencies*, which it defines as digital representations of value that are denominated in their own unit of account, distinct from e-money, which is simply a digital payment mechanism, representing and denominated in fiat money. In contrast to most other policy makers, the World Bank has also defined cryptocurrencies itself as digital currencies that rely on cryptographic techniques to achieve consensus.
Financial Action Task Force (FATF)	Has approached cryptocurrencies as "a subset of *virtual currencies*, which it defines as digital representations of value that can be digitally traded and function as (1) a medium of exchange; and/or (2) a unit of account; and/or (3) a store of value, but do not have legal tender status (i.e., when tendered to a creditor, are a valid and legal offer of payment) in any jurisdiction."

Source: Modified from (Houben & Snyers, 2018).

This is the most interesting time for Islamic countries, especially for the Organization of Islamic Countries (OIC), to harness this opportunity that blockchain and the concept of cryptocurrencies offer. OIC must think and work on the uniform digital currency for the entire Islamic world. This will be a breakthrough for the Islamic finance industry as well, which is continuously facing criticism for following conventional benchmarks since its inception.

One of the major breakthroughs in the crypto world is the emergence and rise of initial coin offerings (ICOs). It would be clearer if we refer to this term as initial cryptoassets offerings, as the word "coin" implies that it includes only currencies. This is defined as a type of crowdfunding that uses blockchain or other distributed ledger technology as a decentralized P2P network as an underlying system with the cryptoassets (cryptocurrencies, cryptotokens, and cryptosecurities) on the top.

Crowdfunding and ICO, both have several similarities and differences. The similarities are: first, both are used as a way of raising funds for a project or company; second, in the fundraising process due to a public call for funds, everyone can invest; third, in both approaches, internet provides the basis for payment and communication and anyone from anywhere can contribute to any project; and finally, mostly in both ways of fundraising, contributors get something as a reward for their contribution. There are some differences in both approaches: foremost, the difference of an employed system as crowdfunding platforms use centralized and regulated systems and in contrast, an ICO utilizes a blockchain based decentralized P2P network to

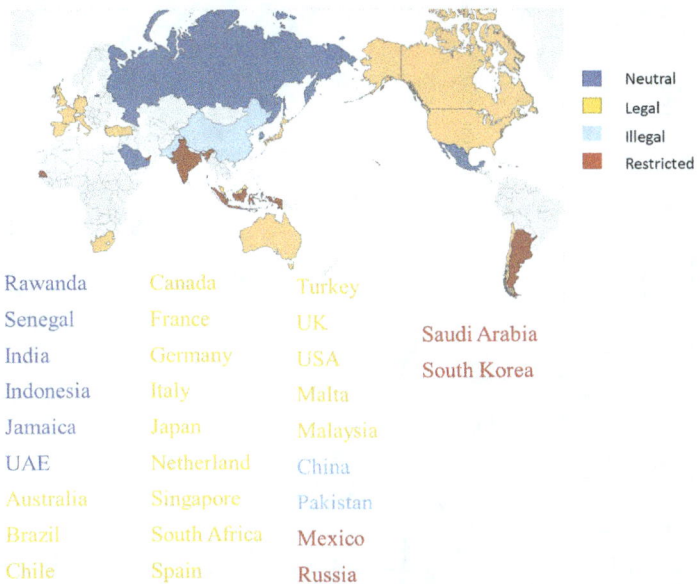

Figure 2.3: Legality of Cryptocurrencies, 2018.
Source: Modified from CoinGecko, 2018; Shafi, Patel, Collins, & Haidermota, 2018.

conduct operations. And in a crowdfunding campaign, the platform and banks act as trusted parties while, in an ICO, a network wide consensus mechanism is involved to verify the transactions.

The first successful ICO was the result of an experiment done by a software developer, J.R. Willet in 2013. He was excited by the opportunities offered by blockchain technology and cryptocurrencies like bitcoin and also wanted to do more with them. He explored that this technology can be used for some complex functions rather than just sending and receiving payments. He tried to raise funding in the shape of cryptocurrency by using a blockchain-based decentralized channel. He built a mechanism through which anyone could send or contribute a bitcoin to the team for the project (MasterCoin) and in return the contributor would receive tokens as rewards. Finally, Willet's idea succeeded and in July 2013, his team had a fund of 5,000 bitcoins with a worth of $500. This process of raising funds was known as an ICO like the term initial public offering (IPO). After this first ICO, in 2014, Ethereum raised funding for their project in bitcoin (BTC) valued at $18 million at the time. This was followed by many successful ICOs like new web browser called "Brave" that in May 2017 generated the amount of US$30 million.

30 — Chapter 2 Fintech – Definition, History, and Global Landscape

Interest	Research	Experimentation	Implementation

Sverige's Risk Bank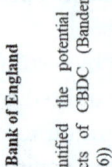

Detailed research plan on issuing retail CBDC (e-krona) as a complement to cash. Decision on issuing CBDC will be made by 2019

Bank of Estonia

Announced intention to launch "estcoin" via initial coin offering (ICO), as part of its e-Residency program (established in 2014) that allows foreign investors to virtually site them busines in the country.

Bank of Japan

Collaborating with the European Central Bank to explore how DLT could be applied to financial market infrastructures (e.g. interbank payment system) Less optimistic about readiness of DLT for real-world application and to be used by central banks

Bank of England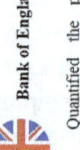

Quantified the potential macroeconomy effects of CBDC (Banden and Kumhof (2016))

U'S Federal Reserve

Staff research on applications of DLT on payments, clearing, and settlement.

European Central Bank

conceptual framework on potential CBDC

Bank Negara Malaysia

Staff research on the framework of CBDC and also applications of DLT and cryptocurrencies on payments etc.

Bank of Canada

Simulated a decentralized CBDC for Large interbank settlements using DLT, beat found some gaps. Next phase is focused on building a modified DLT to address gaps (Project Jasper) (Dec 2016)

Monitory Authority of Singapore

Successfully simulated a decentralized CBDC for Large interbank settlements (Project Ubon) (Mar 2017). Next phase is focused on fixed income securities trading and settlements and cross border payments

People's Bank of China

Exploring technologies to establish a CBDC. Reported to have begun conducting trial runs of its prototype cryptocurrency among retailers (Feb 2017)

Central Bank of the Russian Federation

Conducting pilot runs to proof the viability of different CBDC schemes on various technological platforms (June 20)"

Central Bank of Ecuador

First central bank to implement centralized CBDC for the public ("Dinero Electronic"). Under this scheme. the CBE exclusively manages e-money, and allows citizens to hold an e-money account at the central bank (Dec 2015) Implementation met with mixed success, riddled by slow take-up rates and concerns raised on its reliability

Figure 2.4: Milestones in CBDC by Central Banks.
Source: Modified from Bank Negara Malaysia, BNM, 2017.

Figure 2.5 shows the total investment amount and number of projects, depending on country of registration.[4] Current leading countries are the United States, UK, and Singapore, while in 2017 the leaders were the United States, Switzerland, Singapore, Estonia, and the UK.

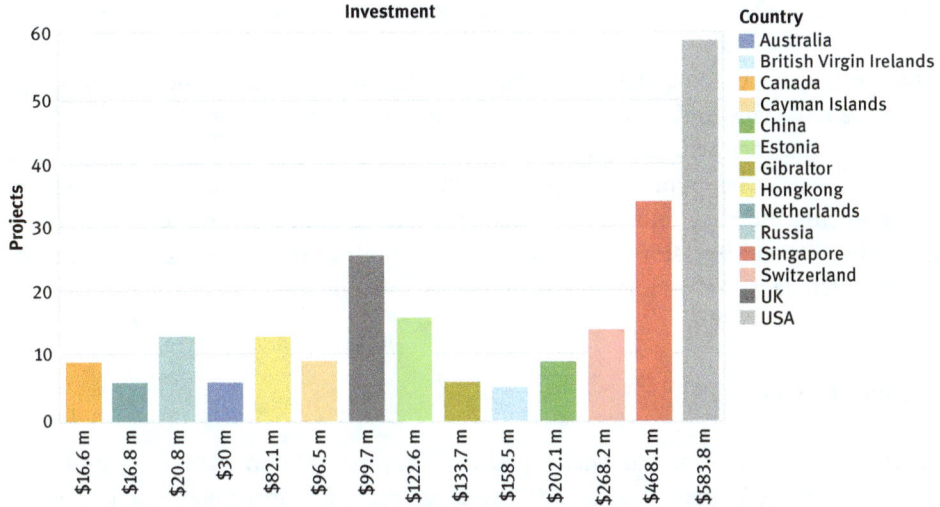

Figure 2.5: Geographical Distribution of Projects by Country Registration.
Source: Modified from ICORating, 2018, *ICO Market Research Report Q1 2018*.

According to the report provided by PwC (2018), the ICO volume between January 2018 and May 2018 is twice as much as it was in the entire year of 2017. The PwC report states that:

In total, 537 ICOs with a total volume of more than US$13.7 billion have been registered since the beginning of the year. In comparison, in 2017 there were a total of 552 ICOs with a volume of just over US$7.0 billion. Also, the average size of an ICO has almost doubled from US$12.8 million to over US$25.5 million since last year.

In the first quarter of 2018, the projects related to blockchain infrastructure and the financial services industry are raising more funds through ICOs followed by gaming, augmented reality (AR) and wallets. The funds raised by cryptocurrencies in that quarter were accounted to be US$4.5 million (ICORating, 2018).

Due to the explosive growth of ICOs, various countries have started to think about their regulations. In Switzerland, the Crypto Valley has launched its ICO code of

---

[4] Country of registration means the country where the company's legal entity is registered at the time of the ICO. If a project does not have a legal entity, it is not included in this table. Country of project registration is determined on the basis of open data, including projects' official websites and open databases of registered companies.

conduct, Thailand is taking the initiative to regulate ICOs, the state of Arizona in the United States has aimed to define when ICOs would be considered as securities in Arizona law, UK crypto companies are teaming up to form a self-regulatory body, German regulatory authorities will publish a note on ICOs, Austria has planned to make new regulations for ICOs, the United States also announced that money transmitter rules will be applied to ICOs, the Dutch finance ministry also called for ICO regulations, Japan authorities have cracked down against illegal ICO operators, and Gibraltar has announced policies to regulate ICO tokens as commercial products (CoinGecko, 2018).

ICOs have emerged as a new and relatively easier way of raising funds and it is expected that they will need more regulations in place as various innovative ICO structures enter the cryptomarketplace. Some argue that ICOs will disrupt the overall financing industry, but others consider them as additional options to venture capitalists, angel investors and crowdfunding platforms due to their unique features of P2P decentralized networks, use cases and agility.

Cryptoexchanges

As the number of cryptocurrencies has gone beyond 1700 in 2018, the number of cryptoexchanges is also expanding in the same trend. Cryptocurrency exchanges are "persons or entities who offer exchange services to cryptocurrency users, usually against payment of a certain fee (i.e., a commission). They allow cryptocurrency users to sell their coins for fiat currency or buy new coins with fiat currency. They usually function both as a bourse and as a form of exchange office." As compared to only 70 exchanges in 2015, currently, this number exceeds 190 exchanges around the globe. This is due to an increase in demand to buy and trade cryptocurrencies. Majority of the top cryptoexchanges allowed consumer to buy, sell and trade cryptocurrencies be it bitcoin, Ethercoin, or Litecoin and also sovereign fiat currencies like Euros, U.S. dollars, or Yen. Different exchanges support different types of cryptocurrencies, and some are suited for retailers while others seem geared toward full time traders or institutions. Table 2.6 exhibits the top 15 cryptoexchanges operating at global level.

From the regulatory perspective, each exchange is governed by law based on the location of the exchange. An international exchange must follow the law of multi-jurisdictions. Not all the exchanges are regulated, some of them are still unregulated and vulnerable to regulatory issues. In 2017, due to the complete ban by the Chinese government on trading of cryptocurrencies, the exchanges based in China had to move their offices outside the country. At the end of 2017, Japan's regulatory authority also suspended these services of cryptoexchanges to the customers within the country as per new guidelines issued by the Japanese Financial Services Agency. As for the United States, the exchanges in different states of America are subjected to State regulations, which vary from state to state, on top of compliance to Federal regulations. In New York, the state has implemented "BitLicense" in 2015 that issued

Table 2.6: The Top 15 Cryptoexchanges (1st half of 2018).

Name	Location	Year Found..	24-Hour Tradin..	Tradeable c..	Accepts fiat
Bibox	China with Global operati..	2017	$205.97 million	62	No
Bity-Z	Hongkong, Beijing, Singa..	2016	$226.78 million	74	No
Bitfinex	Hongkong	2012	$424.61 million	79	Yes
Bithumb	South korea	2017	$266.51 million	37	Yes
BitMEX	Hongkong	N/A	$1.71 billion	1	No
Coinbase	San Francisco, California	2012	N/A	4	Yes
GDAX	San Francisco, California	N/A	$130.141 million	4	Yes
Gemini	New York	N/A	$21.97 million	3	Yes
HitBTC	Hongkong	2013	$263.93 million	22	No
Huobi	Multiple Asian Offices, Un..	2013	$685.60 million	248	Yes
Kraken	San Francisco, California	2011	$135.69 million	17	Yes
OKEx	Hongkong	N/A	$1.15 billion	145	Yes
UPbit	South korea	2017	$265.75 million	142	Yes
ZB.COM	Samoa	2017	$261.35 million	61	Yes

Source: Modified from (Hansen, 2018).

licenses to approved virtual currency businesses. Unlike the traditional regulated exchanges, decentralized exchange users have to protect their details of transactions with their own private keys. Being unregulated, the protection afforded by traditional exchanges are not in place or enforced. Such decentralized exchanges include EtherDelta, Hodi Hodi, and AirSwap, but enthusiasts of these decentralized exchanges claim that decentralized exchanges are less susceptible to cyberattacks by virtue of their decentralized network (Olagoke, 2018).

e-Wallets

Historically, the digitization of payments started in the 1960s when electronic computing penetrated the government and business world. In the meantime, the banking and finance industry was among the early adopters of digitization. The consumers of the developed world were able to make payments in the form of papers and plastic cards. The payment infrastructure was established, where the major players were banks and the government (central bank). The second domain or stage of evolution of e-payments arrived with the advent of internet and ecommerce. In the initial period, the old players offered their services (credit transfers, direct debits, etc.) online. The old payment services or payment infrastructure was not developed for the internet and these systems were not optimal in terms of security and usability. This situation opened up an opportunity for new entrants and for new services that fit the needs of the internet era. PayPal is the best example of that era, and still is today. Due to the emergence of new platforms, especially in the payments industry in 2005, the banks and banking communities started to introduce their own online banking systems. Banks built their online websites to attract and engage the tech savvy customers and also to compete with the emerging platforms. In the meantime, the behavior of consumers was changing and they were becoming increasingly more tech savvy. The merchants, in a push to remain competitive, offered a diverse range of payment methods and options to keep their customers and acquire new ones. But these involved agreements with banks and payment platforms, which had to comply with financial regulations. At this stage, the payment service providers (PSPs) used this opportunity to lower the burden of merchants. They made the necessary arrangements with the banks and payment platforms to reach consumers. Merchants only had to connect once with any PSP and they were dialed in. This new segment in payments facilitated the rise of digital payments around the globe. In 2009 the PSPs were regulated under Payment Services Directive 1 (PSD1). With the emergence and appearance of smartphones in 2007, the new stage in the evolution of e-payments began. Smartphones with near field communication (NFC) technology and QR codes offered a new channel of making payments, which was called mobile payments, and this laid the foundation for mobile commerce.

The ubiquity of the smartphone removed frictions for all the players in the payments industry. The myth of "anytime, anywhere, and any device" became a reality, and made shopping on the go easy and convenient. Amidst these developments in the payment industry, the big social media channels (Facebook, WeChat), mobile commerce giants (Alibaba, Amazon), search engine (Google), and telecoms (Apple and Samsung) started offering their own channels (via apps and interfaces) for payments on these platforms. Now, we have Apple Pay, Alipay, Amazon Pay, Google Pay, Samsung Pay, and also Facebook payments. Though most of these payment options have certain limitations, they mark a great potential to develop and grow in the future as more and more customers are engaging with these modes of payments.

Along with these new modes of payments, these channels provide the option of e-wallets to the consumers (The Paypers, 2017) to facilitate payments using cryptos. At the global level, the proliferation of e-wallets has intensified with these brands (Samsung Pay, Apple Pay, and Android Pay). Banks have also started to compete by developing their in-house e-wallets and merchants are also partnering with banks and fintech start-ups to develop their own e-wallets. According to a report (Research and Markets, 2018) the global mobile wallet market was valued at US$594 billion in 2016 and is estimated to reach approximately US$3.14 trillion by 2022, with CAGR of around 32% between 2017 and 2022.

Table 2.7 exhibits the details related to the general description (definition of e-wallets), payment instruments, payment guarantee, brands, and market reach of e-wallets.

Table 2.7: All You Need to Know About an e-wallet.

General Description	An e-wallet is a digital and virtual tool (app or software) that offers consumers the opportunity to store their payment credentials and methods. It stores users' credentials of credit, debit cards and also other alternative payment methods. Some e-wallets are also able to store loyalty programs. An e-wallet permits an individual to make electronic transactions with an improved checkout and payment experience compared to reentering and keying in all payment credentials every time a purchase is conducted. An e-wallet can function both in physical and online stores. – e-wallet providers can also be global payment method providers, for example, Visa and Mastercard; or maybe independent, for example, Seamless/SEQR – The term "wallet" is also frequently used for e-money, that is, a stored-value account for which a license is required
Functions	The functions of e-wallets are: – Interaction alternatives (through social media, e-mail, text messages, and voice) – Information access (app search, mapping, or service discovery, price comparison, information shopping list) – Security, payments, and financial services (identity storage [ID card, driving license or passport], mobile banking, financial services, P2P payments, financial details, Instore NFC proximity, security management) – Shopping (digital coupons, promotions, transit tolls, food, ticketing, travel, entertainment, gift cards and vouchers) – Customer relationship building (location-based marketing, loyalty programs, and targeted advertising)
Types	On the basis of creation of e-wallets, there are three types: – Closed e-wallets: These are created by an entity for facilitating the purchase of goods/services from it, for example, GrabPay. – Semi-closed e-wallets: These are similar to closed e-wallets but users can get financial services at specific merchants, which have signed a contract with the developer to accept them, for example, AirTel Money in India. Closed and semi-closed e-wallets do not permit cash withdraw or redemption. – Open e-wallets: Open wallets can be used to purchase goods and services at any merchant location that accepts e-wallet (point of sale) and also to withdraw cash from ATMs and banking correspondents, for example, M-Pesa.

Table 2.7 (continued)

Payment instrument	Depending on the e-wallet provider, several payment methods can be used: debit card, credit card, gift card, online banking e-payment, direct debit and recently, cryptocurrencies as well. As of 2017, there were over 150,000 merchants worldwide accepting bitcoin as one of their payment methods. These are the major retailers like Microsoft, Apple, Amazon, Walmart, Expedia, eBay, and even coffeehouse giant Starbucks.
Payment guarantee	The chargeback risk of an e-wallet depends on the payment instrument used to top up the e-wallet. For example, PayPal provides consumers a protection if they are charged for goods they did not purchase or if the order did not arrive or if the order did arrive but was significantly different than what was ordered. On the other hand, merchants are protected by PayPal when selling physical goods that are sold and shipped with proof of delivery from within the United States to buyers around the globe.
Brands	PayPal, Alipay, WeChat Pay, Apple Pay, Samsung Pay, Android Pay, Master-pass, Paylib, Amazon Pay, SEQR, MobilePay, Lyf Pay, Yoyo Wallet, Chase Pay, Allied Wallet, Dwolla, Paytm, MobiKwik, Pay by Bank App, PayBack
Market reach	United States/Europe: Adoption of e-wallets is slower than initial forecasts predicted. However, it is expected that their share will increase in the next three-five years. India: Rapidly growing market due to the conjunction of rising smartphone usage and lack of access to financial services of a large part of the population. Also, demonetization in India has proved to be a lucrative opportunity for e-wallet players (Paytm, Mobiwiki, Snapdeal) in the country. China: For online payments, the e-wallets (particularly Alipay and WeChat Pay) are the most popular form of payment.

Source: Modified from Aite, 2016, *The Evolution of Digital and Mobile Wallets*; The PayPers, 2017, *Payment Methods Report 2017*.

As mentioned in Table 2.7, the rise of e-wallets is comparatively slow on the American continent and in European countries as compared to Asia. This is justified by the exploding use of e-wallets in two populous and large economies, namely India and China. Other Asian countries in that region like Japan, Malaysia and Indonesia also have active users of e-wallets. Figure 2.6 elucidates this phenomenon more clearly.

The adoption of e-wallets is increasing globally with the rising access to smartphones and the internet. Distrust of e-wallets, lack of awareness and the lack of acceptability among FMCG merchants, especially at the grassroots level, will be needed to be overcome in order for it to truly become indispensable. However, the future looks promising for e-wallets.

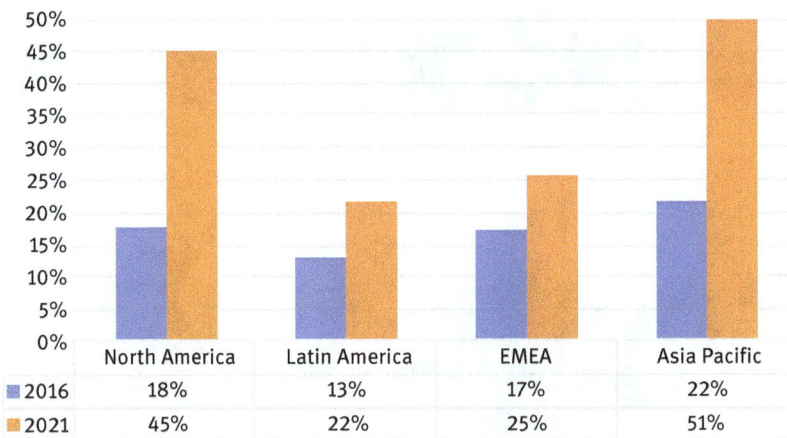

Figure 2.6: The Adoption of e-Wallets Worldwide.
Source: Modified from WorldPay, 2017, *Global Payments Report 2017*.

ICOs versus STOs

An Initial Coin Offering (or ICO for short) is an innovative form of raising capital or investments by issuing tokens or alternative cryptocurrencies, that does not necessarily involve any equity being acquired by the token buyers or investors. ICOs act to raise funds, where a company can raise money via tokenization of their business venture. Investors in ICOs are typically speculators who expect the tokens to skyrocket in value, and therefore only relying on the team behind the project, to improve the value of the tokens.

Unfortunately, ICOs are often likened to stocks or shares in the venture. In effect, many of the tokens issued are more like a utility to be exchanges for a product or utilized as a service. So ICOs do not grant the token-holder any right to equity or profit-sharing of the company's revenue, unlike stocks. ICOs were a duplication of the IPO (initial public offering) without having built the venture to a level of maturity that would represent some form of substantial value from revenue performance. Instead, it was meant to fast-track the venture's ability to raise capital just based on the strength of its idea and the team behind that idea. Needless to say, it raised many concerns, especially in an unregulated environment (Figure 2.7).

Then in 2018, after several mishaps and complaints, the SEC "issued a guideline (constantly being updated) mentioning that all Coin Offerings are security tokens. Many regulators followed suit shortly after, which led to the development of a new form of Coin Offerings dubbed the STOs or Security Token Offerings" (SEC, 2019). Still utilizing the tokens issued as a representation of an investment, the STO security token now signifies a "contract into an underlying investment asset, such as stocks, bonds, funds and real estate investment trusts (REIT)." Like a typical security, it is a

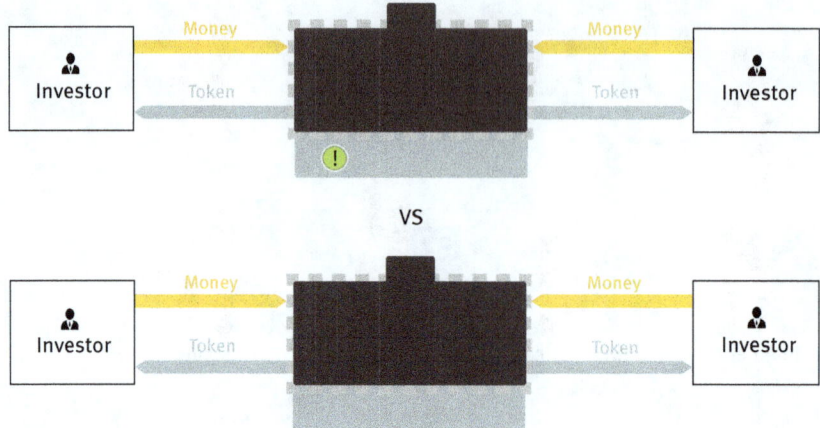

Figure 2.7: Fundamental Differences between ICOs and STOs.

"fungible, negotiable financial instrument that holds some type of monetary value, or an investment product that is backed by a real-world asset such as a company or property" (SEC, 2019).

The additional requirements included that the venture must prove that they are viable through proof of data, proof-of-concept (POC)/minimal viable product (MVP) or prototype, and other elements like traction to show evidence of viability.

Unlike the ICO market where two-thirds of the projects failed or turned out to be scams, the STO market had higher survival and success rates. The mandatory regulatory and legally enforceable requirements imposed on STOs deterred entities with fraudulent intentions from using the DeFi movement for their dishonest purposes. Looking ahead, such steps are necessary if this channel of securitization can be an option for mainstream adoption (Table 2.8).

Also, it is critical to distinguish between private securities and public securities. If a token is considered and handled solely as a private security, in many jurisdictions there will be the possibility of using certain regulatory exemptions. In these cases, the comprehensive IPO (Initial Public Offering) requirements will only come into force if a private token (STO) violates the restrictions related to the exemptions in question and begins to act as a public security (IPO share).

But an advantage of an STO over an IPO is that the security token can behave like a programmable share and offers a set of functionalities and attributes that a traditional public IPO share does not have. For instance, an STO can be created into an investment product that is better than traditional stocks (and bonds) by way of rewarding investors both from the forefront through risk-sharing model to share profit (and losses) and from the back through dividend payments. STO companies that can offer profits from the front and back of the business simultaneously, have the potential to become the new darlings of profit-driven investors.

Table 2.8: Important Distinctions between IPOs, ICOs and STOs.

IPO	ICO	STO
IPO gives you ownership of the company based on the number of shares acquired	ICO give rights of project, not the company equity	STO tokens represent a share of an underlying asset.
Financial data according to exchange of IPO issued	As outlined within the white paper and investor agreement.	A security offering under the qualification of an investment contract.
Subject to taxes, with investors liable to capital gains tax	ICO company may not be taxed; investor subject to capital gains tax.	Subject to taxes, with investors liable to capital gains tax
An IPO is a onetime sale with multiple intermediaries	ICOs can have multiple rounds with no intermediaries, the white paper as the blueprint.	STOs have limited intermediaries (lawyers, advisors, no bankers)
Stock exchanges and companies listed by IPO are heavily regulated	ICO exchanges are not regulated	STO are somewhat regulated

Fiqh View on Coins and Tokens

There is a plethora of studies available that discuss the cryptocurrencies especially bitcoin and its Shariah appraisal. These studies only focused on cryptocurrencies and Shariah ruling about them and leave the two main types of cryptoassets out of the discussion. They mainly conclude that cryptocurrencies like bitcoin have all the important and basic characteristics of a currency but their main concerns were articulated around regulatory issues and authority, and high volatility in prices caused by speculation. Some of the studies also highlight the issue of criminal use of these cryptocurrencies like terrorism funding thus violating the antimoney laundering (AML) regulations. In this section, our focus is cryptoassets, which include cryptocurrencies, cryptotokens, cryptosecurities, and the *fiqh* (Islamic jurisprudence) view on them.

As per the definition of *mal* (asset or wealth) according to the *fiqh* interpretation of the Shariah, the scholars of the four famous schools of *fiqh* (Hanafi, Maliki, Shafi'e, Hanbali) agree that *mal* can be anything of (1) commercial value means having natural desirability, (2) having storage ability, and (3) can be owned. Shariah provides flexibility in the form of *mal* – it may be tangible or intangible. As such, cryptoassets can be considered as *mal*.

For cryptocurrencies, some scholars (especially the gold dinar proponents) have expressed opinions that they should be backed by a real asset like gold. Now, we have cryptocurrencies like Onegram as it is claimed that this cryptocurrency is backed by gold. Currently, there are also many ICOs that are tokenizing real assets like real estate, and gold. These ICOs are viewed as less volatile (Fry, 2018). However, in the categorization of cryptocurrencies (coins and alt coins), its function is like that of sovereign fiat currency, which is a means of exchange.

To attain proper acceptance and full Shariah-compliance, there are some important conditions that have to be followed. A Shariah-compliant asset cannot be from the list of *haram* (prohibitions); for example, wine is an asset but it is not permissible so it is not Shariah compliant (Nordin et al., 2017; Nurhisam, 2017). Another consideration is that its use case cannot violate the *Maqasid Al Shariah* (objectives of the Shariah) regardless if the asset is tangible or not. Hence, the usage of the asset (including goods and services, virtual or real) must conform to the spirit of the Shariah, not just its forms. Though the asset itself has Shariah legitimacy, its eventual usage and practice has to be in accordance with its intended design.

The first step to recognize the legitimacy of cryptocurrencies is through categorizing the 1700+ cryptos that are out there. First, we make a distinction between the two broad categories of the cryptocurrency – coins and tokens:
– A coin is a digital currency, which is used like existing currencies to pay for goods and services. They are usually built using Bitcoin's open-sourced protocol, and typically have no other purpose than to pay for goods and services.
– A token is another form of cryptocurrency (with more features than just currency), that is usually issued on top of another blockchain. Generally, tokens represent utility or an asset, or sometimes both. Most tokens exist to be used with decentralized applications, or dApps.

The critical difference between the two is that tokens are issued through an ICO, and can take various forms, that is, digital asset (digital rights), means for accounting (number of API-calls, volume of torrent uploads), share (stake) in a specific start-up, incentive for using a system or payment among participants.

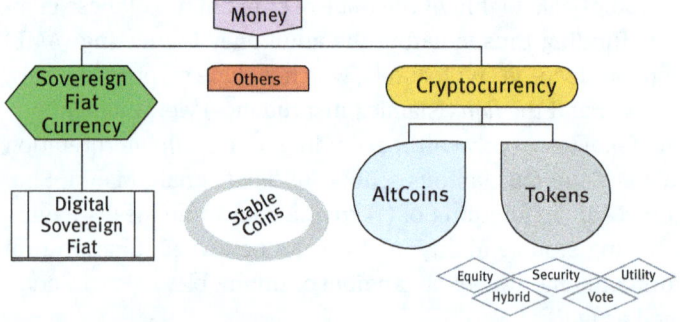

Figure 2.8: Categorization of Cryptocurrencies.

From a *fiqh* perspective, since coins are straight-forward forms of digital currencies, Shariah rules on currency will be applied to them (e.g., cannot be treated like a commodity to be traded like Forex). ICOs, however, are not so straight-forward. These types of cryptocurrencies (see Figure 2.8) need to be clear in their use case and purpose of issuance in order to remove confusion and/or deceptive ambiguity (*gharar*).

The use of the token must be specified clearly – currently, tokens usage can be generally categorized as (but not limited to):
- *Asset-backed token* – token that represents some physical asset like gold or real estate but can also be intangible like talk-time for telcos or GBs of storage.
- *Equity token* – token that represents some stock or equity in the company that issues it. However, few companies have attempted such an ICO because it is tedious, and follows guidelines similar to IPOs.
- *Security token* – tokens that are securitized are security tokens. Investors buying them expect profits in form of dividends, revenue share or (most commonly) price appreciation. However, they are subjected to securities regulations and limitation on who can invest in these tokens and how they can be exchanged.
- *Utility token* – also called application tokens. They are used to provide people with access to either a product or service. Depending on the ICO strategy, most tokens are expected to gain in value based on their limited supply.

Each token will be treated differently according to the *fiqh* understanding of the Shariah as well as the regulatory authorities because of its nature and usage. Due to this, its treatment by the regulators as well as the Shariah will be in accordance with its nature and usage – the way they are used as well as the way they were intended to be used.

As such, it is impossible to give a blanket *fatwa* (religious ruling) on tokens when their usage and intended use case can be highly divergent and cross multiple Shariah rulings. Also, token/ICO design are also constantly evolving; so are regulations from the appropriate authorities.

As mentioned, these are the guidance notes for the contemporary Islamic scholars to consider when it comes to the legitimacy of cryptoassets according to the Shariah. The assessment of Shariah-compliance too should include the procedural processes from creation to the result of any cryptoassets and its mechanisms. For Muslim participation, before launching a project of any cryptoassets it should be scrutinized as per Shariah guidelines, and clarification should be sought from Shariah experts who have the relevant economic, financial and technical (blockchain and token experience) capability.

Stablecoins and Central Bank-Issued Digital Currencies

Stablecoins are cryptocurrencies that are pegged to a stable entity of value such as commodities or sovereign fiat currencies. The main criticism of cryptocurrencies was that they were volatile and this caused their value to fluctuate drastically. Pegging them to entities of stable value controlled this volatility.

Central Bank-issued digital currencies (CBDCs) are digital currencies issued by central banks and are pegged to national sovereign fiat currencies, typically 1:1. Because CBDCs are pegged to a stable fiat currency which is guaranteed by the governments that issue them, they are a form of stablecoins. There are several formats of CBDCs that are being experimented and trialed in various countries and at various scales.

The Central Bank-issued digital currency (CBDC) is a digital alternative to cash that is also peer-to-peer (P2P), but it gives more flexibility in the treatment of the other three features:

1. They can be anonymous (like cash) or identifiable (non-anonymous like current accounts). The first corresponds to the idea of token-based CBDCs, and the second to account-based CBDCs.
2. They can be universal or restricted to a particular set of users. Likewise, distributed ledger (DL)-based tokens can be public (open) or private (closed), for instance, limited to banks or financial institutions.
3. They can be designed to pay or not give returns (in the absence of interest). The delinking of cash from paper–money opens the possibility of including yield as a feature, either in the account based or in the DL-based variant (or crypto-tokens).

These options can be melded in different ways to generate useful formats of the CBDCs for practical applications. Such amalgamation for purposeful solutions may involve these objectives:

i. to enhance the operations of wholesale payment systems
ii. to replace or support cash with a more proficient substitute
iii. to broaden and enrich tools for monetary policy, especially when confronted with the zero lower bound
iv. to strengthen overall financial stability by decreasing the occurrences of banking and financial crises

Traditionally, the Central Banks (CBs) provide banks and other financial institutions with electronic accounts for its functionality in the financial system. The public does not have such access and is only permitted to keep CB money in physical forms (i.e., coins and/or notes). If a CB would issue a universal Central Bank-issued digital currency (CBDC), all the economic actors (regardless of if they are individuals, firms, institutions, governments, and central banks) could store assets and make payments using the Central Bank issued digital currency (Cerqueira et al., 2017). In consequence, this could have important shifts and repercussions for financial stability, monetary policy, and the relation of economic actors to the financial system (see Chapter 9, Mohamed 2021).

Critical Importance of CyberSecurity

The growth of cryptoassets and cryptoexchanges around the globe is growing to be relentless. At the same time, cyberattacks have increased, including scamming, and hacking attempts, and these events have become inevitable if money and wealth is at stake.

The first historical heist happened in the cryptoworld in 2014 when the largest bitcoin exchange of that time, Mt Gox, was hacked by cyberhackers and the cryptoexchange was attacked so badly that it had to be declared bankrupt. This hack was followed by the DAO hack faced by Ethereum in 2016 when the criminals siphoned away one-third of funds – about US$50 million dollars. The second largest bitcoin heist happened in the same year in 2016 at a Hong Kong-based cryptoexchange, Bitfinex, which lost 120,000 BTC that day, worth US$72 million. They have since bounced back into the cryptoworld and back into the mainstream.

The year 2017 suffered its own attacks when the data from thousands of servers and nodes were attacked in an unprecedent manner. The entire year of 2017 saw the cryptoexchanges lose around US$66 million in cyberattacks, but it was much worse in the first half of 2018 according to Roh (2018). So far, it is recorded that a total of US$761 million has been stolen by hackers from the various cryptoexchanges. It is also estimated by the report that this value will hit US$1.5 billion by the end of 2018. The two major cryptoexchanges attacks in the first half of 2018 were the Coincheck hack in Japan, which lost US$500 million and the Coinrail hack in South Korea where the exchange lost US$40 million (CCN, 2018).

It has also been reported that cryptocurrency is being used as a tool for cyber extortion payments. With regard to this, the U.S. Financial Crimes Enforcement Network (FinCen) has banned one of the largest unregulated cryptoexchanges – BTC-e. The CEO was arrested for his involvement in a 300,000 bitcoin heist. In that exchange, only 5% of the total transactions were actual bitcoin transactions and 95% of them were cyber extortion payments (University of Cambridge, 2018).

There are many factors behind the increasing number of cyberattacks including lack of right and skilled talent in cybersecurity, especially for exchanges. The attacks expose massive security concerns on cryptoexchange systems, and their lack of protection for the assets on their platforms and robustness to respond to attacks and reduce loopholes within their systems. This requires a clear strategy of cybersecurity by cryptoexchanges to decipher and defend from attacks in a decentralized anonymous network.

References

Aite. (2016). *The Evolution of Digital and Mobile Wallets*. http://www.paymentscardsandmobile.com/wp-content/uploads/2016/10/The-Evolution-of-Digital-and-Mobile-Wallets.pdf

Arner, D. W., Barberis, J. N., & Buckley, R. P. (2015). The Evolution of FinTech: A New Post-Crisis Paradigm? University of Hong Kong Faculty of Law Research Paper No. 2015/047; UNSW Law Research Paper No. 2016-62. October 2015.

Bank Negara Malaysia, BNM. (2017). *Central Bank Digital Currency: A Monetary Policy Perspective*. http://www.bnm.gov.my/index.php?ch=en_publication&pg=en_staffinsight&ac=45&bb=file

Bettinger, A. (1972). FINTECH: A Series of 40 Time Shared Models Used at Manufacturers Hanover Trust Company. *Interfaces*, 62–63.

Burniske, C., & Tatar, J. (2017). *Cryptoassets: The Innovative Investor's Guide to Bitcoin and Beyond* (1st ed.). McGraw-Hill Education.

CB Insights. (2018). FinTech Trends to Watch in 2018. research/report/FinTech-trends-2018

CCN. (2018, July 4). $731 Million Gained by Hacking Crypto Exchanges in 2018, Can it be Prevented? Retrieved August 6, 2018, https://www.ccn.com/731-million-stolen-from-crypto-exchanges-in-2018-can-hacks-be-prevented/

Cerqueira, Gouveia Olga, Dos Santos, Enestor, de Lis, Santiago Fernández, Neut, Alejandro, & Sebastián, Javier. (2017). Central Bank Digital Currencies: Assessing Implementation Possibilities and Impacts. BBVA Research, March 2017.

Chishti, S., & Barberis, J. (2016). The FinTech Book: The Financial Technology Handbook for Investors, Entrepreneurs, and Visionaries. West Sussex: John Wiley & Sons. http://public.eblib.com/choice/publicfullrecord.aspx?p=4451913

CoinGecko. (2018). *Cryptocurrency Report Q1 2018*. CoinGecko. https://assets.coingecko.com/reports/Q1-2018-Cryptocurrency-Report-by-CoinGecko-large.pdf

Deloitte. (2016). *Connecting Global FinTech: Hub Review 2016*. http://thegfhf.org/wp-content/uploads/2016/10/Connecting-Global-FinTech-Hub-Review-2016-.pdf

Desai, F. (2015). The Evolution of FinTech. Retrieved February 2, 2017, http://www.forbes.com/sites/falgunidesai/2015/12/13/the-evolution-of-FinTech/

Evans, C. (2015). Bitcoin in Islamic Banking and Finance. *Journal of Islamic Banking and Finance*, 3(1), 1–11.

FinTech Switzerland. (2016a, April 16). TOP FinTech Startups Over Last Decades. http://FinTechnews.ch/FinTech/top-FinTech-startups-over-last-decades/3160/

FinTech Switzerland. (2016b, October 3). World FinTech Landscape. http://FinTechnews.ch/FinTech/world-FinTech-landscape/7235/

Freedman, R. S. (2006). *Introduction to Financial Technology*. Academic Press.

Freedman, D. M., & Nutting, M. R. (2015). A Brief History of Crowdfunding Including Rewards. *Donation, Debt, and Equity Platforms in the USA*, 1–10.

Fry, J. (2018). Rise of Crypto Exchanges and Why it Is Important. Retrieved August 1, 2018, https://www.linkedin.com/pulse/rise-crypto-exchanges-why-important-jonny-fry/

Hahn, L. (2016, June 6). DO NOT Count on the ANT Financial IPO to Lift BABA Stock. http://investorplace.com/2016/06/alibaba-baba-stock-ant-financial-ipo/

Haley, S. (2016, May 18). Surging Ahead: FinTech Startups in the Middle East. Retrieved February 4, 2017, https://www.entrepreneur.com/article/275938

Hansen, S. (2018, June). Guide to Top Cryptocurrency Exchanges. Retrieved August 1, 2018, https://www.forbes.com/sites/sarahhansen/2018/06/20/forbes-guide-to-cryptocurrency-exchanges/

He, D., Habermeier, K. F., Leckow, R. B., Haksar, V., Almeid, Y., Kashima, M., & Kyriakos-Saad, N. (2016, January). Virtual Currencies and Beyond: Initial Considerations. http://www.imf.org/external/pubs/cat/longres.aspx?sk=43618

Henning, K. (2013). Recommendations for implementing the strategic initiative INDUSTRIE 4.0. http://thuvienso.dastic.vn:801/dspace/bitstream/TTKHCNDaNang_123456789/357/1/Recommendations%20for%20implementing%20the%20strategic%20initiative%20INDUSTRIE%204.0.pdf

HiveEx. (2018). *Global Cryptocurrency Exchange Trends, Report & Statistics March 2018*. https://www.hiveex.com/hiveex-cryptocurrency-report

Houben, R., & Snyers, A. (2018). *Cryptocurrencies and Blockchain*. Policy Department for Economic, Scientific and Quality of Life Policies European Parliament. http://www.europarl.europa.eu/RegData/etudes/STUD/2018/619024/IPOL_STU(2018)619024_EN.pdf

ICORating. (2018). *ICO Market Research Q1 2018*. https://icorating.com/ico_market_research_q1_2018_icorating.pdf

Ken Research. (2016). US FinTech Market Size. https://kenresearch.wordpress.com/tag/us-FinTech-market-size/

Keynes, John Maynard. (1919). *The Economic Consequences of the Peace* (1st ed.). London: Macmillan & Co., Limited. 10–12.

Keynes, J. (1920). *The Economic Consequences of the Peace*. New York, USA: Harcourt, Brace, and Howe, 10–12.

KPMG & H2. (2016b). *The Pulse of FinTech – Q3 2016 | KPMG | GLOBAL*. https://assets.kpmg.com/content/dam/kpmg/xx/pdf/2016/11/the-pulse-of-FinTech-q3-report.pdf

KPMG & H2. (2017). *The Pulse of FinTech – Q3 2017 | KPMG | GLOBAL*. https://assets.kpmg.com/content/dam/kpmg/xx/pdf/2017/07/the-pulse-of-FinTech-q3-report.pdf

KPMG & H2. (2018). *The Pulse of FinTech – H1 2018 | KPMG | GLOBAL*. https://assets.kpmg.com/content/dam/kpmg/xx/pdf/2018/07/h1-2018-pulse-of-fintech.pdf

Mohamed, H. (2021). Beyond Fintech: Technology Applications for the Islamic Economy. *World Scientific*, 165–192.

Nordin, N. S., Hassan, R., & Nor, R. M. (2017). Cryptocurrency from Shariah Perspective. *Google Docs*. https://drive.google.com/file/d/0B1d0lcOY3R9BcXJXVDBQSWM2Zjg/view?usp=embed_facebook

Nurhisam, L. (2017). Bitcoin: Islamic Law Perspective. *QIJIS (Qudus International Journal of Islamic Studies)*, 5(2), 85–100.

Olagoke, O. (2018, February 19). The Rise of Decentralized Crypto Exchanges. Retrieved August 1, 2018, https://cryptona.co/rise-decentralized-crypto-exchanges/

Research and Markets. (2018). *Global Mobile Wallet and Payment Market Report 2018*. https://www.researchandmarkets.com/research/3xvsh3/global_mobile?w=5

Roh, C. (2018, July 5). Cryptocurrency Exchange Theft Rising in 2018 According to CipherTrace. Retrieved August 6, 2018, https://cryptoslate.com/cryptocurrency-exchange-theft-rising-in-2018-according-to-ciphertrace/

Santarelli, E. (1995). *Finance and Technological Change: Theory and Evidence*. Springer.

SEC. (2019). Framework for "Investment Contract" Analysis of Digital Assets. https://www.sec.gov/files/dlt-framework.pd

Shafi, A., Patel, K., Collins, A., & Haidermota. (2018, July 13). Cryptocurrency Laws and Regulations in UAE 2018 | *Asia Business Law Journal*. Retrieved August 3, 2018, https://www.vantageasia.com/cryptocurrency-law-uae/

Schueffel, P. (2016). Taming the Beast: A Scientific Definition of FinTech. *Journal of Innovation Management*, 4(4), 32–54.

Shubber, K. (2016). Abu Dhabi and Dubai put FinTech first. *Financial Times*. https://www.ft.com/content/87d48142-53e5-11e6-9664-e0bdc13c3bef

Sparklabs. (2016). *FinTech Industry Report 2016*. http://www.slideshare.net/bernardmoon/FinTech-industry-report-2016?ref=https://fin2tech.wordpress.com/2016/08/03/FinTech-industry-report-2016-sparklabs/

Statista. (2016). Topic: FinTech. Retrieved February 3, 2017, https://www.statista.com/topics/2404/FinTech/

Statista. (2018). Fintech. Retrieved October 31, 2018, https://www.statista.com/topics/2404/fintech/

Su, J. B. (2016). The Global FinTech Landscape Reaches Over 1000 Companies, US$105B in Funding, US$867B in Value: Report. Retrieved February 3, 2017, http://www.forbes.com/sites/jeanbaptiste/2016/09/28/the-global-FinTech-landscape-reaches-over-1000-companies-105b-in-funding-867b-in-value-report/

The PayPers. (2017). *Payment Methods Report 2017 (Insights into the e-Wallets Landscape)*. http://aaa.ccpit.org/Category7/Asset/2017/Jul/28/onlineeditimages/file71501224154406.pdf

Traxpay Team. (2016). FinTech: A Revolution 150 Years in the Making (Part 2 of 3). http://traxpay.com/2016/01/fintech-revolution-150-years-in-the-making-part2/

University of Cambridge. (2018). *Cyber Risk Outlook 2018*. Center for Risk Studies, University of Cambridge. https://www.jbs.cam.ac.uk/fileadmin/user_upload/research/centres/risk/downloads/crs-cyber-risk-outlook-2018.pdf

Waupsh, J. (2016). *Bankruption: How Community Banking Can Survive Fintech* (1st edition). Hoboken, New Jersey: Wiley.

WorldPay. (2017). *Global Payments Report 2017*. https://worldpay.globalpaymentsreport.com/wp-content/uploads/reports/GPR-English-2017.pdf

Zimmerman, E. (2016). Evolution of FinTech. https://www.nytimes.com/2016/04/07/business/dealbook/the-evolution-of-FinTech.html?_r=1

Chapter 3
Importance of Fintech and its Applications

Introduction

This chapter covers the importance of fintech within two important perspectives: the financial services industry perspective and digitalization or technological perspective. Financial innovation is reshaping the different areas of the financial services industry, that is, finance and investment, financial operations and risk management, cost, price, and return, payments, and remittances and crowdfunding.

New digital innovative and advanced technologies are reshaping the value proposition of existing financial products and services. Fintech is becoming more and more disruptive by leveraging the latest and advanced technologies such as blockchain, cloud computing, big data analysis, internet of things (IoT), robo-advisory, and artificial intelligence (AI). In this section, technologies that are being used by fintech to provide financial services and products are discussed in detail. By deploying these technologies, financial innovations can provide agility, transparency, cost effective and customer centric products and services.

Today, we live in a connected global world with the availability of the internet and the beginnings of 5G. The world is going to be better connected and "smarter" due to the emergence of new innovative and digital tools including smart wearables and devices, smart houses, smartphones, mobile health care, and much more. In this era of the IoT, the psychological behavior of customers and consumers of every industry has been changed. They demand services, wherever they are, whenever they want and at any time, quickly. Their approach, thought-process, and decision making about products and services have changed.

Financial innovation is rising because technological advancement has enabled a deeper understanding of consumer behavior and customer preferences. Getting to the heart of how people buy and receive information to make their buying decisions is critical to any business today. Cognitive analytics can also help financial service providers reach out to unbanked and underbanked people and provide better access to finance for them when psychological biases are determined, understood, and overcome. This will lead to a great leap toward financial inclusion.

There has been a storm of financial innovation from the customers' perspective, enabled by rising customer expectations for more personalized and digital experiences, enhanced access to venture capital funding, reduced barriers to entry and accelerated advancements in technology.

Financial Innovation within the Financial Services Industry Perspective

Payments Industry

Payments in historical perspective have been utility products; basically, transactional and tactical in nature and volume-driven. The reality is that a payment was often deemed as merely the final and last step in a transaction, with limited and restricted opportunity to provide value-added solutions or services (BNY Mellon, 2014).

But today it is not the same; the payments industry now is in a state of continuous change, underlying several cutting-edge economic, technological, and demographic factors across the length and breadth of the value chain. The industry is witnessing rapid development in innovations across the value chain, thus making it more splintered. New entrants called nonbanking payment systems in the form of fintech companies and established big tech giants (PayPal, Apple, Facebook, Google, Amazon) have caused major disruptions and have nullified the traditional intermediation in major parts of banking and the payments landscape. The first and most effective symbol of the fintech revolution can be perceived within the payments services industry. PayPal is identified as the most successful and strongest player in the field of the payment industry. Statistics shows the net revenue of PayPal during, Q4'16, at 2.98 billion U.S. dollars (Statista, 2016).

Eventually, a payment solution in 2020 will be about providing strategically important solutions and transferring value in support of broader activity in several areas including investment, trade, retail, public and commercial sectors. The PwC Market Research Center forecasts that the number of noncash transactions will also grow by 69% from 2013 to 2020 and the transactions value per minute will be one million (PricewaterhouseCoopers, 2016).

Cloud computing, open-source software, big data and analytics, developers on demand, social media, open app stores for distribution, and blockchain can, or will, enable rapid technology adoption and deployment in the financial services industry especially in the fintech sector and in particular, the payments industry. These technologies could leapfrog antiquated payments mechanisms and systems in several areas such as cross border payments. In addition, the use of Bluetooth, NFC, QR codes in contactless merchant-based payments is also threatening the existing payments models (PricewaterhouseCoopers, 2016).

Digital payments can be defined as noncash transactions processed through digital channels and include digital commerce, mobile payments and peer-to-peer (P2P) money transfers. Figure 3.1 illustrates the definitions of these types.

The global market size of digital payments at the end of 2016 is expected to be US$2.221 trillion. Among the different regions United States accounted for 29% of global digital payments, followed by China who led the mobile payment transaction value with US$467.7 billion in 2016. Statista forecasts that U.S. mobile payments

Figure 3.1: Digital Payments.

will grow at an annual rate of 62% between 2016 and 2021. Digital payments were one of the main drivers of all fintech transaction value and accounted for at 85% in 2016 (Statista, 2016). In 2017, with a global transaction value of US$2.754 trillion, the digital payment segment remained the biggest segment in the fintech industry (Statista, 2017a). In Figure 3.2, we see their continuing trends and in Figure 3.3 we see an upward trajectory.

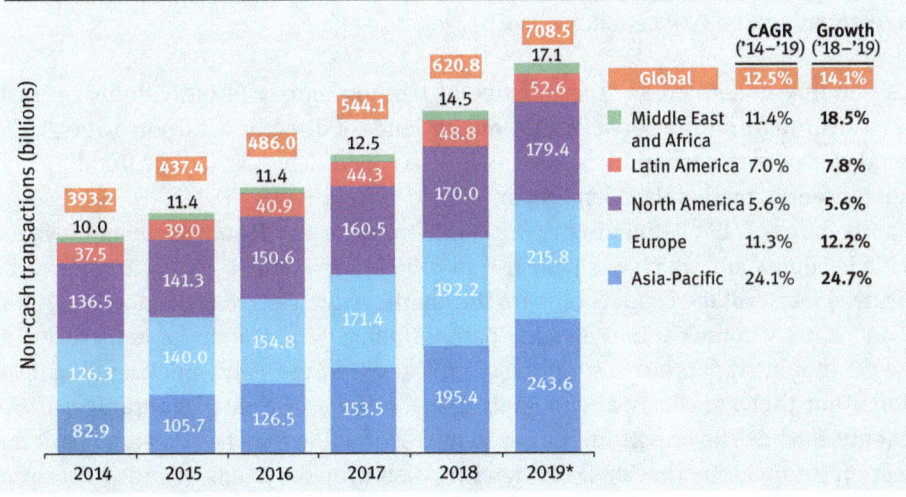

Figure 3.2: Digital Payments Transactions Value between 2014–2019 (US$ Billion).
Note: *Non-cash transaction data for 2019 is sourced the from countries' central banks. In case of data unavailability, forecasted figures are used.
Sources: Capgemini Financial Services Analysis, 2020;ECB Stational Data Warehouse, 2018 figures released November 2019; BIS Statistic Explorer, 2018 figures released December 2019; countries' central bank annual reports, 2019.
Source: Consultancy.uk, 2020.

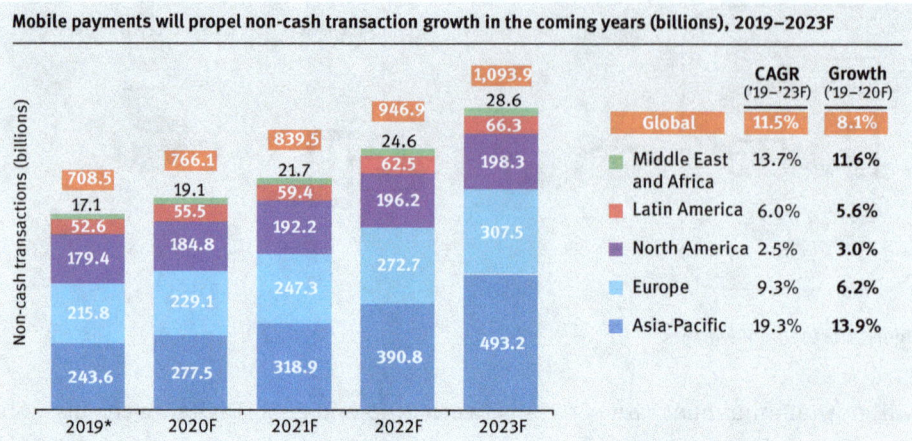

Figure 3.3: Mobile Payments will Drive Growth of Digital Payments (US$ Billion).
Note: *Non-cash transaction data for 2019 is sourced the from countries' central banks. In case of data unavailability, forecasted figures are used.
Sources: Capgemini Financial Services Analysis, 2020;ECB Stational Data Warehouse, 2018 figures released November 2019; BIS Statistic Explorer, 2018 figures released December 2019; countries' central bank annual reports, 2019.
Source: Consultancy.uk, 2020.

Crowdfunding and P2P Lending

P2P lending is defined as "the practice of lending money to individuals or businesses through online services that match lenders directly with borrowers." P2P stands for peer to peer and P2P lending is also called debt-based crowdfunding and more recently, marketplace lending or MPL.

The largest P2P platform in the world in terms of issued loan volume and revenue is the Lending Club, which was launched in 2006 in San Francisco. Table 3.1 shows the financial results of the Lending Club for the quarter, which ended September 30, 2016.

This is a vigorous and interesting part of financial innovation for lenders due to the potentially high returns, simplified application process, and quick lending decisions, but these are linked with high risks because of limited guarantee of the amount repaid. The opportunities posed by P2P lending may have a significant impact on financial institutions. P2P lending also provides loans to those entrepreneurs and small and medium-sized enterprises (SMEs) who cannot get loans from regulated financial institutions, for example, banks. According to Morgan Stanley, it is expected that marketplace lending will approximate US$290 billion by 2020, averaging 51% growth per year. But in a more optimistic case, this sector is seen to be exceeding US$490 billion by 2020 (Coraggio, 2017).

Crowdfunding is a term that refers to a practice of generating funds or capital investments for a reasonable cause, project, or enterprise by getting funds from

Table 3.1: Financial Results of Lending Club Q3'2016.

($ in millions)	Three Month Ended		Nine Months Ended September 30, 2016		
	September 30, 2016	June 30, 2016	September 30, 2015	2016	2015
Organizations	1,972.0 $	1,955.4 $	2,235.6 $	6,677.5 $	5,782.5
Operating Revenue	112.6 $	102.4 $	115.1 $	366.3 $	292.2
Net Income/ (Loss)1	(36.5) $	(81.4) $	1.0 $	(113.7) $	(9.6)
Adjusted EBITDA	(11.1) $	(30.1) $	21.2 $	(16.0) $	45.2

(1) *Includes US$1.7 million of goodwill important in the quarter ended September 30, 2016 and US $37.1 million year to date in 2016.*
Source: Lending Club Report, Q3'2016.

many individuals or organizations. Crowdfunding is adopted when an innovative and new idea that has the potential to generate revenue and create jobs demands financial support to become a reality. It mostly takes place on crowdfunding platforms (CFPs), that is, internet-based platforms that connect fundraisers to funders with the objective of funding a particular campaign from typically many individuals (Belleflamme, Omrani, & Peitz, 2015). These CFPs provide access to funds and capital for a segment of the population who cannot easily access it through traditional means.

Crowdfunding was started by a Boston musician and computer programmer (Brian Camelio from the United States) who for the first time launched a project based on the website ArtistShare in 2003. Maria Schneider's jazz album "Concert in a Garden" was the first project of ArtistShare. This campaign raised about US$130,000 that enabled her to produce music, pay her musicians, etc. Eventually, her album won the 2005 Grammy Award (Freedman & Nutting, 2015). After the success of this first CFP, many CFPs have emerged in the market. The key players in the present global crowdfunding market are Patreon, Gofundme, Indiegogo, Kickstarter, and Teespring. Other prominent vendors in the market are CircleUp, Causes, Crowdfunder, Crowdrise, FirstGiving, Fundable, DonorsChoose, GiveForward, FundRazr, Gust, Innovational Funding, FundRazr, Kiva, Innovational Funding, RocketHub, and Youcaring (Research and Markets, 2016).

A research firm provides an overview of the American crowdfunding CFP as of January 2017, which shows that as of that month, the number of launched projects on Kickstarter amounted to 335,396, and the success rate among those amounted to 35.75% (see Table 3.2). Kickstarter is one of the largest platforms in terms of projects and revenue.

Analysts forecast the global crowdfunding market to grow at a CAGR of 26.87% during the period 2016–2020 (Research and Markets, 2016). Statista forecasted that transaction value in the crowdfunding segment would amount to US$7.23 billion in 2017 and is expected to show an annual growth rate (CAGR 2017–2021) of 27.3% resulting in the total amount of US$18.97 billion in 2021. It is also estimated that the

Table 3.2: Key Statistics for Kickstarter.

Projects and dollars	Projects U.S dollars. Success rates in percent
Launched projects	335,396
Live dollars millions U.S dollars	18
Live Projects	3,788
Success rate (%)	35.75
Successful dollars (billion U.S. dollars)	2.49
Total dollars pledged (billion U.S. dollars)	2.84
Unsuccessful dollars (million U.S. dollars)	3.26

Source: Collated from Statista (2017b) and Kickstarter.

average funding per campaign in the crowdfunding segment amounted to US$992.66 in 2017. In addition, Statista also forecasts that in the crowdfunding segment, the number of funding campaigns will amount to 13,784,220 by 2021 (Statista, 2016).

The crowdfunding sector has brought innovative disruptive models to giant existing industries like transportation and real estate, leveraging advanced technologies and the internet to generate massively scalable businesses. Crowdfunding is an easy-to-access alternative for entrepreneurs as compared to regulated traditional financial institutions.

Neo-Banking

The emergence of neo-banks is considered as a paradigm shift in the banking industry (Oracle, 2017). These neo-banks are also called digital only banks, app-only start-up banks, and challenger banks. Neo-banking is not merely the distribution of data through the internet. It has in-built vision and aims to reach customers through digital omni channels and provide the services they want to them and through the channel of their choice. They do not have a separate digital team for digital-based projects; rather neo-banks have digital integration in their core. Neo-banks offer banking services in a simpler way and with a cost edge as compared to traditional banking products.

There are now about fifty-seven neo-banks operating in different jurisdictions and mostly located in the United Kingdom, like Atom, Monzo, Tandem, and Metro. These banks have raised millions of dollars of funding from different investors. Tandem has raised US$77 million, Starling US$70 million, Atom US$268 million, and Monzo has raised US$46 million (Skinner, 2017).

These banks are attracting customers in real time with their cheaper and better offerings to the tech savvy generation of this digital era. These challenger banks are a very promising avenue for reaching more and more customers through innovative business models and digital channels.

Asset under Management

It is no doubt that a new wave of disruption is making its way into asset management. Contextual insights from massive data analytics can be utilized by fund and wealth managers to help them engage their clients to identify opportunities for them in a timely manner whilst all the time remaining compliant to regulations (Mohamed, 2021). AI-driven services for wealth management have the capacity to craft new business models, provide incredible insights, and spin off value-added products and services through massive data that can inform decisions better and quickly. This generates better financial prediction and sentiment analysis at a much lower cost through an optimal combination of intelligence from data analytics from economic factors, market conditions and investor sentiment. Blockchain can be leveraged to build a client profile in a much more efficient way. Storing client profile data on blockchain allows for data points – profile data, preferences, net worth, account information, social media profiles – to be shared as needed, with each individual block of data being stored securely, but permissioned for access by the individual (read, write, edit) as needed. Also, blockchain applications bring efficiencies in eliminating redundant functions, reducing operational expenses, and increasing client ease-of-use experience. One way to help ease compliance burdens is to build and deploy identity management solutions using blockchain. An identity management system based on verification cryptography can be built using AML, CTF, and KYC requirements according to the country-specific regulations. The same is stored virtually and a part of this information is released to the counterparty at the time of transaction to suffice the counterparty's requirement.

The integration of blockchain and AI into a decentralized intelligence system has profound possibilities to employ data in the asset and wealth management industry.

InsurTech

InsurTech is one the segments of financial innovation addressing existing insurance opportunities, potentials, and challenges.

A 2016 PwC survey (Figure 3.4) showed that insurance companies are very much aware of the fintech revolution and that 74% of the survey's respondents deemed financial innovations as a threat for their industry (PricewaterhouseCoopers, 2016b). It is the effect of an external factor, such as use of advanced technologies like big data and analytics and blockchain as well as the rise of the sharing economy and the ability to improve operations.

PwC'S global survey 2016 depicts that 68% of insurance industry players are dealing with financial innovation and have taken concrete steps to tackle upcoming challenges and/or embrace opportunities. However, only the players who are most

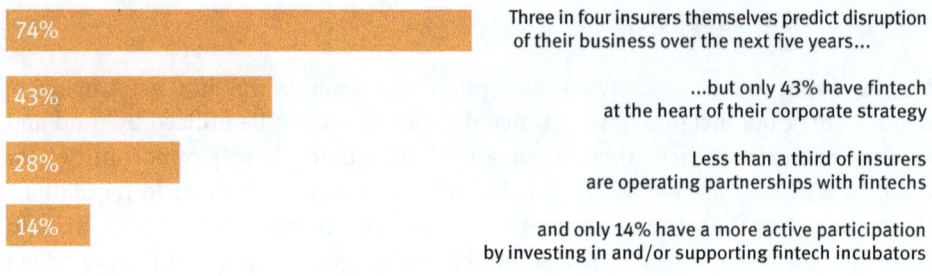

Figure 3.4: PwC's Global Survey of Innovation in the Insurance Industry.
Source: PwC (2016) Payments in the Wild Tech World: Digitization and changing customer expectations.

innovative have fintech at heart and want to explore more active ways to participate in the ecosystem, such as incubators and venture funds.

Insurers are introducing lifestyle apps that give additional consumer value on a continuing and constant basis. The constant consumer involvement will begin to reshape price as the key buying criterion. There is the example of Knip, which is an innovative digital insurance manager that provides users with an easy-to-understand analysis and overview of existing insurance policies, and services in an app. Clark is another insurance platform that works similarly to Knip. Insurance companies should transform digitally and understand the needs of a tech-savvy generation. Big data analytics can play a major role in this area through generating intuitive policies from processing massive data of users' behavior, which can provide insights into customer needs and forecast their requirements.

Deploying smart contracts powered by blockchain, customers and insurers can manage claims in a more transparent, responsive, and irrefutable manner. Some start-ups such as Blockstream, Everledger, and Tierion are working in this direction. Several companies such as insPeer, Peercover, Friendsurance, Lemonade are effectively using social media. Social media activities are helping insurance companies to improve their business and connect with customers. InsurTechs, with the help of IoT, are equipped to offer relevant packages based on real use and behavior rather than averaged statistics. Domotoz is an IoT solution for the connected home that offers a platform for home insurers to rate risk and manage claims (Let's Talk Payments, 2016).

Fintech Within the Technological Perspective

New digital innovative and advanced technologies are, in a way, reshaping the value proposition of existing financial products and services. Financial innovation is becoming more and more disruptive by leveraging the latest and advanced technologies. In this section, we elaborate on the technologies being used by fintech companies to provide better financial services and products.

Blockchain and Its Applications

Blockchain is also called *distributed ledger technology*. Blockchain is a public ledger of business transactions. A blockchain network works as intermediator in a decentralized system for the exchange of assets and information. The two main technology components are "P2P" or shared data storage and public-key cryptography (Mainelli & Milne, 2016).

According to an Accenture report, blockchain is one of the most talked about topics in the present financial services industry. There are 90% of bank executives who are interested in blockchain and currently their banks are exploring the use of blockchain in the payments industry. Moreover, this report also highlights the benefits of using this technology in the payments industry: lower frictionless cost, shorter settlement time, reduced errors, new revenue opportunity, and lower administrative cost (Accenture, 2016a).

More than fifty banks including Barclays and JPMorgan Chase have joined the R3 consortium. This consortium has objectives to find ways to use the blockchain as a decentralized ledger to track money transfers and other transactions. R3 has plans to make its technology open source, which could speed up its wider adoption. Nasdaq Inc. is already using blockchain in collaboration with start-up Chain.com for trading securities in private companies. The Australian Stock Exchange has started working with blockchain start-up Digital Asset Holdings to catalyze its clearing and settlement services in the equities market (Kharif, 2016). Fintech start-ups including Chainalysis and IdentifyMind Global are helpingbanks comply with KYC (Know Your Customer) and AML (anti-money laundering) regulations in the deployment of blockchain for banking services (Deloitte, 2016b). Santander, UniCredit, Reisebank, UBS, ATB Financial, CIBC, and the National Bank of Abu Dhabi are all working with Ripple's technology, which deploys a distributed ledger of the sort that also underpins bitcoin. HSBC and State Street have successfully tested blockchain in bond transactions in 2016, while Bank of America announced a partnership with Microsoft to experiment with the system (Shen, 2016).

Blockchain technology has a big potential beyond cryptocurrencies such as in the payments industry, trade finance, capital markets, insurance, and investment management. There are three main blockchain benefits for the payments industry: efficiency, disintermediation, and transactions cost reduction. Blockchain can provide an efficient infrastructure for the speedy settlement of money movement and decrease the need to use intermediator entities, like banks, for cross border payments.

We will delve much deeper into this truly revolutionary technology in Chapter 5 as well as its extended use cases in Chapter 6.

Cloud Computing

Cloud computing is the on-demand delivery of compute power, database storage, applications, and other information technology (IT) resources through a cloud services platform via the internet with pay-as-you-go pricing. Rather than owning their own computing infrastructure or data centers, companies can rent access to anything from applications to storage from a cloud service provider (CSP). One benefit of using cloud computing services is that firms can avoid the upfront cost and complexity of owning and maintaining their own IT infrastructure, and instead simply pay for what they use, when they use it. In turn, providers of cloud computing services can benefit from significant economies of scale by delivering the same services to a wide range of customers.

Building the infrastructure to support cloud computing now accounts for more than a third of all IT spending worldwide, according to research from IDC.[1]

Meanwhile, spending on traditional, in-house IT continues to slide as computing workloads continue to move to the cloud, whether that is public cloud services offered by vendors or private clouds built by enterprises themselves.

Gartner Research[2] predicts that around one-third of enterprise IT spending will be on hosting and cloud services for the next few years indicating a growing reliance on external sources of infrastructure, application, management, and security services. Analyst Gartner predicts that half the global enterprises using the cloud now will have gone all-in on it by 2021.

Cloud computing has become necessary to our economy due to our need for storing large amounts of data and the requirement to have it accessible easily. The U.S. National Institute of Standards and Technology (NIST) has defined it as "as a model for enabling convenient, on-demand network access to a shared pool of configurable computing resources that can be rapidly provisioned and released with minimal management effort" (Hawes, 2010). There are three major categories of cloud computing as services: Infrastructure as a Service (IaaS), Platform as a Service (PaaS), and Software as a Service (SaaS). These cloud services offer on-demand data access and ubiquitous communications. Cisco forecasted that CSPs will process more than three-quarters (78%) of IT workloads by 2018. In TechTarget's forecast, 80% of the financial services institutions will run on hybrid cloud architecture by 2018 (TechTarget, 2016).

---

[1] https://www.idc.com/getdoc.jsp?containerId=prUS42831017.
[2] http://www.gartner.com/smarterwithgartner/cloud-computing-enters-its-second-decade/.

Big Data Analysis

International Data Corp (IDC) defines big data as "the intelligent economy produces a constant stream of data that is being monitored and analyzed. Social interactions, simulations, mobile devices, facilities, equipment, research and development (R&D), and physical infrastructure all contribute to the flow" (IDC, 2012).

According to IDC, the market for big data technology and services will grow at a CAGR of 23% through 2019. IDC further predicted that annual spending will also reach US$48.6 billion in 2019 (Olavsrud, 2015). The volume of data is growing exponentially, and it is expected that, by 2020, there will be more than 16 zettabytes (16 trillion GB) of useful data generated (Turner et al., 2014).

There are many ways for the financial services industry to achieve business advantages by mining and analyzing data. These include enhanced detection of fraud, retail customer service, and improvement of operational efficiencies. Many fintech companies are also leveraging on big data to provide more customer-focused and intuitive services.

In 2016, the White House published a report exploring that big data can be used to reveal or possibly reduce employment discrimination by promoting efficient and ethical mechanisms for mitigating discrimination in employment opportunities. The White House report also showed that by using big data, educational opportunities can be further increased, while improved algorithms that can potentially help law enforcement become more effective, transparent, and less discriminatory (The White House, 2016). The potential for big data is expected to impact all sectors, from healthcare to media, from energy to retail (Manyika et al., 2011).

There are several ways for the financial services industry to achieve business advantages by mining and analyzing data. These include enhanced detection of fraud, retail customer service, and improvement of operational efficiencies. Big data can also be used to identify exposure in real time across a range of sophisticated financial instruments like derivatives. Predictive analysis of both internal and external data results in good, proactive management of a wide range of problems from credit and operational risk (e.g., fraud and reputational risk) to customer loyalty and profitability. Many organizations are building their core business on their ability to collect and analyze information to extract business insights. Big data technology adoption within industrial sectors is not a luxury but an imperative need for most organizations to survive and gain competitive advantage.

Internet of Things

The IoT is becoming an increasingly popular topic of conversation in the digital age. It is a concept that not only has the potential to impact how we live but also how we work. But what exactly is the IoT and what impact is it going to have?

The IoT, refers to billions of physical devices around the world that are now connected to the internet, collecting, and sharing data. Thanks to cheap processors and wireless networks, it is possible to turn anything, from a phone to a drone, into part of the IoT. This adds a level of digital intelligence to devices that would be otherwise dumb, enabling them to communicate without a human being involved, and merging the digital and physical worlds.

Processors that were cheap and power-frugal enough to be all but disposable were required before it became cost-effective to connect billions of devices. The adoption of radio-frequency identification (RFID) tags – low-power chips that can communicate wirelessly – solved some of this issue, along with the increasing availability of broadband internet and cellular and wireless networking.

The adoption of IPv6 – which, among other things, should provide enough IP addresses for every device the world is ever likely to need – was also a necessary step for the IoT to scale. Adding RFID tags to expensive pieces of equipment to help track their location was one of the first IoT applications. But since then, the cost of adding sensors and an internet connection to objects has continued to fall, and experts predict that this basic functionality could one day cost as little as 10 cents, making it possible to connect nearly everything to the internet.

According to the *Ericsson Mobility Report*, 84 million new mobile subscriptions were added in 2016 Q3, hitting to a total of 7.5 billion. The number of mobile subscriptions is continuing to rise across regions. It is also estimated that by the end of 2022, there will be 8.9 billion mobile subscriptions. Mobile broadband subscriptions will also reach 8 billion, with a 90% growth rate. Many tablets have also been sold currently, but their use is limited without a mobile subscription. The reason of this is that the price difference between WiFi only models and those with mobile capabilities is still quite significant. Despite this, the number of tablets and PCs with mobile capabilities through subscription will increase 30% by 2022. The report also forecasts that by 2022, the number of smartphone subscriptions will reach 6.8 billion, with 95% of the subscriptions registered on LTE, WCDMA/HSPA, and 5G networks (Ericsson, 2016).

The IoT is an emerging and new paradigm in the science of computers and technology in a general sense. In recent years, it has invaded our lives without us being aware of it, yet it is gaining ground as one of the most promising technologies. The European Commission defines IoT as "things having identities and virtual personalities operating in smart spaces using intelligent interfaces to connect and communicate within social, environmental, and user contexts" (Atzori, Iera, & Morabito, 2010, p. 2).

The deployment of IoT devices was initially limited to business and manufacturing, where its application is sometimes known as machine-to-machine (M2M). The number of objects able to record and transmit data to other objects is continually growing. It is forecasted that the number of devices connected to the internet will increase from 10 billion today to 50 billion by 2020 (Payvision, 2016). IoT applications could give retailers, sellers, and their banks access to real-time data on assets and services that they monitor as well as transparency on their goods in transit (Santander, 2015).

Robo-Advisors

Robo-advisors are digital platforms that provide automated and algorithm-driven financial planning services like investing. This service boasts of its ability to require little to no human supervision. A robo-advisor collects information from clients about their financial situation as well as their future goals. To do this, you are asked to answer a survey or a couple of online questions. From this, they use the data you have entered to offer advice.

The advent of modern robo-advisors has completely changed that narrative by delivering the service straight to consumers. After a decade of development, robo-advisors are now capable of handling much more sophisticated tasks, such as tax-loss harvesting, investment selection and retirement planning. The industry has experienced explosive growth as a result; client assets managed by robo-advisors hit US $60 billion at year-end 2015 and are projected to reach US$2 trillion by 2020. Other common designations for robo-advisors include "automated investment advisor," "automated investment management" and "digital advice platforms." They are all referring to the same consumer shift toward using fintech applications for investment management.

There are emerging firms that are leveraging on client algorithms and information to develop automated portfolio allocation and investment recommendations tailored to the individual customers. Such firms have been termed as "robo-advisors." Clients can easily access robo-advisory through digital user channels for very low fees and sometimes for free (Deloitte, 2016a).

Robo-advisors can eliminate behavioral biases and handle routine account maintenance without human involvement. They quickly attained market traction, overseeing US$19 billion by the end of 2014. KPMG and CGI forecast that the number will hit US$2 trillion in assets by 2020 (Patpatia & Association and CGI, 2016). In addition, KPMG's 2016 survey forecasted that 75% of survey's respondents are interested in robo-advisory services (KPMG, 2016). MyPrivateBanking, a research firm, estimated that hybrid robo services will rise by 2020 to a size of US$3.7 trillion assets worldwide; by 2025 the total market size will grow to US$16.3 trillion (MyPrivateBanking, 2016).

A Japanese insurance company, Fukoku Mutual Life Insurance, has replaced more than 30 of its staff by using IBM Watson cognitive computing software robot known as Amelia, which can understand the semantics of the language and can answer business queries like a human. The Japanese company has plans to use Amelia to read medical documents that are used to assess payments. Although the robots will eventually calculate payment amounts, the final approval decisions will still be made by qualified human personnel (Computer Weekly, 2017).

The main advantage of robo-advisors is that they are low-cost alternatives to traditional advisors. By eliminating human labor, online platforms can offer the same services at a fraction of the cost. Most robo-advisors charge an annual flat fee of 0.2% to 0.5% of a client's total account balance. That compares with the typical rate of 1% to 2% charged by a human financial planner, and potentially more for commission-based accounts.

Robo-advisors are also more accessible. They are available 24/7 if the user has an internet connection. Furthermore, it takes significantly less capital to get started, as the minimum assets required to register for an account are typically in the hundreds to thousands (US$5,000 is a standard baseline). One of the most popular robo-advisors, Betterment, has no account minimum at all.

In contrast, human advisors do not normally take on clients with less than US$100,000 in investable assets, especially those who are established in the field. They prefer high-net-worth individuals who need a variety of wealth management services and can afford to pay for them.

Efficiency is another significant advantage these online platforms have. For instance, before robo-advisors, if clients wanted to execute a trade, they would have to call or physically meet a financial advisor, explain their needs, fill out the paperwork, and wait. Now, all of that can be done with the click of a few buttons in the comfort of one's home.

Robo-advisors hold the same legal status as human advisors. They must register with the U.S. Securities and Exchange Commission to conduct business, and are therefore subject to the same securities laws and regulations as traditional broker-dealers. The official designation is "Registered Investment Adviser," or RIA for short. Most robo-advisors are members of the independent regulator Financial Industry Regulatory Authority (FINRA) as well. Investors can use BrokerCheck to research robo-advisors the same way they would a human advisor.

In the United States, assets managed by robo-advisors are not insured by the Federal Deposit Insurance Corporation (FDIC), as they are securities held for investment purposes, not bank deposits. This does not necessarily mean clients are unprotected however, as there are many other avenues by which broker-dealers can insure assets. For example, Wealthfront, the second largest robo-advisor in the United States, is insured by the Securities Investor Protection Corporation (SIPC).

Artificial Intelligence

In 1956, the fathers of modern AI, John McCarthy, Marvin Minsky, Allen Newell, Claude Shannon, Nathaniel Rochester, and Herbert Simon came together for summer school at Dartmouth College (New Hampshire) under the hypothesis that every aspect of intelligence and learning can in principle be so precisely explained that a machine can be made to simulate it. That date is considered the birth of AI because after that time numerous research groups around the globe began to engage in the construction of artificial systems with the avowed goal of equaling, emulating, or even surpassing human mental and physical abilities (Lungarella et al., 2007). In the 1960s, the U.S. Department of Defense took interest in this type of work and began training computers to mimic basic human reasoning. For example, the Defense Advanced Research Projects Agency (DARPA) completed street mapping projects in the 1970s and produced intelligent virtual assistants in 2003.

AI is an area of computer science that emphasizes the creation of intelligent machines that work and react like humans. AI makes it possible for machines to learn from experience, adjust to new inputs and perform human-like tasks. Using modern technologies, computers can be trained to accomplish specific tasks by processing large amounts of data and recognizing patterns in the data.

As such AI has become a hot topic, with many talking about the advantages that it can bring to the highly regulated financial services industry. AI can help banks in their anti-money laundering (AML) and counter-terrorism financing (CTF) screening or employee misconduct detection efforts by replacing costly functions that are currently done manually by humans (Arslanian, 2016).

Another example is that of the Swedish bank, SEB, which is using AI software from IPsoft for its customer service function, after achieving success in an internal project. While a customer service experience of the future may involve automation of some kind, the help of a virtual human called a cognitive agent may be the next evolutionary step. Cognitive agents are virtual assistants that can supposedly think and act like humans, be able to handle complex interactions and learn from situations. SEB in Sweden is the first bank that has decided to use IPsoft's cognitive technology for customer services (Flinders, 2016). For SEB, it is all about scalability and the fact that they now have customer service solutions that they can roll out quickly.

Machine Learning and Deep Learning

Machine learning (ML) is a branch of AI based on the idea that systems can learn from data, identify patterns, and make decisions with minimal human intervention. It was born from pattern recognition and the theory that computers can learn without being programmed to perform specific tasks; researchers interested in AI wanted to see if computers could learn from data. The iterative aspect of ML is important because as models are exposed to new data, they can independently adapt. They learn from previous computations to produce reliable, repeatable decisions and results. Essentially it works on a system of probability – based on data fed to it, it can make statements, decisions, or predictions with a degree of certainty. The addition of a feedback loop enables "learning" – by sensing or being told whether its decisions are right or wrong, it modifies the approach it takes in the next iteration (future).

ML applications can read text and work out whether the person who wrote it is making a complaint, making a contractual agreement, offering congratulations or simply making a declaration. They can also listen to an instruction, decipher the speaker's accent, and find pieces of information to match the request, or decide what to do next if the information is unavailable. The idea was to be able to communicate and interact with electronic devices and digital information, as naturally as we would with another human being through ML and neural networks. Think Siri, Alexa, or Cortana.

Within the field of data analytics, ML is a method used to devise complex models and algorithms that lend themselves to prediction; in commercial use, this is known as predictive analytics. These analytical models allow researchers, data scientists, engineers, and analysts to "produce reliable, repeatable decisions and results" and uncover "hidden insights" through learning from historical relationships and trends in the data.[3] In the current AI revolution, ML has entrenched itself to eventually develop human-like AI. In the last few years, we have begun to hear about deeper concepts than ML – *deep learning*.

Deep learning is used by Google in its voice and image recognition algorithms, by Netflix and Amazon to decide what you want to watch or buy next,[4] and by researchers at MIT to predict the future.[5] MIT designed a predictive system, a deep-learning method called adversarial learning, wherein two neural networks try to outsmart each other. Using this technique, the researchers were able to generate predictions that were deemed to be realistic 20% more often than a baseline model of other computer-generated methods.

Because deep learning work is focused on developing big data neural networks, they become what are known as deep neural networks – complex logic networks to deal with classifying very large datasets, like Google's massive image library, or Twitter's never-ending barrage of tweets. With datasets as comprehensive as these, and logical networks sophisticated enough to handle their classification, it becomes trivial for a computer to specify something (a lot of things really) with a high probability of accuracy in what it presents to human beings.

---

3 https://www.sas.com/en_sg/insights/analytics/machine-learning.html.
4 https://www.forbes.com/sites/bernardmarr/2016/12/08/what-is-the-difference-betwee-deep-learning-machine-learning-and-ai/#1980ca7b26cfn.
5 https://www.ibtimes.com/artificial-intelligence-mit-researchers-create-deep-learning-algo-ithm-can-peer-2452024.

Quantum Computing

Quantum computing (QC) is another landmark development in the technological world. It introduces an efficient and appropriate way for unfolding and then resolving complex problems on computing systems that uses the concepts of superposition and entanglement. Since the 1940s, the systems we have been using in various shapes and forms – laptops, cloud servers, smartphones, supercomputers – are known as classical computers. Those classical computers are based on bits (zeros and ones), a unit of information that does every computation that happens in the device. In quantum computers, there are quantum bits also known as qubits. These qubits are different than bits used in classical computers and the qubits are made up of quantum particles found in the nature. The property of qubits is that they can use for superposition which is major component of QC. This allows the quantum particles to exist in different states at the same time. For example, in classical computers, in case of coin, there will be head or tail at one time, but in case of quantum computers, there may be head and tail both at the same time, it means quantum particles related to the coin exist even while coin is flipping. This is the reason why QC is important because using qubits, the quantum computer can run several problems at one time and find out the answer.

In today's world of big data, QC has great implications for large firms and financial institution who want to leverage the large size data and by computing that data they can valuable information and find out solutions. Qubits can also be inextricably linked together using a phenomenon called quantum entanglement. Quantum entanglement is a quantum mechanical phenomenon in which the quantum states of two or more objects must be described with reference to each other, even though the individual objects may be spatially separated. The implication of quantum entanglement is that measurements performed on one system seem to be instantaneously influencing other systems entangled with it.

QC has applications for financial services industry. By applying QC to resolve financial problems, specially, those dealing with constrained optimization and uncertainty. First movers can take huge advantage by implementing this technology as they will be able to make complex calculations and unveil dynamic arbitrage possibilities that other are unable to observe. Moreover, by using behavioral data, the financial institutions can enhance customers' engagement and do faster assessment of the market volatility.

The combination of QC, AI and ML can prove to be a complete package for financial institutions and bring great advantages to them. The fraud detection is a challenging problem for institutions, by using this combination of technology, this problem can be resolved. It is estimated that financial institutions are losing between US$10 billion and US$40 billion in revenue a year due to fraud and poor data management practices. Fraud detection systems remain highly inaccurate, returning 80% false positives, causing financial institutions to be overly risk averse.

To help ensure proper credit scoring, the customer onboarding process can take as long as 12 weeks. In today's digital age, where 70% of banking takes place digitally, consumers are just not willing to wait that long (Yndurain et al., 2019). Financial institutions too slow in engaging effectively with new customers are losing them to more nimble competitors. For customer targeting and prediction modeling, quantum computing could be a game changer. The data modeling capabilities of quantum computers are expected to prove superior in finding patterns, performing classifications, and making predictions that are not possible today because of the challenges of complex data structures. The other use cases of QC for financial industry are trading optimization, risk profiling, optimal feature selection in credit scoring (Orús et al., 2019), post-quantum cryptography and blockchain for smart cities (Chen et al., 2021) and financial transactions.

Due to the importance of QC, financial institutions have started experimenting this technology. Presently, the major Wall Street banks are leading the charge in the quantum realm. J.P. Morgan and Citigroup, meanwhile, have set up quantum computing initiatives and even bought stakes in computing start-ups. In the late 2019, Wells Fargo joined the IBM Q program, a community of companies, startups, academic institutions, and research labs working to explore practical applications. European banks are also exploring quantum computing opportunities. BBVA has formed a partnership to explore portfolio optimization and more efficient Monte Carlo modelling. Also, in Spain, Caixa Bank is running a trial hybrid framework of quantum and conventional computing with the aim of better classifying credit risk profiles. In mid-2020, UK's Standard Chartered revealed its exploration of quantum computing applications, such as portfolio simulation, in collaboration with US-based Universities Space Research Association (Backes et al., 2020).

References

Accenture. (2016a). Blockchain Technology-How-Banks-Building-Real-Time-Global-Payment-Network. https://www.accenture.com/t20161019T015506w/us-en/_acnmedia/PDF-35/Accenture-Blockchain-How-Banks-Building-Real-Time-Global-Payment-Network.PDF

Accenture. (2016b). Unbanked Population Market Opportunity. https://www.accenture.com/us-en/insight-billion-reasons-bank-inclusively

Arslanian, H. (2016, December 12). 10 FinTech Predictions for Asia in 2017. https://letstalkpayments.com/10-predictions-for-asia-in-2017/

Atzori, L., Iera, A., & Morabito, G. (2010). The Internet of Things: A Survey. *Computer Networks*, *54*(15), 2787–2805.

Backes, J., Dietz, M., Henke, N., Moon, J., Pautasso, L., & Sadeque, Z. (2020). How quantum computing could change financial services. In McKinsey (Issue December). https://www.mckinsey.com/industries/financial-services/our-insights/how-quantum-computing-could-change-financial-services

Belleflamme, P., Omrani, N., & Peitz, M. (2015). The Economics of Crowdfunding Platforms. *Information Economics and Policy*, *33*, 11–28.

BNY Mellon. (2014). *Global Payments 2020: Transformation and Convergence.* https://www.finextra.com/finextra-downloads/featuredocs/bny_mellon.pdf

Chen, J., Gan, W., Hu, M., & Chen, C. M. (2021). On the construction of a post-quantum blockchain for smart city. *Journal of Information Security and Applications, 58.* https://doi.org/10.1016/j.jisa.2021.102780

Coraggio, G. (2017, January 5). P2P lending boosted by new Italian FinTech rules? http://www.gamingtechlaw.com/2017/01/p2p-lending-fintech-italy.html

ComputerWeekly. (2017, January). Robots replace staff at Japanese insurance firm. http://www.computerweekly.com/news/450410454/Robots-replace-staff-at-Japanese-insurance-firm

David, S. (2016). Asset Management: The Next Frontier for FinTech? *Asset Management: The next Frontier for FinTech? – FinTech News.* http://www.ukFinTech.com/future-of-FinTech/asset-management-the-next-frontier-for-FinTech

Deloitte. (2016a). *Blockchains: Enigma. Paradox. Opportunity.* https://www2.deloitte.com/content/dam/Deloitte/uk/Documents/Innovation/deloitte-uk-blockchain-full-report.pdf

Deloitte. (2016b). *Robo-Advisors: Capitalizing on a Growing Opportunity.* https://www2.deloitte.com/content/dam/Deloitte/us/Documents/strategy/us-cons-robo-advisors.pdf

Ericsson. (2016). *Ericsson Mobility Report.*

Flinders, K. (2016, October). Swedish Bank Uses Amelia the Robot for Customer Services. https://www.computerweekly.com/news/450400413/Swedish-bank-uses-Amelia-the-robot-for-customer-services

Freedman, D. M., & Nutting, M. R. (2015). A Brief History of Crowdfunding Including Rewards. *Donation, Debt, and Equity Platforms in the USA*, 1–10, 1–8.

Hawes, K. (2010, November 15). Cloud Computing. Retrieved January 11, 2017, https://www.nist.gov/programs-projects/cloud-computing

International Data Corp. (IDC). (2012). *Worldwide Big Data Technology and Services Forecast, 2012–16.*

Kharif, O. (2016, May 19). Blockchain Goes Beyond Crypto-Currency. *Bloomberg.Com.* https://www.bloomberg.com/news/articles/2016-05-19/built-for-bitcoin-blockchain-goes-beyond-crypto-currency

KPMG. (2016). *Robo Advising: Hype or Opportunity?* https://home.kpmg.com/content/dam/kpmg/pdf/2016/07/Robo-Advising-Catching-Up-And-Getting-Ahead.pdf

Let's Talk Payments. (2016, April 4). 10 Reasons Why InsurTech Is Going to Be Important. Retrieved February 7, 2017, https://letstalkpayments.com/10-reasons-why-insurtech-is-going-to-be-important/

Lungarella, M., Iida, F., Bongard, J., and Pfeifer, R. (2007). *50 Years of Artificial Intelligence: Essays Dedicated to the 50th Anniversary of Artificial Intelligence* (Vol. 4850). Switzerland: Springer. https://books.google.com/books?hl=en&id=xeFtCQAAQBAJ&oi=fnd&pg=PP2&dq=50Years+of+Artificial+Intelligence+Essays+Dedicated+to+the+50th+Anniversary+of+Artificial+Intelligence&ots=m3tbYe224u&sig=ljT5iFvtkGblY5CgWxXeHVJOZr8

Mainelli, M., & Milne, A. (2016). The Impact and Potential of Blockchain on Securities Transaction Lifecycle. http://papers.ssrn.com/sol3/papers.cfm?abstract_id=2777404

Manyika, J., Chui, M., Brown, B., Bughin, J., Dobbs, R., Roxburgh, C., & Byers, A. H. (2011). *Big data: The next frontier for innovation, competition, and productivity.* New York, NY, USA: McKinsey & Co.

MyPrivateBanking. (2016). *Robo Advisors Are Gaining Popularity with High-Net-Worth Investors.*

Olavsrud, T. (2015, November). IDC Says Big Data Spending to Hit $48.6 Billion in 2019. https://www.cio.com/article/3004512/big-data/idc-predicts-big-data-spending-to-reach-48-6-billion-in-2019.html

Orús, R., Mugel, S., & Lizaso, E. (2019). Quantum computing for finance: Overview and prospects. *Reviews in Physics*, 4(September 2018). https://doi.org/10.1016/j.revip.2019.100028

Oracle (2017), Banking in the Connected World, http://www.oracle.com/us/industries/financial-services/fs-banking-connected-world-wp-4082001.pdf.

Patpatia & Association and CGI. (2016). *Beyond Robo-Advisors: Using Technology to Power New Methods of Client Advice and Interaction*. USA: Patpatia & Associates, Inc.

Payvision. (2016). The Mobile Payments Report 2016. http://www.payvision.com/the-mobile-payments-report-2016-an-omnichannel-evolution

PricewaterhouseCoopers. (2016). *Payments in the Wild Tech World: Digitisation and Changing Customer Expectations*. https://www.pwc.com/gx/en/financial-services/FinTech/assets/payments-in-the-wild-tech-world.pdf

PricewaterhouseCoopers PwC. (2016a). *How FinTech Is Shaping Asset and Wealth Management*. http://www.pwc.com/gx/en/industries/financial-services/publications/how-FinTech-is-shaping-asset-and-wealth-management.html

PricewaterhouseCoopers PwC. (2016b). *Opportunities Await: How InsurTech Is Reshaping Insurance*. http://www.pwc.com/gx/en/industries/financial-services/FinTech-survey/insurtech.html

Research and Markets. (2016). *Global Crowdfunding Market 2016–2020*. Research and Markets. http://www.researchandmarkets.com/reports/3608989/global-crowdfunding-market-2016-2020

Santander. (2015). *The FinTech 2.0 Paper: rebooting financial services*. USA: Santander InnoVentures.

Shen, L. (2016). Blockchain Could Start Making Some Real Waves the Banking Industry Next Year. Retrieved February 6, 2017, http://fortune.com/2016/09/28/blockchain-banks-2017/

Skinner, C. M. (2017, March 8). 57 Banks and Nothing Wrong? Retrieved July 3, 2018, https://thefinanser.com/2017/03/57-banks-nothing-wrong.html/

Statista. (2016). *FinTech: Digital Payments*. Retrieved from https://www.statista.com/download/outlook/whitepaper/FinTech_Payments_Outlook_0117.pdf

Statista. (2017a). Statista Report on Fintech 2017. http://static2.statista.com/download/pdf/Statista_Report_2017_FinTech_Excerpt.pdf

Statista. (2017b). Topic: Kickstarter. Retrieved October 31, 2018, https://www.statista.com/topics/2102/kickstarter/

TechTarget, C. (2016). *What Does Cloud Computing Look Like in 2016?* (E-guide).

The White House. (2016). *Big Data: A Report on Algorithmic Systems, Opportunity, and Civil Rights*. Washington.

Tapscott, D. (2016, May). How Blockchains Could Change the World | McKinsey & Company. http://www.mckinsey.com/industries/high-tech/our-insights/how-blockchains-could-change-the-worldinfrastructure-an-ambitious-look-at-how-blockchain-can-reshape-financial-services

Turner, V., Gantz, J. F., Reinsel, D., & Minton, S. (2014). The digital universe of opportunities: Rich data and the increasing value of the internet of things. *IDC Analyze the Future*, Asia Pacific: International Data corporation, IDC. 5.

World Economic Forum. (2016). The Future of Financial Infrastructure: An Ambitious Look at How Blockchain Can Reshape Financial Services (p. 130). http://weforum.org/reports/the-future-of-financial-infrastructure-an-ambitious-look-at-how-blockchain-can-reshape-financial-services

Yndurain, E., Stefan Woerner, & Daneil J. Egger. (2019). Exploring quantum computing use cases for financial services. In IBM.

Chapter 4
Emergence of Islamic Fintech and its Developments

Introduction

Shariah rules and regulations are the underlying tenets of Islamic finance products. The terms and conditions of these contracts are always written in legal documents and these documents need to be executed in the right way to ensure proper compliance. At the moment, the mechanisms are manual, and the processes take a lot of time and are costly. Advanced technologies such as artificial intelligence and automatable smart contracts have the potential to significantly improve the overall process, efficiency, transparency, and saving of time.

With the digitalization and technological revolution, the financial services industry is witnessing the most significant transformational development of the era, one that is certainly positive and inclusive for these populations. Thus, automation is increasingly developing not only as a tool that can improve financial performance, but also functioning as an effective tool to enhance sustainability and efficiency. Technology has the potential to contribute effectively, particularly in the area of financial inclusion and sustainable development, offering new ways for integration for those who are excluded from the financial services industry and have a superior financial and social status, while ensuring that they have access to a wide range of financial products in line with their values. Rather than looking at the fintech revolution as unwelcoming, we should leverage on it to advance economic and social goals in embracing it as an opportunity, because its potential for social impact is enormous.

Over the last five years, Islamic fintech has grown from infancy with very limited number of platforms to over a hundred credible ventures. Still, when compared to the global (conventional) fintech landscape, the size of Islamic fintech is significantly smaller and less market-leading. But the start-ups that have emerged in these last three–four years, have shown credible performance and acceptability by the Islamic markets. Islamic crowdfunding has been the main segment of Islamic fintech still, but these are relatively low-tech when compared to more sophisticated firms. Four Islamic countries, Brunei Darussalam, Malaysia, Bahrain, and UAE, have issued regulatory frameworks for fintech to allow the banks, institutions, and start-ups to collaborate and develop innovative business models and test them within controlled guidelines. These developments show that the global landscape of fintech adoption will continue to evolve as the regulators and industry work together in key areas of regulatory implications on new technological advances in the financial sector for responsible development of products and services.

What Is Islamic Fintech?

As Shariah-compliant finance grows and institutions embrace mobile and internet banking, the sector believes it offers strong opportunities with meaningful steps being taken to develop fintech ecosystems in key markets to grow the industry. But how does one really define Islamic fintech? How does it differ from conventional fintech for that matter?

Islamic fintech can be defined as the technologies that are deployed in Islamic finance to uphold and entrench Islamic rules and values in order to build a just, resilient and sustainable economy. It utilizes all the necessary elements of technology, which will disrupt cumbersome processes, bottlenecks, and inaccessibility of funds by the underserved segments of society. In the subsequent sections, we categorize the current existing Islamic fintech platforms and analyze their use cases and applications for the industry in order to serve their target markets more efficiently.

Etymologically, Islamic fintech is the amalgamation of technology and Islamic finance, which means that any product or service that spawns from fintech must abide by the rules extracted from the Qur'an and Sunnah known as the Shariah. True to its fintech label, its digital distribution of Shariah-compliant financial products and services is delivered through innovative digital channels known as omnichannels. Islamic fintech platforms utilize revolutionary technologies like artificial intelligence (AI), blockchain, big data, extensive cloud computing and internet of things (IoT) devices in providing Islamic financial services in a more sophisticated and transparent way. Its activities will involve deploying new tech-based business models to promote economic, environmental, financial and social goals, which include better services across all Islamic financial services and product performance, and broader benefits like financial inclusion, poverty alleviation and social justice. Islamic fintech would enable greater access to Islamic financial services in cheaper, easier, and more efficient ways to provide opportunities for financing, payments, and investment aligned to the intended objectives of the Islamic Divine Laws (*Maqasid Al-Shariah*).

Alignment between Islamic Finance and Fintech

The Islamic financial system has an in-built and inherent character of risk sharing and rule-compliance. In practice, however, Islamic banking and finance is no different from the conventional finance industry, which relies heavily on risk transfer and/or the shifting of risk from lender to the borrower. This incongruency does not sit comfortably on the different sections of the Muslim society with regards to Islamic banking and financial services. Since the emergence of Islamic banking in the 1960s and 1970s, this industry has faced much criticism due to its mimicking of conventional interest-based risk-transfer/shifting modus operandi of banking. Likewise, the consumers of Islamic banks expect guaranteed or fixed returns similar to existing conventional banks. This is a poor understanding of the profit-and-loss-sharing mechanism that an ideal Islamic finance system should uphold. The consumers, like the banks, should be willing to undertake the risk and share the outcome, be it profits or losses. This is the basis of risk-sharing or having "skin-in the-game." Both parties have a vested interest in a transaction or investment and will likely work closely to achieve shared objectives. The core values of caring, cooperating, preventing possible harm, etc. are then ingrained in such agreements.

Today, Islamic banking and finance is heavily based on risk transferring and risk shifting. The balance sheets of Islamic banks show the concentration of two products, that is, *murabahah,* which is trade based mark-ups and *ijarah,* which is a lease-based product. Islamic banks have very low percentage of truly risk sharing products on their balance sheets, which are *mudarabah* (silent partnership) and *musyarakah* (joint venture). Also, Islamic banking and finance, which should have operationalized the ideals of the Shariah to pursue capitalistic goals *alongside* social aims, have made little headway in financial inclusion among the underbanked and unbanked population. The democratization of formal financial services is indeed crucial for the economic empowerment of the Muslim ummah, or the general public. The true soul of Islamic finance is to instill inclusivity and shared prosperity; at this stage, the current Islamic banking model does not seem fit to the bill. The transformation of Islamic banking institutions from a risk transferring to risk sharing model, should be built on norms and rules, which are the essence of a truly Islamic economy. It should not be a system to compete with the existing interest-based risk-transfer/shifting conventional system. The rhetoric of Islamic finance literature and conferences are enriched with the discussion of risk sharing but the real understanding and implementation of the risk sharing model is very limited and requires a disruption.

Islamic fintech provides the opportunity for the adoption and application of a risk sharing model in Islamic financial institutions through small innovative start-ups who want to contribute to the Islamic finance industry. One example is neo-banking or virtual banks. This Islamic neo-banking model provides the opportunities for financers and investors who are looking for true Islamic risk-sharing, interest-free products and services, which are not currently possible through existing Islamic banks. The modus operandi of the Islamic fintech should be highly congruent with the asset-backed, interest-free, risk sharing, under-leveraged real sector model of the ideal Islamic economy.

Islamic fintech can then be articulated through the democratization of financial services and the delivery of financial services via new digital channels. Its essence should include the elimination of asymmetric information, fraud, no-confidence and distrust between counterparties, be they financial institutions, regulators, family offices and customers. It also reduces the deceptive ambiguity in the operations and business models of not only counterparty transactions but creates positive ripple effects throughout the entire supply chain within the Islamic economic ecosystem. For instance, monitoring through a public distributed ledger (blockchain) in the application of smart contracts, Islamic fintech companies can bring more efficiency and transparency in their operations. Similarly, the usage of IoT devices in takaful can make insurance claims submission and processing more nimble and agile. The cash *waqf* (Islamic endowment) model on blockchain also could be a great breakthrough in *waqf* management, too.

Social and ethical impacts of financial services are also one of the main promises of Islamic fintech. For example, the financing for a welfare project is often not possible through traditional banking and financial institutions, but now through crowdfunding, take, for example, LaunchGood and GoFundMe, it is possible for individuals and small businesses of any sector to get funding for their social impact projects.

Islam and Fintech in History

History has witnessed that Islamic banking at the commercial level started and emerged in the 1970s. From the banking perspective alone, Islamic finance started very late in the game as compared to conventional banking, which started in the 1660s with the formation of the Bank of England.

However, in the twentieth century, Islamic revivalists worked to define interest as *riba*, to enjoin Muslims to lend and borrow at "Islamic Banks" that avoided interest-bearing fixed rates. By the twenty-first century this Islamic Banking movement had created "institutions of interest-free financial enterprises across the world" (Choudhury, 1992). The movement started with activists and scholars in the late 1940s and early 1950s (Siddiqi, 1981). They believed commercial banks were a "necessary evil," and proposed a banking system based on the concept of *mudarabah*, where shared profit on investment would replace interest.

And this revival of greater Islamic observance was not unjustified. The developments in the fields of social sciences, humanities, and natural sciences made by past Muslims were remarkable. They were the best innovators and inventors of their times. Their focus was serving time and money on learning, education and making inventions. Muḥammad ibn Mūsā al-Khwārizmī[1] was one of the first to have

---

[1] Al-Khwarizmi's treatise on algebra (*The Compendious Book on Calculation by Completion and Balancing*, ca. 813–833 CE [8]:171) presented the first systematic solution of linear and quadratic equations. One of his principal achievements in algebra was his demonstration of how to solve quadratic equations by completing the square, for which he provided geometric justifications. He was known as the Father of Algebra. The term algebra itself comes from the title of his book (specifically the word *al-jabr* meaning "completion" or "rejoining"). His name gave rise to the terms algorism and algorithm. His name is also the origin of (Spanish) *guarismo* and of (Portu-guese) *algarismo*, both meaning digit.

introduced algebra, numeric digits, and the basic notions of algorithms to the world. These basics of algebra and algorithms are now considered the pillars of technology since every modern device and technology is based on some fundamental algorithm. Freedman (2006), in his book *Introduction to Financial Technology* clearly mentioned that the father and pioneer of the technological revolution was the Muslim Mathematician, al-Khwārizmī. *The Compendious Book on Calculation by Completion and Balancing*, translated into Latin by Robert of Chester in 1145, was used until the sixteenth century as the principal mathematical textbook of European universities.[2] Unfortunately, the Muslims to date have been unable to follow the path of their great ancestors who had made defining and world-changing concepts, which still reverberate, centuries later, until today. Nevertheless, the tide of the fintech revolution seemed to have awoken some segments of the Islamic society. About 120 Islamic fintech players have emerged on the Islamic fintech landscape; most of these 120 players are less than five years old. Comparatively, the conventional fintech global landscape consists of more than 2,000 fintech platforms; half of which have been around more than five years. In itself, it is encouraging to note that massive frustrations with the current Islamic banking and finance models are now being translated to wider innovation for improved models and use cases.

The excitement about fintech is not a just fantasy or a passing fad. Fintech is something that will put the whole financial industry (conventional *and* Islamic) on a level playing field. The segment that gives greater priority to innovation and openness, will capture future market share and dominance. For the Islamic finance industry, this can erase centuries of lagging behind in the banking game, and an opportunity to springboard alongside the conventional system to offer and deploy competitive products that are Shariah-compliant through the effective use of new technologies for innovative business models and capabilities to scale.

Islamic Fintech Developments Around the Globe

Fintech has begun to penetrate into the Islamic finance space, where these new Islamic fintech platforms are leveraging on social media data and analyzing them for practical purposes such as targeted marketing and profiling user behavior. This section looks at the global landscape of Islamic fintech platforms (see Figure 4.1) and we divide them according to the different categories of their services and underlying technologies.

---

[2] Fred James Hill, and Nicholas Awde (2003). *A History of the Islamic World*, p. 55. "'The Compendious Book on Calculation by Completion and Balancing' (Hisab al-Jabr wa H-Muqabala) on the development of the subject cannot be underestimated. Translated into Latin during the 12th Century, it remained the principal mathematics textbook in European universities until the 16th Century."

Figure 4.1: Islamic Fintech Companies and Platforms.
Source: Islamic FinTech Landscape by Red Money (as of March 2022).

Global Islamic Fintech Landscape and Index

The first of its kind index named "Global Islamic Fintech Index" (GIFT) is published in (Global Islamic Fintech Report, 2021). The index applied a total of 32 indicators across five different categories for each country. These five categories are: Talent; Regulation; Infrastructure; Islamic Fintech Market & Ecosystem; and Capital. The index encapsulates an overall ranking of 64 OIC and non-OIC countries. These countries were included based on their existing Islamic Fintech market activity, the presence of Islamic finance capital (a facilitator of growth in Islamic Fintech), or due to their systemic importance to the wider global Fintech ecosystem (e.g., China, Japan).

The results of this index show that Malaysia, Saudi Arabia, and the UAE rated as top destinations. Malaysia scored 87 out of 100, followed by Saudi Arabia (76) and UAE (70). Figure 4.2 shows the scores of top 20 countries.

Interestingly, several non-OIC countries are also listed in the above list and some of them such as UK is performing much better than majority of Islamic countries. The following regional comparison exhibits the median values of different regions.

Figure 4.3 shows that several non-OIC regions are also quite conducive to Islamic Fintech, for example, Americas, Europe.

Islamic Fintech Developments Around the Globe — 73

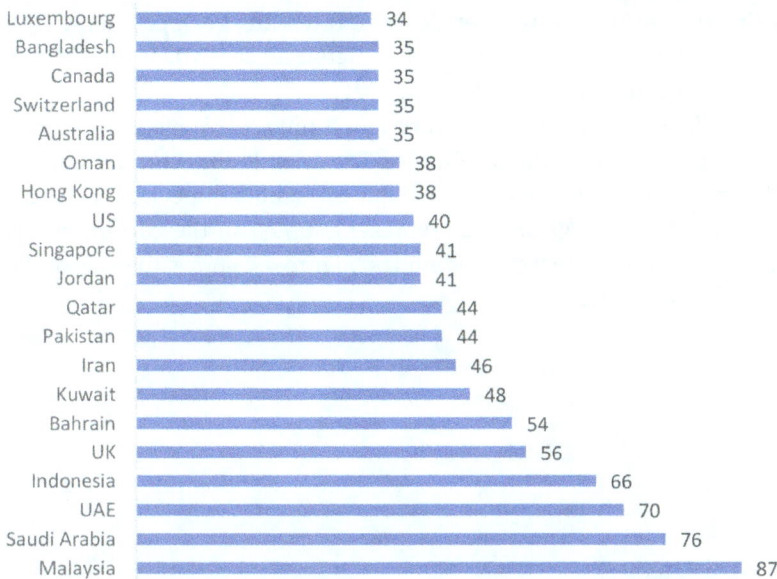

Figure 4.2: Top 20 Islamic Fintech Countries according to GIFT.
Source: Modified from (Global Islamic Fintech Report, 2021).

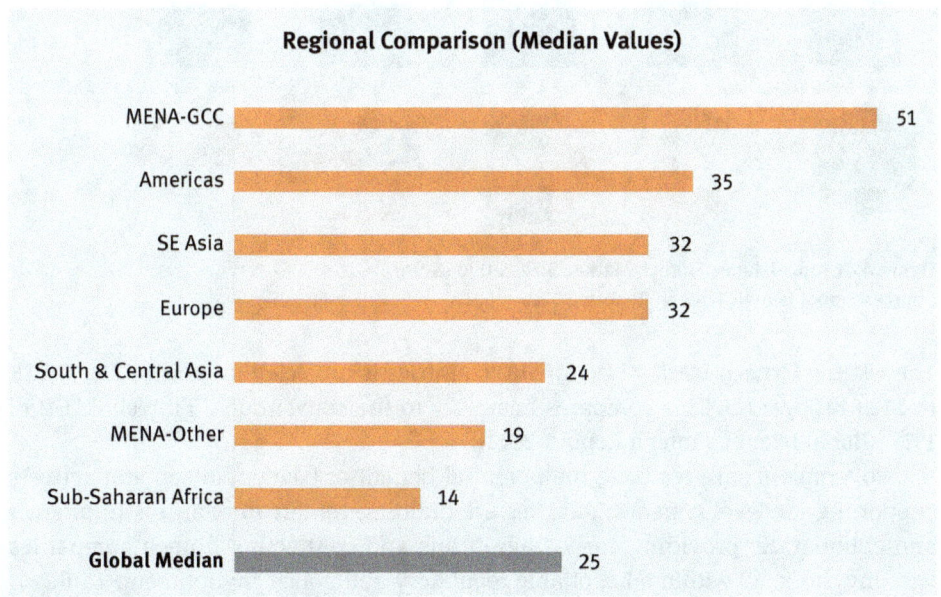

Figure 4.3: Regional Comparison (Median Values).
Source: (Global Islamic Fintech Report, 2021).

The Islamic fintech landscape is expanding with slow speed but with constant pace. The number of Islamic fintech companies has reached to 225 that includes platforms of raising funds (44), followed by deposits & lending (40), payments (37), alternative finance (32), wealth management (32), digital assets (20), social finance (12), insurance (6) and capital markets (2) (GIFR, 2021).

The progress of Islamic fintech is not very much impressive when it is compared with the numbers of conventional fintech. The Islamic fintech landscape is still young and very much fragmented. The estimated Islamic Fintech market size for OIC countries in 2020 was $49 Bn. This represents 0.72% of the current global Fintech market size, based on transaction volumes. Figure 4.4 shows the size of the top five Islamic fintech markets.

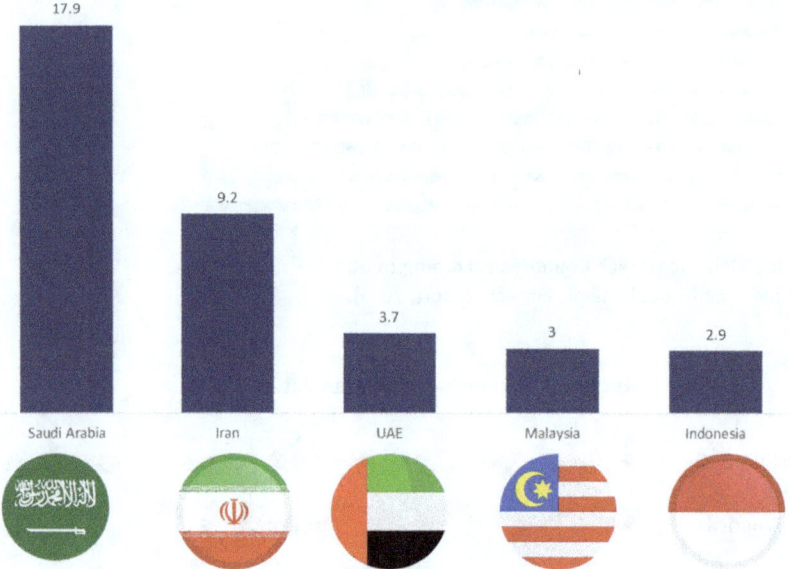

Figure 4.4: Top 5 Islamic Fintech Market Sizes 2020 ($ Bn).
Source: Global Islamic Fintech Report, 2021.

The Islamic Fintech market size for OIC countries is projected to grow at 21% CAGR to $128 Bn by 2025. This compares favorably to the conventional Fintech CAGR of 15% (Global Islamic Fintech Report, 2021).

Governments are realizing the potential benefit of Islamic fintech and actively supporting its development. Countries are building centers for startups to interact and collaborate, providing early-stage funds and connecting fintech companies with investors, all within a hospitable regulatory and policy environment. Table 4.1 shows the facilities providing different governments regarding Islamic fintech:

Table 4.1: OIC Governments or Regulators Facilitating Islamic Fintech.

Organization	Country	Facility Provided
National Islamic Finance Committee (KNKS)	Indonesia	A federal government entity, The National Shari'a Finance Committee (KNKS) is an institution that functions as a catalyst for the development of Islamic finance and wider Islamic Economy on a national and international scale. It was setup to drive the execution of the Indonesian Shari'a Economic Master Plan issued in May 2019
Bank Negara	Malaysia	Investment Account Platform (IAP) established by Bank Negara is the first Islamic P2P initiative established by a central bank.
Malaysia Digital Economy Corporation	Malaysia	Connecting a network of investors with halal business owners and providing halal certifications. Owned by the Malaysian government.
Dubai International Financial Center	UAE	Accelerate the financial technology sector in MEASA through DIFC Fintech Hive program that supports fintech, regtech, insurtech, and Islamic fintech startups. Provides access to a USD 100 million fund and network of financial institutions.
Bahrain Fintech Bay	Bahrain	Provides opportunities for fintech companies to cooperate and develop their technologies. IFIs operating in Bahrain and throughout the GCC are partners with the Bahrain Fintech Bay.
Other	UK, Turkey, and Abu Dhabi	UK Islamic Fintech panel to promote Islamic fintech sector. UK-Turkey Islamic Fintech Working Group to consider opportunities in Islamic Fintech sector. Abu Dhabi General Market's New Fintech Ecosystem.

Source: Modified from (World Bank, 2020).

Islamic Countries' Initiatives for Islamic Fintech

There are several cities around the world accelerating toward building Islamic financial hubs for their region. These leading Islamic financial hubs in different regions are taking the lead in exploring the extended use of Islamic financial technologies within their ecosystems. Although the focus of this section is on Islamic countries' initiatives, we have included London as well since it is a key Islamic finance hub for Europe.

Islamic Republic of Pakistan (Islamabad, Lahore)

In the Islamic Republic of Pakistan, 60% of the total population is made up of youth. Pakistan is suited well to embrace the digital age because of its large ratio of young population and also their disproportionate excitement toward technology adoption. Pakistan Telecommunication Authority (PTA) has recently reported that annual cellular subscribers by October 2020 are more than 174 million (87% of population) (Pakistan Telecommunication Authority PTA, 2020). The Mobile broadband penetration has also improved from 16% to 42% (PTA, 2020). According to Pakistan Economy survey, PTA has unveiled 5G roadmap incorporating the testing of 5G technology and allied services during the FY2021 (Govt. of Pakistan, 2020). The steady growth in the consumerization of IT among Pakistanis shows that their behavior and psychology is also changing with gradual speed that can be translated into a step toward the digitalization of the country.

The level of financial inclusion is very low in Pakistan and it is considered among the least financially inclusive countries in the world. A large proportion of the population is unbanked having no access to formal or informal financial services, and about 85% of the population are underbanked, lacking access to formal financial services. The high cost of banking infrastructure prevents the dissemination of financial services beyond a small portion of the population. However, digitalizing financial services offers a promising solution to overcome problems of reach and scale. This is attested by a fintech survey done in 2016 (Karandaaz Pakistan and FinSurgents, 2017) whereby 92% of senior executives and 80% of middle managers interviewed agreed that fintech has a significant role to play in emerging markets with low financial inclusion. McKinsey & Co. (Manyika et al., 2016) reported that digital finance has the potential to provide access to 93 million people in Pakistan alone which will increase to US$263 billion and US$23 billion in terms of new deposits and credit respectively. It will also provide an opportunity for the Pakistani government to save US$7 billion by preventing leakage of tax and stopping illicit activities. It also has the potential to create 7 million jobs in Pakistan and can boost the percentage of gross domestic product (GDP) 7% ($36 billion) by 2025.

To achieve the goal of digital financial inclusion, the Ministry of IT issued the "Digital Pakistan Policy" in which they mention the establishing of innovation centers for fintech in major cities of the country (Ministry of Information Technology MOIT, 2017). In December 2017, Dr. Umar Ali Saif, the chairman of Punjab Information Technology Board and Vice Chancellor of Information Technology University (ITU), Lahore signed a Memorandum of Understanding (MOU) with Digital Financial Services Research Group (DFSRG) University of Washington (Seattle, USA) for the establishment of the first FinTech Center in Lahore, Pakistan. The chairman explained that this fintech center will be used for activities including authentication, customer experience studies, cyber security, data analytics, financial management and fraud prevention, etc. The center will also work with the financial industry, academia and government and will also promote digitalization of payments especially Government to Person (G2P) and vice versa (Ahmed, 2017). The Islamic financial industry in Pakistan also aims to explore untapped fintech opportunities in the country. For this purpose, the 2nd World Islamic Finance Forum was held on March 19–20, 2018 at Karachi, Pakistan and fintech and blockchain were prominent areas in the conference agenda. To promote the awareness and also to trigger discussions on fintech and blockchain, a conference was held entitled "Role of Blockchain in Emerging Pakistan" under the flagship University of CMOSATS Pakistan on April 28–29, 2018. The potential opportunities that blockchain offers, different models and use cases were discussed among experts, academicians, and government personnel at the conference. These developments in policies, collaborations and also other tech-related events are laying the foundation for a futuristic and robust fintech ecosystem in Pakistan.

Banks and mobile money providers are embracing and going toward the use of digital technologies and channels to make their operations and products more efficient. Meezan Bank Limited, which is one of the Islamic banks of Pakistan with the largest network in the country, signed an agreement with VMware.inc, a global leader in cloud infrastructure and business mobility, to meet the growing demands through IT (Business Recorder, 2017). But, currently, there are only twelve players including banks, fintechs and mobile money providers in Pakistan that have branchless banking licenses. These include UBL, MCB, HBL, JS Bank, Bank of Punjab, Meezan Bank, Tameer Microfinance with Telenor, Waseela Microfinance with Mobilink, U-Microfinance with Ufone, Askari Bank with Zong, Bank Alfalah with Warid and FINCA with Finja. Unfortunately, none has interoperability among their services and wallets (Karandaaz Pakistan & FinSurgents, 2017).

Even though Pakistan is improving in adoption of technology, the fintech ecosystem is still undeveloped and at very nascent stage. With reference to the numbers of Fintechs in Pakistan, the report by (Karandaaz Pakistan, 2021) states: "Our estimates suggest that there are more than 40 prominent Fintechs in the country, that can be categorized into the seven categories based on their products and services portfolio."

Pakistan has some ways to go, and other lessons can be learned from more advanced countries like implementing regulatory sandbox for fintech, modernizing existing digital infrastructure, working on interoperability, coordination, and collaboration, information, and communications technology (ICT) and financial literacy; these are the essential building blocks for developing a robust fintech ecosystem in Pakistan.

Kingdom of Bahrain (Manama)

Bahrain has been a regional financial center for over four decades and has the largest concentration of financial institutions and funds registered and domiciled in the region. The financial services sector is the second largest contributor to GDP (16.5%), and there are over 400 financial institutions licensed in the Kingdom, including almost 80 conventional banks and 25 Islamic banks. Bahrain's strong ICT infrastructure and established platforms for innovation and entrepreneurship, make it well-placed to become a regional hub and breeding ground for fintech investments.

Bahrain's journey toward fintech was officially initiated by the Central Bank of Bahrain (CBB) and they subsequently developed a regulatory sandbox for fintech in June 2017. The CBB aims to provide an innovative and virtual testing environment to new entrants in the region, which will lead it to becoming the fintech hub of the Gulf region (Treki, 2017).

Since the development of the first regulatory sandbox in June 2017, CBB has approved more than five applicants, which included the robo-advisory investment platform Wahed Invest, BitArabia, an online bitcoin exchange Belfrics, a London-based forex cash management solution for businesses called Tramonex; and NOW Money, the Dubai-based account and remittance service for low-income workers in the GCC (Finextra, 2017; Peyton, 2018b).

In November 2017, the Bahrain Economic Development Board, and Fintech Consortium, launched "Bahrain FinTech Bay" (BFB) claiming that it will be the largest fintech hub in the Middle East and Africa. It is an initiative to create the environment and provide the platform to accelerators, investors, fintech startups, entrepreneurs, regulatory bodies, and financial institutions. The BFB will be a building consisting of 10,000 square feet of usable space and situated at Arcapita building overlooking the waters of Bahrain Bay and the Arabian Gulf.

It will be comprised of state-of-the-art facilities, workstations, coworking spaces, communal areas, hot desks, and a variety of shared infrastructure, making it the ideal hub for local and international corporate innovation labs and fintech startups to secure bases for themselves (Bahrainedb.com, 2017).

There is also an establishment of a consortium of three Bahraini banks – KFH Bahrain, a unit of the Kuwait Finance House, Islamic lender Al Baraka Banking Group and Bahrain Development Bank – to facilitate the development of the Islamic fintech ecosystem. This consortium aims to establish a company Algo Bahrain dedicated and specialized for research and development in the area of Islamic fintech. It will grow and promote Islamic banking in the country through Shariah-compliant solutions (Townsend, 2017), and aims to launch fifteen fintech platforms before 2022 (elgilani, 2017).

To further capitalize the opportunity in the Middle Eastern banking industry, the Kingdom of Bahrain has entered a partnership with the fintech incubator and ecosystem builder, Singapore FinTech Consortium (SFC), and the asset management advisory firm Trucial Investment Partners, to initiate, nurture and sustain Bahrain's fintech ecosystem, by leveraging on the expertise of the SFC. These partnerships form the catalyst that will help to grow and develop the Bahraini fintech sector, as it enables them to pull together the experience and know-how of global industry leaders (FinTech Futures, 2017).

The fintech ecosystem is developing in the country with each passing year as the number of fintech companies is increasing. Figure 4.5 exhibits the details:

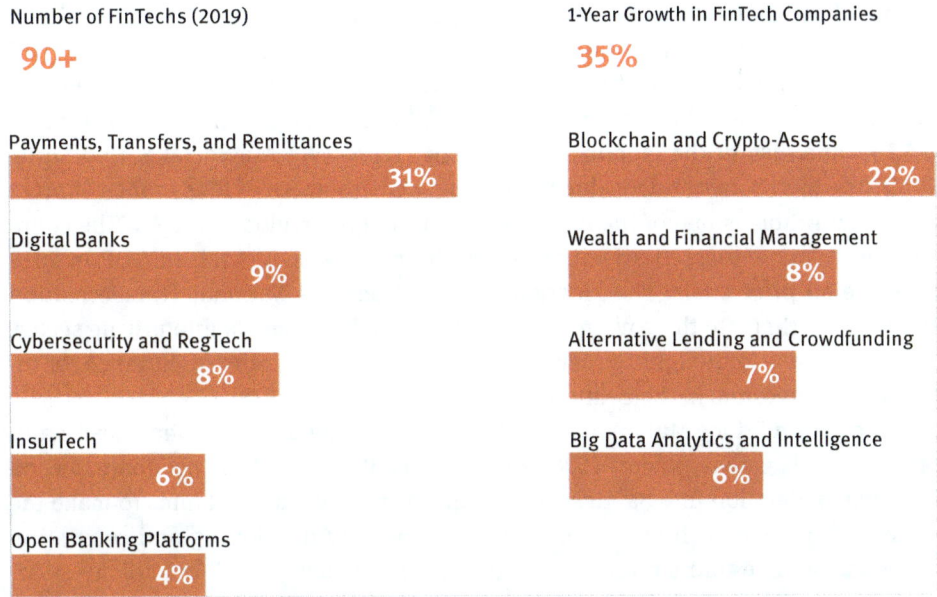

Figure 4.5: Fintech Ecosystem in Bahrain.
Source: https://www.bahrainfintechbay.com/bahrain-fintech-landscape

The central bank of the country also announced in May 2021 to launch a pilot project for the digital currency in partnership with Bank ABC and JP Morgan, as the kingdom is pursuing to achieve the goal of cashless economy. The central bank also launched an innovative challenge called Bahrain Supernova Fintech Challenge with the aim of boosting the growth of fintech ecosystem. The central partnered with different digital platforms in this challenge. The year 2021 saw an exponential growth of fintech platforms such as shariah compliant cryptocurrency platform Rain raised $6 million is series A funding. The central bank also issued an open banking license to a telecom company Batelco, and it became first GCC based company that secured this license (Lewis, 2021).

With these great initiatives, the Kingdom is moving toward becoming the Fintech hub in the region. It can be expected that with this rate of growth, the goal will be achieved within next few years.

Kingdom of Saudi Arabia (Jeddah, Riyadh)

Saudi Arabia has unique demographic and economic features that uphold its status as one of the most attractive, competitive, and sophisticated places for local and international players. The population of the country is about 35.08 million and half of these are under the age of twenty-four. Due to having a high ratio of millennials and digital natives, the country has one of the highest penetrations of internet (95.7%) and also of the mobile subscriptions (112%) (We Are Social & HootSuite, 2021). The high penetration is due to the robust environment of ICTs in the country.

Saudi Arabia is one of the largest economies in the region of MENA. The country's economy witnessed an expansion with an increase of 1.8% in GDP in 2018 after the oil price crisis. The kingdom has launched the National Transformation Program to stimulate the government activities and investments into private sector. This program also brought up new reforms to reduce the barrier of entrance for international investors in the country.

The Crown Prince Muhammad bin Salman has come up with a very clear manifesto which is called "Vision 2030" on the diversification of the economy and on bringing moderation into Saudi social culture. This new blueprint aims to make the country independent from the oil-based economy by developing and promoting other sectors like tourism and entertainment. In "Vision 2030" technology is declared to be the heart of all the sectors.

The upshot of the above is that the Kingdom has and is building all the features which are essential to develop a vibrant fintech ecosystem in the country. In this regard, the Saudi Arabian Monetary Agency (SAMA) has very keen interest in fintech adoption. Their willingness toward adoption of fintech is shown by their investments in the fintech sector locally and globally. For this purpose, a separate fund is re-launched named as Public Investment Fund (PIF). This is a principal vehicle for investments in fintech and also is a part of Vision 2030. One of the major flagship investments of PIF was to invest in the US$100 billion "Softbank Vision Fund" supervised by Softbank. This fund has a key role as an investor in the fintech world. The investment done by the Kingdom in the Softbank fund is part of Softbank's US$1 billion investment in US fintech start-up SoFi in 2015 and also its US$1.4 billion investment in the largest Indian FinTech PayTM initiative in 2017 (Clifford Chance, 2017).

Different initiatives have been taken within the country. One of these main initiatives is to set up a Small and Medium Enterprises Authority in 2016 to achieve the goal of encouraging and involving young and talented entrepreneurs by providing business and innovation friendly regulations, ease of access to financing, global collaborations, and partnerships and also a major share of national acquisition and government bids. Another major element in the Kingdom's fintech ambitions is King Abdullah Financial District situated at the heart of Riyadh. This will be the biggest business area in the Kingdom. The authorities unveiled that this would play a key role in making the country a fintech hub.

Recently in February 2018, SAMA has signed an agreement with Ripple, a global blockchain payments solution provider, to get support for its banks to deploy and test blockchain based payments (Peyton, 2018a). In March 2018, the largest bank of the Kingdom, Riyad Bank partnered with Gemalto, a technology provider, for introducing contactless payment wrist bands for their customers. The bank has also launched Gemalto's contactless sticker that can easily turn a mobile device into a contactless payment device (FinTech Futures, 2018).

In July 2018, the Capital Market Authority CMA of the kingdom approved licenses of the first two fintech players. One is Riyadh-based start-up Manafa Capital and the other one is Scopeer. Both are allowed to provider crowdfunding services on a trial basis. In 2019, SAMA launched a regulatory sandbox for Fintech to provide startups with the platform to test their products, services, and business models (Hamid & Azim, 2021). Currently, under the supervision of Saudi central bank, kingdom holds around 30 fintech platforms which is ten times more than planned by the authority. This shows the vibrance of fintech ecosystem in the country (Arab News, 2021). With the collaboration of Mastercard and IBM, SAMA also introduced new payment system called Sarie in the country (Hamilton, 2021) and the kingdom has also planned to move toward open banking in 2022 (Slieman, 2021).

People's Republic of Bangladesh

Bangladesh is one of the growing economies in Asia region and a neighbor with two Fintech hubs such as China and India. The population of Bangladesh is around 165.5 million and the mobile phone penetration is 100.6%, whereas the internet penetration is very low which is 28.8% (We Are Social & HootSuite, 2021). The percentage of internet users in this populated country is not very satisfactory. This shows a greater level of digital divide existing in the country that needs to be addressed by the authorities. The present startup ecosystem in Bangladesh is accounted for $1.45 billion and has the potential to hit $10 billion valuation in the future. Another important development is that the financial inclusion in the country has increased from 16% in 2011 to 37% in 2018 (GoMedici, 2021). Despite this good progress, Bangladesh still is among the economies with the largest unbanked population.

Considering this whole scenario of high mobile penetration and low internet penetration, the ecosystem of Fintech is at the very early stage in the country. All Finechs collectively process $4 billion in monthly transactions (GoMedici, 2021). The mobile payment sector is on the top followed by lending and personal finance. Table 4.2 encapsulates the details of existing Fintech in the country:

Regulators in Bangladesh have also started taking interest and aiming for the better digital future of the country. The government has issued Digital Bangladesh-2025 policy and adopted the test and learn approach for Fintechs and new entrants. The government needs to try to enhance the technology inclusion by increasing

Table 4.2: Fintech Startups in Bangladesh.

	Platform Name	Founding Year	Sector
1.	bKash	2010	Mobile financial services and payment system for consumers
2.	SureCash	2010	Re-loadable mobile wallet.
3.	PayWell	2012	Online bill payment platform for consumers
4.	iFarmer	2017	Online crowdfunding platform for farming communities
5.	Dmoney	2016	Mobile wallet for payments
6.	Nagad	2018	Correspondent banking services
7.	Emerging Credit Rating	2009	Financial database of credit ratings
8.	SSL Commerz	2007	Online payment gateway
9.	Bankalap	2016	Aggregator platform for financial products
10.	TopUp	2016	Mobile recharge application for consumer
11.	Teek Taka	2020	Ethical trade finance platform

financial technology literacy in the country. As a developing and emerging economy, Bangladesh has the opportunity of harnessing the power of technology to boost the country's growth and empower the poor strata of the country.

Malaysia (Kuala Lumpur)

Malaysia's journey toward a vibrant fintech ecosystem began with its vision for the future of Islamic finance through delivering actions today for a sustainable tomorrow on May 11, 2016. They understood that fintech is challenging the status quo of the financial industry and new business models will emerge. Delivery channels will challenge existing norms, but transaction costs will be significantly reduced. Rather than looking at the fintech revolution as unwelcoming, Bank Negara urged financial institutions to embrace fintech as an opportunity. By June 2016, Bank Negara Malaysia established a group entitled "Financial Technology Enabler Group (FTEG)." The operation of this group is to serve as the focal contact point on fintech-related queries, which involved matters regarding regulation and the adoption of fintech by the financial services sector.

In July 2016, Bank Negara Malaysia reached out to banks, start-ups and other stake holders in order to take comments and suggestions from them for a regulatory framework. Having received over sixty comments and suggestions from banks (conventional and Islamic), start-ups and other stakeholders, Bank Negara Malaysia developed its own financial technology regulatory sandbox framework on October 18, 2016. The framework outlined the objective of facilitating firms which are looking to test out innovative business models and products that can improve efficiency, accessibility, quality and security of financial services and products. The framework also covered opportunities to banks (Islamic and conventional) to take the ideas that can improve risk management mechanisms and discuss gaps regarding investment in the Malaysian economy. For Islamic financial services providers, it is emphasized that the innovative and novel solutions for Islamic financial services must be consistent with and according to the prevailing Shariah standards (Bank Negara Malaysia BNM, 2016).

In 2016, Securities Commission Malaysia in a landmark move, gave approvals to a series of Equity Crowd Funding platforms: Ata Plus, Crowdonomic, FundedByMe (Alix Global), Eureeca, pitchIN and Crowdplus. Securities Commission Malaysia also granted approvals to six P2P lending operators, namely Ethis Kapital, FundedByMe Malaysia, B2B FinPAL, Modalku Ventures, ManagePay Services, and Peoplender ("FinTech Malaysia," 2017).

The year 2017 witnessed and recorded the introduction and launch of numerous key milestones in regulatory development for fintech in Malaysia, as both regulatory authorities, Securities Commission Malaysia and Bank Negara Malaysia, acted quickly to support the on-going financial disruption by introducing regulatory changes and guidelines as described in Figure 4.6.

Another clear and significant development in the fintech industry in Malaysia has been seen in the payments sector in 2017. Major payment players like Alipay and WeChat have entered the Malaysian market. Alipay has arranged participation with three banks of Malaysia, that is, Maybank, CIMB bank, and Public bank. Along with this, Alipay has also received approval from Bank Negara Malaysia to jointly work with the Touch 'n' Go corporation to form TNG Digital. At the same time, WeChat has received its payments license to legally operate in Malaysia, forming a partnership with Hong Leong Bank Malaysia.

On the local front many telecommunication companies, like Axiata and Digi have also jumped into the fray where it is reported that 88 players within the Malaysian fintech space dominated the payments segment, followed by e-wallets, based on the report entitled "Malaysia: fintech Landscape Report Oct 2017."[11] Another Malaysian initiative worthy of mention is the Multimedia Development Corporation (MdeC) which was incorporated in 1996 to oversee the development of the Multimedia Super Corridor (MSC) Malaysia and to advise the Malaysian government on legislation and policies, as well as to set breakthrough standards for multimedia operations.

Established in the same year, MSC Malaysia's primary focus was to create an ideal and conducive platform to nurture Malaysian SMEs in the ICT sector, to become world-class businesses while attracting participation from global ICT companies to invest in and develop cutting-edge digital and creative solutions in Malaysia. Seventeen years on, MSC Malaysia has driven the development of the Malaysian ICT

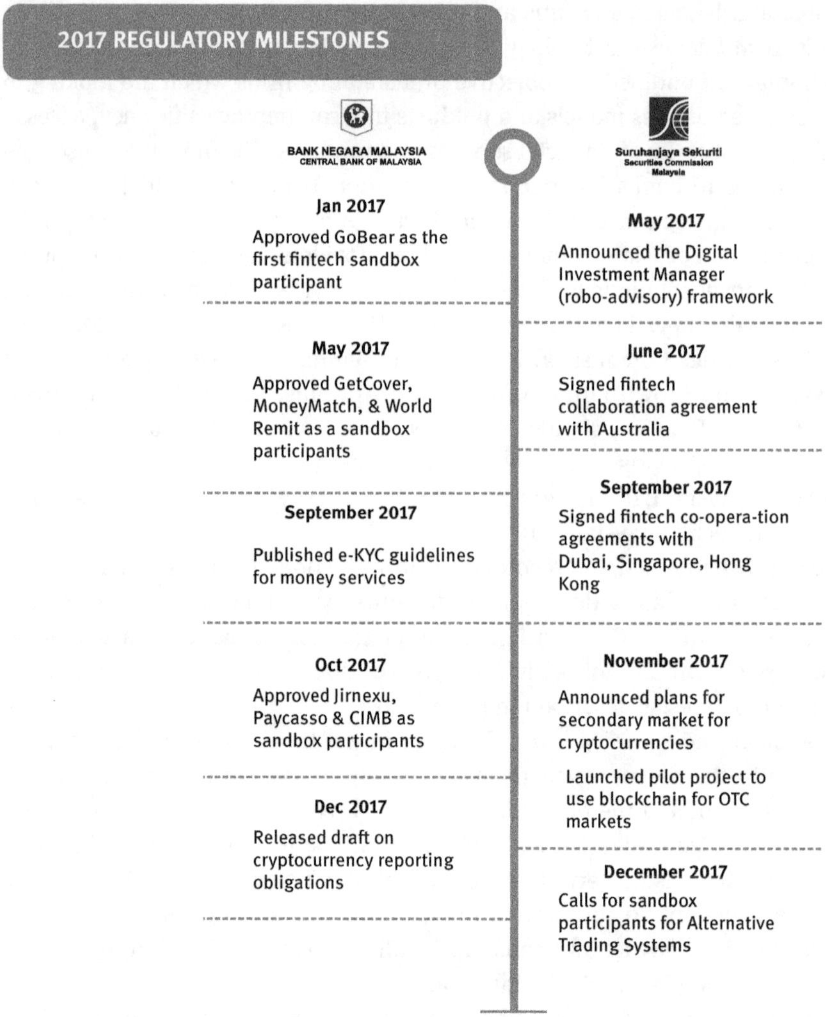

2017 REGULATORY MILESTONES

BANK NEGARA MALAYSIA
CENTRAL BANK OF MALAYSIA

Jan 2017
Approved GoBear as the first fintech sandbox participant

May 2017
Approved GetCover, MoneyMatch, & World Remit as a sandbox participants

September 2017
Published e-KYC guidelines for money services

Oct 2017
Approved Jirnexu, Paycasso & CIMB as sandbox participants

Dec 2017
Released draft on cryptocurrency reporting obligations

Suruhanjaya Sekuriti
Securities Commission Malaysia

May 2017
Announced the Digital Investment Manager (robo-advisory) framework

June 2017
Signed fintech collaboration agreement with Australia

September 2017
Signed fintech co-opera-tion agreements with Dubai, Singapore, Hong Kong

November 2017
Announced plans for secondary market for cryptocurrencies

Launched pilot project to use blockchain for OTC markets

December 2017
Calls for sandbox participants for Alternative Trading Systems

Figure 4.6: Bank Negara's Regulatory Milestones for 2017.
Source: https://FinTechnews.my/15690/alaysia/FinTech-malaysia-2017-in-review

industry, enhanced technology adoption, and has made significan't strides in increasing the economic impact and footprint of ICT for the nation. In October 2010, MdeC was given an additional task by the government, which was to develop a blueprint for a Digital Economy that draws from the huge opportunities created by the Digital world. This resulted in a program called Digital Malaysia that was officially unveiled to the public in May 2012. Digital Malaysia is a natural progression to harness the building blocks already laid by MSC Malaysia. Founded on three strategic thrusts of moving Malaysia from supply to demand, consumption to production and low knowledge-add to high knowledge-add, it ultimately aims to create an ecosystem that promotes the pervasive use of ICT in all aspects of the economy and the first eight projects are already under implementation. This will in turn connect communities globally and enable them to interact in real time, increase the country's Gross National Income, enhance business productivity, and improve the standards of living. Ultimately, Digital Malaysia aims to turn Malaysia into a developed digital economy by 2020, that connects and empowers the government, businesses, and citizens. Today, MSC Malaysia and Digital Malaysia run concurrently to spur Malaysia's ICT industry development and digital economic growth, under the purview of MDEC, which has since been renamed as Malaysia Digital Economy Corporation.

Due to the robust steps taken by the authorities, there are currently 233 fintech companies operating in the country that are offering a wide array of services including digital payments, digital assets, lending, investment, robo-advisory, and so on (Fong, 2021). The digital payments and e-wallets are top services among all. Figure 4.7 encapsulates the percentage of fintech sectors.

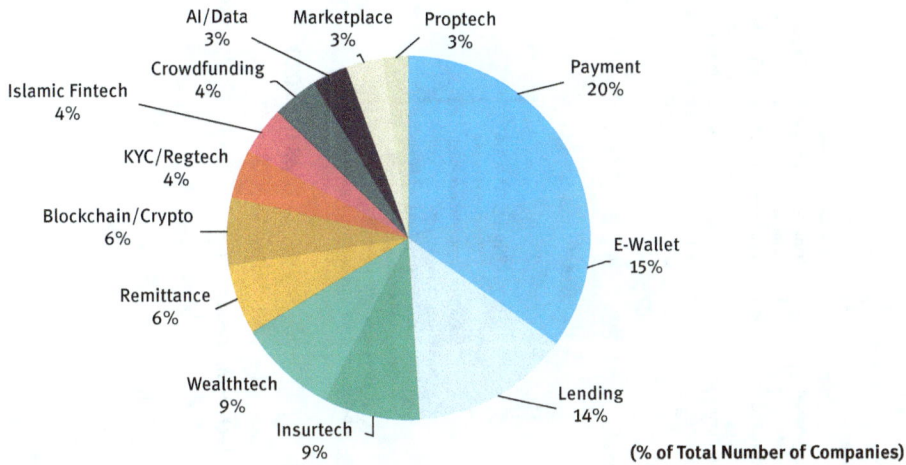

Figure 4.7: Fintech Space in Malaysia.
Source: Fong, 2021.

As the fintech ecosystem is gaining pace in the country, the regulators are also actively supporting the growth with new regulatory initiatives. The authorities have introduced e-KYC, capital marketing started e-payments and e-wallets services, BNM revised guidelines on digital assets, issued licensed to new money lenders and BNM recently issued framework for the digital banks with the aim of issuing five licenses until the end of 2022. Figure 4.8 contains the details on regulatory developments.

86 — Chapter 4 Emergence of Islamic Fintech and its Developments

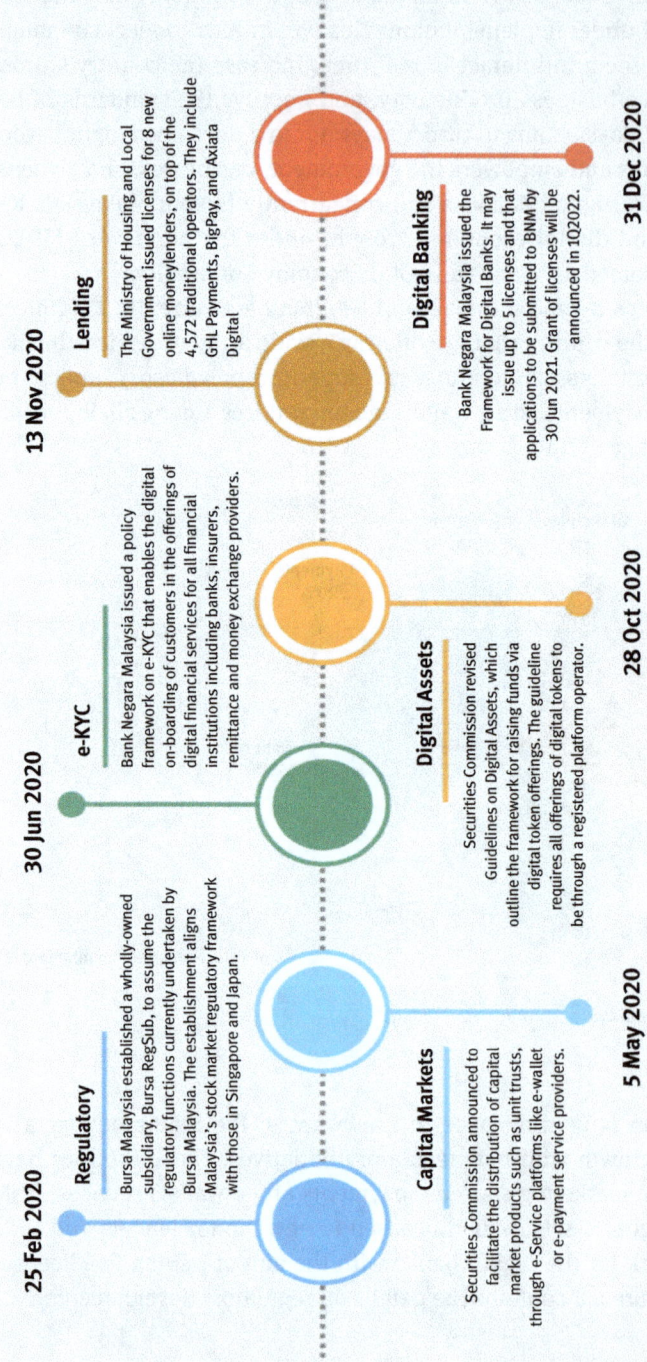

Figure 4.8: Regulatory Developments for Fintech in Malaysia.
Source: Fong, 2021

Republic of Indonesia (Bandung, Jakarta, Surabaya, and Yogyakarta)

The Republic of Indonesia is the largest economy in Southeast Asia Pacific having a population of over 260 million. Sixty percent of the overall population are under the age of thirty-five who are considered as digital natives brought up in the era of internet. There is a high rate of internet and mobile penetration among these millennials and digital natives and this rate of penetration is constantly growing. This makes Indonesia a treasure trove of maiden fintech opportunities. Indonesia is one of the earlier adopters of fintech in the region as Indonesia developed a fintech ecosystem before Malaysia and Brunei Darussalam due to having an edge in market size. The fintech market is steadily growing in the country with the annual growth rate of 16.3%. The exact figure of total investments in the fintech sector cannot be estimated (as majority of the investments are undisclosed); the total disclosed investments alone in 2017 are valued at US$176.35 million. Table 4.3 shows the detail of disclosed and undisclosed deals of 2017 with announcement date, funding stage, fintechs, and investors.

Table 4.3: List of Indonesian Fintech Investments in 2017.

Startup	Stage	Announcement	Value (US$)	Investor
Espay/Unik	Acquired	1-Jan-17	Undisclosed	EMTEK
Cermati	Series A Ext	2-Feb-17	Undisclosed	Orange Growth Capital
Akseleran	Seed	Feb-17	Undisclosed	Angel Investor
Amartha	Series A	3-Mar-17	$2 m	MCI, Lynx Asia Partners, Beenext, Midplaza Holdig
C88/CekAja		11-Mar-17	Undisclosed	Kickstart Ventures, Socrates Capital
Kudo	Acquired	3-Apr-17	$80–100 m	Grab
Ayopop	Seed	4-Apr-17	$1 m	Gree Ventures
Bareksa	Seed	6-Apr-17	Undisclosed	Gernilang Dana Sentosa
Gandeng Tangan		7-Apr-17	Undisclosed	Mariko Asmara, ANGIN
M-Cash		20-Apr-17	Undisclosed	Kresna Graha Investma
Tatalite		12-May-17	$6.3 m	SBI Group Japan
Akulaku	Series B	Jun-17	Undisclosed	Legend Capital, Shunwei Capital, Qiming Venture Partner
Kioson		20-Jun-17	$450 k	Mitra Komunikasi Nusantara

Table 4.3 (continued)

Startup	Stage	Announcement	Value (US$)	Investor
Pasar Dana Pinjarman		4-Jul-17	$50 m	Itochu
Jukir	Acquired	6-Jul-17	Undisclosed	Walezz
Julo	Seed	19-Jul-17	Undisclosed	East Ventures, Skystar Capital, Convergence Ventures
PayAccess	Series A	Jul-17	Undisclosed	Undisclosed
Artawana	Pre-seed	4-Aug-17	Undisclosed	East Ventures
UangTeman	Series A	7-Aug-17	$12 m	K2 Venture Capital, Darper Associates, STI Financial Group, Alpha JWC
Payfazz		8-Aug-17	Undisclosed	Y Combinator, MDI Ventures
Kredivo	Series A	4-Oct-17	Undisclosed	Jungle Ventures, NSI Ventures
Kioson	IPO	5-Oct-17		
Pendanaan	Series A	31-Oct-17	Undisclosed	Legend Capital
M Cash	IPO	1-Nov-17		
OnlinePajak	Series A	9-Nov-17	$3.5 m	Alpha JWC Ventures, Sequoia Capital
Bitcoin.co.id		23-Nov-17	Undisclosed	East Ventures

Source: Daily Social, 2017, *Indonesian FinTech Report*.

The growth in numbers of players in the Indonesian fintech space is remarkable. There were only 50 fintech companies identified in 2015, which has now exceeded 165 fintech companies in Indonesia (Christian König, 2018). The segment of digital payments (38%) is ranked as a top fintech segment followed by lending (31%), personal finance (8%), and so on (Fong, 2018).

Indonesian fintech is mainly regulated by two main regulatory authorities, Bank Indonesia (Central Bank) and Otoritas Jasa Keuangan (OJK or Financial Services Authority). The Bank Indonesia has established a Bank Indonesia fintech office and also launch a fintech regulatory sandbox with the aim of provision of innovation friendly environment to the new entrants that can test their new business models and products in a controlled environment. The OJK also introduced new regulations for peer-to-peer lending and for electronic money.

In Indonesia, the fintech sector can play a significant role in promoting financial inclusion by reaching out to the tech savvy but unbanked population. Users, regardless of gender, race, or religion, can benefit from improved access to streamlined financial services. Amid all of the advantages and opportunities available, Indonesia can effectively capitalize on them through smart regulations, while creating interoperability among financial institutions and open collaboration with young fintech companies to develop new partnerships and strengthen the overall financial and economic position of a country that will be the fifth largest economy by 2030.[12]

Currently, there are around 322 fintechs operating in the country with 73 fintechs in the payment sector, followed by 33 in lending, 26 in Blockchain, 24 in investments, 15 in insurtech, 9 in crowdfunding, 7 in point-of-sale (POS) services and comparison. So, the lending and payment sector on the top among all the sectors. The p2p lending platforms are playing their role in providing access to financing to 23 million MSMEs who were not bankable. In 2019/2020, increased P2P lending companies develop AI-powered credit scoring models and alternative lending solutions to serve the large, underserved population. As per 2020, total funding from P2P platforms reached IDR 113.46 trillion ($7.7 billion) with close to 26 million borrowers. Fintech, banks, platforms, and government authorities have been working together to build innovative digital services and boost financial inclusion in a country where millions are unbanked. Home to a robust population of digital natives, Indonesia becomes a hot spot to fintech players. Digital players have been actively involving in collaborations with leading platforms such as Bukalapak, Tokopedia, Gojek, and Traveloka (Fintech Singapore, 2020).

Republic of Kazakhstan

Kazakhstan (KZ) is a country having population around 18.89 million. Respective to the population, the level of technology adoption is not developed enough as the digital readiness level of the country is low and ranked at 94th position in the global innovation index. The mobile penetration in the country is around 86% and internet penetration is 81.9% (We Are Social & HootSuite, 2021). Although the country has high level of mobile and internet penetration, the country is also facing the problem of financial exclusion as the 40% of the total population is financially included. Giving these facts and figures, it can be observed that the Fintech ecosystem in the country is underdeveloped. After embracing digital transformation, traditional banks turned into the Fintechs. Kaspi.kz, a giant Fintech player in KZ is controlled by Kaspi Bank, the third largest bank in the country. This is the ecommerce banking app which holds a 65% market share of digital payments in Kazakhstan, is aiming to expand its offering into neighboring commonwealth independent states (CIS) – starting with Azerbaijan. In 2019, Kaspi made a $515 million profit. Whilst $74 million of this was through its marketplace, $369 million came from its fintech platform, and another $73 million came from its payments business (FOCUS, 2019).

To trigger the development of digital financial ecosystem in the country, the government took solid initiatives. In 2018, the government established the Astana

International Financial Center (AIFC) as a financial hub to hasten the development of local stock and bond markets as alternative sources of funds for firms and innovative financial products including Islamic banking & finance and developing the fintech industry (ADB, 2021). After the launch of AIFC, the Kaspi is also listed on Astana International Exchange (AIX). AIX is an international platform that has shareholders from Shangai Stock Exchange, Nasdaq, China's Sil Road Fund and Goldman Sachs (FOCUS, 2019).

AIFC is a really pushing the new entrants in the country for developing their firms and fostering the growth of new fintechs in the country. AIFC is also playing its role in the propagation of Islamic finance in the country as the country has considerable percentage of Muslim population. The government also issued a policy document with the title "The Concept for the Development of Digital Payment Technologies in the Kyrgyz Republic for 2020–2022" (KPMG, 2020). These kind of steps from the government are acting as supportive agents for the businesses and payment platforms. Under these guidelines, new entrants can also come up with the innovative solutions. Apart from Kapsi, there are other fintech players in the country such as ULES: a platform that act as intermediator between borrowers and lenders, Panda Money: working for the promotion of financial literacy in the country, Pay24: a paytech startup providing digital payment capabilities, payment terminals, and Svetofor: an e-commerce platform (Zephyrnet.com, 2020).

The regulatory sandbox issued by AIFC in 2018, under this sandbox, more than 16 companies with projects in the field of banking services, blockchain and other financial technologies have already been accepted into the sandbox of the AIFC. Moreover, in 2019, AIFC also joined the Global Financial Innovation network. This network allows the entrants to test their innovative business models in associated countries such as UK, Singapore, and United States. The National Bank of Kazakhstan has also announced that it is working on creating a digital version of its national currency. As part of the first step toward this goal, the National Bank is in the process of investigating similar kind of projects in other countries, especially Sweden and China (FOCUS, 2019).

In a nutshell, it can be expected that the country is paving its way toward the development of fintech ecosystem in the country. With the constant endeavors and effective planning, the country will achieve the goal of becoming hub for the Fintechs in the region.

Republic of Turkey (Istanbul)

Turkey has some unique demographic features with a population under 25 (41%), highest mobile penetration (95%), growing rate of internet users (67%) and also remarkable adult literacy rates (95%). Turkey has made exceptional growth in mobile banking and mobile payment transaction. In online retail, Turkey has also outperformed Spain,

Germany, and the United States in digital payment transactions share during 2016 (BKM, 2017).

Turkey embarked its fintech journey in 2012, where the fintech sector has since grown at an exponential rate (see Figure 4.9). The local Turkish banks also invested in fintech companies. The amount of fintech investment in Turkey was recorded as US$4.6 million in 2012, which grew by 175% in 2016 and the value of fintech investments hit US$29 million.

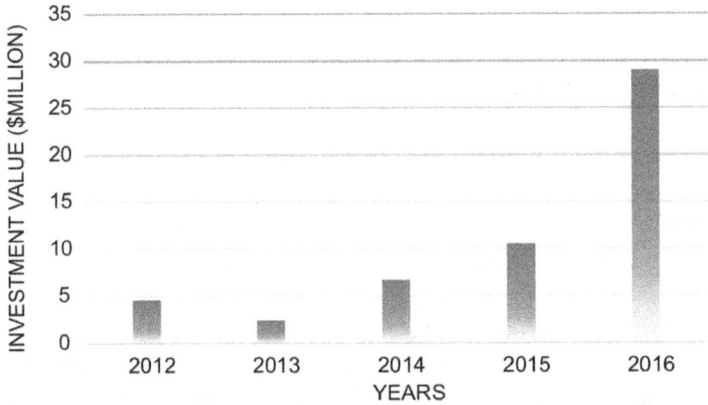

Figure 4.9: Fintech Investments in Turkey (2012–2016).

The size of the overall fintech market in Turkey encompasses more than 200 fintech companies and start-ups. The digital payment segment is at the top among all the fintech segments as 72 fintechs make up this category.

In 2016, the formation of fintech Istanbul through the support of Turkish regulatory authority Interbank Card Center (Bankalararasi Kart Merkezi, BKM), opened the Turkish fintech ecosystem to the world of international players – establishing partnerships with six international organizations, namely Innovate Finance, Level 39, Global FinTech Hubs Federation, Swiss FinTech, Holland FinTech and FinTech Headquarters (FinTech Istanbul & BKM, 2016).

FinTech investments are growing in Turkey due to the robust structure of financial institutions, particularly in the banking sector. At the end of 2019, there were more than 300 start-ups operating in 13 different verticals that include banking, payments, finance, corporate finance, personal finance management, insurance, asset management, crowdfunding, investment, big data, hubs, crypto coins, and blockchain in the field of fintech in Turkey (Sakarya & Aksu, 2021). The new regulations on information system of banks and e-banking services have been issued in March 2020 and implemented as of July 2020. These regulations also include an article on open banking that will be the starting point for digital banks in the country (Chambers and Partners, 2021).

Turkey has great potential in making Istanbul a hub of fintech. The Turkish government has launched the Istanbul Financial Center initiative with the aim of making Istanbul a global financial leader by 2023. The Turkish government also announced the formation of a Finance Technopark in Istanbul with the cooperation of a Turkish exchange and a leading university. The interoperability, cooperation and coordination among Turkish government regulatory bodies, incumbent banks and fintech start-ups is an important element that will vindicate its position in the global arena.

Sultanate of Brunei (Brunei Darussalam)

Brunei is one of the unassuming countries in Southeast Asia that has joined the fintech race. The tiny nation, one of two Islamic sultanates left in the world, is looking to develop its own fintech sector amid strong neighbors like Singapore, Malaysia, and Hong Kong, who are traditional financial hubs, due to its commitment to Islamic values and the Shariah.

In November 2016, Brunei vowed to build a strong economy based on the principles of Islam, and the government of Brunei Darussalam has made an agreement with South Korea to work on the development of Islamic financial technologies. The Brunei government made this agreement for the deployment of new and advanced technologies for the development of Islamic finance and has allocated B $2 million for this. The demonstration of this first step was seen in the form of a seminar entitled "Exploring Islamic FinTech Seminar" organized by the Energy and Industry Department at the Prime Minister's Office (EIDPMO) in partnership with the Embassy of the Republic of Korea. In this seminar authoritative representatives of both countries expressed their views about developing Islamic fintech sector in Brunei Darussalam through cooperation in terms of skills, advanced technologies and expertise in Islamic finance industry. Both countries felt that Islamic fintech is a good example of where we can find avenues for international collaboration and investment to create and generate capital, spinoffs in the local market for employment opportunities and, ultimately, diversify and boost their respective economies (Norjidi, 2016). This also signals Brunei's vision of diversification of economic pathways from just the oil and gas sector.

In 2019, the Digital Economy Council (DEC) was established by Monetary Authority of Brunei Darussalam (AMBD) to guide policy formulation and coordinate efforts of government bodies toward Brunei's drive to become a Smart Nation. DEC's top priorities include making the society cashless by embracing digital payments, digitalizing government services, and initiating export-driven initiatives supported by growing talent (AMBD, 2020).

Moreover, initiatives such as the national digital identity (e-Darussalam Account) have allowed fintech companies to leverage digital capabilities provided by the government to create innovative and convenient digital financial services.

Brunei Darussalam has the Digital Payment Roadmap 2019–2025 (DPR), which sets out key strategies toward the digital transformation in payments and identifies initiatives for implementation. Digital financial innovations in Brunei Darussalam are mainly led by banks, although recent years have seen independent startups providing digital payments and remittance services (Sinay et al., 2021).

AMBD established Fintech Unit, a dedicated office for fintech, and issued a regulatory sandbox in 2018. At the end of 2020, digital payments start-up BruPay, digital remittance companies MoneyMatch, and AliPay merchant acquirer Beep Digital Solutions, are approved participants of the AMBD FinTech Regulatory Sandbox. Several other FinTech companies are working closely with AMBD and are undergoing the assessment and evaluation process toward obtaining the required approvals for participation in the market (AMBD, 2020).

United Arab Emirates (Dubai)

The Financial Services Regulatory Authority (FSRA) of Abu Dhabi Global Market (ADGM) took its first step toward fintech development by publishing a consultation paper for a proposed "Regulatory Laboratory" (RegLab) on May 10, 2016. This was a very exclusive framework, which allowed the new entrants who want to deploy innovative and new technology into financial services sectors (particularly named as fintech participants) to test their activities in a cost effective and controlled environment.

Under the framework of the RegLab, fintech participants have up to two years for testing and experimenting with their products within the sandbox environment, where throughout this period the participants have not had to submit a regular progress report to the FSRA. At the end of the testing period, viable business models will get the final authorization and approval for the full launch of the business model to the market. Failing to fulfill the authorization criteria will exclude the applicants from the framework of the RegLab (ADGM, 2016). Since the establishment of the ADMG RegLab in May 2017, five fintech participants from total of 11 applicants have been approved:
1. CapitalWorld, primarily based in India, is a one-stop digital platform that automates the entire loan value chain from application to credit appraisal and post-disbursement credit monitoring. They remove the traditional hindrances of the process, like having to physically visit bank branches to apply for a loan. CapitalWorld completes the whole process online and they match the loan seeker with their partner bank. Banks disburse the loan once the applicant matches the risk appetite and other criteria set by the disbursing lender.

2. Finalytix is a U.S.-based robo-advisory platform for wealth management applications that seeks to help clients optimize their holdings, mitigate risks and costs, and identify new investment opportunities.
3. NOW Money based in UAE, which offers mobile technology to permit low-income migrant workers in the UAE to access banking and remittance services, otherwise out of reach. Users get direct access to an account, debit card and remittance capabilities from a smartphone app and support from a service center.
4. Rubique is an India-based online platform that links banks and fund seekers/borrowers through a smart online financing process that connects to a range of loan, credit card, and financing options that helps to fill the gap between lenders and borrowers.
5. Titanium Escrow is a UAE-based automated escrow service that enhances trust in counterparties and stabilizes the cash-flows of small businesses.

Since 2017, more fintech participants have been selected from over twenty applications from multiple countries. Among the newly selected participants, four are blockchain firms, namely UK-based EquiChain, Hong Kong-based OKLink, UAE-based Pyppl, and a Canadian firm, Remitr (CNBC.com, 2017).

As of 2021, the landscape of fintech in UAE encompasses 134 fintechs. There are 34 fintechs in payment sector, followed by 17 in blockchain/cryptocurrency, 14 in insurtech, 10 in e-wallet, lending, wealthtech, and 7 in neo-banks. The key drivers of this growth in UAE are high penetration of smartphones and internet that supported financial inclusion, receiving attraction from the investors, and COVID-19 triggered the adoption of digital financial services. The UAE government has decentralized its approach to Fintech by introducing more than 40 "free zones" among the seven Emirates. Each free zone operates under separate regulatory and governance structures, largely independent of the "mainland" (or known as "onshore") authorities. As such, the rules and regulations applicable to companies situated in free zones differ from the rules and regulations applicable to companies operating in the mainland. In April 2019, the UAE Cabinet announced the National Artificial Intelligence Strategy 2031, a 10-year strategy aims to develop frameworks for AI adoption across selected sectors and make UAE a global leader in AI by 2031. The UAE is making ties with foreign partners, establishing agreements with China, India, and Israel. In 2019, Chinese firm UBTech Robotics clinched a US$362M contract to set up AI labs for Emirati students. In Dec 2020, the Central Bank of UAE (CBUAE) launched its fintech office to support Fintech activities in the banking sector and facilitate the establishment of a UAE-approved regulatory framework in cooperation with other FinTech authorities in the UAE (including in the DIFC and ADGM). The new office aims to develop a mature fintech ecosystem within the UAE and position the nation as a fintech hub regionally and globally (News & East, 2021).

UAE is paving its way to not become regional hub of fintech but a global for fintech by taking proactive participation and formation of policies.

United Kingdom (London)

Although the UK is not an Islamic country, London is one of the world's biggest and largest centers for international financial institutions having headquarter of 251 foreign banks and 588 foreign quoted companies with deep aspirations to be an Islamic finance hub. Hence, we have included it in our list of countries as their initiatives will significantly impact the growth of the Islamic digital economy, particularly in Europe.

The UK is the global leader in the cross-border lending and the second center for asset under management after the United States (EY, 2014). The availability of highly skilled financial and tech talent, well developed world class technology and financial services infrastructure, a market that is open to innovation, access to capital, mercantile and welcoming culture for international financial institutions, and innovation friendly regulatory approach are the drivers that maintain its position as a global leader of banking and finance centered in London.

The factors that lead the emergence and development of the fintech ecosystem in the UK are super digital connectivity, the trust loss after the financial crisis and introduction of new regulations by the UK government. The UK has the highest level of smartphone and internet penetration globally and is also ranked as a leader in offering financial services online. The economic crisis of 2008 had plummeted the customers' sentiments and they started to adopt new products offered by the new entrants. Meanwhile, financial institutions also seemed to fail in showing the adaptation and agility regarding technology and innovation. Finally, this financial crisis forced the regulators to monitor and supervise the banks' activities more rigorously. The UK regulators took the dynamic and openminded approach and introduced new regulations while providing for opportunities to new entrants and companies to capitalize on their innovative products and new business models. These changes and drivers in the UK market have made London the hub of fintech for Islamic finance in Europe.

The investments in London-based fintech start-ups hit £800 million in 2017, showing a double-digit growth as compared to 2016 (Knight, 2018). The total funding attracted by the UK fintech start-ups in 2017 is valued at US$1.34 billion (London & Partners, 2018). Among the top ten European fintech deals in the last quarter of 2017, there were seven deals linked with London-based fintech companies. Those are TrayPort (US$726.5m), TransferWise (US$280m), TradeTech Alpha (US$150m), Just Giving (US$127m), Monzo (US$93.8m), Salary Finance (US$52.8m), and WorldRemit (US$40m). Out of these seven fintech startups, five were included in the top fifty hottest European fintech start-ups (KPMG 2018).

In March 2018, the UK Government Fintech Strategy announced that the government is going to make a new "fintech bridge" with Australia and a £7.5 billion public-private fintech investment fund allocated for this purpose (Knight, 2018). These steps were unveiled to uphold London's position as a global hub and leader of fintech. The investments and close alignment and connection between regulators and Islamic finance industry in UK is leading to great developments. This shows the aim of the UK government to ensure that London remain *the* hub of Islamic fintech in the world.

Currently, there are 2,500 FinTechs in the UK. The growth of UK FinTechs accelerated between 2011–2016 where the number of FinTechs increased up to 21% year on year. UK is by far leading in Europe in terms of investments in fintech companies: $4.1 billion invested across 408 deals in 2020 (Deloitte, 2021). The UK FinTech sector raised $5.7bn in the first half of 2021, outstripping the total investment secured in 2020 ($4.3bn) by 34% and breaking the record year set in 2019 ($4.6bn) by 26% (Innovative Finance, 2021). The fintech companies in the country are moving toward the adoption of voice technologies, open banking, AI and ML and autonomous finance. The driving factors for the fintech are foreign talent, large investments, supporting industries, and regulatory environment.

Obstacles for Islamic Fintech

We know that innovation is a key foundational aspect in the development of Islamic finance in the digital economy. Fintech has the potential to play a major role, primarily to improve processes and cost effectiveness while maintaining strict Shariah compliance for the benefit of the industry. FinTech is necessary for Islamic finance to maintain and grow its market share – a failure to keep pace would weaken the players' competitiveness. What then impedes the adoption of Islamic fintech by Islamic financial institutions?

The principal challenge is still the regulatory environment, which is constantly evolving. A good example is the highly evolving nature of the Initial Coin Offering (ICO) market. The Islamic finance industry already has a lot on its plate, be it standardization, developing regulation and innovating new products. Regulatory limitations and concerns could hinder the ability of Islamic finance institutions to forge ahead in adopting new models linked to various fintech themes such as decentralization and privacy. Another factor is that fintech has its significant cost and integration requirements before any economic benefit can be derived. This could push fintech to the backburner, as resources may be limited to work on disruptive initiatives within the company.

Impediments to change and its challenges are a part and parcel of any industry and organization in any sector. It requires significant mindset and organizational realignment, and sufficient resources to support it. In the end, the eventual winner is the one who is able to tackle those challenges with the appropriate strategy, plan, and change management.

To balance the use of new technology to provide better services while controlling new operational risks, the Islamic fintech industry may overcome such challenges through:
1. Regulatory support: The financial industry is considered one of the most regulated industries. To foster the environment of innovation and entrepreneurship, supportive regulations and policies having great importance.
2. Financial support: There are a large number of companies and firms that finance conventional fintech platforms at seed, angel and venture levels. But, for Islamic fintech platforms, opportunities of financing are not enough and its very hectic as well.
3. Shariah compliance: This is the top priority for Islamic fintech and its basic element, which makes them Islamic. Shariah advisory scholars now need to be adept with the underlying technology, which drives digital Shariah solutions to adequately assess Shariah compliance. These Shariah scholars also need to be versed in economics and finance to make sound decisions and would require future scholars to be multidisciplinary, just like their predecessors in the past Golden Age of Islam.
4. Agility and adaptation: Agility and adaptation is very important in the fast-changing technology world. Without agility and adaptation, Islamic fintech cannot compete with its conventional counterpart in an industry where virtually every segment is being reimagined.
5. Entrepreneurial courage and persistence: This is intuitively essential, although it is not widely discussed in traditional financial literature. Any entrepreneurial endeavor requires immense courage and persistence. The Islamic world needs its young people to have these qualities and develop entrepreneurial efforts to overcome the challenges of the future of Islamic finance.

Overcoming the Digital Divide in the Islamic Digital Economy

Digital technology has been seen as a key source for economic growth and human development by various economists around the world. The penetration of digital technology instigates access to huge flow of information, knowledge, and online businesses. The increasing role of Information Communication Technologies (ICTs) and the internet leads to the new economy, in which transactions are done in a very efficient way by using automation and at low cost. However, the uneven distribution of ICTs within or between societies may result in their having a very uneven impact on economic development and on wealth (Srinuan & Bohlin, 2011). The notion of "digital divide" is gaining more importance and is considered as a big challenge by different international economic institutions and organizations. It is seen as a major challenge for various policy makers and academic researchers (Várallyai, 2015). The digital technology, which is often referred to as ICTs, plays a significant role in advancing economic growth and reducing poverty (Jamwal & Padha, 2009). It is reported that ICT using enterprises in developing countries have 3.4% sales growth, 1.2% more employment growth, 5.1% more profitability, 2.5% more investment rate, 6% more reinvestment rate and produce $3,423 more value-added per workers than enterprises that do not use ICT (Acılar, 2011). It is believed in general that digital technology enables attracting and opening new markets for developed countries at the expense of developing countries. It allows developed countries to raise their domination on the international markets by exploiting their competitive advantage over developing countries which are less competitive (Bahrini & Qaffas, 2019).

Digitalization is also important for the development of Islamic economy in general and digital Islamic economy in particular. Hence, the digital divide within Islamic countries is a concerned challenge that can be a major obstacle for Islamic economy to attain stability if the issue is not resolved timely and effectively. The Muslim community that represents a bigger proportion (24%) of the world population, plays a significant role in the global economy. The current progress in the Islamic economy reveals the great technological potential and role of digitalization in enhancing the global Islamic digital economy, even though it is still at its earlier phases. There are many substantial opportunities that are being availed and utilized at certain level to develop and enhance the efficacy of Islamic digital economy. For example, Blockchain, FinTech, Augmented reality (AR), Virtual reality (VR), and IoT technologies. To harness the power of the said technologies, a paramount step for the sustainability of Islamic economy, the availability and existence of technological infrastructure such as installation of telephone lines, access of internet and mobile to everyone especially in remote areas is pre-requisite.

The literature available so far in this area reveals the fact that the research done on Middle East, Sub-Saharan African regions, or on OIC member countries in general, is still in its preliminary phase. And it requires further exploration and deliberations in order to achieve a clear picture of digital divide in OIC countries.

Implications for Islamic Digital Economy

The tremendous development of digital technology has substantially impacted our lifestyle and the way of doing business globally. The use of internet has become one of the most significant and basic requirements in the present-day world (Bahrini & Qaffas, 2019). The digital developments will have inferences for almost all the sustainable development goals (SDGs) and will impact all sectors and stakeholders globally (Digital Economic Report, 2019).

In OIC member countries, the situation in terms of digital divide is very complex and almost same in nature as in case of other developing countries. Geographically, the OIC member countries are comprised of different regions across the globe.

And within each region, the countries are further categorized into rich (mostly oil-producing countries) and the economically marginalized Muslim countries. The data available on technology penetration and internet users in these regions, reveals that there are about 500 million internet users in Muslim countries. However, there are still more than a billion people without any access to the internet. There are 43% people in average from the Muslim majority countries who have access to the internet, and since 2015, near about 20 to 25 million internet users have been added to the virtual network in these regions. In some larger Muslim countries, regardless of having the high-speed internet facilities and supercomputers available, the internet penetration rate is seen very low. For example, in Pakistan and Bangladesh, the internet penetration is measured about 15% only (OIC Statistics Database (OICStat), 2017).

The impediments confronting the Islamic economies vary from one country to another based upon their economic and administrative capabilities. Though, the chief factors that are recognized in general and are responsible for the gloomy ICT scenario within and across the OIC member countries include: widespread poverty, high illiteracy rates, and poor infrastructure (Karatas & Tunca, 2010).

The Islamic economy with digital technologies is generating a new panorama for trade and development in which the net gains are probably to be unevenly dispersed for both developed and developing countries. Therefore, to avert the emerging digital Islamic economy from aggravating digital divides, there should be a strong modus operandi to improve the capabilities and readiness of the countries so that they may seize the maximum benefit from digitalization especially in the rural and underdeveloped regions of the world. There are sizable differences in automation potential between countries, based mainly on the structure of their economies, the relative level of wages, and the size and dynamics of the workforce. It is intuitive that as machines become more advanced and exceed human abilities, their adoption becomes imperative to gain industrial competitive advantage. However, the technical feasibility to automate does not automatically translate into the deployment of automation in the workplace and the automation of jobs due to many factors. Given the importance of innovation for achieving a competitive and sustainable economy, governments and their stakeholders needs to address concerns on job losses and mental blockages preventing appropriate innovation and knowledge diffusion from taking place.

In order to boost the growth of Islamic economy and overcome its existing difficulties, there needs to be a complete overhaul in the digital approach that involves developing a proper digital ICT infrastructure to talent and skill development by providing the necessary STEM[3] education and mentorship to the underprivileged or people living in rural areas who have poor access to traditional modern facilities.

---

3 STEM stands for science, technology, engineering, and mathematics.

The digital inequalities within and across the OIC countries may be leveled if enough attention is focused on collaborative digital technology initiatives and empowerment.

Technological innovation is a critical issue that needs to be addressed by Islamic countries, perhaps more than it realizes, as it still trails in innovation statistics due to its comparatively weak innovation spirit in global terms. The limited amount of research and development (R&D) activity is reflective of a national innovation system that lacks formality, integration, and not well-functioning. This has resulted in only minor changes in capabilities, with few channels for knowledge and skills diffusion, except for FDI or joint venture arrangements, or technical assistance from foreign buyers.

The basic innovation building blocks are underdeveloped in Islamic countries unlike in advanced countries, where there are highly developed innovation policies within full-fledged innovation systems. Directly applying innovation policies of developed countries would fail dramatically in Islamic countries as it lacks compatibility due to the mismatch of basic science and technology (S&T) and innovation base and resources. The focus should first be on removing the obstacles for innovation and ensuring that a basic enabling environment for innovation is established and given room to grow through simpler technical innovation policies. Technological innovation will continue to change how companies organize work, as well as the mix of work in any given sector. A successful implementation and execution of such a nation-wide strategy will require ongoing adaptation and transition by both employers and workers in terms of processes, activities, enterprise, skills and even the environment they work in.

Recommendations

To fully utilize technical capabilities and enhance the Islamic economies through technology innovation, there must be several deep policy and infrastructural changes that we recommend and must take place:

1 FDI and Competition Policy
Considering Islamic countries' shallow innovation and technological base, it is not surprising that at this stage of development, FDI and joint venture arrangements with multinational enterprises (MNEs) have been the most important channel for innovation, particularly knowledge or technological diffusion, to Islamic firms. This is true at both the aggregate and micro levels. Islamic countries still require more FDI to spur innovation because FDI firms possess the necessary innovation capital (primarily in technology and management processes) that is closer to the frontier. By engaging in FDI or joint ventures, local firms can access not only the principals'

innovation capital but also their other capital indirectly, leading to more innovation. This capital includes, inter alia, marketing links, and global market access.

FDI can promote diffusion through direct technology transfer, technical licensing, R&D facilities, and even the movement of workers from MNEs to other local firms. It creates imitation and demonstration effects and, when used properly, can be an important basis for building up domestic technological capabilities. Having said that, the types of FDI also matters. An export-oriented FDI compared to domestic-oriented FDI is more desirable because firstly, an FDI that participates in global value chains (GVCs) has higher and more demanding technical standards and requirements usually call for more complex technology and production methods. Secondly, exposure to the global market creates more intense competition from similar firms in other countries, which in turn incentives the proper transfer of the necessary technology to their facilities in Islamic countries, for fear of losing their competitive edge over rivals in other producing countries.

However, Islamic countries should not remain reliant on FDI in the long run. Instead, Islamic countries should envision to improve its technological attainment and capabilities to perform major product change and eventual own products. Alongside measures to attract FDI, the government must also ensure that after sufficient technology transfer takes place, its labor force can translate them to its own ideas for change and improvements.

2 Improved Key Innovation Enablers and Infrastructure

To coordinate the full benefits of FDI and other policies, the diffusion of knowledge of technology and management of processes must be followed through. To prepare for such absorption of knowledge, several key enablers must be laid down too:

I. Building Capacities

The rapid pace of technological change with the development of Industry 4.0, requires academic training in universities to be more agile and flexible in adapting to new technological shifts. Similarly, the providers of vocational or technical labor, such as technical and vocational schools, need to be necessarily allied with actual job and skills requirements. The "government must ensure that basic scientific, language, and computer skill attainment is achieved, and the vocational school curriculum should be aligned with modern industrial needs."[4] Therefore, the government can influence entrepreneurship by infusing effective innovation programs in universities, as well as incentivize privately-run accelerators and incubator programs. "New ideas and the entrepreneurial

---

4 In the agricultural sector, "there are 1,800 schools that provide vocational training across Indonesia. However, the training is outdated. For example, students learn how to milk a cow manually, while the industry uses machinery. The Ministry of Trade provides some training, for example, a course on export, but the services provided by government-funded training centres are very limited and often irrelevant to the needs of the industry" (Tijaja & Faisal 2014).

spirit thrive best in an environment that features free circulation of brains and money, competitive solutions, (and) a sound institutional environment" (Aghion et al., 2010). An important requisite for entrepreneurial activity is the creation of a culture that rewards experimentation, risk taking, and therefore tolerates failure. There are some possible measures that can help the attractiveness of entrepreneurship. For example, governments can offer innovation grants that promote the creation of a national product (e.g., a locally-made mobile phone) so as to inspire the innovative spirit of entrepreneurs and instill national pride. For the local innovator, the large Islamic local market brings adequate revenue and profits.

II. Science and Technology (S&T) Infrastructure

The government can avail more research facilities, grants for industrial innovation and public-private partnerships on employment and other collaborative initiatives, as well as technology support services, including metrology, standards, testing, and quality assurance (MSTQ) facilities and various technology information services. According to Pietrobelli and Rabellotti (2010), MSTQ facilities play an essential role in upgrading a country's ability to participate in the market and modular types of GVC, which require higher supplier competence and, thus, require more innovation and promote knowledge diffusion. So far, MSTQ facilities in Islamic countries are poor in quality and insufficient in quantity. National standardization processes and certification will become difficult.

In a large country like Indonesia, it is unreasonable to expect the government to develop all S&T infrastructure using its own resources. Inviting the private sector to participate in building public innovation facilities and running innovation programs, which eventually will benefit the private sector as well as employability is crucial. Attractive and effective public–private partnerships are needed to make this happen.

III. Protection of Intellectual Property

We recommend improving intellectual property rights (IPR) protection and its enforcement. These are probably the most crucial factors for ensuring sufficient technical licensing, technology transfer, and other diffusion activities to germinate. In Islamic countries, few FDI firms are willing to transfer their best technology to prevent duplication or the loss of competitive advantage, due to the currently weak IPR enforcement. As is the case of China, IPR protection remains the key to stimulating more knowledge diffusion into the economy while protecting the rights of the foreign entity. Although the regulatory framework on IPR in Islamic countries exists, its enforcement must be elevated and implemented effectively to encourage further knowledge and technology transfer.

IV. Financing Ideas

Ideas are usually not enough and requires capital support to carry them to fruition. Hence, policies to enhance the availability and enable access to capital must be formulated. A system should be devised to overcome the natural risk aversion of the financing sector (particularly banks) toward innovation activities that involve plenty of risk. The government needs to creatively facilitate and mobilize innovation finance via incentive structures to encourage them to participate in funding firms' R&D activities. Alternative financiers like business angels, venture capitalists (VCs) or corporate VCs need to be attracted to potential viable investments. Alternatively, direct funding by the government into alternative capital can also be initiated but such moves involve either establishing public venture finance firms, or indirectly investing into private alternative fund vehicles. Key performance indicators (KPIs) of the fund will focus on survival and subsequent expansion of the start-up. Such vehicles can provide strong validation for the ventures and start-ups that eventually get funded.

V. Regulatory and Legal Efficiencies

Besides policies and public-private collaboration, there are regulatory bottlenecks that impede knowledge diffusion activities, including those regulations that are not directly related to innovation policy on the outset. Salam et al (2018) pointed out a prominent example, which is the regulation on the movement of labor and experts. The successful technology diffusion does not only happen from importing capital goods but more importantly through the transfer of skills from technical experts by foreign firms or suppliers. They do so by training local workers and/or engineers in the operation of newly installed technology or machinery. Regulatory burdens, such as unnecessary drawn-out procedures and lengthy processes needed to bring in foreign technical experts, will eventually deter future technology transfer visit applications. For example, a two-day visit by foreign experts which requires weeks or months of administrative processes will discourage future transfer visits from such experts.

3 Private Innovation Initiatives

To promote local innovation, we recommend that inspiring innovation literacy and energizing local leaders with the benefits and practical know-how of innovation is essential. Given Islamic countries' fluid political structure, the development of innovation-related initiatives, programs, and infrastructure in cities is greatly influenced by tangible political support (or lack thereof) from their governing authorities. Effective triple-helix collaboration should exist not only at the national level but also at the provincial level.

Programs to connect universities' technical skills with local entrepreneur projects under public initiatives and support need to be encouraged. Furthermore, given the limited innovation capital in the public sector, local governments should instead deploy strategies to attract and invite the private sector within or outside cities to participate in local innovation projects that bring about diffusion, such as training and collaboration provided by firms. Both factors are behind the success of the most innovative regions in Islamic countries. Some local industries, especially the food, tourism, and creative industries, have shown excellent potential to be promoted and to benefit from the diffusion of knowledge at the local level.

A critical aspect of local innovation initiatives is entrepreneurship development. In large cities, start-ups should be encouraged and facilitated by the provision of coworking spaces, creative hubs for the exchange of ideas through training and workshops, and start-up incubator programs. For the less-developed regions or parts of cities, however, providing access to entrepreneurship skills and finance for residents through entrepreneurship training and mentoring should be embedded in local development plans. Connecting them to the technical expertise of nearby universities will yield more diffusion. Given that diffusion requires frequent and extensive interactions with sources of knowledge, simply allocating more budget for entrepreneurship programs is not enough.

Also, we are of the opinion that "industrial clustering" is an important medium for horizontal and vertical diffusion and, therefore, needs to be facilitated. A more effective strategy – in implementation and incentives – to attract firms are essential to avoid the fate of special economic zones, which have largely failed to attract firms and generally been unsuccessful at invigorating innovation. The government should aim to gradually increase the budget for R&D activities, and it should complement this with a well-planned strategy and well-conceived incentives for firms.

References

Acılar, A. (2011, April). Exploring the Aspects of Digital Divide in a Developing Country. Issues in Informing Science and Information Technology, 8, 231–243. Retrieved from https://www.researchgate.net/publication/228295762

ADB. (2021). Kazakhstan Development Transforming Power Finance Assessment. https://www.adb.org/sites/default/files/publication/664451/kazakhstan-development-finance-assessment.pdf

ADGM. (2016). The Financial Services Regulatory Authority (FSRA) of Abu Dhabi Global Market (ADGM) today published a public consultation paper setting. Retrieved February 25, 2018, from http://www.adgm.com/mediacentre/press-releases/abu-dhabi-global-market-sets-out-proposal-for-FinTech-regulatory-framework-in-the-uae/

Aghion, P., Dewatripont. M., Hoxby, C.M., Mas-Colell, A. and Sapir, A. (2010). The Governance and Performance of Universities: Evidence from Europe and the US. Economic Policy, Vol. 25, No. 61, 7–59.

Ahmed, Z. (2017, January 31). ITU Announces Building Pakistan's First FinTech Center in Lahore. Retrieved July 31, 2018, from https://pakwired.com/a-memorandum-signed-for-setting-up-pakistans-first-FinTech-center-in-lahore/

Arab News. (2021). Saudi Arabia 'holds 10 times more fintech companies than planned'. *Arab News.Com*. https://www.arabnews.com/node/1893086/business-economy

References

Bahrainedb. (2017, November 5). Bahrain and FinTech Consortium Launch the Largest Dedicated FinTech Hub in the Middle East and Africa| Invest in Bahrain. Retrieved February 21, 2018, from http://bahrainedb.com/latest-news/bahrain-and-FinTech-consortium-launch-bahrain-FinTech-bay/

Bank Negara Malaysia BNM. (2016, October). Financial Technology Regulatory Sandbox Framework. Retrieved from http://w2.bnm.gov.my/guidelines/50_others/pd_regulatorysandboxframework_Oct2016.pdf

BKM. (2017). *Cashless Turkey by 2023*. Retrieved from https://bkm.com.tr/wp-content/uploads/2017/05/cashless-2023.pdf

Business Recorder. (2017). VMware partners with Meezan Bank. Retrieved October 6, 2017, from http://fp.brecorder.com/2017/09/20170913217179/

Bahrini, R., & Qaffas, A. (2019). Impact of Information and Communication Technology on Economic Growth: Evidence from Developing Countries. Economies, 7(21), 2–13. https://doi.org/10.3390/economies7010021

Chambers and Partners. (2021). *Fintech 2021: Turkey*. https://practiceguides.chambers.com/practice-guides/employment-2020/jordan

Choudhury, M. A., & Malike, U. A. (1992). *The Foundations of Islamic Political Economy*. London: Macmillan; New York: St. Martin's Press, p. 104.

Christian König. (2018, May). *FinTech Indonesia Startup Report*. Business. Retrieved from https://www.slideshare.net/ChristianKnig1/FinTech-indonesia-startup-report-66696864?ref=http://FinTechnews.sg/FinTech-startups-in-indonesia/

Clifford Chance. (2017). *FinTech in the Middle East: An Overview*. Retrieved from https://talkingtech.cliffordchance.com/content/micro-cctech/en/FinTech/FinTech-in-the-middle-east/_jcr_content/text/parsysthumb/download/file.res/FinTech%20In%20The%20Middle%20East.pdf

CNBC.com, N. A., Writer at. (2017, May 17). Abu Dhabi Global Market Admits First Five FinTech Start-Ups into its Reglab Sandbox. Retrieved February 25, 2018, from https://www.cnbc.com/2017/05/17/abu-dhabi-global-market-admits-first-five-FinTech-start-ups-into-its-reglab-sandbox.html

Deloitte. (2021). *The UK FinTech landscape*. https://www2.deloitte.com/uk/en/pages/financial-services/articles/uk-fintech-landscape.html

Digital Economy Report. (2019). Digital Economic Report. United Nations Conference on Trade and Development-UNCTAD. Geneva: United Nations Publications. Retrieved from https://unctad.org/meetings/en/SessionalDocuments/tdb66_d5_en.pdf

elgilani, M. (2017, December 6). ALGO Bahrain – The World's First FinTech Consortium of Islamic Banks. Retrieved February 21, 2018, from http://www.bizbahrain.com/algo-bahrain-worlds-first-FinTech-consortium-islamic-banks/

EY. (2014). Landscaping UK FinTech (p. 20). Retrieved from https://www.ey.com/Publication/vwLUAssets/Landscaping_UK_FinTech/%24FILE/EY-Landscaping-UK-FinTech.pdf

Finextra. (2017, August 29). Bahrain Welcomes First FinTech Sandbox Entrants. Retrieved February 21, 2018, from https://www.finextra.com/pressarticle/70491/bahrain-welcomes-first-FinTech-sandbox-entrants

FinTech Futures. (2018, March). Riyad Bank Launches Saudi Arabia's first Contactless Payment Wristband. Retrieved July 30, 2018, from https://www.bankingtech.com/2018/03/

FinTech Istanbul, & BKM. (2016). *The Turkish FinTech Ecosystem*. Retrieved from http://FinTech.istanbul/en/wp-content/uploads/2018/03/FinTech-Progress-Report.pdf

FinTech Malaysia: Key Developments & Opportunities in 2017. (2017). Retrieved from http://www.banktechasia.com/FinTech-malaysia-2017-highlights/

Fintech Singapore. (2020). *Indonesia Fintech Report 2020*. https://fintechnews.sg/wp-content/uploads/2020/12/Fintech-Indonesia-Report-2020.pdf

Fong, V. (2018, June 26). The State of Play for FinTech Indonesia. Retrieved July 30, 2018, from http://FinTechnews.sg/20712/indonesia/FinTech-indonesia-report-2018/

Fong, V. (2021). Malaysia FinTech Report 2021. *Fintech News Malaysia*, 92. https://de.statista.com/statistik/studie/id/44591/dokument/fintech-report/

Freedman, R.S. (2006). *Introduction to Financial Technology*. New York: Academic Press, Elsevier.

FOCUS. (2019). Kazakhstan poised to be a centre for fintech startups | The World Federation of Exchanges. https://focus.world-exchanges.org/articles/kazakhstan-poised-be-forge-fintech-startups

Global Islamic Fintech Report. (2021). Global Islamic Fintech Report. *Cdn.Salaamgateway.Com*, 56. https://cdn.salaamgateway.com/special-coverage/islamic-fintech-2021/Global-Islamic-Fintech-Report-2021-Executive-Summary.pdf

Government of Pakistan. (2020). *Pakistan Economic Survey 2020–21*. http://www.finance.gov.pk/survey/chapters_21/PES_2020_21.pdf

GoMedici. (2021). Bangladesh – The Rising FinTech Star in South Asia. https://gomedici.com/bangladesh-the-rising-fintech-star-in-south-asia

Hamid, T., & Azim, N. A. (2021). *Can Saudi Arabia become the region's fintech frontrunner?* Wamda.Com. https://www.wamda.com/2021/06/saudi-arabia-regions-fintech-frontrunner

Hamilton, A. (2021). *Saudi Arabia launches new payments system with IBM and Mastercard*. Fintechfutures.Com. https://www.fintechfutures.com/2021/04/saudi-arabia-launches-new-real-time-payments-system-with-ibm-and-mastercard/

Innovative Finance. (2021). *Innovate Finance reports 2021 as a record-breaking year for UK FinTech*. IBS Intelligence. https://ibsintelligence.com/ibsi-news/innovate-finance-reports-2021-as-a-record-breaking-year-for-uk-fintech/

Jamwal, S., & Padha, D. (2009). ICT as an stimulus for development in developing countries. Proceedings of the 3rd National Conference; INDIACom-2009 Computing For Nation Development. New Delhi: Bharati Vidyapeeth's Institute of Computer Applications and Management, India.

Karandaaz Pakistan & FinSurgents. (2017). *Seeding Innovation – A Framework for Rooting FinTechs in Pakistan*. Retrieved from https://www.karandaaz.com.pk/media-center/news-events/seeding-innovation-a-framework-for-rooting-FinTechs-in-pakistan/

Karandaaz Pakistan. (2021). *Fintech Ecosystem of Pakistan: Landscape Study*. https://karandaaz.com.pk/wp-content/uploads/2021/06/Fintech-Ecosystem-of-Pakistan.pdf

Karatas, M., & Tunca, M. Z. (2010). Sustainable Development and the Digital Divide in OIC Countries: Towads a Collaborative Digital Approach. In M. Karatas, & M. Z. Tunca, Sustainable Economic Development and the Influence of Information Technologies: Dynamics of Knowledge Society Transformation. Hershey New York: Information Science Reference (an imprint of IGI Global).

Knight, M. (2018). 12 Companies at the Heart of London's FinTech Boom. Retrieved July 10, 2018, from https://www.fathomlondon.com/2018/04/23/12-companies-at-the-heart-of-londons-FinTech-boom.html

KPMG. (2018). The Pulse of FinTech Q4'17, Retrieved from https://assets.kpmg.com/content/dam/kpmg/xx/pdf/2018/02/pulse_of_FinTech_q4_2017.pdf

KPMG. (2020). Overview of Fintech Development in Central Asia FinTech market in Central Asia.

Lewis, S. (2021). *5 Fintech Initiatives To Follow In Bahrain – Fintechnews Middle East*. Fintechnews.Ae. https://fintechnews.ae/9017/bahrain/5-fintech-developments-to-follow-in-bahrain/

London & Partners. (2018). 2017 Record Year for London and UK Tech Investment.

Manyika, J., Lund, S., Singer, M., White, O., & Berry, C. (2016). *Digital Finance for All: Powering Inclusive Growth in Emerging Economies*. New York, USA: McKinsey & Co. Retrieved from http://www.mckinsey.com/global-themes/employment-and-growth/how-digital-finance-could-boost-growth-in-emerging-economies

Ministry of Information Technology MOIT. (2017). *Digital Pakistan Policy 2017*. Retrieved from http://moit.gov.pk/policies/DPP-2017v5.pdf

News, F., & East, M. (2021). *Fintech News Middle East: UAE Fintech Report 2021.*

Norjidi, D. (2016, November 11). Islamic FinTech can Take Brunei to New Heights. Retrieved February 21, 2017, from http://borneobulletin.com.bn/islamic-FinTech-can-take-brunei-new-heights/

OIC Statistics Database (OICStat). (2017). Retrieved from SESRIC- Statistical, Economic and Social Research and Training Centre for Islamic Countries: https://www.sesric.org/oicstat.php

Pakistan Telecommunication Authority, P. (2020). *Annual Report 2020.* https://www.pta.gov.pk/en/annual-reports

Pietrobelli, C., & Rabellotti, R. (2011). Global Value Chains Meet Innovation Systems: Are There Learning Opportunities for Developing Countries? In World Development (232, Vol. 39, Issue 7). https://doi.org/10.1016/j.worlddev.2010.05.013

Peyton, A. (2018a, February). Saudi Arabian Monetary Authority Pilots Ripple Payments.

Peyton, J. A. (2018b, January). Central Bank of Bahrain's FinTech Sandbox Heats Up. Retrieved February 21, 2018, from http://www.bankingtech.com/2018/01/central-bank-of-bahrains-FinTech-sandbox-heats-up

Sakarya, Ş., & Aksu, M. (2021). *Fintech Ecosystem in Turkey: An Evaluation in Terms of Financial Markets and Financial Stability.* 11–31. https://doi.org/10.1007/978-981-33-6811-8_2

Salam, U., Lee, S., Fullerton, V., Yusuf, Y., Krantz, S., & Henstridge, M. (2018). Indonesia Case Study: Rapid Technological Change-Challenges and Opportunities Final Report. Pathways for Prosperity Commission. http://www.pathwayscommission.bsg.ox.ac.uk

Sinay, J. B., Tumengkol, E. A., & Zendra, O. (2021). *Payment Systems in the Digital Age: Case of ASEAN* (Issue 04). https://asean.org/storage/ASEAN-Policy-Brief-4_FINAL-06Apr2021.pdf

Siddiqi, M. N. (1981). Rationale of Islamic banking. International Centre for Research in Islamic Economics King Abdulaziz University, Kingdom of Saudi Arabia. This can be accessed here: https://iei.kau.edu.sa/Files/121/Files/152672_06-MNSiddiqi.pdf.

Sleiman, M. (2021). *Saudi Arabia's fintech regulations can speed up Open Banking | Analysis – Gulf News.* Gulf News.Com. https://gulfnews.com/business/analysis/saudi-arabias-fintech-regulations-can-speed-up-open-banking-1.1627542469157

Srinuan, C., & Bohlin, E. (2011). Understanding the Digital Divide: A Literature Survey and Ways Forward. 22nd European Regional Conference of the International Telecommunications Society (ITS2011), Budapest, 18-21 September, 2011: Innovative ICT Applications - Emerging Regulatory, Economic and Policy Issues. International Telecommunications Society (ITS), USA.

Tijaja, J., & Faisal, M. (2014). Industrial Policy in Indonesia: A Global Value Chain Perspective. SSRN Electronic Journal. https://doi.org/10.2139/ssrn.2515775

Townsend, S. (2017, December). Bahrain Banks Launch R&D Firm to Drive Growth of Islamic FinTech. Retrieved February 21, 2018, from https://www.thenational.ae/business/banking/bahrain-banks-launch-r-d-firm-to-drive-growth-of-islamic-FinTech-1.681737

Treki, R. E. (2017). Central Bank of Bahrain (CBB) Launch Regulatory Sandbox for FinTech Firms. Retrieved February 21, 2018, from http://www.tamimi.com/law-update-articles/central-bank-bahrain-cbb-launch-regulatory-sandbox-FinTech-firms/

Várallyai, L. (2015). Statistical Analysis of Digital Divide Factors. Procedia Economics and Finance, 364-372. Retrieved from https://www.researchgate.net/publication/278726455

We Are Social, & HootSuite. (2021). Digital 2021. In *Global Digital Insights.*

World Bank. (2020). Leveraging Islamic Fintech to Improve Financial Inclusion. In *World Bank Group.* https://doi.org/10.1596/34520

Zephyrnet.com. (2020). Kyrgyzstan Wakes up to Fintech Potential. https://zephyrnet.com/kyrgyzstan-wakes-up-to-fintech-potential/?__cf_chl_jschl_tk__=pmd_32e4396933fdd8871792597dc65958391a8253a0-1627664866-0-gqNtZGzNAo2jcnBszQe6

Chapter 5
Blockchain and the Digital Economy

Introduction

Over the last decade, disruptive innovation in financial services has emerged from financial technology (fintech) start-ups. These new firms have been quicker than banks to take advantage of advances in digital technology, developing banking products that are more user-friendly, cost less to deliver, and are optimized for digital channels.

This relative success is unsurprising. These new players are less burdened by the demands of regulatory compliance which banks are subject to. They are unencumbered by complex and costly to maintain legacy systems. They can focus on creating single-purpose solutions, designed to offer an improved experience within just one product or service. They are more in tune with the peer-to-peer (P2P) culture engendered by the explosion of social media. And they are smaller organizations, designed for innovation.

Confidence in fintech has accelerated venture capital (VC) financing in the industry to a record level of US$27.4 billion in 2017 – a growth of 18% from 2016. According to a recent report from consulting firm Accenture, the growth in fintech investment has been driven by a surge in deal value in the United States, UK, and India.

In the United States, the value of VC investment deals jumped 31% to US$11.3 billion in 2017. Meanwhile, in the UK, deal values almost quadrupled to US$3.4 billion, while India saw a near quintupling of investment to US$2.4 billion in 2017. The volume of global fintech deals also rose greatly, in 2018 and 2019 as shown in Figure 5.1. Much of the growth, particularly in the United States and UK, has been driven by big new investment flows from China, Russia, the Middle East, and other emerging economies. Figure 5.2 takes a closer look at the capital investment by region between 2018 and first quarter of 2021. The EMEA region has been closing the gap over the past three years with the leading U.S. market due to investors attractiveness in European assets after the surge of European unicorns over the past decade.

Investments in Blockchain

Major firms across the financial services landscape have made investments in blockchain-based start-ups, continuing into 2018. The herd of new strategic investors is playing an increasingly important role in the health of the financing market for these start-ups. While quarterly deal activity dropped to its lowest point since Q2'14 in Q4'16, the quarter's top two financing deals featured investments by major corporate and financial services players.

More specifically, distributed ledger developer Axoni saw Wells Fargo lead its US$18M Series A offering, which included JP Morgan, Goldman Sachs, F-Prime Capital,

Introduction — 109

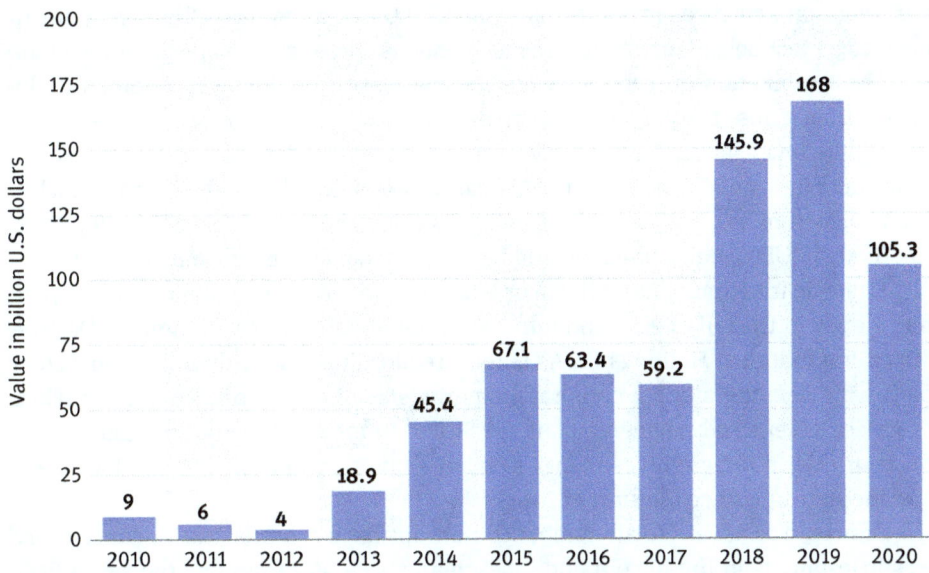

Figure 5.1: Total Capital Flows into Fintech Worldwide.
Source: Statista, 2021.

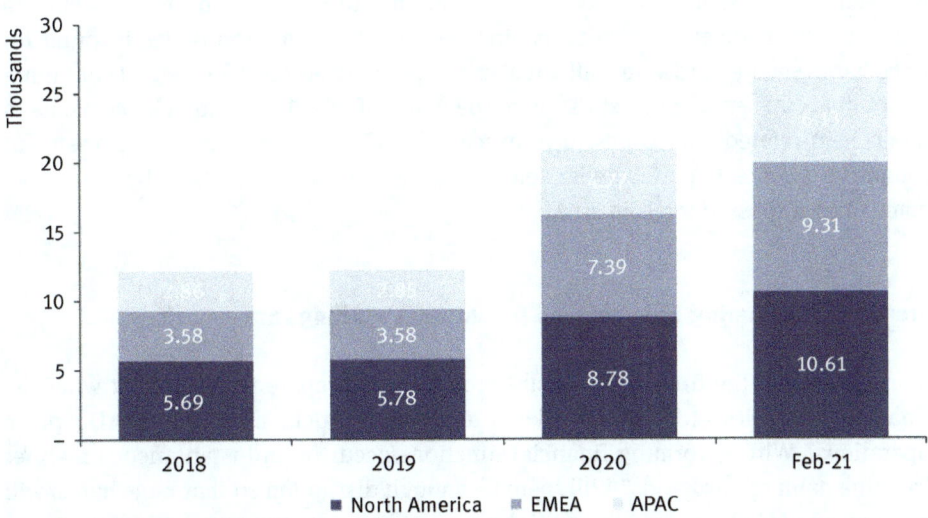

Figure 5.2: Venture Capital Fintech Investment by Region.
Source: Statista, 2021.

and Thomson Reuters as investors. As Axoni CEO Greg Schvey said, "Deploying distributed ledger technology in production at this scale is a watershed moment for the industry. The combination of technology and business expertise being contributed to this project from across the participating firms is unparalleled and the benefits are clear."[1] Among the financial services investors are insurance providers such as TransAmerica, New York Life, and Mitsui Sumitomo Insurance Group (MSIG); payments giants including Visa, MasterCard, and American Express; as well as banks like Mitsubishi UFJ Financial Group (MUFG), Citi, Santander, and Canadian Imperial Bank of Commerce (CIBC).

Strategic investment into bitcoin or blockchain start-ups over the past three years hit its apex in the fall of 2015 and into the winter of 2016. In recent months, Deloitte, Miami International Holdings (MIAX), and Credit China placed their first blockchain bets, with Deloitte taking a corporate minority stake in appropriately named blockchain settlement and payments platform SETL.[2] In total, over fifty financial services firms or their strategic investment arms have invested in a bitcoin or blockchain-specific start-ups since the start of 2014.

Of note, a relatively small number of start-ups have captured most financial services investments in the bitcoin and blockchain space. For example, the seven firms listed below – Circle Internet Financial, Coinbase, Ripple, BitFury Group, Blockstream, Digital Asset Holdings, and Chain – have received nearly US$625M in funding and are all listed among the top ten most well-funded bitcoin and blockchain companies. Between Circle's Series E round of US$110 million, US$118 million raised by Orbs, a purported "consumer-ready blockchain" service, US$75 million Series B round for Paris-based secure hardware wallet-maker Ledger, they account for a significant number of financial services investors. As of the first half of 2018, the total investments in blockchain-related companies have exceeded US$1.3 billion across all investment rounds worldwide. Reported dollar volume invested in VC rounds raised by blockchain companies surpassed totals in 2017.

Trends of the Sharing Economy and the Internet of Things Era

Many people in the financial industry are trying to prepare for or predict what the financial services sector will look like in 2020. Will artificial intelligence (AI) replace operations? Will performing financial functions occur in an instantaneous manner from the palm of our hands? Will there be enough disruption so that large banks will no longer exist? The following principles are not just our forecasts for the future, but are widely shared.

---

[1] http://www.dtcc.com/news/2017/january/09/dtcc-selects-ibm-axoni-and-r3-to-develop-dtccs-distributed-ledger-solution.
[2] https://www.cbinsights.com/research/financial-services-corporate-blockchain-investments/.

Open Platforms

Most platforms already built or being built are installed or web-based, but few have been completely open. Most very successful companies are completely obsessive about keeping the system closed. In most cases, this worked very well. However, the current trend is to open, and for good reason. Recently, Google, which had frantically protected its search algorithms, opened its AI algorithms for everyone to see and interact with. And perhaps even more astonishing was Microsoft's purchase of open-source leader, GitHub.

We can project the open system materializing in two related areas: first, new platforms can be built with proven open-sourced financial services-oriented software. Examples include databases a company uses, such as Hadoop, PostgreSQL, and MongoDB. Second, open API (application programming interface) systems can be an enabler. Open APIs provide future flexibility as well as the ability to have other non-influenced voices providing continuous feedback to suggest new ways to approach a problem. An open API also allows third-party vendors to build additional features and enhancements without getting stuck in the company's resource constrained pipeline and prioritizations.

An open system fits perfectly into the overarching need for transparency in the financial markets system, and more transparency will lead to better product and cost control. However, the main problem with an open system is information leakage. How do you have a fully open system to increase transparency and at the same time make sure the amount of information leakage is minimal? How do you financially capitalize on your investment in your API? The solutions to these two questions will be the fine art that will need to be mastered by tomorrow's industry leaders.

Web and Mobile (Internet of Things Devices)

There have been many iterations of web-based front-end technologies, from Microsoft's Silverlight to Adobe's Flash, yet they are fading into the history halls of technologies. The Web and HTML 5 are here to stay.

The advent of financial markets-specific containers such as Openfin, which create ease of integration among platforms and institutions by making an application native to any screen, allows the transformation to mobile to be extremely easy. The more institutions standardize on the usage of these infrastructures, the easier application deployment and integration will be.

Open-sourced efforts in this space are impressive, but only if they lead to further standardization of front-end development. As for mobile, it is easy to say a platform will be mobile, but it is harder to execute transitioning to mobile if all features of an application must be made mobile. Having the luxury to build a mobile strategy from scratch is rare.

Looking at certain areas in the world, such as parts of Africa and China, the desktop model has been completely bypassed. Hence, the importance of offering the consumer full capabilities using a mobile platform. For the average financial services executive on the street, mobile means more frequent and immediate transparency. The ability to know about an issue in real time and solve that issue on a mobile platform is key for future potential users.

Cloud-Based (Internet of Things Infrastructure)

Public clouds, private clouds, cloud as a disaster recovery (DR), and cloud communications are here to stay and will increase as the adoption of cloud-based computing accelerates. All companies, regardless of size, should build with a cloud-based infrastructure in mind, and seriously consider a server-less environment with adequate cybersecurity measures.

Banks are very concerned about security, and the safety to store their sensitive information in the cloud. It should be noted that most of the high-visibility hacks in the past ten years have affected networks but fewer on cloud providers. It is much easier to protect small amounts of connection points than it is to guard large amounts of entry points coming into a system. Financial institutions need to find ways to mitigate security fears on the path to future computing, which appears to be in the cloud.

Cloud computing also serves as an opportunity to consolidate platforms and connectivity. However, it is the role of vendors to provide further efficiencies using cloud computing rather than financial institutions believing that if they simply move everything to the cloud, their processes would be cheaper and easier to maintain.

Moving operations fully to the cloud will be akin to disconnecting from cable and going wireless, but it needs to have a justified use case and may not necessarily make sense for every business. Some cloud services' pricing is flexible in that they charge by the number of minutes used on the platform. This is very encouraging and innovative, as making an upfront commitment for usage is a burden on cashflows and no longer necessary. Such technological shifts allow the financial institutions to focus on their core business areas which are managing balance sheets, providing credits and financing, trading, and risk management while using whatever tools they have at their disposal to provide mobility and maintaining competitive advantage in their space.

Clearing Trades and Settlement Transactions

A recent poll showed that 60% of participants believe that further digitization and clearing of the over-the-counter (OTC) world is certain. The recent numbers published by the largest clearing houses support this migration mainly due to crippling regulatory burdens of keeping larger amounts of capital for OTC trades. There are many factors working against full migration of OTC products to standardized clearable products. Some include the basic fact that there is no single model to price these products. Therefore, disagreements on the amount of required collateral prevents the full migration into clearing.

Another obstacle is that banks do not want to create too much transparency in these products, as they provide the bank with huge margins on trading in the current opaque market. Some financial institutions have created direct links to clearing houses and other advancements in the cleared processing of trades. New regulation around trades requires immediate processing activity on these products, and some regulations require full reporting within 10 minutes.

However, what is obviously being missed is that even in the cleared space, 50% or more of the transactions are still voice trades made over the phone. If we do not fully automate that part of the cleared trade process, we will not achieve the full compliance needed to create the efficiencies predicted by many.

Therefore, automation of the voice trade is key to the advancement of trade processing. We expect technologies in this space to rapidly advance. However, 98% accuracy is simply *not* enough in this use case. We need to be right all the time when it comes to sensitive information. By 2020, this concern will be likely addressed, and we will reach full automation of the trading process from an OTC digitization standpoint as well as from the voice trade perspective.

Widespread Use of Artificial Intelligence

If you are a vendor or start-up and want to be funded, unless you can come up with a better idea, you will need to explain how your platform will use either AI, cognitive components such as chat bots, or behavioral-based insurance underwriting, and of course you must explain how you could use blockchain in your future vision.

The short-term prediction is that AI, cognitive platforms, and blockchain will all be a major part of any meaningful solution going forward. With the explosion of big data, AI technologies are key to understanding and improving the use of this big data. AI has advanced at a rapid pace and will integrate into our daily lives, often unseen, by 2020.[3] For example, we see the use of AI in our platform as a means to achieve two major goals: data quality, and trade breaks reconciliation and remediation. All of the catalysts for increased data usage are clear, but the biggest problem is the quality of the data itself. If the quality of the data coming in is

---

[3] Fintech AI Revenue to Grow 960% by 2021, Driven by Big Data, Distributed Computing & Connectivity. *Juniper-Research, August 2, 2016*. https://www.juniperresearch.com/press/press-re-leases/fintech-ai-revenue-to-grow-960-by-2021-driven-by.

poor, then you will also have poor output – quality of output is highly dependent on the quality of input.

The Holy Grail in terms of our platform's goals is to improve data quality, improve data matching of nonstructured data, and help our AI algorithms correct data impurities on their own. We have seen an explosion in the interest around blockchain and the way it could simplify the complexities of the market infrastructure.

Blockchain would drastically reduce costs while improving the ability of financial institutions to synchronize data and transactions. Some experts believe the way to prepare for it is by installing a private node distributed ledger and then preparing to expose it to other players if and when they are ready. Herein lies the main problem with the implementation of blockchain – it will only work if all the participants implement the technology until effective solutions to this problem are found. To reach this network effect or its true scale potential, one factor that is very important is the ability to define the right use case for the technology.

A main concern today is that institutions are not very selective in the choice of use case when implementing AI or blockchain. This dilutes the importance of the technology and sometimes leads to large investments in solutions being disbanded mid-way. If we are selective in our use cases, and are choosing the right technology partner, we should have full verification of the success of such technologies in the early 2020s, which will set clear key performance indicators toward the implementation of these technologies.

Regulatory Controls

If we could all agree on one area that controls the narrative of the financial institution business model and its future viability, it would be the immense amount of new regulations controlling investment capital in the market for the past decade.

Complying with the regulations became costly in the global arena. If you were local and thought you could escape the reach of the regulators, you were wrong. Furthermore, the regulatory attitude toward financial market participants was do or die, leaving no choice or time to think about future strategies.

One of the main criticisms is that most regulators were interested in collecting large fees for noncompliance issues rather than working to reduce systematic risk. New technology was patched on like band-aids put on an open wound.

Although some efforts are on the way for deregulation in the United States, many new regulations and even tighter frameworks were approved in the European Union. It is likely that we will continue to suffer higher level of regulations globally, which will distract us from the strategic views of our institutions. It will be interesting to see how regulators from less developed nations follow advanced nations to add further regulatory burdens on fintech companies.

Managing global compliance with these regulations and adjusting the financial institutions' systems to be flexible enough to deal with the newest breed of regulation is not the best way to approach this issue strategically. Utilities could provide a meaningful stepping stone for further compliance with the ever-changing regulatory environment.

Institutional Investment

The paradigm of the separation of buy-side (institutional investors) functions and sell-side (investment banking industry) functions is rapidly changing. Functions such as market making or direct clearing were not considered a real threat to the sell-side model until recently. This trend will continue to grow and therefore we believe that by 2020, at least one or two large buy-side firms will decide to enter the market making business (e.g., Citadel Securities) and direct clearing.

What this means from a technology platform perspective is that the full automation of workflows that were once deemed to be impossible to automate are now possible. Buy-side firms have no interest in becoming banks, as they are always at the forefront of creativity in financial instruments and, most important, they have the power of the user. When building our platform, we are constantly reaching out to innovative institutional investors to get their input on product development. If there is one major risk to the banks' future business model, it is the evolution of the buy-side model.

Conversely, institutional investors have benefited from the fact that investment banks pay for most of the costs involving clearing, processing, and even trading securities. Furthermore, institutional investors are used to the banks performing functions on their behalf, such as reporting. These functions will not be handled by the banks beyond 2020; therefore, the flip side of buy-side dominance is the extra expense in technology and resources to comply with this new level of importance. The positive aspect is that institutional investors, especially the nimbler hedge fund industry, tend to think about problems with no legacy bias, and are thus part of creating new and improved workflows to deal with the new financial responsibilities.

Diversity and Choices

To get where we want to be in the fintech future, we will have to continue the simple function of mobility. Competition is good for the market and we believe that we are in an era when it will only increase, offering a diverse competitive landscape for fintech but raising other issues. One issue is currently very apparent in many parts of the industry, where there are at least six to ten choices of vendors for one problem.

Blockchain, advanced AI algorithms, and payment platforms are just some examples of this proliferation.

If we provide the ecosystem in which many participants can easily integrate their services, then financial institutions would be able to "try out" any service they would like with minimal technological effort. Frequency of usage and new functionality would often be deployed in a seamless way to market participants. Take the Amazon or iTunes models, for example. Apps come and go, succeed and fail, but the user never needs to spend more time or effort on them beyond a simple download or small fee. The other important factor to reaching diversity and choice is that you do not want the framework that gets you the ability to choose to be just another toll taker on the way to a perfect environment. The commercial business model of participants and vendors needs to change and this should happen over the next five years.

User Defined and User Experience

We have seen too many systems and technologies created by the financial industry that seem to have thought about the use case and the technology needed to achieve its goals, but at the same time neglected the user experience (UX). When the UX is poor, eventually the user will look for another alternative. Looking at the current technological offerings, some of the major platforms that support the market infrastructure are simply terrible to use, as an average function might take a long list of manual steps to complete. There is a shift in power that is moving to the users, and vendors should assign UX a much higher importance, as it does other features. Basically, behind the traders that make money sit great people who have had to deal with inferior and cumbersome UXs.

Financial institutions rarely make that experience better unless they think it will directly affect their bottom-lines. However, by 2020, most institutions will address this issue; otherwise their competitors will do so and benefit with an increased market share because of it. Another important part of improvement to UX is the clear definition and support for user rights. Users are looking for clear rights and a flexible method to add or take away from entitlements and user preferences. Letting the user define his own trade matching algorithms is one way we are addressing this issue for 2020.

Trust in the New Sharing Economy

As Adam Smith, the father of modern economics, pointed out, a base level of trust in society is necessary for specialization and the economic growth that accompanies it. If we did not trust the butcher to give us quality meat without having to inspect the cow every time – or worse yet, if we needed to litigate after every grocery run – the whole system would come to a screeching halt.

This concept is even more critical in the sharing economy – which is often, quite appropriately, referred to as the trust economy. The sharing economy requires an incredibly high degree of trust, often based off little more than a profile picture and rudimentary reputation system. Sharing saves people time, money, and aggravation. But what really greases the wheels of this fast-growing economy is trust; it is what allows someone to take a ride from a stranger or rent a room in a house from someone they have never met. These successes in the sharing economy startled more than a few cynics who assumed that this reliance on trust, reputation, and goodwill would quickly become a giant scam or worse.

The sharing economy matches under-utilized assets with potential users. Uber and Airbnb have transformed idle assets (inventory) into economic value – by drastically changing social behavior and replacing transaction costs in order to match users with the assets. In the sharing economy, people must become comfortable enough trusting others that they will forego the expense of takaful contracts, lawyers, security systems, and even private ownership enforcement, to enjoy the benefits of sharing assets. The global population has become entrenched in the dominant ownership mindset. People are wading through an asset-heavy lifestyle engineered by the rise of hyper-consumption with material possessions, most of which are not really wanted, needed, or even used. While established businesses continue to hammer consumers with various iterations of the same proven formula – create product, sell it, collect money, repeat – a new, grassroots model of doing business is emerging, providing consumers with the power to get what they want and need at less personal and environmental cost (Gansky 2010).

As advanced trust mechanisms develop, the first "transaction costs" to disappear will be the redundant ownership of assets. As the mechanisms develop further, other opportunities will arise. Airbnb and asset rental companies are, in many ways, still working off the paradigm of scale economies, the low-hanging economic fruit of our time. Trust metrics will offer even greater economic value down the road, when massive economic gains can be reaped by applying them to things like:
- Releasing business value trapped in excess capacity and unnecessary transaction costs
- Altering traits of reliability and integrity to deliver on a commitment
- Collaborate to make trust data more viable and widespread

At the same time, the sharing economy represents a significant and growing business opportunity that will play a much grander fundamental shift in economic transactions. It is a shift from an infrastructure that *protects* people *from* each other, to an infrastructure that *helps* people *trust* each other.

Trust and Reciprocity in the Economy

Institutional economists, economic sociologists, political economists, and others concerned with the social organization of economic life have long maintained that trust and confidence are crucial to effective economic functioning, not only in underwriting specific exchanges between particular agents, but in terms of a generalized foundation of trust that underpins a wider socioeconomic system. In instrumental terms, resources of trust promote economic efficiency by reducing the transaction costs of economic exchange, on the assumption that others will behave according to common norms of economic conduct. It may be possible to transact without such an underpinning of trust – in contexts where cheating, fraud or corruption are rife – but the risks and associated costs of doing so are much higher than where individuals have a reasonable expectation that others will deal plainly. Trust leads a double life as a social value and an economic resource; as such, it is a critical concept for linking social arrangements with economic outcomes.

As financial markets have grown more complex, and exchanges within them made impersonal through electronic communications, the problem of trust has become more acute. Systemic risk requires systemic trust, and the ways in which risk has been distributed across the system via complicated and often opaque instruments has tested systemic resources of trust to breaking point. Tighter credit requirements – inter-bank, business, and mortgage lending – are a signal example of a crisis in confidence inside the financial system. The proliferation of crowdfunding platforms, for example, seems to indicate the market seeking alternative means to traditional lending.

It should also be noted that poor and tyrannical countries find themselves entrapped in continuing mistrust, inequality, and dysfunctional institutions. High levels of inequality contribute to lower levels of trust, which lessen the political and societal support for the state to collect resources for launching and implementing universal welfare programs in an uncorrupted and nondiscriminatory way. Unequal societies find themselves trapped in a continuous cycle of inequality, low trust in others and in government, policies that do little to reduce the gap between the rich, and the poor and create a sense of equal opportunity. Demands for radical redistribution, as we see in many transitioning countries, exacerbate social tensions rather than relieving them.

However, we know that extending trust to people inspires them. It brings out the best in them and it motivates them. In fact, the reason that extending trust is so powerful is because trust is a compelling form of positive human motivation. This is a key source of economic growth and collaboration. Extending trust also in turn increases trust. It is somewhat ironic that one of the best ways to increase trust is to simply extend it. Trusting people inspires them to want to be worthy of that trust. It brings out the best in them. It makes it safer to risk and innovate, and extending trust generates reciprocity. When we give trust to people, they tend to give it back. There are many reasons for this, and the fundamental reason why the sharing economy has succeeded so far is because its positive (and counter-intuitive) outcome helps show that people are more trusting than skeptics usually assume, especially when someone else goes out on that limb first. This helped fuel much of the early optimism of a utopian trust economy where we could all operate on a system of goodwill toward mankind. But when we withhold trust, people generally will in return withhold it. In teams and organizations, giving trust manifests in greater employee engagement and retention, increased customer loyalty and referrals, and other economic benefits.

Trust and Trustworthiness (Reciprocity) in Islam

In Islam, man is entrusted with an *amanah* (trust) to establish responsibility on earth by means of virtues and bounties endowed to him by God, his initiative, creativity, and labor (*isti'mar*). Nature has been created for human beings, but man is also required to establish a moral social order on earth. The concept of *amanah* implies that in all his actions, man should choose to prosper the earth (*islah*) by making the best use of resources and to fully utilize the virtues inherent in him to *isti'mar* the earth. *Ifsad* (*fasad*) or adversity or corruption, is to be avoided in managing one's role as a *khalifah*. Being a *khalifah*, man has also been granted authority to freely manage nature/universe and to cooperate with his fellow beings to complete the task of *khalifah*. As our world and the economy evolves, we seek new ways (innovate) to cope with the challenges evolution brings. We believe technology is a great way to do this, and the main building block to enable trust in impersonal financial transactions in a highly globalized environment can be identified as blockchain. This innovation that will shape the future will not only play a crucial role in boosting the financial sector (banking, takaful, investment, etc.) including the Islamic finance sector but also other economic transactions that will characterize the sharing economy.

Religious tenets, in general, could be viewed as the force behind the "invisible hand" that Adam Smith had probably alluded to, where in the pursuit of self-interest, the "invisible hand" will safeguard the collective interest. There always has been a moral and ethical obligation to pursuing one's own interest because we do not live in isolation. If we choose to ignore these obligations, the unspoken social contract breaks down and it would lead to the tragedy of commons. Building trust by upholding ethical and moral obligations, hence, reinforces public civility and communal solidarity, removes fears and mistrust in public and private institutions for a harmonious and profitable existence, by reducing risk in highly uncertain times through shared goals and reciprocal undertaking. And as we will see in the next few sections, specific technology, like blockchain, will be a key enabler to further encourage this and play a significant role in the new sharing economy.

What is Blockchain?

Blockchain is a P2P public ledger maintained by a distributed network of computers that requires no central authority or third-party intermediaries. It consists of three key components: a transaction, a transaction record, and a system that verifies and stores the transaction. The blocks are generated through open-source software and record the information about when and in what sequence the transaction took place. This "block" chronologically stores information of all the transactions that have taken place in the chain, and therefore the name – blockchain. In other words, a blockchain is a database of immutable time-stamped information of every transaction in that chain that is replicated on servers across the globe. This technology is the foundation of cryptocurrencies[4] such as bitcoin. In fact, blockchain technology was first introduced in 2009 with bitcoin, a cryptocurrency-based distributed payment protocol.

Blockchain's main innovation is a public transaction record of integrity without central authority. The technology offers everyone the opportunity to participate in secure contracts over time, with a secure record of what was agreed at that time. This innovation carries a significance stretching far beyond cryptocurrency. Blockchain lets people who have no particular confidence in each other collaborate without having to go through a neutral central authority. Simply put, it is a mechanism for creating trust. Within this open ledger system, blockchain offers an inherent level of trust for the user, eliminating the need for the middleman and mitigating the risk of human error. Its publicly accessible log of transactions ensures that the data is protected against tampering and revision, and it is virtually impossible for individuals to modify or replace parts of the blockchain secretly.

A full copy of the blockchain contains every transaction ever executed, making information on the value belonging to every active address (account) accessible at any point in history. Every block contains a long reference number or hash of the previous block, thus creating a chain of blocks from the genesis block to the current block. Figure 5.3 illustrates how a transaction is recorded on the blockchain, based on the cryptocurrency protocol.

Validation is required for a new block to be added on to the blockchain. This validation process, also called mining, allows pending transactions to be confirmed; enforces a chronological order on the blockchain; protects the neutrality of the blockchain; and enables different computers (or nodes) to agree on the state of the system at any given time (Bitcoin Project, n.d.).

---

[4] Bitcoin and other cryptocurrencies (also called AltCoins) gained significant momentum in 2013 with bitcoin's sharp price rise, the historic high being US$1124.76 on November 29, 2013. High prices and high volatility attracted speculation, as well as proliferation of competitive and complementary cryptocurrencies. Arguably, there were over 500 AltCoins based on blockchain technology as of November **2014**.

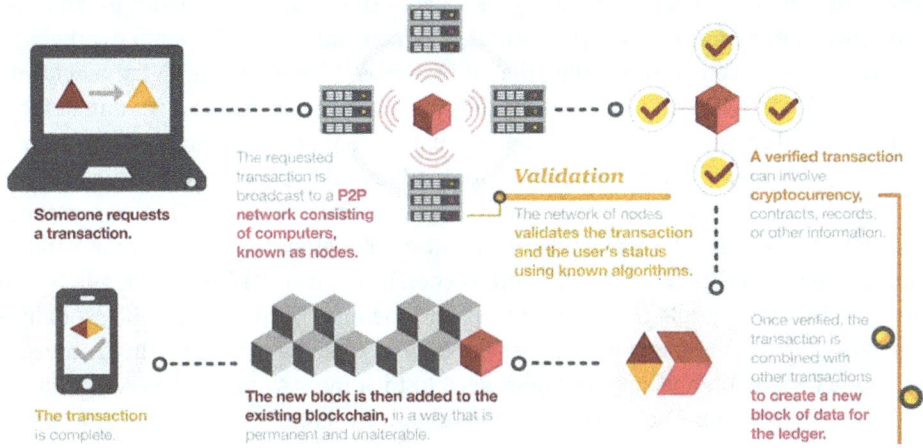

Figure 5.3: How the Blockchain Transaction Works.
Source: http://saphanatutorial.com/introduction-to-blockchain-for-beginners/.

In traditional transactions, such as money transfers or foreign currency, there is usually an intermediary or a centralized entity that records the transmission of money or currency that exist apart from it. In blockchain, the token or digital coin itself is what has value, which is determined by the market. This is what makes the system a truly decentralized exchange. When people buy or sell bitcoins, a secret key or token is broadcast to the system. "Miners" use nodes, computers, or devices linked to a network, to identify and validate the transaction using copies of all or some information of the blockchain, which are accessible publicly. Before the transaction is accepted by the network, miners must show PoW using a cryptographic hash function (that special algorithm), which aims to provide high levels of protection. Miners receive some form of compensation for their computing power contribution, avoiding the need to have a centralized system. New protocols such as Ripple rely on a consensus process that does not need miners nor proof of work and can agree on the changes to the blockchain within seconds. As progress is made in blockchain technology, its use will become more efficient and applicable in many ways, that is, to transact anything of value, not just digitizing currency.

Blockchain as Currency and Payments

Using blockchain as digital currency, like bitcoin, is a way of buying and selling things over the internet without cash. The bitcoin value chain is composed of several different constituencies: software developers, miners, exchanges, merchant processing services, web wallet companies, and users/consumers. From an individual user's perspective, the important elements in transacting coins are a user address, a private key, and wallet software. The address is where others can send bitcoin to you, and the private key is the cryptographic secret by which you can send bitcoin to others.

Until blockchain cryptography, digital cash was, like any other digital asset, infinitely duplicable (like our ability to make copies of an e-mail attachment any number of times), and there was no way to confirm that a certain batch of digital cash had not already been spent without a central intermediary. There had to be a trusted third party (whether a bank or quasi-bank payment platforms like PayPal) in transactions, which kept a ledger confirming that each portion of digital cash was spent only once; this is the double-spend problem. Coin ownership is recorded in the public ledger and confirmed by cryptographic protocols and the mining community. Blockchain is "trust-free" in the sense that a user does not need to trust the other party in the transaction, or a central intermediary, but does need to trust the system: the blockchain protocol software system. The "blocks" in the chain are groups of transactions posted sequentially to the ledger – that is, added to the "chain." Blockchain ledgers can be inspected publicly with block explorers, internet sites (e.g., www.Blockchain.info for the bitcoin blockchain) where you can see a transaction stream by entering a blockchain address (a user's public-key address, e.g., 1BpXJCi5bEjNn6DtoYJhg6wR5JwLCGLbfx).

One of the main issues blockchain can tackle is the high complexity of payments networks, due to the fragmentation of the financial industry itself, which makes it impractical for individual banks to deal directly with all other banks on the planet.

For example, when a bank gets a payment instruction from a client, it needs to find a correspondent bank that is willing to take the client's funds and terminate the payment locally at the receiving bank. And in order to do so, the corre-spondent bank needs to have a nostro[5] or vostro account with the receiving bank (or with another correspondent bank that has access to the receiving bank, thus adding an extra hoop), ideally with enough pre-funded liquidity to complete the payment on the client's behalf.

But when this happens, the receiving bank has no way to verify that the incoming transfer from the (last) correspondent bank, in fact, corresponds to the original client sending the money. That is why a SWIFT message from the sender is needed, so the receiving bank can understand the purpose of the incoming funds, do proper due diligence or antimoney laundering (AML) checks on the payment, and inform the receiver of the funds.

All the parties involved have different ledgers, that is, they do not share a single version of the truth, and the coordination between all these parties is slow and error-prone, many times relying on manual interventions by back-office teams. Furthermore,

---

[5] *Nostro* is a Latin word, which means "our." When a bank holds an account in foreign currency in another bank it is called nostro account, that is, our account with them. Similarly, *vostro* means "your," that is, your account with us. Accounts of other banks in another bank (in domes- tic currency) are known as *vostro* accounts.

someone needs to perform currency conversion at either end, and different parties need to manage liquidity levels at *nostro/vostro* accounts, which involves settling against central bank accounts as well.

One way that cryptocurrencies can provide efficiency is in international trade invoicing and payments. Sourcing liquidity for local currency is a key factor to make international supplier payments more reliable. The problem for importers in emerging economies is that there are fewer buyers and sellers of local currency. This results in fewer bids and asks, making it more difficult for buyers and sellers of local currency to transact, hence, impacting on reliability of international supplier payments and their participation in trade. It is plausible in this respect that bitcoin the currency (BTC) could provide liquidity for local currencies and bitcoin the system could act as a means to pay international supplier invoices in international currencies. For example, consider a scenario where an international supplier invoices a firm in Kenya in US\$ (Africa has been the fastest growing region in the last decade – and the microfinancing service M-Pesa[6] originated from Kenya). Technically, the local importer can purchase BTC with local currency (KES) on an exchange that acts as an onramp – in 10 minutes the transaction is confirmed by where the balance is deposited into a bank account. Clearly this is technically feasible, as this is indeed how current remittance flows on bitcoin work – and in this example would avoid the high intermediation costs for converting the KES.

Blockchains as Databases and Public Registries

Blockchains also have a host of other uses because they meet the need for a trustworthy record, something vital for transactions of every sort. One idea is to develop tamper-proof public databases cheaply like land registries (Honduras) and registry of companies (Isle of Man); or registers of the ownership of luxury goods, like diamonds (Everledger) or works of art. Documents can be notarized by embedding information about them into a public blockchain – and you will no longer need a notary to vouch for them. Financial-services firms are contemplating using blockchains as a record of who owns what instead of having a series of internal ledgers. A trusted private ledger removes the need for reconciling each transaction with a counterparty; it is fast and it minimizes errors. Oliver Wyman, Anthemis Group, and Santander Innoventures (2015), estimate that this could save banks up to US \$20 billion a year by 2022.[7]

---

[6] M-Pesa was first launched by the Kenyan mobile network operator Safaricom, where Vodafone is technically a minority shareholder (40%), in March 2007. M-Pesa quickly captured a signif- icant market share for cash transfers, and grew to 17 million subscribers by December 2011 in Kenya alone.
[7] This is quoted from their joint report "The Fintech 2.0 Paper: rebooting financial services."

Public records, too, can be migrated to the blockchain: land and property titles, vehicle registrations, business licenses, marriage certificates, and death certificates. Digital identity can be confirmed with the blockchain through securely encoded driver's licenses, identity cards, passports, and voter registrations. Private records such as IOUs, loans, contracts, signatures, wills, and trusts can be stored.

Physical asset keys can be encoded as digital assets on the blockchain for controlled access to homes, hotel rooms, rental cars, and privately-owned or shared-access automobiles (e.g., Getaround). Intangible assets (e.g., patents, trademarks, copyrights, reservations, and domain names) can also be protected and transferred via the blockchain. For example, to protect an idea, instead of trademarking it or patenting it, you could encode it to the blockchain and you would have proof of a specific invention/innovation being registered with a specific date-time stamp for future proof.

Blockchain as Smart Contracts

Whereas the initial blockchain version is for the decentralization of money and payments, the next evolution of blockchain is for the decentralization of markets, and the transfer of many other kinds of assets beyond currency using blockchain, from the creation of a unit of value through every time it is transferred or divided. The key idea is that the decentralized transaction ledger functionality of blockchain could be used to register, confirm, and transfer all manner of contracts and property. Satoshi Nakamoto (2009) started by specifying escrow transactions, bonded contracts, third-party arbitration, and multiparty signature transactions. All financial transactions could be reinvented on the blockchain, including stock, private equity, crowdfunding instruments, bonds, mutual funds, annuities, pensions, and all manner of financial instruments (futures, options, currency swaps, etc.).

Smart contracts are a complex set of software codes with components designed to automate execution and settlement of contractual agreements. In other words, they are programmable contracts, which self-execute the stipulations of an agreement when predetermined conditions are triggered. Once two or more parties consent to all of the terms within the contract, they cryptographically sign the smart contract and deploy it to a distributed ledger. When a condition specified in the code is met, the program automatically triggers a corresponding action. By removing the need for direct human involvement, a deployed smart contract on a distributed ledger could make contractual relationships more efficient and economical with potentially fewer opportunities for error, misunderstanding, delay or dispute. The smart contract is also automatable and enforceable. It is automatable by a computer or network of computers, although some parts may require human input and control. It is then enforceable by either legal enforcement of rights and obligations or tamper-proof execution.

In contractual agreements within the purview of the Shariah, it is imperative that the clauses be transparent and void of deceptive ambiguity (*gharar*). Certain "expensive" law firms charge a premium to be able to craft clauses such that in cases of dispute, these clauses allow unfair advantage to them. If you really think about it, smart contracts are meant to be "dumb" such that they ideally have no hidden loopholes and terms and conditions are plain enough to be executed automatically by code. Such is the spirit of the Shariah.

In addition, reliance on physical documents leads to delays, inefficiencies and increases exposure to errors and fraud. Financial intermediaries, while providing interoperability for the finance system and reducing risk, create unnecessary overhead costs and increase compliance requirements. Smart contracts on blockchain have the capacity to inject greater efficiency and productivity while saving costs associated with traditional contracts.

Blockchain as Clearing and Settlement of Securities Transactions

In their analysis, Boston Consulting Group (Evans et al., 2016) noted that one of the most scrutinized uses of blockchain is for the clearing and settlement of securities transactions, currently a complex network of brokers, custodian banks, stock transfer agents, regulators, and depositories. A single transfer can require a dozen intermediary transactions, and typically takes three days to settle, of which about 20% generate errors, which must be corrected manually.

With blockchain, two trading parties could read and write to a common, trusted, and error-free database. The transaction could be written in legal language as well as in computer code, so that the data exchange itself is the settlement. And it could be visible to regulators. The brokers (as agents of the buyer and seller) could trade on a larger blockchain to remove custodians as intermediaries, thereby reducing total transaction costs. Institutions issuing securities, such as corporations and municipalities, could issue them directly onto the blockchain, thereby removing the need for stock transfer agents.

Reduction of Fraud

It is commonly acknowledged that one of the main challenges facing the banking industry today is the growth of fraud and cyberattacks. Traditionally, bank ledgers have been created within a centralized database. This model has been more susceptible to hackers and cyberattacks as all the information is located in one place – usually secured behind outdated legacy information technology (IT) systems. Hackers and cybercriminals are well aware of evolving digital technology and have been able to bypass these security systems to commit data breaches and fraud.

In contrast, as blockchain is decentralized it is less prone to this type of fraud. By using blockchain there would not only be real-time execution of payments but also complete transparency, which would enable real-time fraud analysis and prevention. A blockchain is checked at every step of a transaction by independent miners, with all data being open and publicly available, there is a real-time analysis and verification of every bit of data and all information during the transaction. The blockchain ledger can provide a historical record of all documents shared and compliance activities undertaken for each banking customer. Mali-cious attempts to view or change the data become part of the data itself, making third-party hacks immediately obvious.

For example, this record could be used to provide evidence that a bank has acted in accordance with the requirements placed upon it – should regulators ask for such clarification. It would also be of particular use in identifying entities attempting to create fraudulent histories. Subject to the provisions of data protection regulation, the data within it could even be analyzed by the banks to spot irregularities or foul play – directly targeting criminal activity. This would be an advantage over the current banking and payments systems, which are more susceptible to fraud and hacking. There would need to be collaboration to achieve this within the blockchain ecosystem. Banks would need to partner with regulators and fintech companies to develop credible, decentralized ledgers permitting rapid adoption of global real-time payments and settlement.

On December 30, 2015, Nasdaq announced that it had made its first ever share trade using blockchain technology. Nasdaq used its proprietary Linq platform (developed in collaboration with Chain.com and global design firm IDEO) to sell shares. As Nasdaq has pointed out, within the multistep manual process used today in banks and financial institutions there is not only plenty of room for error but also for fraud. By utilizing blockchain, organizations can reduce risk and administrative burden, as well as saving time and money. Nevertheless, banks must consider that blockchain does not yet eliminate all types of fraud.

Know Your Customer

Know Your Customer (KY) requests currently can cause delays in banking transactions, typically taking thirty to fifty days to complete to a satisfactory level. Current KYC processes also entail substantial duplication of effort between banks (and other third-party institutions). While annual compliance costs are high, there are also large penalties for failing to follow KYC guidelines properly.

The average bank spends US$56 million a year on KYC compliance, according to a recent Thomson Reuters survey, which also revealed that some banks spend up to US$420 million annually on KYC compliance, AML checks and customer due diligence (CDD). Since 2009, regulatory fines, particularly in the United States, have followed an upward trend with record-breaking fines levied during 2015. Ongoing regulatory change, with no one internationally agreed standard, makes it increasingly hard for banks to remain compliant. Thus, as it can take such a long time to on-board a new customer because of lengthening KYC procedures, this is having an increasingly negative effect on customer experience.

A blockchain specialist at Rabobank proposed that KYC statements can be stored on blockchain. Once a bank has KYC-ed a new customer they can then put that statement, including a summary of the KYC documents, on a blockchain that can then be used by other banks and other accredited organizations (such as insurers, car rental firms, loan providers, etc.) without the need to ask the customer to start the KYC process all over again. These organizations will know that the customer's ID documents have been independently checked and verified so they will not need to carry out their own KYC checks, reducing their administrative burdens and costs. As data stored on blockchain is irreversible, it would provide a single source of truth thereby minimizing the risk of duplication or error. There is also the advantage for the customer that they only must supply KYC documents once (until they need to be updated) and that they are not then disclosed to any other party (except for their own bank) as the other organizations will not need to see and check the ID documents but will just rely on the blockchain verification. SWIFT has established a KYC Registry with 1,125-member banks sharing KYC documentation – however, this is only 16% of the 7,000 banks on their network. The KYC Registry meets the need for an efficient, shared platform for managing and exchanging standardized KYC data and it's free to upload the documentation to the Registry and to share it with other institutions. SWIFT validates the data rigorously, informs the client if it is incomplete or needs updating, and sends out alerts to correspondents whenever the data changes.

There will still be issues surrounding security and privacy of customer's KYC information but, as long as all KYC is held on a private blockchain rather than a public one, these issues should be minimal from a bank customer's point of view. The data on the blockchain will merely be a reference point with a digital signature or cryptographic hash – which would give individuals access to the relevant client information in a repository separate to the blockchain, ensuring a secure and private way of conducting and storing a customer's KYC information. Equally important, though, is ensuring financial institutions only have permissioned access on a temporary basis so that access to KYC information is only granted when strictly necessary for that purpose, and for no other ancillary reason. Therefore, it is evident that blockchain could have a major role in streamlining these KYC and AML processes – although this may require cross-border consensus as to what is regarded as acceptable KYC documentation and what needs to be done in terms of acceptable verification of those documents.

According to a Goldman Sachs Report,[8] the banking sector can achieve 10% headcount reduction with the introduction of blockchain in the KYC procedures.

---

8 Schenider, J. (2016). *BlockChain: Putting Theory into Practice. Goldman Sachs.*

This amounts to around US$160 million in cost-saving annually. Blockchain will also reduce the amount of budgetary resources allocated for employee training, there will be 30% headcount reduction amounting to US$420 million. Overall operational cost savings are estimated to be around US$2.5 billion dollars. AML penalties will also be reduced by an estimated US$0.5 to US$2 billion dollars.

Blockchain Infrastructure

The elements of computing are storage, programs, and communications. Mainframes, PCs, mobile, and cloud all manifest these elements in their own unique ways. So, what are the main elements of a blockchain? Just like the "cloud" that does not simply exist as a magical entity by itself, a blockchain does not exist as a chain on its own. Rather, the blockchain application is really made up of building blocks of computing that can be used together to create effective decentralized applications.

In a centralized system, programmers may use Amazon S3 for raw data storage, MongoDB Atlas for databases, and Amazon EC2 for processing. In the storage element, they may have file systems and databases, where file systems are for storing raw data like mp3s with a hierarchy of directories and files, and databases are for storing structured metadata with a query interface like SQL.

In creating decentralized apps (Dapps), the main building blocks of decentralized computing are (see Figure 5.4):

STORAGE	PROCESSING	COMMUNICATIONS
TOKEN STORAGE Bitcoin, Zcash, .*	**STATEFUL BIZ LOGIC** Ethereum, Lisk, Rchain, Tezos, .. Client-side compute (JS, Swift)	**DATA** TCP/IP, HTTP, Tokenized Tor
FILE SYSTEM or BLOB IPFS/FileCoin, Eth Swarm, Storj, Sia, Tieron, LAFS	**STATELESS BIZ LOGIC** Crypto Conditions (e.g,BigchainDB). Bitshares, Eos, and all stateful biz logic	**VALUE** Interledger, Cosmos
DATABASE BigchainDB + IPDB, IOTA		
DATA MARKET Ocean Enigma, DataBroker, Datum	**HIGH PERF. COMPUTE** TrueBit, Golem, iEx.ec, Nyriad, VMs, client-side compute	**STATE** PolkaDot, Aeternity

Figure 5.4: The 3 Main Elements of Decentralized Computing.
Source: https://blog.bigchaindb.com/blockchain-infrastructure-landscape-a-first-principles-framing-92cc5549bafe.

- Storage: token storage, database, file system/raw data
- Processing: stateful business logic, stateless business logic, high performance programs
- Communications: connect networks of data, of value, and of state

In this section, we intend to provide an illustrative understanding of the key elements of decentralized computing. Despite trying to make it as simple as we can, these sections may appear to be too technical for some readers, but insightful for others.

Storage

The fundamental computing element of storage has the following building blocks:

Token storage: Tokens are stores of value (e.g., assets, securities) whether it is air miles, bitcoins (alt coins), digital art copyrights, or telco talk time. The main actions on a token storage system are to issue and transfer tokens (with many variants), while preventing double-spends, fraud, etc.

Bitcoin and Zcash are two prominent coin systems focusing solely on transactional exchange. Ethereum happens to use tokens in service toward its mission of being a world computer. These are all examples of tokens given out as internal incentives to run the network infrastructure.

Other tokens are not internal to a network to power the network itself, but are used for incentives in a higher-level network where the lower-level infrastructure actually stores the tokens. One example is ERC20 tokens like Golem (GNT) running on top of the Ethereum main net. Another example is Envoke's IP licensing tokens, running on the IPDB network.

Finally, it is important to note that most blockchain systems have a mechanism for token storage.

Database: Databases specialize in storing structured metadata, for example, as tables (relational DB), document stores (e.g., JSON), key-value stores, time series, or graphs; and then rapidly retrieving that data via queries (e.g., SQL).

Traditional distributed (but centralized) databases like MongoDB and Cassandra routinely store hundreds of Terabytes and even Petabytes of data, with throughput that can exceed 1 million writes per second. Query languages like SQL are great because they separate implementation from specification, and are, therefore, not constrained to any particular application. SQL has been a standard for decades. This is why the same database system can be used across many different industries.

File system/Raw data storage: These are systems to store large files (movies, mp3s, large datasets), organized in a hierarchy of directories and files.

IPFS and Tahoe-LAFS are decentralized file systems that wrap decentralized or centralized raw data storage. FileCoin, Storj, Sia, and Tieron do decentralized raw data storage. The file-sharing BitTorrent also does the same, although it uses a "tit-for-tat" scheme rather than tokens. Ethereum Swarm, Dat, and Swarm-JS do basically both.

Data marketplace: These systems connect the data owners (e.g., enterprises) with data consumers (e.g., AI startups). While they are higher-level than databases and file systems, they are nonetheless core infrastructure because the countless applications that need data (e.g., anything AI) will depend on such services. Ocean is an example "protocol and network," on which data marketplaces can be built. There are also application-specific marketplaces: Enigma Catalyst for crypto markets, Datum for personal data; and DataBroker DAO for Internet of Things (IoT) streams.

Processing

The fundamental computing element of processing for Dapps is the smart contract. "Smart contracts" systems are the popular label for systems that do processing in a decentralized fashion. This actually has two subsets with very different properties: stateless (combinational) business logic and stateful (sequential) business logic. Stateless versus stateful gives revolutionary differences in complexity, identification, verifiability, etc. There is a third decentralized processing building block: high-performance compute (HPC), which we discuss at the end of the chapter.

Stateless (combinational) business logic: This is any arbitrary logic that does not retain state internally. In electrical engineering terms, it can be structured as combinational digital logic circuits. The logic is represented as a truth table, schematic diagram, or code holding conditional statements (combining if/then, and, or, not). Because they do not have state, it is easy to verify large stateless smart contracts, and therefore to build large verified/secure systems.

The interledger protocol (ILP) contains the crypto-conditions (CC) protocol to cleanly specify combinational circuits (where the output is a pure function of the input). CC is important to know of because it is becoming an internet standard via the Internet Engineering Task Force (IETF), and because ILP is getting widespread adoption among centralized and decentralized payments networks (e.g., > 75 banks via Ripple). CC has standalone implementations in JavaScript, Python, Java, and more. BigchainDB, Ripple, Stellar, and other systems use CCs; and thus support combinational business logic and smart contracts.

Because stateful logic is a superset of stateless logic, hence systems that support stateful logic also support stateless logic (at the expense of additional complexity and verifiability challenges).

Stateful (sequential) business logic: This is any arbitrary logic that does retain state internally – it has memory. Or, it is a combinational logic circuit with at least one feedback loop (and a clock). For example, a microprocessor has an internal register that gets updated according to machine-code instructions that are sent to it. More generally, stateful business logic is a Turing machine that takes in a sequence of inputs, and returns a sequence of outputs.

Ethereum is the best-known blockchain system that manifests stateful business logic and smart contracts running directly on-chain. Lisk, RChain, DFINITY, Aeternity, Tezos, Fabric, Sawtooth, and many more also implement it. Running code that is "just out there, somewhere" is a powerful concept, with many use cases. Trent McConaghy[9] believes that this helps explain why Ethereum took off, why its ecosystem has grown such that it is almost a platform in its own right, and why so much competition has arisen in this building block.

Because sequential logic is a superset of combinational logic, these systems also support combinational logic.

For many use cases in decentralized processing, McConaghy deems there is a simpler approach: by simply having the processing on the client side within the browser or the mobile device, running JavaScript or Swift. This architecture is easy for mainstream web developers. For example, all that many web apps need is an application state. To build this you just need JS + IPDB (using js-bigchaindb-driver). For raw data storage and payments additions, then include the JS client versions of IPFS (ipfs.js) and Ethereum (web3.js).

HPC: This is processing to do "heavy lifting" programming for things like rendering, machine learning, circuit simulation, weather forecasting, protein folding, and more. A programming job here might take hours or even weeks on a cluster of machines (CPUs, GPUs, even TPUs[10]).

McConaghy imagines that some blockchain engineers envision these approaches to decentralized HPC:
- Golem and iEx.ec frame it as a combination of decentralized supercomputer along with associated apps.
- Nyriad frames it as storage processing. Basically, the processing sits next to decentralized storage (which Nyriad also has a solution to).
- TrueBit allows third parties to program, but then does post-compute checking (implicitly checking when possible; explicitly checking if questions get raised).
- McConaghy thinks some programmers are simply running heavy computation on VMs or Docker containers, and putting the result (final VM state, or just

---

9 Founder of OceanProtocol and BigchainDB.
10 The CPU controls all of the other parts of a computer. The GPU can only handle graphics, although it can be used for calculations by some special scientific applications. A TPU is a special chip for machine learning.

computed results) into raw data storage with restricted access. They can then sell access to these containers using, for example, tokenized read permissions. This approach asks more of clients to verify results, but it is good to know that such tech is already possible today.

Communications

The third and final fundamental decentralized computing element is communications. There are many ways to frame communications but we will focus on connecting networks. It comes in three levels: data, value, and state.

Data: In the 1960s, ARPAnet was created as a data network, and its success spawned several similar networks like NPL and CYCLADES. However, they did not have the ability to communicate with each other. Cerf and Kahn invented TCP/IP in the 1970s to connect them, to create a network of networks, which we now call the internet. TCP/IP is now the de-facto standard to connect networks. Despite its age, TCP/IP can be viewed as a decentralized building block for connecting networks of data.

Value: TCP/IP only connects networks on a data level. You can double-spend packets – send the same packet to more than one destination at once. But what about connecting networks where someone can send value across the networks? For example, from bitcoin to Ethereum, or even SWIFT payments network to say Ripple's XRP network. In such cases, the token is intended to be able to go to one destination at a time. One way to connect networks while preventing double-spends is to use an exchange, but that is more complicated than it needs to be. Instead, blockchain engineers have stripped an exchange to its essence and removed the need for a trusted middleman, by using cryptographic escrow. Peter can send money to Charlie via Victoria, where Victoria is passing on the funds but cannot spend them (and there is a time constraint so that Victoria cannot delay or stall). This is the essence behind the ILP. It is the same conceptual idea as two-way pegs (like sidechains) and state channels (like Lightning and Raiden); but the focus is solely on connecting networks with respect to value. Besides ILP there is Cosmos, which adds a bit more complexity for convenience on certain use cases.

State: Beyond connecting networks of value, engineers are pondering something with its own crypto-wallet that can hop from one network to another. These ideas include a smart contract in one Ethereum main net that can move its state to another Ethereum net, or another compatible net. Also, removing restrictions from an AI DAO to just one net and enable it to connect to others.

Some systems are already getting there; Polkadot is one that is able to connect networks of state, and Aeternity fits somewhere between the network-of-value and network-of-state spectrum.

Furthermore, as we speak, the blockchain community is starting to build systems that manifest combinations. There are many combinations of two blocks at once, usually IPFS + Ethereum or IPFS + IPDB. And there are even engineers using three or more blocks. Such is the level of experimentation and innovation that is happening in the decentralized digital ecosystem.

References

Evans, P., Aré, L., Forth, P., Harlé, N., & Portincaso, M. (2016). *Thinking Outside the Blocks: A Strategic Perspective on Blockchain and Digital Tokens*. Boston, Massachusetts, USA: Boston Consulting Group. December 1.

Gansky, L. (2010). *The Mesh: Why the Future of Business Is Sharing*. Portfolio Penguin, NY. GitHub. *Blockchain Based Proof of Work*. GitHub. March 2014.

Nakamoto, S. (2009). *Bitcoin: A Peer-to-Peer Electronic Cash System*. White paper, 2009, 1–9.

Oliver Wyman, Anthemis Group and Santander Innoventures (2015). The Fintech 2.0 Paper: Rebooting financial services.

Schenider, J. (2016). *BlockChain: Putting Theory into Practice*. Goldman Sachs.

Szabo, N. (1996). *Smart Contracts: Building Blocks for Digital Markets*. Extropy, no. 16.

Chapter 6
Expanded Use Cases of Blockchain

Smart Contracts in Islamic Transactions

Contractual agreements are key enablers for trade and commerce which record mutually agreed upon terms for execution or dispute resolution. The Quranic verses (Surah Al-Baqarah: 282–283) enjoin Muslims to put contracts in writing for fairness and accountability. As such, Muslim traders rely upon an Islamic legal and institutional framework for the purposes of accounting and accountability, while Muslim scholars define legal norms and act as mediators in commercial disputes. Possessing written records is vital to the efficiency and transparency of commerce and for monitoring trade and agreements. Islamic law is the central institutional framework of being Muslim, and its inherent legal framework dictates, among other things, the ethical norms of business behavior, to form the foundation for trust, equality, and fairness.

As the world evolves, we use technology to operationalize the specific intents of the Shariah so that Islamic economic actors can be adept at more efficient (and less risky) ways of doing business. Reliance on physical documents leads to delays, inefficiencies, and increases exposure to errors and fraud. Financial intermediaries, while providing interoperability for the finance system and reducing risk, create unnecessary overhead costs and increase compliance requirements. Smart contracts, on distributed ledger technologies (blockchain) that have the capacity to inject greater efficiency and productivity while saving costs associated with traditional contracts. Many financial enterprises are exploring the use of smart contract technology for various applications across the banking, financial services, and insurance (including takaful) sectors (EY, 2017). As of now, prototypes developed have been simplified versions of a smart contract, but more work needs to be done in key areas, which will tackle legal and regulatory compliance, scalability and security, and the ability to code complex contracts which currently dominate the financial services landscape.

How Does a Smart Contract Work?

Smart contracts are complex software solutions with components designed to automate execution and settlement of contractual agreements. In other words, they are programmable contracts that self-execute the stipulations of an agree-ment when predetermined conditions are triggered. Once two or more parties consent to all the terms within the contract, they cryptographically sign the smart contract and deploy it to a distributed ledger (Buterin, 2013). When a condition specified in the code is met, the program automatically triggers a corresponding action. By removing the need for direct human involvement, a deployed smart contract on a distributed ledger could make contractual relationships more efficient, reliable, and economical with potentially fewer opportunities for error, misunderstanding, delay or dispute.

Smart contracts do not have to be contracts at all. They can be processes that can be administered electronically (Szabo, 1996). So, there are a wide array of applications of smart contracts. It also should be pointed out that contract technology has changed dramatically the past twenty years with companies like DocuSign providing an electronic signature platform that meant you no longer had to send your contract out to many signers and a certain amount of automation can be built in. The main difference that blockchain can afford is to add in secure measures that can ensure that the terms are upheld, often using a third-party *oracle* (not the database company), which is an electronic data feed that signals a provision of the contract has been met so that the blockchain changes state accordingly (see Figure 6.1).

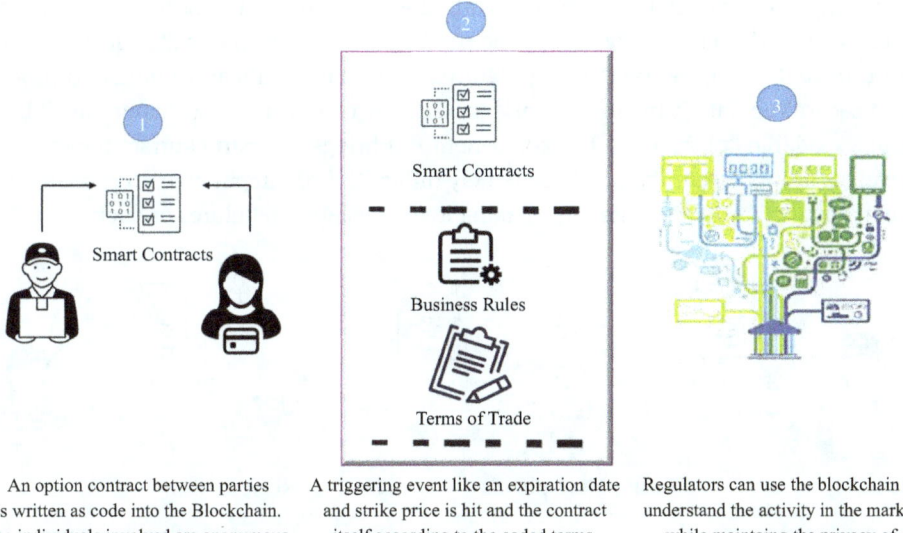

An option contract between parties is written as code into the Blockchain. The individuals involved are anonymous, but the contract is the public ledger.

A triggering event like an expiration date and strike price is hit and the contract itself according to the coded terms.

Regulators can use the blockchain to understand the activity in the market while maintaing the privacy of individual actors' positions.

Figure 6.1: Smart Contracts on Blockchain.

1. An option contract between counterparties is written as code into the blockchain. The individuals involved can be anonymous, but the contract is a public ledger.
2. A triggering event like an expiration date or strike price, and the contract executes itself according to the coded terms.
3. Regulators can use the blockchain to understand the activity in the market while maintaining the privacy of individual actors' positions.

Key features of smart contracts are: programmability, multisignature (or multisig) authentication, escrow capability, and oracle inputs:

- A smart contract automatically executes based on programmed logic.
- Multisig allows two or more parties to the contract to approve the execution of a transaction independently – a key requirement for multiparty contracts.
- Escrow capability ensures the locking of funds with a mediator (e.g., a bank or an online market), which can be unlocked under conditions acceptable to the contracting parties. Sometimes, external inputs such as prices, performance, or other real-world data may be required to process a transaction, and oracle services help smart contracts with inputs such as these.

There are several models of smart contracts being prototyped today, but the basic blockchain-based technology uses public key encryption infrastructure (PKI) to encode the terms and conditions of a contract. PKI is a method of cryptography that uses of two types of keys. The first is a public key that all parties are aware of, and the second is a private key known only to its recipient. In a smart contract transaction initiated on a blockchain depicted in Figure 6.2, the sending recipient encrypts their message into an unreadable "cipher text" using algorithms or mathematical formulas, to protect and secure the data. Only the use of a private key can decrypt the "cipher text" back into a readable "plain text." The key benefit PKI brings to smart contract transactions revolves around security, as it is extremely difficult, if not impossible, to reverse engineer a public key to a private one, making it very resilient to failures or hacks.

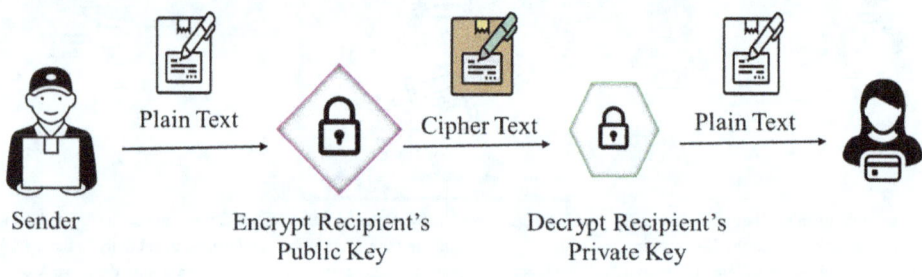

Different keys are used to encrypt & decrypt messages

Figure 6.2: How the Blockchain Cryptography Works for Smart Contracts.

Automation and Enforceability

The smart contract is automatable and enforceable. It is automatable by a computer or network of computers, although some parts may require human input and control. It is then enforceable by either legal enforcement of rights and obligations or tamper-proof execution.

The legal prose is linked via parameters (name-value pairs) to the smart contract code that provides execution. An executable software agent on the shared ledger will proceed to undertake various transfers of value in accordance with the legal prose. The parameters are a succinct way to inform the code of the final operational details.

The legality of financial smart contracts is yet to be established even in the conventional system. Initial steps have been taken in some countries to recognize distributed ledgers in their state courts, as should courts in Islamic jurisdictions. Accurate translation of legal terms according to Islamic law of contracts into software logic is another key aspect to consider. The landscape to be explored includes increasing the sophistication of parameters from base types to complex higher-order types to business logic that could be admissible in court and potentially replace the corresponding legal prose into contract code. In Islamic economies, legislators, regulators, and governments should realize the potential for distributed ledgers in increasing transparency and ease of compliance and reporting. The push from these authorities will be instrumental in overcoming legal and administrative hurdles.

Benefits and Evolution of Blockchain-Based Smart Contracts

Contracts or records stored on blockchains eliminate the need for a central intermediary to provide trust in the system. For markets that do not use intermediaries, it is still more trust than existing operations. By automating parts of business processes in the short run and possibly entire processes in the long run, smart contracts would significantly reduce the costs associated with areas such as compliance, record keeping, and manual intervention. A significant benefit from the power of the technology is in reducing costs, risks, error rates, and reconciliation processes while allowing everyone to have a shared infrastructure. It frees up capital and assists with compliance and regulatory reporting.

In trading securities, for example, most securities have a delayed settlement, with settlement times of T+2 or longer being common. Smart contracts have the potential to bring this down to minutes. This would also free up capital in the system by reducing mandatory collateral requirements for the trading of equities and would thereby improve return on capital. With smart contracts, workflow can be made more efficient by providing each of the people or points in the workflow with greater visibility into the state of an asset in the workflow. At the next level, this could be possible among a group of companies with proper governance. Ultimately, when these smart contracts become admissible in courts, it would make the entire system operational and efficient.

Applications of Smart Contracts

Smart contracts on the blockchain could and will create efficiencies and therefore savings for every category of monetary markets, investments, and other financial services like insurance/takaful but more important, they will reorganize how certain services are run within the economy. To illustrate this, we focus on some financial service areas, which could benefit from immediate sizeable savings:

Capital Markets and Investment Banking

With the deployment of smart contracts, software can be created to extrapolate specific data or carry out specific instructions if certain parameters are satisfied or triggered. Authorized matching of trades during the settlement process can be done via smart contracts. With smart contracts, trade agreements such as collateral, loan, swap, sukuk, and other agreements could be met by writing specific instructions via code onto the ledger.
- Structured finance, like settlements of syndicated loans, sukuk, etc. A long settlement period creates greater risk and a liquidity challenge in loan markets.
- Stock exchange market infrastructure like clearing and settlements of equities.

Commercial and Retail Banking

The smart contract also facilitates automatic payment processing, only if certain parameters within the agreed upon contract are satisfied. Because of smart contracts, costly errors from the manual processing of contractual terms, including settlement instructions, can be reduced considerably. If an Asian bank has transacted a trade or swap contract with a U.S. bank, the settlement details would only be provided if the financial details of the trade match between the two banks.
- Trade finance like supply-chain documentation, invoicing, and payments in letters of credit, trust receipts, etc.
- Mortgages for housing. The mortgage loan process relies on a complex ecosystem for the origination, funding, and servicing of mortgages, with considerable costs and delays.
- Loans of any kind, including crowdfunding for start-ups and small and medium-sized enterprises (SME). Distribution of equity of micro, small, and medium-sized enterprises (MSMEs) to investors.

Takaful

By moving insurance claims onto an immutable ledger, blockchain can help eliminate common sources of fraud in the insurance industry. A shared ledger and insurance policies executed through smart contracts can bring an order of magnitude improvement in efficiency to property and casualty insurance. Through the blockchain, medical records can be cryptographically secured and shared between health

providers, increasing interoperability in the health insurance ecosystem. By securing reinsurance contracts on the blockchain through smart contracts, the blockchain can simplify the flow of information and payments between insurers and reinsurers.
- Automated claims processing in commercial insurance, motor insurance, etc. Smart contracts that bring insurers, customers, and third parties to a single platform will lead to process efficiencies, and reduced claim processing time and costs.
- New products like peer-to-peer insurance/takaful.

The migration of traditional contracts to smart contracts can be estimated to save billions of dollars in the global Islamic finance markets. They are indeed significant, but do not come without challenges to be overcome, but it will be possible with the determination and resources to do so.

Islamic Trade Financing

Trade is the lifeblood of the global economy, and banks have long played an important role in mitigating risk and offering financing for domestic and international trade. Trade finance and supply chain finance provide companies with the funds and security they need to buy and sell products and services domestically and across borders. The use of open account trading has increased in recent years due in part to the ease of communication and exchange of information between businesses over the internet. However, even with open account trading, there is still a strong demand for bank services for financing, risk mitigation, data trans-fer and data matching. These bank services are aimed at reducing the risk SMEs and large corporations face when trading, such as counterparty risk, the complexity of complying with laws and regulations in multiple jurisdictions, the risk of goods being lost or damaged in transit, and foreign exchange risk.

As technology shifts and the popularity of open account trading[1] has expanded (making up about 90% of global trade today), banks and corporations require solutions that will enable them to overcome the pain points found in trade finance today. The use of distributed ledgers or blockchains has been explored in areas such as payments and securities settlement, and these technologies could also be used to improve service in trade transactions.

---

[1] An open account transaction in international trade is a sale where the goods are shipped and delivered before payment is due, which is typically in 30, 60, or 90 days. Obviously, this option is advantageous to the importer in terms of cash flow and cost, but it is consequently a risky option for an exporter.

Blockchain-Based Trade Finance

The exchange of trade data serves as the backbone for the trade finance workflow, making it an ideal starting point for the use of blockchains. The approval and matching of data found in trade documents such as invoices can be a trigger for events that follow such as the transfer of ownership or execution of a payment. By facilitating easy access to data and end-to-end transparency of the entire value chain, blockchains can create a level playing field for all parties involved in a trade transaction and facilitate improved exchange of trade information.

Settlement of securities or interest in securities are delivered, usually with a simultaneous exchange of money, to fulfill the contractual obligation. As part of the performance of delivery obligations of the trade, settlement involves the delivery of the securities and the corresponding payment. On top of that, settlement is increasingly moving toward the DVP method (delivery vs. payment) – the simultaneous and irrevocable exchange of security and cash, to minimize the seller's and buyer's risks involved in delivering one asset without receiving the contra asset at the same time. This is sometimes referred to as dependent deliveries of security or dependent payments of cash. In other words, the delivery of security will not be implemented without simultaneous payment of cash and vice versa.

The exchange of trade data and auditability of a trader's credit history can also help increase speed, efficiency, and security in financing between buyers, sellers, and their banks. The real-time visibility of events along a supply chain means that financing triggers can be identified sooner, which means that funds can be released faster. Blockchains can also help improve credit ratings and risk assessment procedures.

The lack of integration of trade financing to the trade cycle is the lack of transparency surrounding trade and trade finance today. Trade finance also suffers from costly and time intensive information matching, often with paper documents that can lead to delays in the transfer of goods, initiation of payment, or release of funds as part of a financing agreement. These manual processes, together with the lack of transparency, also raise the risk of error or even fraud in the case of duplicate invoice financing.

Industry stakeholders have made efforts to reduce the impact of some of these issues (such as the development of the bank payment obligation [BPO] for open account trading), but the difficulty with these solutions is two-fold: a lack of adoption and a proliferation of different platforms that lack interoperability.

As the use of blockchains in trade finance takes hold, all parties involved can save time and resources by eliminating the need for some of the manual processing and data matching they do today and allowing them to focus on more profitable propositions such as creating better products, which can be vital to businesses involved in domestic and international trade. Figure 6.3 details the connecting parties in a blockchain-based trade transaction.

Islamic Trade Financing — 141

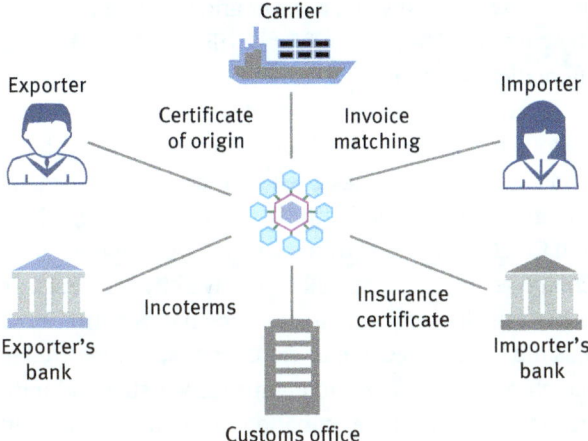

Figure 6.3: Using Distributed Ledger (Blockchain) in Trade Transactions.

With real-time visibility into events along a supply chain, financing triggers can be identified sooner. This means that funds can be released much faster (between a buyer and seller, as well as to a bank as part of a factoring agreement). In addition, the blockchain allows the ability of nonbank actors (shipping companies, customs agents, etc.) to update ledgers immediately once a transaction has been finalized.

Enablers to Blockchain-Based Trade Financing

To help improve trade financial services offered by banks to their corporate clients, there are some required enablers to systematize these services. The use of smart contracts and the development of instant payment infrastructures are two such enablers that will greatly enhance the benefits for banks, financial institutions and businesses using digitally distributed ledgers in trade finance.

Blockchain-Based Smart Contracts

The transparency of events along the supply chain via the blockchain is itself a major enabler of faster payment and improved financing, increased efficiency, reduced risk of fraud, and lower costs. Smart contracts are self-executing programs that automatically carry out functions once a triggering event has taken place. They are linear contracts that can include multiple parties (buyer, seller, banks, takaful companies, etc.) that cannot be altered.

For example, if a smart contract is written between a buyer and a seller to say that once goods have been cleared by customs, 20% of the funds will be released to the seller, a smart contract would automatically disburse payment once confirmation is entered in a distributed ledger that the customs office has cleared the goods. The confirmation of approval by customs is not a triggering event requiring action by a bank; the payment is automatically made once confirmation has been entered into the system. With a smart contract, legal stipulations are embedded in the computer code, which enables the automatic execution of functions defined by a legal contract, though smart contracts may be simply transactional as well, as originally conceived by Nick Szabo's vending machine model which today translates roughly to blockchain cybercurrency.

Smart contracts can be seen as the future of economic transactions, as they enable more efficiencies in legal contracts through a decrease in manual processing and initiation of contract terms, risk reduction through the elimination of manual errors and duplicate invoice financing. However, legal and regulatory challenges surround smart contracts in many jurisdictions, and many companies exploring the use of smart contracts are still in the proof-of-concept stage. To accelerate maturity of this technology, smart contract terms need to be standardized and small scale B2B smart contract applications need to succeed. Adoption for use in trade finance will pave the way to the actualization of the theoretical benefits.

Instant Payment Structures

The development of instant payment infrastructures is another key enabler that will add speed and efficiency to trade transactions that currently may require human interactions. Over twenty countries around the world have already implemented instant payment infrastructures (like Ripple and Stellar), and major markets such as Australia, the United States, the Eurozone, and Asia are in the process of developing and testing instant payment systems. With the ability to send and receive domestic payments within seconds, the movement of money triggered by events along the supply chain can proceed more rapidly, which means that shipping companies, customs offices, and sellers have quicker access to funds. Instant payments can also enable buyers and sellers to obtain funding from their banks faster than they do today, which can lead to a further optimization of working capital and unlock liquidity from supply chains.

Current Challenges

The adoption of blockchain-based trade finance still faces several challenges, including an unclear legal and regulatory environment, the need to extend the speed and the scalability of the technology, and the challenge of creating a network effect to spur adoption of distributed ledgers in the trade finance space. If Islamic countries and industry stakeholders work together to meet these challenges, they stand to realize significant tangible benefits. Distributed ledgers can ensure full transparency of the value chain, reduced error rates and credit risk, lower costs, improved convenience, and provide a level playing field for all participants. This in turn can help corporations improve liquidity and working capital, upgrade the reconciliation process, and provide additional financing opportunities, while allowing banks to meet customer expectations, modernize information technology (IT) systems, enable the development of new products, and avoid disintermediation. In Islamic economies, legislators, regulators, and governments should harness the potential for distributed ledgers in increasing transparency and ease of compliance and reporting. The push from these authorities will be instrumental in steadily developing advanced trading, legal enforcement and administrative systems that are crucial to empower justice as well as prosperity.

Takaful (Islamic Insurance) on the Blocks

As a niche section of the insurance sector, the takaful segment is significantly impacted by the disruptions occurring within the insurance sector. The global insurance market had a reasonable growth rate, with global real premium growth rates of 2.9% in the advanced economies and 7.4% in the emerging and developing countries in 2014, an improvement over the 2012 and 2013 rates (IFSB, 2016). Likewise, the growth rate of gross contributions in the takaful sector demonstrated a recovery in 2014 from 2013, when the growth rate of premiums was by far the lowest historically.

In its Islamic Financial Services Industry (IFSI) Stability 2017 report, the Islamic Financial Services Board (IFSB) observed that the reinvigorated gross contributions of the takaful sector reached US$22.1 billion in 2014, up from only around US$5 billion in 2006. In 2016 the global insurance market reported steady growth rates, supported mainly by emerging markets. Nonlife premiums in emerging Asia expanded at a rate of 7.3% in 2016, after a strong 9% growth in 2015.[2] Another notable trend in emerging Asia was the slowdown in motor insurance uptake following lower car sales. Similarly, anecdotal evidence points to lower sales of new cars in the key takaful domain of Saudi Arabia in 2016,[3] and to a 13% decline in car sales in Malaysia in the same year.[4] Meanwhile, medical expense premiums in emerging markets continued to grow at double-digit rates in 2016, attributable to operators in China where private medical insurance is gaining traction alongside state medical support schemes. Of importance, policy makers in selected Gulf Cooperation Council (GCC)

---

2 Swiss Re, Global Insurance Review 2016 and Outlook 2017/2018.
3 Recession cripples car sales, *Saudi Gazette* (October 2016).
4 MAA expects slight increase in car sales this year, *The Star Online* (January 2017).

countries have recently pushed for mandatory medical coverage requirements, thus supporting the uptake and premiums of medical takaful in the region.

The biggest share of the takaful sector belonged to GCC countries, followed by Iran and the East Asia and Pacific region. The other three regions (Africa, South Asia, and Levant) had a very much lesser share of the total. As takaful's share of the insurance sector is only 1%, there is a long way to go for the takaful sector. Indeed, the low penetration rates in certain countries in which the takaful industry operates, indicate an available market for the takaful sector. Since many of the target markets like Turkey, Saudi Arabia, Pakistan, Qatar, and Egypt, have a growing middle-class and young populations with solid growth prospects, there is promise for the takaful sector to grow further.

Three jurisdictions account for 84% of the global takaful contributions: Saudi Arabia (37%), Iran (34%), and Malaysia (14%). However, the types of takaful provision are different for different jurisdictions, for example, in Malaysia nearly two-thirds of the takaful contributions are for family takaful (which features a strong savings/investment component). In Saudi Arabia and Iran, insurance such as medical/health or motor takaful is prevailing. The current low propagation of takaful services indicates there is ample opportunity for further growth of the insurance/takaful industry, combined with high population growth and a growing middle class.

Also, the IFSI report revealed that the business profiles of takaful operators differ among the countries. They found that in Malaysia, family takaful is 68.1% of the total business line, which is the highest number in the sample. The combination of a relatively young population, a high percentage of working population, a vibrant social security system, and saving incentives for retirement, play a part in the high proportion of life insurance in its society, including family takaful. Behind Malaysia is Pakistan and the UAE, which comprise a reasonable share of family takaful – around 30%. This is not so in Saudi Arabia, where health coverage is compulsory and a tradition of long-term saving using insurance/takaful products is nonexistent. Other countries with low shares of family takaful are Kuwait (at 8.6%) and Bangladesh and Qatar (both at 0%). Given the rising birthrates and growing middle class, policies geared toward increasing public awareness of such services, as well as those encouraging long-term savings such as unit-linked instruments could grow the family takaful business.

Motor takaful is the second most important business line in the sample countries of the IFSI report, with an average of 27.7% over the entire sample of countries. Kuwait has the highest share of motor takaful, followed by Sri Lanka, Pakistan, and Qatar.

The third most important business line for takaful was Fire, Property and Accidents, with the highest levels in the domestic markets of Qatar and Bangladesh. Other business lines in the takaful sector include the Workmen's Compensation and Energy Takaful, which has a considerable traction in the UAE and Sri Lanka.

A Model for a Blockchain-Based Takaful

Smart contracts deployed through the blockchain will provide customers and takaful (insurance) companies a system to manage claims in a transparent, quick, and indisputable manner. Takaful policies, along with its terms and conditions, and potential claims can be recorded onto the blockchain and validated by the network, ensuring valid claims are dispensed and false claims are rejected.[5] For example, the blockchain will reject multiple claims for one accident because the network would know that a claim has already been made. Smart contracts would also process claims efficiently by triggering payments automatically when certain conditions are met and validated. To effectively detect identity fraud, falsified injury or damage reports, etc., blockchain can be used as a cross-industry, distributed registry with external data and customer data to:
- Confirm authenticity, ownership, and origin of goods as well as the legitimacy of documents (e.g., medical reports)
- Check for police reports indicating theft, claims history as well as a person's verified identity and expose patterns of deception related to a person or identity
- Proof of date and time stamps of policy issuance or purchase of a product/asset
- Validate ownership and site changes

Still, to attain full blockchain-specific benefits from these applications above what is achievable with traditional solutions and other current types of cooperation, for example, via industry associations, broad cooperation between insurers, customers, manufacturers, and other stakeholders is needed. This is an example of an ecosystem growing beyond the traditional industry practice in the sharing economy of the digital era. Emerging blockchain applications and four key areas where we see the most potential for evolution and transformation are:

Fraud Detection and Risk Mitigation

Blockchain has the potential to eradicate mistakes and detect deceptive activity because of its ability to be a public ledger across multiple unknown parties. A distributed digital depot can autonomously confirm the legitimacy of customers, policies, and transactions (such as claims) by presenting a comprehensive historical record. As such, insurers would be able to spot fake or counterfeit transactions involving doubtful people and suspect entities.

---

5 An estimated 5 to 10% of all claims are fraudulent. According to the estimated global size of the takaful industry, this costs takāful operators more than US$2billion per year.

First-mover insurers are already evaluating the use of blockchain to mitigate scams and risks related to cross-border payments and transactions linking multiple currencies. In forte insurance and reinsurance segments, where insurers are often disconnected from the clients, blockchain may be used to tackle the significant inefficiencies, disparities and errors caused by bad data quality from the front and back offices. In the United States, health insurers and regulators view blockchain as a powerful tool for fighting Medicare deceit. Validation and verification form the nucleus of the blockchain business case, which can improve many insurance processes.

Blockchain will lessen administrative and operational costs through automated verification of policyholder identity and contract validity, auditable records of claims and information from third parties (e.g., encrypted patient data between a doctor and an injured party manageable by the insurer to authenticate payment), and disbursement for claims through a blockchain-based payments infrastructure or smart contracts-linked escrow account. Providing reinsurers controlled access to claims and claims histories recorded on the blockchain increases transparency for the reinsurer in an automated yet auditable manner.

Claims Processing and Management
In addition to mobile and digital technologies, blockchain is essential to establishing an efficient, transparent, and customer-focused claims model based on higher degrees of trust through transparency. Within claims management, new data streams can enhance the risk selection process by combining location, external risk and data analytics. A distributed ledger integrated with existing systems can enable the insurer and various third parties to easily and instantly access and update relevant information (e.g., claim forms, photo evidence, police reports, and eyewitness or third-party accounts).

The use of data from a mobile phone can simplify claims submissions, reduce loss adjustment costs, and increase client satisfaction, with blockchain systems connecting communications to all parties.

Correspondingly, the use of mobile technologies, satellite imagery, sensor data, and blockchain could facilitate claims payments and rescue services when natural disasters occur in remote areas. Information collected from weather stations could establish claim amounts based on actual climate readings, with blockchain facilitating more efficient data sharing and stronger protection against fraud.

In addition, this advanced technology will be able to work effortlessly with the internet of things (IoT) where massive numbers of devices are linked via the internet. For example, accident claims can be made through an app provided by the insurer by taking pictures or sending videos of accidents which are time-stamped. Together with blockchain solutions for know-your-client (KYC) data, a client can send the verified identity data to other companies for confirmation with the same app, avoiding the need to repeat the verification process, thus expediting efficiency in the on-boarding of new users.

New Distribution and Payment Models
Some international insurers are already developing partnerships and exploring new payment systems and business models (cryptocurrencies and digital wallets) to achieve capital efficiencies through a truly public global ledger system. Increased computerization used to acquire risk information in contracts also suggests new opportunities to build market intelligence, simplify payments and build financial risk models. At the very least, global insurers can use blockchain to remove asset management costs or hedging fees required for mitigating currency fluctuations in cross-border and international transactions.

In the new business model, the focus of the insurers would be on matching supply and demand and to risk calculation research, instead of asset management. The insurer could create a marketplace-like platform where customers can post their insurance demand, which could be either a standardized product or even a specific demand. The insurer then would use its risk models along with "risk assessment intelligence," based on available historical information, to perform a premium calculation for the expected return. With this expected return, interested investors can bid or subscribe to the demanded insurance.

With the use of smart contracts and records on a decentralized ledger, the payment from the investor to the customer in the event of an insurance claim becomes cheaper, transparent, and more efficient than long-established ways. In addition, the investors know their maximum exposure as the amount defined in the smart contracts.

The insurer can also now play the role of assessor of the damage to validate the authenticity of the insurance claim. But this could as easily be outsourced to a third party and by connecting blockchain to other ledgers where verification can be done automatically.

Reinsurance
Property and casualty insurers seeking clearer visibility into their reinsurance contracts and risk exposures may gain it through blockchain. Consider the case of an insurer seeking to offload an equal amount of risk to two separate reinsurers. A blockchain ledger could provide insight and notification if one of those reinsurers then tried to offload some of its portion to a subsidiary of the other reinsurer. It also would help insurers gain confidence that, as they pay out claims, they are appropriately rebalancing their capital exposures against specific risks.

Within reinsurance, the benefits of blockchain include more accurate reserve calculations based on actual participating contracts and automatic calculation updates once the primary information and data are updated. On top of that, insurers obtain more room to move capital and improve transparency into known risks, capital productivity and compliance. Operationally, the process of audit trails becomes simpler to chart, modeling requirements are significantly reduced and there is less coordination required between the finance and IT functions.

Blockchain-Based Islamic Capital Markets

An Islamic bank could set up a new trading platform (or move across an existing trading platform) on a blockchain protocol. Blockchain technology offers the potential to support a new medium to exchange assets without centralized trusts or intermediaries – and without the risk of double spending. As already discussed, blockchain can eliminate the threat or the risk of fraud in all areas of banking, and this could equally apply to a trading platform. Furthermore, blockchain would also address issues such as operational risk and administrative costs as it can be made transparent and immutable. The traceability and the permanent historic record that would exist on the blockchain backing up every asset or item of value that was traded, would provide assurance and authenticity all the way through the supply chain. This, again, will be determined by the advances in technology needed to speed blockchain transactions.

In practice, when a high-value item is first created, a corresponding digital token is issued by a trusted central authority which acts to authenticate the product's point of origin. Then, every time the product is bought and sold the digital token is moved in parallel so that a real-world chain of ownership is created and mirrored by the blockchain history of that digital token. The digital token is acting as a virtual "certificate of authenticity," which would have the advantage that it is far harder to steal or forge than a piece of paper, database, or spreadsheet. Upon receiving the digital token, the final recipient of the product will then be able to verify the chain of custody all the way back to the point of creation. Blockchain gives the benefit of distributed and verifiable trust that was not present before.

As a nonbanking example, Everledger, a permanent ledger for diamond certification, has adopted the use of bitcoin as a mark of authenticity providing transparency for all parties involved – a clear attempt to prevent diamond fraud. Similarly, the immutability and digital uniqueness inherent in blockchain offers the ability to provide a secure transfer of value and endorsement of authenticity. The challenge of maintaining data privacy among counterparties to trade transactions is also overcome by utilizing blockchain technology where tokenization, in the form of cryptography, is used to protect the trade data with parties only allowed access to permissioned information with the correct security key.

This should enable the most confidential of transactions, especially financial transactions, to still take place on such a trading platform.

Clearing and settlement costs billions and, according to Santander's 2015 joint report[6] produced in collaboration with Oliver Wyman and Anthemis Group, it is estimated that moving this into a digital record, near real-time and over the internet,

---

[6] http://www.finextra.com/finextra-downloads/newsdocs/The%20FinTech%202%200%20Paper.PDF.

will save the industry US$20 billion a year or more in overhead costs due to D+3. D+3, or T+3, the three-day clearing and settlement cycle common to most investment markets today. Many firms are leading the charge to digitize the clearing and settlement structures from Blythe Masters' Digital Asset Holdings with the Hyperledger to Overstock with T-0, along with many other key and emerging players such as Epiphyte, Clearmatics, and SETL.

McKinsey[7] expects that adoption of blockchain technology in capital markets will be marked by four stages of gradual development: single-enterprise adoption across legal entities; adoption by a small subset of banks as an upgrade to manual processes; conversion of inter-dealer settlements; and, finally, largescale adoption across buyers and sellers in public markets.

The likely adoption of blockchain in capital markets by industry participants would be in these four key actionable areas:

- Assessment of business impact and plan for the long term. Firms should invest now in technology and expertise related to blockchain, and push for industry-wide cooperation.
- Industry cooperation and engagement with regulators. Industry participants will need to work together to design solutions for specific asset classes and processes. Banks and other market participants must form consortia and work with regulators early in the design process to iron out consumer protection, fair market practice, disclosure, privacy, and security.
- Consolidate internal ledgers on the blockchain. Internal ledger synchronization is a persistent challenge, and regulatory pressure to consolidate those ledgers is mounting. A private blockchain-based enterprise solution would allow fintech companies to help financial institutions.
- Modernize post-trade and manual processes: Updating legacy systems and processes of post-trade activities such as asset booking, and transfer can make workflow more efficient and productive while being less disruptive to existing business standards.

The blockchain revolution will not happen overnight, and will require cooperation among market participants, regulators, and technologists. The unlikelihood of simultaneous, large-scale adoption will initially confine blockchain application to subsets of financial market participants and specific use cases. However, the potential for rapid uptake once open questions are resolved means all market participants must be aware of the potential benefits and threats and have a plan in place to respond.

---

[7] http://www.mckinsey.com/industries/financial-services/our-insights/beyond-the-hype-blockchains-in-capital-markets.

Payments and Settlements

The main use case that is focused on when looking at the possibilities of blockchain for banking is that of payments.

Blockchain could be used as another way of paying each other, not depending on SWIFT and other payment schemes. There is a potential role for blockchain in payments and that blockchain could have benefits for not only bank customers, but this could also lead to operational efficiencies and cost savings for banks themselves. Payment systems collectively are currently under a lot of pressure, as there has been an urgency to modernize payments and to address the questions of safety and security since the 2008 financial crash. This has led to new market entrants, such as fintech companies, looking to solve these problems using blockchain. The existing payment system has always gone through banks and central banks, a process that was first put into place in the 1970s and 1980s. Apart from speeding up money transfers, blockchain could also help banks to operate continuously, 24 hours a day. This is now somewhat expected by customers who want an omni-channel banking experience at any time of day or night. Rabobank has been heavily involved in the on-going development and use of Ripple Lab's blockchain Ripple protocol.

As of December 2017, many banks have partnered with Ripple to use blockchain technology in making payments to customers and cross-border transactions. Ripple has said that its technology could give banks a 33% reduction in their operating costs during the international payment process and allow lenders to move money "in seconds." Ripple is a "real-time gross settlement system" (RTGS), currency exchange and remittance network. Released in 2012, Ripple purports to enable "secure, instant and nearly free global financial transactions of any size with no charge-backs." It supports tokens representing fiat currency, cryptocurrency, commodity, or any other unit of value. While traditional bank wire services use a handful of intermediaries to process overseas payments, Ripple allows two banks to connect with each other without any intermediaries. Ripple uses a dynamic currency conversion technique that allows Ripple to always offer the lowest exchange rate. Using Ripple's blockchain banks can offer competitive transaction fees as well as currency conversion fees. Ripple can be used by banks for an open-source approach to payments to replace many of the common intermediaries in the payments industry, thereby passing on savings to partner institutions, and thus by extension, to their customers. Currently, Ripple recognizes a few fiat currencies like USD, GBP, EUR, etc., commodities like gold, silver, platinum and a handful of popular cryptocurrencies like BTC, LTC, the native cryptocurrency XRP, etc. Ripple transactions are very fast – in general, it takes only about 5 seconds for a Ripple payment to go through. Currently, Ripple can also process 1500 transactions per second, a number that is 500x higher than Bitcoin's TPS. Ripple also can scale this even further and reach as much as 50,000 transactions per second.

Thus, blockchain can be used to make payments in real-time globally, with real-time execution, complete transparency, real-time fraud analysis and prevention and at a reasonable cost. The main issue with Ripple now is that it is a proprietary blockchain network that cannot yet connect with other systems. To connect Ripple to other blockchain protocols an interledger protocol will have to be developed, tested and put in place.

VISA Europe Collab and BTL Group are working on a separate concept to make cross-border payments between banks using distributed ledgers. The project will use BTL's cross-border settlement platform Interbit to explore the ways in which a distributed ledger-based settlements system (utilizing "smart contracts") can reduce the friction of domestic and cross-border transfers between banks. This is a similar goal to Ripple but, as it is based on the Ethereum smart contracts concept, it is not proprietary like Ripple and thus is potentially more scalable.

Similarly, UBS, Deutsche Bank, Santander and BNY Mellon have teamed up with blockchain developer Clearmatics and trading company ICAP to create a new digital representation of fiat currency called the "Utility Settlement Coin."[8]

Although this is still proof of concept, it could potentially reduce friction in delivery versus payment scenarios by providing a faster and less expensive settlement mechanism than existing funds transfer and currency exchange mechanisms.

In July 2018, Stellar, the seventh-largest cryptocurrency network, became the first digital ledger technology (DLT) protocol to obtain Shariah certification for payments and asset tokenization. The Stellar Development Foundation announced that, following a review of the technology's properties and applications, the Shariyah Review Bureau (SRB) – which is licensed by the Central Bank of Bahrain and operates an international Shariah advisory practice – had certified Stellar as a Shariah-compliant vehicle for conducting monetary transfers and tokenizing real-world assets. According to the foundation, this certification[9] from SRB will enable Stellar to forge partnerships with Islamic financial institutions throughout the Middle East and Southeast Asia.

Sukuk on the Blockchain

One important application in Islamic capital markets for blockchain is the *sukuk* (Islamic bonds) market. Sukuk are securitized, and hence tradable on secondary markets much like a stock can be traded on a stock exchange. Islamic finance prohibits interest payments on loans and the sale of debt; sukuk markets evolved to securitize Islamic modes of financing such as profit sharing through asset ownership for a given tenure.

---

8 https://www.finextra.com/blogposting/14459/ubs-and-the-utility-settlement-coin.
9 https://www.stellar.org/wp-content/uploads/2018/07/stellar-compliance-sharia.pdf.

There are a variety of sukuk structures based on various Shariah-compliant contracts: profit sharing (*sukuk al-mudarabah*), deferred-delivery purchase (*sukuk al-salam*), leasing of assets (*sukuk al-ijarah*), joint venture (*sukuk al-musyarakah*), *sukuk al-istisna* (project based), and cost-plus asset purchase (*sukuk al-murabahah*). A notable difference between bonds and sukuk can be seen in the case of default: bond holders are left with bad debts, but sukuk holders have recourse to valuable underlying assets.

Sukuk has been a popular approach for governments seeking to finance infrastructure projects, but the legal complexity and overall cost to issue sukuk has kept it out of reach for smaller corporations and MSMEs. It has been an excellent way to raise much needed capital, but investors have also been always restricted to the much larger institutional investors due to the high barrier of entry, which usually starts in the millions. However, the inability to lower these barriers of entry at the retail level to thousands or hundreds of dollars to enable wider participation (and access to more funds) for sukuk participation, and hence wider risk and profit-sharing in the Islamic capital market, is still persistent and remains an impediment to true shared prosperity.

A new approach announced in May 2018 by Blossom Finance[10] aims to change that by using the blockchain. Blossom Finance's "Smart Sukuk" platform leverages Ethereum blockchain smart contracts to increase the efficiency and reach of sukuk issuance globally. Smart Sukuk standardizes and automates much of the legal, accounting, and payment overhead of conventional sukuk offerings – all backed by fully licensed legal entities in the issuing jurisdiction. Blossom's Smart Sukuk supports issuance of the sukuk in local currency and eliminates the need for institutions to add cryptocurrency to their balance sheet, and is only issued in jurisdictions with clear and viable legal frameworks to support it. Figure 6.4 illustrates a lease (*ijarah*) sukuk for a hospital construction project.

Distributed Ledger Technology and the Over-the-Counter Market

Distributed ledger technology could introduce transparency into the opaque unlisted and OTC market space, while still maintaining transaction confidentiality. The Securities Commission (SC) Malaysia has embarked on a pilot project to explore the usage of DLT or blockchain in the unlisted and over-the-counter (OTC) market space through its aFINity Innovation Lab. SC Malaysia expanded its Alliance for FinTech community or aFINity program this year to include "innovation labs," which act as a platform to facilitate the testing of new digital innovations within the finance industry.

---

10 https://blossomfinance.com/press/islamic-finance-upgraded-smarter-sukuk-using-block-chain.

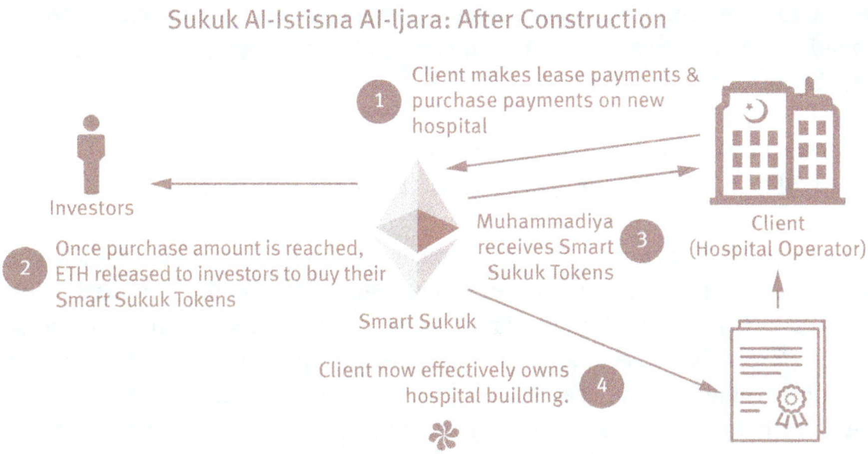

Sukuk Al-Istisna Al-Ijara: After Construction

1. Client makes lease payments & purchase payments on new hospital
2. Once purchase amount is reached, ETH released to investors to buy their Smart Sukuk Tokens
3. Muhammadiya receives Smart Sukuk Tokens
4. Client now effectively owns hospital building.

Investors — Smart Sukuk — Client (Hospital Operator)

Figure 6.4: Illustration of a Leasing Sukuk for a Construction Project.
Source: Blossom Finance https://blossomfinance.com/press/ islamic-finance-upgraded-smarter-sukuk-using-blockchain

OTC markets are decentralized markets, without a central physical location, where market participants trade with one another through various communication modes such as the telephone, email, and proprietary electronic trading systems, as opposed to trading through a centralized exchange.

Traditionally, the unlisted and OTC market space have operated in an opaque fashion due to limited information availability. By using a distributed ledger as the technology underpinning the market infrastructure, all transactions and market activities would be recorded and made available to all market participants, while still maintaining transaction confidentiality.

Media Rights, Intellectual Property, and Trademark Protection

Today, media users are largely accustomed to having free access to a wide variety of content, and most of them are still reluctant to pay subscription fees for "premium" content behind paywalls. In addition, all media segments have suffered significantly from digitization, since content can be copied and distributed easily and without loss of quality. So far, the introduction of digital rights management (DRM) systems has not substantially reduced copyright infringements. The ensuing revenue "leakage" has been only partially recovered through new consumption models such as streaming subscriptions and micropayments for articles. The subsequent "commoditization" of content has been undermined by widespread piracy of intellectual property (IP).

Blockchain-based technologies have the potential to resolve some of these current challenges:

- Paid content can receive a boost from new, micropayment-based pricing models
- Monetization options emerge for an increasingly fragmented content inventory (e.g., blogs, news bites, photos)
- Allocation of advertising budgets becomes more accurate and targeted as media usage can be directly linked to the respective content items
- Copyright infringements and piracy would be nearly impossible

Sealed in the chain, blocks can no longer be changed: the prevention of deletion, editing, or copying creates true digital assets. These multiplied and decentralized blockchain processes lead to a high level of robustness and trust. Every participant in the network can verify the correctness of transactions. Network consensus methods and cryptographic technology are used to validate transactions. Thus, trust is not established externally by a central authority or an auditor but continuously in the network. Furthermore, the decentralized storage in a blockchain is known to be very failure-resistant. Even in the event of the failure of many network participants, the blockchain remains available, eliminating the single point of failure. New information stored in a blockchain is immutable. Its method of recordkeeping prevents deletion or reversal of transactions added to the blockchain, once further blocks have been added. However, the technology and the mechanisms are still evolving, and industry-wide adoption of standards is most probably still a few years off.

With the advent of blockchain, the media industry structure could change significantly. Blockchain technology permits bypassing content aggregators, platform providers, and royalty collection associations to a large extent. Thus, market power shifts to the copyright owners. While some applications of blockchain technology may still seem farfetched and require further technological advancements, payment-focused use cases have already been proved to work. Parts of the media value chain are therefore already endangered by new blockchain-based payment and contract options. These can fundamentally reset pricing, advertising, revenue sharing, and royalty payment processes. Payments or advertising revenues no longer need to be centrally collected. Payment transactions become less costly, and the distribution of revenues is automated, based on predefined smart contracts. Table 6.1 depicts the potential blockchain-based opportunities in the media industry.

Generating Advertising Revenues

Blockchain facilitates customer relationships. Based on the blockchain, everyone from leading media houses to small bloggers can easily generate advertising revenues. As blockchains permit an exact tracking of content usage, they also enable a direct allocation of advertising budgets. Together with new, blockchain-enabled micropayments, content creators can establish direct relationships with their customers. In an extreme scenario, aggregators could even become obsolete in the future.

Table 6.1: Potential Blockchain-Based Opportunities in the Media.

Potential	Cost-effective Pricing Options for Paid Content	Bypassing Aggregators/ Distributors	Distribution of Royalty Payments	Monetization of Consumer-to-Consumer/ Peer-to-Peer Content sharing	Cross-Border Consumption of Paid Content
Focus Areas	As micropayments become economically efficient and digital content is harder to copy illegally, new pricing opportunities arise	Blockchain allows everybody to become a marketer as reach of lead generation becomes trackable and can be compensated	Content consumption/ usage is captured in blockchain and a precise consumption-based analysis of playtimes is possible	Consumer-to-consumer (C2C)/Peer-to-peer (P2P) content sharing and usage becomes transparent and monetizable through the blockchain	Cross-border limitations of paid content subscriptions and DRM complexities will be decreased by the block-chain
Industry Benefit	Low-price content (< US $1.99) can efficiently be settled between seller and buyer	Liberalization of advertising market More precise performance tracking of advertising efforts	Near real-time allocation of royalty payments Alternative to imprecise estimates	Transparent and "controllable" P2P transactions Automated "real-time" billing Automated "real-time" billing	Decreased complexity of rights management Direct linkage of consumption to user through blockchain authentication

As soon as artists tie up digital copies of their songs or videos in a blockchain they will be able to sell them directly to their fans without any intermediaries such as record labels. Moreover, a fair allocation of revenues from music streaming becomes possible, whether advertising-based or paid content-based. Artists can market their songs independently of big platform providers wherever they want, since a blockchain permits easy tracking of usage and deduction of the associated payments.

Collections and Copyright Tracking

Collection associations could use a blockchain to create a permissioned blockchain ecosystem for musical rights. Based on a broad consensus amongst the parties involved, the industry bodies would act as "gatekeepers" to grant and/or withdraw access to the closed ecosystem. In addition, collection associations, typically acting domestically for one or a handful of countries, could use blockchain as an enabler to enter new markets, since established measurement and disbursement mechanisms in use with radio stations, broadcasters, and other parties, which, for instance, play music commercially, could become obsolete through the introduction of smart contracts.

In a different scenario, blockchain could also become a threat to traditional collecting bodies. Up to now they have been "chasing" certain commercial users who "do not pay their bills," as exemplified by YouTubers illegally using copyrighted music in their videos, or royalty dues incurred by an event DJ. With the help of blockchain, every play of a song is recognized, counted, with royalties tracked and allocated to specific users. The role of the collecting body, collecting and distributing royalty payments, could soon become obsolete, as blockchain-based smart contracts take over the work instead.

In a nutshell, blockchain's potential benefits for the media industry primarily relate to payment transactions and copyright tracking. Possible applications and technical innovations will have a far-reaching impact: content creators may be able to keep a close track of their playtimes, royalties and advertising revenues could be shared in an exact and timely manner based on consumption, and low-cost content could be purchased efficiently, even if priced at a mere fraction of a cent. However, there are several fundamental issues and technical obstacles, which may undermine the realization of our use cases:

- Opaqueness of blockchain platforms and standards due to quickly changing market participants
- Usability and reach of blockchain technologies in everyday environments
- Interoperability of platforms and various standards needs to be harmonized

Media players need to consider blockchain-based applications and their potential impact on the whole industry: micropayment-based pricing options for paid content, a shift of market power caused by content bypassing aggregators, and an improved distribution of royalty payments, to name just a few. To ensure continued competitiveness because of digital disruption consequences to existing media business models, companies should lose no time in identifying applicable blockchain-based opportunities as a fundamental component of their future business strategy.

LegalTech and the Evolution of Legal Services

The digitization of legal data constitutes another megatrend transforming workflows and business models. The volume of data used in legal advice has increased exponentially – a pattern seen in many other industries as well. A variety of legal technologies has emerged, enabling the digitization and automation of these and other legal-work activities (Veith et al., 2016). In fact, findings from a survey of law firm partners and legal-technology providers by The Boston Consulting Group suggest that legal-technology solutions could perform as much as 30–50% of tasks carried out by junior lawyers today. LegalTech is defined as companies that provide software and tech-enabled services to the legal vertical (including law firms and internal counsel) as well as tech-enabled legal services delivered to businesses and consumers. It is the reaction to the disruption that technology is having across all sectors of the economy. Although the legal sector is one of the most resistant to change due to its conservative nature, access to justice is a fundamental human right; while most cannot afford to hire legal representation when the need arises, there is immense potential for tech companies who are able to provide such services. Emerging start-ups like Case Text, Judicata, Rocket Lawyer, DragonLaw and LegalTech products like LegalZoom and DocuSign have lowered the barrier to entry for legal protection that was previously confined to law offices. Now anyone can assign shareholding agreements, write their will or incorporate a company without having to seek legal counsel. The disbanding of the traditional legal business model is good news for the public interest in affordable and accessible legal protection.

To better accommodate market demands, many nontraditional legal service providers (tech-enabled firms, software automating legal work, nontraditional law firms, etc.) have emerged. The five key areas of LegalTech according to ABA (2016) are:

Legal Research

The technology that enables the process of identifying and retrieving information necessary to support legal decision making.
- Blockchain-based referencing non-Word files (audio, pictures, etc.)
- Using predictive analytics to filter and recommend relevant documents
- Artificial intelligence (AI)-enabled virtual assistants and chatbots performing research tasks on par with a paralegal

Contract Management

The technology that enables the management and automation of legal contract creation and review.
- Automatically produce customized templates based on limited input
- Review documents for key and nonstandard clauses
- Organize and classify volumes of contracts (e.g., during due diligence for M&A projects)

Intellectual Property Management

Software used to research, manage, and protect IP including trademarks, copyrights, trade secrets and patents.
- In the near term, IP management professionals will benefit from the same incremental improvements AI is providing in the legal research space.
- In the intermediate term, machine learning will enable the automation of the entire IP infringement detection process.

Automation and Analytics

The emerging class of technology that leverages big data, AI, machine learning, and other technologies to perform predictive analytics and automate legal work.
- Analyzing bodies of historical legal decisions to predict the outcome of ongoing litigation
- Enabling clients to assess the performance of their counsel by reviewing their history of outcomes
- Assessing arbitrators, jury members, and judges for objectivity

eDiscovery

The technology that facilitates the identification, collection, preservation, processing, review, analysis, and production of electronically stored information (ESI).
- Progressing from screening for keywords to predictive coding where algorithms use predictive analytics to determine the most relevant documents based on search

Blockchain coupled with the artificial intelligence cluster of technologies (AI as well as machine learning, natural language processing, machine vision, etc.) are especially applicable to the legal services space. This is because AI has been proven to be most useful/profitable when it is fed large volumes of data (e.g., legal research archives, eDiscovery ESI). They are also useful in automating time-consuming mundane formulaic tasks like screening research and filling out legal templates. As such, AI can save the consumer massive legal fees from expensive man-hours that traditional lawyers charge.

The opposition to putting data/applications in the cloud, which in turn was largely driven by fear of security breaches, has largely diminished over the last few years. Entrepreneurs and early-stage venture capitals have gotten in front of the positive tailwinds and are starting and investing in more LegalTech companies than ever before. The number of LegalTech start-ups listed on AngelList has increased from 15 in 2009 to 400 in 2017.[11] Figure 6.5 describes the evolution of the legal business models in the years to come.

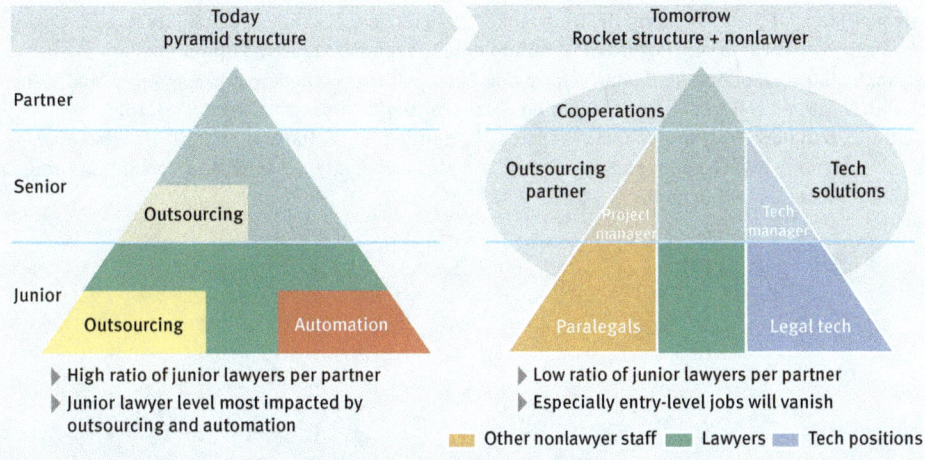

Figure 6.5: Evolution of the Legal Business Model.
Source: How Legal Technology Will Change the Business of Law. Boston Consulting Group and Bucerius Law School (Veith et al. 2016).

The market size for LegalTech is quite sizeable, and in the United States, it is US$16 billion in total addressable market (TAM) – US$9.4 billion from selling to law firms and US$6.5 billion from selling to corporate legal departments. The current actual spend[12] of only US$3 billion reflects a less than 20% market penetration, leaving a significant potential of opportunity for LegalTech firms as well as investors. The largest areas of spend today include enterprise legal management, contract management, and eDiscovery; while the fastest growing areas over the next few years will include knowledge management, legal analytics, and contract management.

References

American Bar Association (ABA). (2016). Report on the Future of Legal Services in the United States. ABA Commission on the Future of Legal Services. August 2016.

Buterin, V. (2013). *Ethereum White Paper: A Next Generation Smart Contract & Decentralized Application Platform*. White Paper, Ethereum, Ethereum.

---

11 ABA Report on the Future of Legal Services in the United States (2016).
12 Legal Services Market Global Market Report 2017, Business Research Company.

Ernst and Young (2017). Blockchain in Insurance: Applications and Pursuing a Path to Adoption. https://webforms.ey.com/Publication/vwLUAssets/EY-blockhain-in-insurance/$FILE/EY-blockhain-in-insurance.pdf

Gansky, L. (2010). *The Mesh: Why the Future of Business Is Sharing*. New York: Portfolio Penguin.

Islamic Financial Services Board (IFSB), Islamic Financial Services Industry Stability Report. (2016). https://www.ifsb.org/docs/IFSI%20Stability%20Report%202016%20(final).pdf

Swan, M. (2015). *Blockchain: Blueprint for a New Economy*. Massachusetts, USA: O'Reilly Media, Inc.

Szabo, N. (1996). *Smart Contracts: Building Blocks for Digital Markets*. Extropy, no. 16.

Veith, C., Bandlow, M., Harnisch, M., Wenzler, H., Hartung, M., & Hartung, D. (2016). *How Legal Technology Will Change the Business of Law*. Massachusetts, USA: Boston Consulting Group and Bucerius Law School.

Chapter 7
Data Risk Management For Advanced Islamic Financial Institutions

Introduction

Artificial intelligence (AI) has taken the present industrial revolution by storm and transformed many sectors by enabling explosive growth in the last five years, particularly after the pandemic hit in early 2020. AI start-ups have been established globally during these years, making significant strides and "representing a 175% increase relative to the previous 12 years" (Mohamed, 2021). Operationally, the AI improves its accuracy and precision when it is fed with more valuable data, as it uses new data-sets to update its engine to improve decision process automatically. As for the blockchain, several key areas are making it work – tokenization of real-world assets, maturity of stablecoins and the improved acceptance of regulations and standardization. We are witnessing two fast-growing trends merge and complement each other: The first one is tokenization, where all illiquid assets in the world, from private equity to real estate and luxury goods, become liquid and all liquid assets can be traded more efficiently. The second is the rise of a new tokenized economy where inevitably new rules will develop to establish transactional rules that will guide economic behaviors that are productive, efficient, and just. There is an immense potential for Islamic Finance to contribute to this area with its values-based principles in financial transactions (fiqh muamalat). By unlocking the economic potential of the blockchain, these two complementary and correlated trends will complete the decentralization of finance and the way financial services of the future will be implemented.

The inevitable integration of AI and blockchain will benefit the economy, including the supporting financial industry. Finance should be viewed in its original role of supporting all other industries through capital provisions. The digital transformation of the economy, and the disruption of finance via FinTech has transformed data into the fuel to the digital engines that drives today's economy. The datafication of various information relevant for improving efficiency and productivity has generated huge amounts of data which we call now Big Data. Datafication was first described by Cukier and Viktor Mayer-Schoenberger (2013) as a process of "taking all aspects of life and turning them into data." Facebook datafies personal networks, sensors datafy all kinds of environmental conditions, smart phones datafy personal communication and movements, wearables datafy personal conditions. This is leading to a situation of almost ubiquitous collection and availability of data.

Until only recently, authorities and officials have started to discuss the issue of Big Data at a strategic level. There is not yet a common and widely shared understanding of the way forward, whether this is a challenge or opportunity, whether it is small or big, etc. Typically, a first SWOT analysis, accompanied by a rough risk/benefit analysis, are usually conducted. However, a thorough risk analysis should also include aspects such as likelihood and impact, and be expanded to outline strategies to mitigate and manage risks.

The objective of this chapter is to analyze the additional data risk management required when artificial intelligence coupled with blockchain technology are utilized within the financial management and services industry. With data volumes increasing, real-time and complex data streams (structured and unstructured) become more and more important for financial risk control. AI through Big Data and real-time analytics "can optimize financial strategies by processing new market data and consequently using them for much attuned risk management, advisory and customer-centric service" (Mohamed, 2021).

In this chapter, the identified data risk management for DeFi applications and services are in the electronic client onboarding process, real-time financial prediction, advanced management of model portfolios, digital payment systems, AI-driven trade clearing and settlement. These techniques of data risk management encompass various risks that are associated with traditional finance that will impact asset and liability management (ALM) risk, credit risk, market risk, operational risk, liquidity risk, regulatory and Shariah risk compliance across all financial sectors.

Consumer-Related Risks

AI fueled by big data can assist financial institutions to significantly improve risk management, through improved and (more) real-time insights in the customer behavior as well as market movements. We list the most common risks associated with consumers where AI can be most useful:

i. Identity theft deterrence
   The huge amounts of transactional data can be used to feed fraud-detection AI modules, that will continuously monitor the risk of fraud and activate additional security measures like further verification steps or the restriction of access are necessitated.

ii. Liquidity management efficiency
   From big data, financial institutions can get much better visibility on in-flows and out-flows of cash, to optimize liquidity management, which includes both tangible money at branches as well as the total liquidity of the institution, be it a bank or an insurer.

iii. Credit risk management
Credit rating models for customers can be improved through more accurate credit scoring from AI-processed consumer behavior data. Such discernments can be obtained from transaction records, publicly available information (such as online professional bios or media reports), tax returns, even social media data. This information can also help in collateral management of credits, which in turn improves the credit risk management for the bank.
iv. Card fraud detection
Card transactions can be analyzed by their patterns (in terms of transaction amount, location, frequency, etc.) to detect suspicious activity to be verified by cardholder. Any fraudulent transaction can be stopped swiftly.
v. Insurance fraud detection
The detection of potential fraud at the onboarding of new insurance policies (i.e., policy not corresponding to reality) as well as fraud prevention when claims are made can be improved via AI. Sources of data that can be used as indicators are IoT data (i.e., sensor data from car accident or home damage), incongruence in information provided for claims, excessive views to the insured amount or fire/theft insurances preceding a claim, etc.

In modernized payment systems, payments from customers are being consolidated into one centralized account regardless they purchase via online or from physical outlets. Omnichannel payment is integrated with application programming interface (API) which helps simplify the reconciliation process to reduce time spent and minimize operational and execution risks. The new ecosystem suggests a lesser touchpoint as both cash and digital payments are process through a single window. In Singapore, United Overseas Bank (UOB) is another example of a brand that uses big data to drive risk management. One specific initiative involving risk management that the bank has incorporated in their system that is based on big data is to reduce the time needed to calculate the value at risk. According to the bank, the process which initially took about 18 hours has been reduced to a few minutes using the AI-driven risk management system. Through this initiative, it is deemed possible to carry out almost real-time risk analysis moving forward.

Drivers for AI-Driven Risk Management

The phenomenon of big data is driven by its ability to provide insights in a strategic and timely manner. Its wide acceptance is very much determined by several key factors, which strengthen each other, resulting in an exponential increase of data analysis to derive actionable insights and value:

i. Change in Customer Behavior and Expectations
   a. Customers are interacting with their bank or insurer digitally these days, reducing personal interaction, but at the same time it is possible to collect in an automated way much more data about the customer (e.g., his browsing history, geo-location data on his mobile phone, exact timing of the interactions) than when he visits a branch. This data should be leveraged to compensate the reduced customer engagement, caused by the loss of personal interaction.
   b. Customers use more and more social media: where these media used to be limited to closed private circles of friends, customers now use these media more and more in their day-to-day live, for example, to interact with companies. This means banks and insurers should interact more through these channels to offer services and to gain insights about their customers.
   c. Customers expect more and more a high-quality, low-friction, around-the-clock, customer-centric experience across multiple channels. In order to deliver such a personalized service, an in-depth holistic knowledge about the customer is required. This can only be achieved by leveraging all available customer data through Big Data techniques.
ii. Technological Evolution Leading to Larger Amounts of Data
   a. With the rise of IoT data, the amount of customer data will escalate, resulting in new streams of data, even if customer is not interacting with the bank or insurer.
   b. New advanced authentication techniques, such as biometric authentication and consumer preferences (e.g., via finger/mouse movements, accelerometer, and gyro sensor readings on mobile phone), will also considerably increase the amount of data to be processed in near real-time.
   c. The acceptance of Open Architectures (via APIs) allows banks and insurers to be connected to valuable data collected by other parties.
   d. Advanced data visualization: tools which enable users to visually understand large amounts of data in ways where insights can be usefully derived from (e.g., through bubble charts, geospatial heat maps, projected spread).
   e. Cloud-based solutions: offer affordable and scalable data storage and infrastructure to support effectively enable these Big Data technologies.
iii. Competition of Fintech players
   The overwhelming success of the robo-advisory startups which offer automated digital investment advice based on low-barriers to entry with minimal investment sum and selected profile information, show innovative use of market sentiment data toward new compelling customer services that is shifting financial investment services. The competition between Fintech companies will only further enhance the services they provide, taking more market share away from traditional financial service providers.

iv. Regulatory pressure
The constant tsunami of financial regulations (i.e., Basel III, FRTB, MiFID II, updated AML/KYC, FATCA, etc.) requiring banks to disclose more attenuated data to central banks and regulators, have pushed financial institutions to adopt technology (Regtech) in order to avoid fines imposed when failing to comply. The fine line between data privacy and data for consumer insights make banks accountable when collecting data, so that consumer rights are not infringed, or their private information leaked in cases of breach. Also, any necessary regulatory reporting can be generated automatically, while specific data can be made available in cases of investigation by the regulators.
v. Increased cybersecurity
As digital transformation takes hold, it is a given that online fraud and electronic crimes will increase. Banks need to protect their most valuable asset – the trust – from the customers that they hold. The ability to secure communication channels and sensitive customer data through whatever security means necessary is top priority. One way is through risk-based authentication where a fraud-detection AI engine determines the required level of security (authentication) by calculating a risk profile for each channel request. This engine can also identify fraud via irregularities in the user's behavior from customer analytics.
vi. Pressure to reduce operational cost
Increased competition and extremely low interest rate regimes are affecting profit margins in financial services. Hence, banks and insurers are forced to reduce operational costs, by improving efficiency and productivity. Many of these efficiency gains can be gained from big data insights within their operations.

Risks in Data Sources and Big Data Processes

The various techniques of risk management within the financial industry will include all risks faced by traditional financial institutions- asset and liability management (ALM) risk, credit risk, default risk, market risk, operational risk, liquidity risk, regulatory and Shariah compliance risk. Particularly when processes become more digitized, the sources of data from which AI modules generate the desired outcomes become crucial. As Big Data will leverage a multitude of internal and external data sources, it is important to ensure the purity and relevancy of such data to produce the desired outcomes with a high-level of accuracy and precision. Tainted or irrelevant data will affect the expected results and negatively impact decision-making from inaccurate analyses.

Generally, these Big Data are categorized as structured data that is present in the company's databases, structured and unstructured data transiting through the organization (but often not stored), information gathered from external partners, and publicly available information.

In the following section, we describe where the data sources are derived from:
- Structured Data Present in Company's Databases
  - Customer-relationship management (CRM) information (e.g., they contain onboarding data such as KYC and AML information)
  - Product-specific silo information (e.g., credits, accounts, payments, securities, insurances)
  - Security information (e.g., authentication, authorization, and signature data)
  - Structured data gathered by new compelling services, like personalized financial management (like budget plans, categorization of expenses and saving goals), digital investment advisory (such as investment profiling questionnaires and financial plans), and IoT sensor data (like information from car telematics, wearables, home sensors, and geolocation data).
- Structured and Unstructured Transiting Data
  - Unstructured communication like recorded emails, chat sessions, voice and video meetings (e.g., between branch or contact center employees and customers). This also includes unstructured summaries of communication, like call logs or comments written by call center employees.
  - Customer behavior on websites, that is, browsing patterns.
  - Meta-data on channel interactions, like browser name and version, IP address, customer operating system, cookie data, URL redirects, geo-location data.
  - Customer survey or feedback information.
- Information Gathered from External Partners
  - Social media data, that is, comments, likes, (re-)tweets, shares, feeling toward a company's brand, or a broader topic or a particular keyword.
  - Data gathered from API ecosystems, for example, data collected by partners, which deliver services on top of APIs exposed by the financial services company or data collected from APIs publicly exposed by competitors (e.g., PSD2 account information stored by competing banks)
  - Financial market news, analyst reports, securities data.
- Publicly Available Information
  - Demographic data
  - Financial data about companies (like annual reports)
  - Media feeds (blogs, news agencies, newspapers)

Subsequently, a framework for Big Data in Modernization of Financial Processes should distinguish between three phases of the business process, input, throughput, and output. The input phase corresponds to the "design" and "collect" phases of the business process, the throughput to the "process" and "analysis" phases while the output is equivalent to the "dissemination" phase. Quality dimensions are nested within a hierarchical structure called hyperdimensions. The three defined hyperdimensions are "source," "metadata," and "data." Quality dimensions are nested within these hyperdimensions and are assigned to each of the production phases. For the input phase, the additional dimensions "privacy and confidentiality", "complexity" (according to the structure of the data), "completeness" of metadata and "linkability" (possibility to link data with other data) should be added to the standard quality model. For each of the quality dimensions, factors relevant for their description should be assessed together and separately.

Risk Management in Various Financial Processes

AI and blockchain experts are sure that technology can be used to manage client profiles more efficiently and reliably. Confidential client data such as profile data, behavioral preferences, wealth net worth, personal account information, social media profiles can be shared as needed, through permissioned access as needed.

i. Managing Technological Risks
Besides organizational challenges, we want to emphasize that that using AI itself adds another dimension of risk in the financial risk management framework – Cybersecurity Risk. As such, we recommend some effective ways to protect computerized systems against cyber threats through integration of security into every step of the digital transformation or implementation. This spans the entire lifecycle from initiation, to development, to deployment and eventual disposal of the system to ensure complete financial risk management. Control Gates or decision points are specific milestones where the security implementations are evaluated. They specify to the corporation that "security considerations are addressed, adequate security controls are built in, and identified risks are clearly understood before the system development advances to the next lifecycle phase" (NIST, 2008). The Agile approach can be adopted to continuously update and improve on standards. The "security planning is to be conducted as part of integrating security, and should include:
– Identifying and confirming key security roles in the system development project
– Outlining key security milestones and activities for the system development.
– Connecting the use of secure design, IT architecture and coding standards.
– Warranting all key stakeholders have a shared understanding of the goals, implications, considerations, and requirements of performing security.

These values integration is crucial in responding to potential security threats as it highlights to key stakeholder important areas of systems development progress, and that critical decisions made will have security implications" (Mohamed & Ali, 2021).
Other technological risks associated specifically to the DeFi applications are:

– Oracle Risks

Without oracles, blockchains are completely self-encapsulated and have no knowledge of the outside world other than the transactions added to the native blockchain. Many DeFi protocols require access to secure, tamper-resistant asset prices to ensure that routine actions, such as liquidations and prediction market resolutions, function correctly. Protocol reliance on these data feeds introduces oracle risk. Oracles, as they exist today, represent the highest risk to DeFi protocols that rely on them. All on-chain oracles are vulnerable to front-running, and millions of dollars have been lost due to arbitrageurs. Additionally, oracle services, including Chainlink and Maker, have suffered crippling outages with catastrophic downstream effects (Harvey et al, 2021). Until oracles are themselves blockchain native, hardened, and proven resilient, they represent the largest systemic threat to DeFi today.

– Protocol Governance Risks

Programming risk is the sole threat to the protocol because the application is autonomous and controlled by smart contracts. Other DeFi applications rely on more than just autonomous computer code. For example, MakerDAO, the decentralized credit facility described earlier, is reliant on a human-controlled governance process that actively adjusts protocol parameters to keep the system solvent. Many other DeFi protocols use similar systems and rely on humans to actively manage protocol risk (Harvey et al, 2021). This introduces a new risk, governance risk, which is unique to the DeFi landscape.

Protocol governance refers to the representative or liquid democratic mechanisms. To participate in the governance process, users and investors must acquire a token that has been explicitly assigned protocol governance rights on a liquid marketplace. Once acquired, holders use these tokens to vote on protocol changes and guide future direction. Governance tokens usually have a fixed supply that assists in resisting attempts by anyone to acquire a majority (51%), nevertheless they expose the protocol to the risk of control by a malicious actor.

The founders often control traditional fintech companies, which reduces the risk of an external party influencing or changing the company's direction or product. DeFi protocols, however, are vulnerable to attack as soon as the governance system launches. Any financially equipped adversary can simply acquire a majority of liquid governance tokens to gain control of the protocol and steal funds. We have not yet experienced a successful governance attack on any Ethereum-based DeFi project, but little doubt exists that a financially equipped adversary will eventually attack a protocol if the potential profit exceeds the cost of attack.

– Smart-Contract Risks

Blockchains can remove traditional financial risks, such as counterparty risk, with their unique properties, but DeFi is built on code. This software foundation gives attackers a larger attack surface than the threat vectors of traditional financial institutions. Since public blockchains are open systems, virtually anyone can view and interact with code on a blockchain after the code is deployed. Given that this code is often responsible for storing and transferring blockchain native financial assets, it introduces a new, unique risk—smart contract risk (Harvey et al., 2021).

Smart Contract risk can take the form of a logic error in the code or an economic exploit in which an attacker can withdraw funds from the platform beyond the intended functionality. The former can take the form of any typical software bug in the code. For example, let's say we have a smart contract which is intended to be able to escrow deposits from a particular ERC-20 from any user and transfer the entire balance to the winner of a lottery. The contract keeps track of how many tokens it has internally, and uses that internal number as the amount when performing the transfer. The bug will belong here in our hypothetical contract. The internal number will, due to a rounding error, be slightly higher than the actual balance of tokens the contract holds. When it tries to transfer, it will transfer "too much" and the execution will fail. If there was no failsafe put into place, the tokens are functionally locked within the protocol. Informally these are known as "bricked" funds and cannot be recovered.

Smart-contract programming still has a long way to go before best practices are developed and complex smart-contracts have the resilience necessary to handle high-value transactions. As long as smart-contract risk threatens the DeFi landscape, application adoption and trust will suffer as users hesitate to trust the contracts they interact with and that custody their funds.

– Scaling Risks
Compared to Visa, which can handle upward of 25,000 transactions per second, Ethereum is capable of handling less than 0.1% of the throughput. Ethereum's lack of scalability places DeFi at risk of being unable to meet requisite demand. Much effort is focused on increasing Ethereum's scalability or replacing Ethereum with an alternative blockchain that can more readily handle higher transaction volumes. To date, all efforts have proven unsuccessful.

Vertical and horizontal scaling are two additional general approaches to increasing blockchain throughput. Vertical scaling centralizes all transaction processing to a single large machine. This centralization reduces the communication overhead (transaction/block latency) associated with a PoW blockchain such as Ethereum, but results in a centralized architecture in which one machine is responsible for a majority of the system's processing. Horizontal scaling, however, divides the work of the system into multiple pieces, retaining decentralization but increasing the throughput of the system through parallelization. Ethereum 2.0 takes this approach in combination with a Proof of Stake consensus algorithm.

Many approaches aim to decrease the scalability risks facing DeFi today, but the field lacks a clear winner (Harvey et al, 2021). As long as DeFi's growth is limited by blockchain scaling, applications will be limited in their potential impact.

ii. Managing Credit Risk with Improved Client Onboarding Process

In the current system, prospective patrons are required to show identification and residency documents, prove matrimonial position, founts of wealth, pronounce commercial interests and official occupation (and even declare political ties in order to set up certain accounts) for financial transactions. In this basic onboarding process, financial institutions may take weeks to verify information and conduct due diligence with reliable accuracy. In such cases, the blockchain presents a strong use case for client onboarding in wealth management.

The integration of AI-enhanced onboarding processes for new customers or finance-seekers and the use of smart contracts to automate terms and conditions will improve bottlenecks caused by document consolidation and funds approval. Along with the development of instant payment infrastructures, funds in escrow and its eventual release upon fulfillment of trade agreements will advance facilitation in trade finance in a timely and cost-efficient manner, hence maximizing capital allocation and cashflows for businesses.

iii. Managing Asset and Liability Risk in Financial Portfolios

A robo-advisor is an AI-driven digital guide that offers automated financial advice or simple investment consultation. Robo-advisors (and chatbots) are increasingly popular because they can lower costs and increase the quality and transparency of financial advice for consumers – helping consumers choose investments, banking products and insurance policies (Buchanan, 2018). Robo-advisory services can be viewed in the following ways: (1) "access to and rebalancing of passive and rule-based investment strategies" (Mohamed, 2020a), (2) "cost-efficient implementation of a diversified asset allocation" (Rohner & Uhl, 2017), and (3) overcoming behavioral biases. According to Rohner and Uhl, (2017), robo-advisors can save costs of up to 4.4% per year and improve the quality of financial consultation compared to traditional investment advisory.

For financial predictions in portfolio management, new innovation in AI and machine learning are developed as tools to recognize indicators to predict price movements and to generate insights from massive datasets to improve market assessment and decision acumen compared to existing models. "The key task is to identify signals from data on which predictions relating to price level or volatility can be made, over various time horizons, to generate higher and uncorrelated returns" (FSB, 2017). Portfolio construction with probabilistic (risk) calculations, stochastic modelling and scenario testing are some of the numerical models (including statistical and geometrical analysis) that are mathematically rigorous.

Technology again will provide that leap forward with "cloud computing streamlining existing infrastructure and at the same time enabling many new, previously unimaginable or unimplementable, applications" (Kaplan, 2016). In addition to the currently available on-demand cloud computing, "recent progress in quantum computers could soon provide the next disruptive chapter in humanity's unbounded appetite for computational processing" (Buchanan, 2019).

Data mining techniques use algorithms to discover hidden patterns, relationships, dependencies and unusual records or dependencies. Predictive analytics use a variety of techniques to make predictions (determine likelihood of future events, i.e., future trends or likely behavior) from historical and current data patterns. Often based on time-series analysis, this type of analysis is typically used for determining the "next-best-offer" and implementing adaptive user interfaces.

Machine learning is a group of techniques consisting of applying one of the above techniques but adding the element of automated learning to it. This means the analytic technique will learn itself to provide better insights into the data, that is, the model compares expected outcome with the real outcome and adapts accordingly to better align for future predictions.

Social network analysis utilizes a group of techniques that will typically use a combination of above techniques, but due to their widespread usage, it is often considered as a separate group. It allows to represent, analyze, and extract patterns and trends from social media data. A typical example is sentiment analysis, which aims to derive conclusions from the subjective information of the customer sentiment.

Digital asset management (like investment portfolio companies and robo-advisors) use automation to process copious amounts of asset data like economic indicators and their interaction with market movements. Applying sentiment analyses via advanced AI techniques to various advisory utilities by analyzing historical data, market patterns and market dependencies have given drastically better financial predictions. With improved algorithms running enhanced AI systems for better projections and predictions, traditional finance concepts like the "Efficient Market Hypothesis" (EMH), portfolio diversification and portfolio rotation may work together to produce new theories and strategies to produce better returns and improve overall risk management.

iv. Managing Market Risks Through Advanced Interbank Payment Systems
"The current settlement of payments is costly because it needs strict monitoring to avoid any double spending or sudden default. As a result, payment systems currently used by CBs are tiered: only Tier1 banks can open a settlement account in the CB (which needs to remain continuously funded) for immediate settlement purposes. Banks in other tiers must open accounts in Tier1 banks and go through them to settle their transfers in the CB. Thus, top-tier banks intermediate other banks' transfers while also managing their own customers' accounts" (Mohamed, 2020b) (see Figure 7.1, left).

In a tech-enhanced model (Figure 7.1, right), the interbank settlement system infrastructure is replaced by an AI-driven blockchain or a distributed ledger technology, "such that the accounts of the participants in the Central Bank are replaced by digital wallets and the CB becomes just another node of the network, although with certain privileges. The CB can still access information on all the transactions as a supervisor, decides who can join the system and is the issuer of the cryptocurrency" (Mohamed, 2020b). "The main advantages of this scenario lie, on the one hand, in the increased efficiency of the interbank payment system (i.e., cost reduction and speed increase)" (BIS, 2018). "On the other hand, in the greater resilience of a system of this type to cyberattacks since there is no vulnerable central point. The less efficient and insecure the system is, the greater the net benefits of adopting a central bank-issued digital currency, discounting the cost of implementing the new infrastructure and, therefore, the more probable its adoption" (Mohamed, 2021).

The creation of a shared payments ledger system would allow for real-time and traceable transactional information about capital flows, which is progressing toward active monitoring and trigger alerts of creeping systemic risk that may impair financial stability. In fostering competition, it will expand accessibility without incurring traditional payment infrastructure costs. The cost of adding a new participant is technologically and operationally simpler and would be considerably cheaper since it just means adding a new node to the blockchain network.

"Since the transactional part of payments can then be provided by any payments player from the direct access to the CB settlement system, the future value creation in the payment business would likely be a broad range of value-added services, mainly built upon the payment insights and knowledge extracted from transactional data" (Mohamed, 2021) based on a seamless and intuitive user experience. "One area where there is a huge potential for efficiency gains is in cross–border payment systems. Cryptocurrencies offer an opportunity for dramatic cost reductions, which may translate into faster and less expensive transactions, for instance in remittances" (IMF, 2017). With the increasing use of cryptocurrencies in cross-border transactions, Central Banks may cooperate to integrate their respective payments systems to increase cross–border exchange using their systems. All in all, customers would end up with more options for money transfers that are likely cheaper, safer, and faster.

v. Managing Operational Risks in Transactional Interoperability
Since financial service companies have already deployed several of these "older" technologies, it is essential that the analytical solutions from different generations work effectively together, rather than having to perform a big-bang replacement of the existing data architecture. Several financial service companies have been aggregating data from different channels and silos, by creating operational data stores (ODS) and data warehouses (DWH), which are based on relational databases.

Afterwards these companies created OLAP (On-Line Analytical Processing) cubes (i.e., multi-dimensional data tables) on these data warehouses or used Business Intelligence (BI) tools like Business Objects to slice and dice the data, to calculate KPIs and to better understand customer behavior. More recently these BI tools have also evolved toward more statistical and mathematical analysis. The combination of these

Introduction — 173

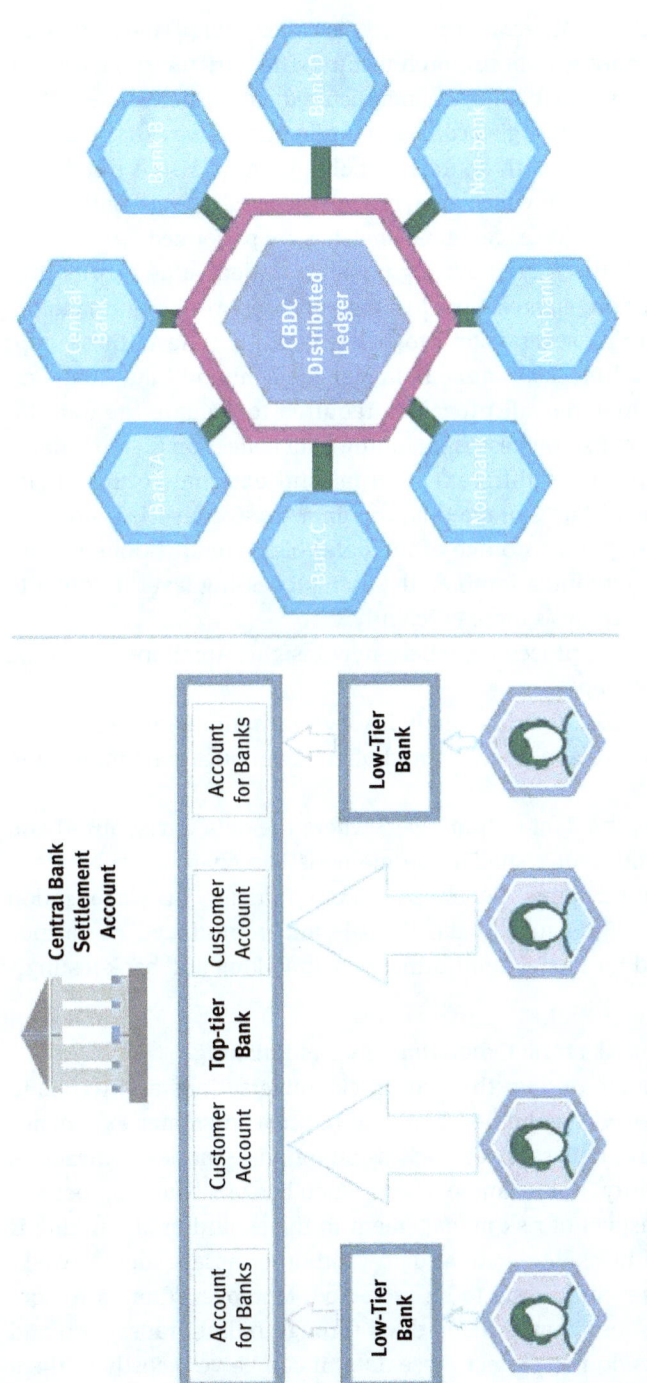

Figure 7.1: Tiered Payment Model versus Distributed Payment Model.

new technologies, with the current technology stack, is called a Big Data Warehouse (BDW), which is a hybrid data warehouse architecture. The structured data is still using the conventional DWH setup, but for the unstructured data a more modern ODL approach is taken. Big Data technologies can be setup in such a way that they can aggregate and analyze data from both sources. Finally, there is also a trend from batch-oriented replication of data on which analytics are executed, toward online real-time streaming of data, on which (near) real-time analytics are performed.

From collecting data all the way to getting business added-value results (i.e., discovering useful information, suggest conclusions and support decision-making) is a complex process, requiring several steps to go executed. High level these steps can be split in two high level blocks, that is, Data Management and Data Analytics, where Data Management includes all processes required to prepare the data for analysis. This involves a series of processes including data collection (i.e., the data source layer), gathering from different internal and external sources (data scraping) the raw data. Next, data storage (i.e., the data storage layer) where storage and/or staging (i.e., temporary storage of the data) of the data is done for further processing. Then data manipulation (i.e., the data processing layer) in order to prepare the data to perform analysis more efficiently.

Data Analytics includes all processes, where new insights are gained from the data. This includes two sub-steps:
– Modelling and analysis (i.e., the data analytics layer) where there are a variety of techniques to model and analyze data, and often techniques are combined to get the best result.
– Data visualization (i.e., the data output layer) where the data is visualized and insights drawn from different visualization methods like charts, graphs, decision trees, traffic light indicators, heatmaps or more intricate 3-D visualization techniques, typically aggregated in dashboards and reproduced in various types of reports needed for model monitoring, benchmarking and back testing.

vi. Managing Operational Risks from Cybercriminals and Phishing

Social media is a huge source of data that can track conversations and trends to analyze consumer behavior. It has helped banks to improve customer experience by listening and improving their services such as simplifying money transaction with the same level of security. But it can be a bane when hackers listen in, too.

Hence, an important aspect of risk management to the evolution of banking is cybersecurity. Banks hold massive personal data (and other assets such as cash) which is an important asset that needs to be protected. Moreover, there are more and more cashless transactions that is being done through online transaction and physical scanners. If banks do not protect these data, it can be very costly to them and their customers. According to Hewitt (2020), the top emerging cyber threats for banks are malware that is targeted to end-user devices, social engineering by exploiting human behavior to gain access to company servers, and data manipulation that makes changes in target system to make undetected changes or extraction of data for illegal purposes. Scorching examples are phishing of information by fake banking websites that try to retrieve customers' usernames and passwords without them being aware of it.

By having an updated firewall, banks will be able block malicious activities before they reach other parts of the network. While a firewall upgrade increases protection, updated anti-virus and anti-malware applications will help in preventing projected attacks. But a big concern is with respect to mobile banking apps. Here, the adoption of a multi-factor authentication (MFA) is extremely important to protect consumers whose passwords are hijacked or become

compromised. Utilizing MFA will stop cybercriminals from reaching the network as multiple layers of protection (such as a six-digit code sent to individual's mobile phone) will form additional security function. Other risk management solutions include automatic log out and biometric utilization.

Apart from that, digital banking processes need to have a cyber-risk framework that includes a cyber risk management program. A Cyber Risk Management Program has:

a. Identify Valuable Digital Assets
   These assets might include computers, systems, networks, or data.
b. Identify and Prioritize Digital Risks
   Look at the risks associated with every threat that can affect your organization, from unintentional ones (like unsecured Amazon Web Services buckets) to outright attacks (like Denial of Service and Ransomware attacks). Every potential threat, including new and emerging risks, should be identified.
c. Track Security Metrics
   These metrics can also help identify ways to mitigate risk and guide future risk prioritization. The efficacy of your metrics program relies heavily on what you decide to measure, so it is crucial that you are tracking metrics that affect your company from both an operational and strategic standpoint.
d. Implement Automated Cybersecurity Solutions
   Using automated cybersecurity solutions to monitor your network gives time back to IT teams, allowing security professionals to focus their efforts on high-risk threats.
e. Security Training for all Employees
   Security training should be administered to every employee during the onboarding process, with curriculum varying based on job function and seniority. Regular testing of employees' cybersecurity literacy will allow you to evaluate the effectiveness of the education programs you have in place.

f. Incident Response Plan
In the event of a breach, you need to have a response plan in place as this can help reduce potential damage and allow for a quick return to normal operations. A checklist of action items should be prioritized during an attack to ensure no time is wasted. This plan will vary depending on the severity of the attack and the size of your organization.

vii. Managing Regulatory and Shariah Risks Through Better Compliance

AI-enhanced blockchain-based platforms can be used to address the challenges involving identity, privacy and security across regions and platforms by decentralizing and distributing databases while leveraging on AI for improved administration and processing of private information. These automated decentralized platforms give integrated systems an identity, make and "receive payments, enter into complex agreements and transact without an intermediary" (Mohamed and Ali, 2019) in a trusted manner.

One way to help ease compliance burdens is to build and deploy identity management solutions using both AI and blockchain technologies. The ability of the blockchain to authenticate and verify information through a consensus mechanism allows a trusted way to identify persons or parties that makes the entire transaction become reliable and trustworthy. Intuitively, identity management systems based on cryptography are being developed using AML, CTF, and KYC requirements according to the regulations set in each region or country. Some solutions that are being built exist on privately distributed ledger where one enterprise can be assigned as a node in the blockchain network and the platforms developed by asset management companies is driven by an AI-engine that checks on AML, CTF, and KYC compliance remotely connected to a data lake (an off-chain database) of records. These Big Data technologies require also new ways of storing the data, which gave rise to Operational Data Lakes (ODL). These data lakes store all data (i.e., data in use today, but also data that may be used someday), both structured and unstructured, in their raw unprocessed form (allowing easy adaptation to change). This in contrast to data warehouses, which only store the data required by the business and store this data specifically structured for flexible querying and intuitive viewing and analysis (i.e., data is denormalized with a lot redundancy). Operational Data Lakes form a modern replacement for Operational Data Stores (ODS), supporting both structured as unstructured data and handling much larger volumes of data. Often companies consider the replacement of an ODS with an ODL as a good first step toward a Big Data architecture.

The combination of these new technologies, with the current technology stack, is called a Big Data Warehouse (BDW), which is a hybrid data warehouse architecture. The structured data is still using the conventional DWH setup, but for the unstructured data a more modern ODL approach is taken. Big Data technologies can be setup in such a way that they can aggregate and analyze data from both sources.

Automated audits, scheduled reporting, and simplification of processes are among the benefits offered by such AI integrated blockchain platforms to address regulatory compliance, where technology is assisting financial service providers with regulatory requirements and compliance management.

As for Shariah compliance, Islamic requirements necessitate transactions to be in line with Shariah principles to ensure financial stability, economic prosperity, and social justice. In order to operationalize the values of the Shariah, technology can be used as an enabler to systematize preferred behaviors to uphold fairness and justice for all parties. For example, smart contract platforms can be used to underwrite the contractual relationship between fund managers and investors in the delivery of services, and AI algorithms can be programmed for Shariah-compliance screening to sieve through various investments or companies. Also, the roles of Shariah boards, Shariah governance mechanisms involving Shariah reviews and

audits, can be automated when enhanced with a repository of religious fatwas and ijtihad rulings from previous transactions. Such a module does not put Shariah scholars out of a job but instead will help them overcome repetitive mundane tasks and focus on high-level considerations to improve the regulatory and compliance processes that may hinder current practices. Furthermore, robotic process automation (RPA), which is a form of AI, can be used to calculate the portion of impure income and determine its purification value to adhere to Shariah requirements more closely. Such is the possibilities that technology holds to bring us closer to the spirit of the Shariah, which is essentially to maximize the utility of this world without forgetting the responsibility to maximize the utility of the next world.

Conclusion

The future of financial industries will heavily utilize automation and AI-driven technology integrated to blockchain-based systems to help financial service providers uplift existing processes and realize new revenue streams and business models to serve their customers better. With competition in the financial services sector getting fiercer, banks need to adopt a data-driven approach if they want to stay competitive. As opportunities for incumbent banks and insurers from these insights are almost unlimited, big data will be a strong differentiator in the future competitiveness of financial institutions.

While operational efficiency and profitability may be key drivers for technology adoption, AI's ability in combatting financial crime such as monitoring trader recklessness, anti-fraud and anti-money laundering needs to be acknowledged and utilized widely through cooperation across jurisdictions. The real-time 24-hour monitoring capabilities and the capacity of machine learning (ML) to examine huge amounts of data allows for greater granular and profound analyses in various financial products and services. When data is managed and processed the right way,

the risk management of automated and decentralized systems can achieve crucial advantages for safer business operations within Islamic financial institutions as we develop into advanced cities of the future. While the developments of AI appear to move faster than we had imagine, the oversight and governance of AI needs to progress in parallel. AI could be as powerful as human or exceeds human capability, but it does not have the ability to do so independently. It still needs to be "trained" and improved by human beings using numerical data sets so that they can handle various tasks. Ultimately, these products of human imagination need to be managed so that unintended consequences result from its misuse and abuse, intentionally or unknowingly.

References

Bank for International Settlements (2019). *Proceeding with Caution – A Survey on Central Bank Digital Currency, Monetary and Economic Department,* January 2019.

Bank for International Settlements (2018). *Central Bank Digital Currencies, Committee on Payments and Market Infrastructures,* March 2018.

Beketov, M., Lehmann, K. and Wittke, M. (2018). Robo Advisors: Quantitative Methods Inside the Robots. *Journal of Asset Management, Palgrave Macmillan, 19*(6), 363–370, October.

Brummer, C., and Yadav, Y. (2019). The Fintech Trilemma. *Georgetown Law Journal, 107,* 235–307.

Buchanan, B., & Cao, C. (2018). Quo Vadis?: A Comparison of the Fintech Revolution in China and the West, No. 2017-0, SWIFT Institute, USA.

Buchanan, B. (2019). Artificial Intelligence in Finance. Seattle University with funding from The Alan Turing Institute. https://doi.org/10.5281/zenodo.2612537

Citi (2018) Bank of the Future: the ABCs of Digital Disruption in Finance. CitiReport March 2018.

Cukier, K., & Mayer-Schoenberger, V. (2013). The Rise of Big Data: How It's Changing the Way We Think About the World. *Foreign Affairs, 92*(3), 28–40. http://www.jstor.org/stable/23526834

Ernst and Young (2017). *Blockchain Innovation in Wealth and Asset Management: Benefits and Key Challenges to Adopting This Technology.*

Financial Stability Board (2017). *Artificial Intelligence and Machine Learning in Financial Services: Market Developments and Financial Stability Implications.* 1 November 2017.

Harvey, C. R. and Ramachandran, A. and Santoro, J. (2021). DeFi and the Future of Finance. https://ssrn.com/abstract=3711777

Hewitt, N. (2020). How to build a security-first culture with remote teams. Imperva. https://www.imperva.com/blog/how-to-build-a-security-first-culture-with-remote-teams/

IMF (2017). "Fintech and Financial Services: Initial Considerations," IMF Staff Discussion Note, SDN 17/05.

Kaplan, J. (2016). *Artificial Intelligence: What Everyone Needs to Know.* Oxford, United Kingdom: Oxford University Press.

Mohamed, H. (2021). *Beyond Fintech – Technology Applications for the Islamic Economy.* Singapore: World Scientific.

Mohamed, H. and Ali, H. (2021). Finding Solutions to Cybersecurity Challenges in the Digital Economy. In Boitan, I. A. and Marchewka-Bartkowiak, K. (Eds.), *Fostering Innovation and Competitiveness with FinTech, RegTech, and SupTech.* Chapter 5, 80–96. Pennsylvania, USA: IGI Global.

Mohamed, H. (2020a). Asset and Wealth Management in the IR4.0 Era. *Journal of Wealth Management and Financial Planning*, *7*, 3–18.

Mohamed, H. (2020b). Implementing a Central Bank Issued Digital Currency: Assessing Economic Implications. International Journal of Islamic Economics and Finance, *3*(1), 51–74.

Mohamed, H. and Ali, H. (2019). *Blockchain, Fintech and Islamic Finance – Building the Future of the New Islamic Digital Economy*. De|G Press, Boston/Berlin.

National Institute of Standards and Technology. (2008). Special Publication 800-64 Revision 2 – Security Considerations in the System Development Life Cycle.

Rohner, P. and Uhl, M. (2017). Robo-Advisors vs. Traditional Investment Advisors – An Unequal Game. *Journal of Wealth Management*, *21*(1), 44–50.

Schär, F. (2021). *Decentralized Finance: On Blockchain- and Smart Contract-Based Financial Markets, Federal Reserve Bank of St. Louis Review*, USA: Early Edition 2021.

Chapter 8
Evolution of Blockchain

Introduction

Blockchain is potentially disruptive to all business intermediaries. Its disruptiveness is proportional to the cost, complexity, and degree of transaction duplication in the existing system of intermediation. Recent technology waves – notably the internet of things (IoT), exploiting the proliferation of smart mobile devices, and augmented reality – may directly endow physical objects with information and intelligence: they make the real virtual. The technologies of token and blockchain, conversely, endow data with continuity: they make the virtual real.

Not only is there the possibility that blockchain technology could reinvent every category of monetary markets, payments, and financial services, it might also offer similar reconfiguration possibilities to a great many industries within the economy. Blockchain is fundamentally a new paradigm for organizing activity with less friction and more efficiency, and at much greater scale than current paradigms (Swan, 2015). Swan believes that it is not just that blockchain technology is decentralized and that decentralization as a general model can work well now because there is a liquid enough underlying network with the web interconnecting all humans. Including centralized or decentralized transactions: blockchain technology affords a universal and global scope and scale that was previously impossible.

The mining process of verifying blockchain transactions is what enables it to be undeniably secure proved by enduring untold numbers of cyberattacks. While bitcoin itself requires going through exchanges to convert hard currency into cryptocurrency and storing it, new blockchain technology programming changes eliminated the need for this. At the rate technology advances, blockchain will eventually run its course and sprout other potential uses along the way.

With blockchain, technology companies have finally broken through to the next leap in business transactions of every kind along with a new concept of the "internet of value" and the rapidly advancing IoT.

When combined with distributed infrastructure technology, the IoT, can significantly expand the return of investment (ROI) of an asset – its utilization. In manufacturing, for example, a distributed infrastructure-based IoT could power efficient product data-keeping. All information pertaining to a product from the point of manufacture through the time it reaches the end user can be stored on the ledger. This would include product history, revisions, warranty information and expiration date (if applicable), thus making the ledger a trusted source of product data. Via access to the maintenance schedules on the ledger, service requests can be triggered when a product requires maintenance.

Home appliances can be designed to interact with each other to reduce energy consumption based on utilization. As an example, a washer can determine when the detergent supply decreases and automatically refills itself. The machine could also trigger a service request if it detects a component malfunction or a maintenance request based on usage and/or maintenance schedule. Blockchain can be the technology to store all of this information.

Within financial services, IoT can link the performance of a manufacturer to its lending potential. Sensors attached to goods produced at the manufacturing plant would monitor the products' retail sales, a good measure of how the business is doing. Banks can use this information to assist in a lending decision.

In 2015 Honduras implemented blockchain technology to develop incorruptible land registries. Blockchain and distributed infrastructure technology also has potential applications in takaful (the tracking of high-value goods to protect against insurance fraud), trade finance, supply chain management (the effective management and tracing of documents and entities participating in the process) and distributed identity, independent of countries or governments.

Transnational Justice Applications for the Economy

The freedom attribute associated with blockchain technologies becomes more pronounced in the future evolution of the blockchain, the next category of application beyond currency and market transactions. Through its global decentralized nature, blockchain technology has the potential ability to circumvent the current limitations of geographic jurisdictions. There is an argument that blockchain technology can more equitably address issues related to freedom, jurisdiction, censorship, and regulation, perhaps in ways that nation-state models and international diplomacy efforts regarding human rights cannot. There is a scale and jurisdiction consideration that certain operations are transnational and are more effectively administered, coordinated, monitored, and reviewed at a higher organizational level such as that of the World Trade Organization (WTO).

The idea is to fortify transnational organizations from the limitations of geography-based, nation-state jurisdiction to a truly global cloud. The first point is that transnational organizations need transnational governance structures. The reach, accessibility, and transparency of blockchain technology could be an effective transnational governance structure. Blockchain governance is more congruent with the character and needs of transnational organizations than nation-state governance. The second point is that not only is the transnational governance provided by blockchain more effective, more likely would be fairer. There is potentially more equality, justice, and freedom available to organizations and their participants in a decentralized, cloud-based model. This is provided by the blockchain's immutable public record, transparency, access, and reach. Anyone worldwide could look up and confirm the activities of transnational organizations on the blockchain. Thus, the blockchain is a global system of checks and balances that creates trust among all parties. This is precisely the sort of core infrastructural element that could allow humanity to scale to orders-of-magnitude larger processes with truly global organizations and coordination mechanisms.

Blockchain technology simultaneously highlights the issue of the appropriate administration of transnational public goods and presents a solution. Wikipedia is a similar international public good that is currently subject to a local jurisdiction that could impose on the organization an artificial or biased agenda. It is possible that blockchain mechanisms might be the most efficient and equitable models for administering all transnational public goods, particularly due to their participative, democratic, and distributed nature.

Coordination and Efficiency in Markets Through Consensus-Building

Blockchain technology can facilitate the coordination and acknowledgment of all manner of human interaction, facilitating a higher order of collaboration and possibly paving the way for human/machine interaction at some level. Further, blockchain technology is not just a better organizational model functionally, practically, and quantitatively; by requiring consensus to operate, the model could also have greater liberty, equality, and empowerment qualitatively. Thus, the blockchain is a complete solution that integrates both extrinsic and intrinsic and qualitative and quantitative benefits.

Despite the many interesting potential uses of blockchain technology, one of the most important skills in the developing industries will be to see where it is and is not appropriate to use blockchain models. Not all processes need an economy or a payments system, or peer-to-peer (P2P) exchange, or decentralization, or robust public record keeping. Further, the scale of operations is a relevant factor, because it might not make sense to have every tiny micro-transaction recorded on a public blockchain; for example, blog-post and tip-jar transactions could be batched into side-chains in which one overall daily transaction is recorded. Sidechains are more broadly proposed as an infrastructural mechanism by which multiblock chain ecosystems can exchange and transfer assets (Back et al., 2014). Especially with made to measure (M2M)/IoT device-to-device communication, there are many open questions about the most effective ways to incorporate market principles (if at all) to coordinate resources, incentivize certain goal-directed behavior, and have tracking and payments remuneration. (Dawson, 2014) Even before we consider the potential economic models for M2M/IoT payments, we must work out general coordination protocols for how large swarms of devices can communicate, perhaps deploying control system and scheduling software for these machine social networks, adding new layers of communication protocols like a "chirp" for simple micro-communications such as on, off, start, and stop (daCosta, 2013).

Pragmatic Approach to Technology Implementation

There is an increasing amount of conversation related to the emerging technology called by the now over-used name blockchain. It seems an ironic use of that name, since much of the actual news these days concerning solutions under development is likely not a blockchain solution at all, but a different form of distributed ledger technology (DLT). If we can put semantics aside, the basis for the excitement is based on the blockchain concept, which underpins the bitcoin platform for a distributed and immutable ledger facilitating the exchange of the virtual currency.

There are several DLT platforms that are receiving interest from the financial services community that leverage some aspects of blockchain. Among them is Corda, which is being developed by R3, a fintech focused on DLT. A visit to the Corda website finds that they do not call their platform blockchain, as that word does not seem to even exist on their website. The message is clear that the platform is designed for financial services – not surprising, as R3 has been heavily funded by several large banks and others. The platform is designed to not share all transaction data across the network, as the access to transactions is restricted to only those needing to view or validate them on a case-by-case basis. This access is limited to the parties to the transaction and potentially regulators or central authorities. This form of private ledger does not share the vision of bitcoin, the public network where the transactional history is shared by all nodes. Corda supports multiple consensus algorithms, which provide flexibility to comply with different regulators but also differs from the use of miners found in the bitcoin world.

Another example are the tools being offered by Digital Asset Holdings. Digital Asset utilizes a form of private DLT, Hyperledger, which is not a true Blockchain. Like Corda, Digital Asset exists to support banking and capital markets and central authorities such as exchanges and central counterparties (CCPs). Like the Corda platform, not all the transaction data stored on the Digital Asset platform is replicated across all the nodes. This data is shared only by those involved in the transaction. Digital Asset differs from other platforms as it employs a form of XML called Digital Asset Modeling Language (DAML) utilized to develop Smart Contracts, which automate the execution of contract terms related to the exchange of assets that interact with the Hyperledger. However, a common thread among these platforms and blockchain is the use of cryptography and some form of consensus algorithm, such as Practical Byzantine Fault Tolerance (PBFT). PBFT is effective in asynchronous environments such as the internet, where the need to maintain high availability and provide the capability to recover from bugs, errors, and malicious cyberattacks is critical.

There is some debate about the development of these private networks, as the focus moves away from bitcoin to a continuous stream of new ventures, alliances, and projects on different platforms. The groundswell of excitement for a technology such as blockchain has created an unsurprisingly opposite reaction as well from cynics who are beginning to line up to rain on the parade. However, both sides seem to suffer from the same hype.

The issue is that they are both looking at blockchain as something being either black or white. Some supporters of this emerging technology believe, unequivocally, that we are on the cusp of a disruption that will change the world as we know it. On the other hand, there are the skeptics. While we would not want to lump them all together, there are certainly some skeptics who are threatened by the new technology. This includes those who may have some vested interest, professional or financial, in alternative or legacy tools and technology, as well as those who fear the focus is moving away from what they believe is the promise that a true public blockchain can provide. Legitimately, there is reason to be cynical from a technology perspective. But frontier technologies are built on healthy skepticism and experimentation.

In the discussions about how the implementation of these private networks such as Corda and Digital Asset are moving, the focus is away from the true decentralized nature of the blockchain. Currently, there are several serious challenges that cause impediments for the large-scale implementation of a true public blockchain. There are issues with scalability and latency with the blockchain model that utilizes cryptographic algorithms and shares the entire transaction history across every node in the network. At the time of this writing, there are few viable solutions to this problem, as most blockchain solutions do not provide the speed that is available using current technology. Use cases involving equity trading execution or card processing require execution cycles that DLT cannot currently provide. This explains why the current focus has been on creating post-trade processing solutions, such as for securities or derivatives settlement.

Another challenge for the technology relates to privacy laws. Several nations maintain data residency requirements. This means that any data that includes personally identifiable information may not reside outside of their national borders (Swan, 2015). Some other countries are not as restrictive but still limit access to personal data requiring strict role-based permissions, data masking and other techniques. These rules have an impact on the potential architecture, functionality and the ability to implement a public blockchain solution. Additionally, if we consider the use of a public blockchain that includes no central authority and is anonymous, how can sanctions and antimoney laundering regulations be monitored and maintained? This creates a major hurdle to obtain regulatory approval of any solution having this issue.

Get it Going First

Obviously, there are several technical and regulatory issues that remain to be solved before a true public blockchain model will become viable. So, what becomes of the work developing private networks that is ongoing with Corda, Digital Asset and others? There is much potential value to be gained from the implementation of a private DLT platform. The implementation of some form of DLT and Smart Contracts for the appropriate use cases may provide advantages in efficiency and maintaining audit trails over other alternatives. However, when considering any information technology (IT) implementation, it is important to choose the appropriate technology for the business problem you are trying to solve. The solution should never try to find the problem.

Thus, banks and other institutions must avoid considering use cases where latency and other technical or regulatory limitations would affect the success of the project. This may include maintaining the status quo by utilizing a central authority to avoid additional and unnecessary regulatory entanglements. Currently, regulators are providing varying degrees of support for the implementation of DLT. The Monetary Authority of Singapore (MAS) is directly promoting both securities settlement and cross-border payments using DLT technology. On the other hand, while some regulators have voiced concern for existing rules such as AML (anti-money laundering), most seem to be taking a more wait-and-see stance. It is critical to perform the appropriate planning, including viability and readiness assessments, prior to any potential rollout to ensure that the appropriate use cases are considered and that the integration to legacy systems is thoughtfully designed and executed. Institutions must be aware that business operating models and processes will be affected. Change management will also be an important consideration.

The discounting by the cynics of efforts being made by those as varied as the Depository Trust & Clearing Corporation (DTCC), the recently announced Enterprise Ethereum Alliance or MAS truly miss the point that this will be an evolution and not a revolution. The fact that these platforms do not provide what many consider a pure blockchain or are being implemented with a profit motive seems to bother some in the blockchain community. Any new technology that is to be implemented successfully on this scale will need investment from many parties. It will need that investment in start-ups and by established players, such as Microsoft and IBM, to overcome the current technological challenges. It will need investment from large institutions to spend portions of their IT budgets already strained from maintaining legacy systems and trying to keep up with emerging requirements of digital banking and changing regulations.

If we look back at the history of other technologies that have brought a paradigm shift, many have taken time; even years to replace legacy business models and systems. The development of a mature DLT platform will take time as well. The current implementations of DLT clearly are not the blockchain that underpins the virtual currency bitcoin. The tools and platforms such as the offerings from Digital Asset Holdings and R3 Corda are offered as a pragmatic answer to a set of current business, technological and regulatory challenges. By implementing the appropriate use cases the potential impact of the current challenges inherent in the bitcoin example – including scalability, latency and privacy – will be reduced. These challenges make the current public blockchain model a non-starter for banks.

In other parts of the world, regulators have been providing regulatory sandboxes for financial technology, such as blockchain. The trend started in the UK in February 2015 when the first Blockchain tech sandbox was launched. The sandbox allowed businesses to test out new and innovative financial services without incurring all the normal regulatory consequences of engaging in those activities, according to the Financial Conduct Authority Director of Strategy, Christopher Woolard, who have since been inundated with interest about their sandbox.

Singapore's Central Bank introduced a similar environment in August 2016, launching a regulatory sandbox to allow local fintech companies to experiment with their solutions. In November, the Thai Central Bank started a major fintech promotion, launching a sandbox that included blockchain tech start-ups. While designed for banks, non-bank technology firms with "sufficient capital and human resources" were invited too.

Big-four professional services firm KPMG released a report[1] attributing many Asian investments in blockchain fintech to this global trend of regulatory sandboxes. The firm pointed out that the governments in Hong Kong, Australia, Indonesia, and Malaysia all created or announced sandboxes for the banking sector during the third quarter of 2016. The firm described the push as part of a greater, worldwide embrace of fintech in general by governments and other monetary authorities.

Overcoming Limitations of Technology

The blockchain industry is still in the early stages of development, and there are many kinds of limitations. Ideally, the blockchain industry would develop similarly to the cloud-computing model, for which standard infrastructure components – like connectivity, processing, storage, and management systems – were defined and implemented very quickly at the beginning to allow the industry to focus on the higher level of developing value-added services instead of the core infrastructure. The current limitations are many but not insurmountable and include those related to technical issues with the underlying technology, public perception, government regulation, and reported thefts and scandals.

---

[1] "Global VC-backed fintech funding declines in Q3'16, but Asia investment reaches new high: KPMG and CB Insights." KPMG, November 16, 2016. https://home.kpmg.com/xx/en/home/media/press-releases/2016/11/global-vc-backed-fintech-funding-declines-in-q3-2016.html.

Technical Challenges

One main challenge with the underlying bitcoin blockchain technology is scaling up from the current maximum limit of seven transactions per second (the VISA credit card processing network customarily performs 2,000 transactions per second and can manage peak volumes of 10,000 transactions per second), especially if there were to be mainstream adoption of bitcoin (Lee, 2013). Some of the other issues include increasing the block size, addressing blockchain latency and bandwidth, countering vulnerability to mining attacks, and implementing hard forks (changes that are not backward compatible) to the code. There have been some significant advancements in this area as we speak.

Another significant technical challenge and requirement is that a full ecosystem of plug-and-play solutions be developed to provide the entire value chain of service delivery (Swan, 2015). For example, there needs to be secure decentralized storage, messaging, transport, communications protocols, namespace and address management, network administration, and archives linked to the blockchain ecosystem.

While it is possible that cryptotechnologies will see more adoption due to their flexibility and wider scope of potential use within banks, the benefits that distributed ledgers can bring to financial institutions and corporations will be dampened if a critical mass of adoption is not reached. If one bank uses distributed ledgers and another does not, a trade transaction involving those two banks will have to rely on legacy products and networks. Interoperability between distributed ledgers (as well as between distributed ledgers and legacy systems) will be key to enabling network effects that can produce benefits for all stakeholders. As banks and others look to the use of the blockchain in trade and finance, they should focus on how to bring industry participants together to create a network effective for blockchain-based platforms.

Business Challenges

At first traditional business models might not seem applicable to the blockchain economy since the whole point of decentralized P2P models is that there are no facilitating intermediaries to take a cut/transaction fee. However, some of the many types of business models that have developed with enterprise software and cloud computing might be applicable, too, for the blockchain economy – for example, the Red Hat model (fee-based services to implement open source software), and SaaS, providing Software as a Service, including with relevant modifications. Optimistically, the new blockchain era could usher in new types of jobs and opportunities.

Any solution will ultimately need to fit into an organization's existing financial ecosystem. Considering this fit beforehand will improve the integration process later, should the concept prove successful. Additionally, many technological partners offer different applications of distributed infrastructure technology. Choosing the partner that fits a business need and desired configuration is vital to the technology's individual success. Data privacy is another technological consideration. For example, while trading assets on an open blockchain may significantly cut costs, it is not a practical solution if all transactions are observable by all parties in the system. Consequently, the design of the technology itself will need to be reviewed depending on the application of choice.

Furthermore, moving any product or service from a centralized to a decentralized mode of operation will have vast impacts on an entire organization. A business' front office, operations, compliance, tax, accounting, legal, and technology offices are likely to be involved. Any strategic identification of opportunities to improve a business using this technology will therefore need to consider the end-to-end operational impact of each solution.

Government Regulatory Challenges

The likelihood of a decentralized system to become commonplace is not obvious as it would have to offer the same or higher level of trust and protection than the current one. For this to happen, the system would have to possess a massive amount of computer power and efficiently cope with the enormous energy consumption required to support it. In addition, it is not clear how this system would deal with legal and regulatory concerns, as well as with matters of national security, such as money laundering, fraud, tax evasion or terrorism. Moreover, digital currencies would not be exempt from potential crashes; like the current system, if their usage reaches substantial levels, these shocks could generate systemic risk and severe economic downturns. In this scenario, monetary policy would not be able to respond effectively if it fails to boost demand among a large share of economic agents that use digital currencies.

Regulatory approval can strongly impact the success of any distributed infrastructure implementation. For example, developing a distributed ledger to assist in the clearing and settlement of financial assets may involve custodial considerations, especially if assets are considered to be held on the network at any point. These custodial considerations may require a party to submit to regulatory requirements, which in turn could increase the compliance costs of such a system. On the other hand, a well-designed, standardized, automatically reconciled ledger could provide immediate real-time access to the relevant regulator for all partner institutions on the network. This could prove to save considerable costs and therefore outweigh the additional compliance costs involved in establishing the system.

One way to comfort regulators is to allow for permissioned access for regulatory audits. The sharing of data (be it with regulators, or other parties) can be done through permissioned access via encryption keys. The access can be granted by the blockchain owner (or system provider) for regulators (and other verified authorities in a particular investigation or audit check) to view the related areas where it would help in their duties. In these early phases of blockchain implementation, the utopian version of a truly public and fully decentralized blockchain system may have to wait until the regulators (and all other authorities) become comfortable with the idea of a digital economic system with decentralized operations.

Bitcoin and blockchain are themselves neutral; as any technology, they can be used for good or evil. Although there are possibilities for the malicious use of blockchain, the potential benefits greatly outweigh the potential downsides. Over time, public perception can change as more individuals themselves have e-wallets and begin to use bitcoin.

Privacy Challenges

There are many issues to be resolved before individuals feel comfortable storing their personal records in a decentralized manner with a pointer and possibly access via blockchain. The potential privacy nightmare is that if all your data is online and the secret key is stolen, lost (forgotten) or exposed, you have little recourse. In the current cryptocurrency architecture, there are many scenarios in which this might happen, just as today with personal and corporate passwords being routinely stolen or databases hacked. Any comprehensive solution must include a biometric measure that forms a bridge across the physical-cyberspace boundary. For complex, high value blockchain transactions, this legally reliable biometric connector will require a third party to confirm that the biometric measure is indeed the one belonging to the physical-space identity. Additionally, the blockchain application must incorporate a digital representation of a person's fingerprint, iris or retina pattern, or a photograph into the blockchain transaction. This means that the person's biometric information will not only exist permanently in cyberspace, it will be stored on hundreds or thousands of blockchain nodes, all beyond the control of the physical-space human being to which it belongs.

However, despite all of the potential limitations with the still-nascent blockchain economy, there is virtually no question that it is a disruptive force and that its impact will be significant. The blockchain economy has provided new larger-scale ideas about how to do things. Even if you do not buy into the future of bitcoin as a stable, long-term cryptocurrency, or blockchain technology as it is currently conceived and developing, there is a very strong case for decentralized models – the internet decentralized information and established the Information Age. The blockchain industry is one of the first identifiable large-scale implementations of decentralization models, conceived and executed to scale the complex levels of human activity, possibly even those that have yet to be imagined. Progressing toward decentralization of economic transactions would make future economic activities less restrictive and increase efficiency. Centralized systems may exist on top of the decentralized system but they will be few and will act as forms of governance or administrators. For governments and corporations that means massive cost reductions, like reducing banks' infrastructure costs attributable to cross-border payments, securities trading, and regulatory compliance by between US$15 and 20 billion per annum by 2022. For the society, this translates to better access, transactional efficiency, and savings. For Islamic finance, instead of developing new rules to control speculative and unrestrained reckless behaviors, blockchain embeds such governance measures within its technology as well as Islamic virtues that uphold the values of trust, honesty and transparency, and those that require fulfilling of obligations and responsibilities.

References

Back, A., Corallo, M., Dashjr, L., Friedenbacj, M., Maxwell, G., Miller, A., Poelstra, A., Timon, J., & Wuille, P. (2014). *Enabling Blockchain Innovations with Pegged Sidechains*. California, USA: Blockstream White Paper.

daCosta, F. (2013). *Rethinking the Internet of Things: A Scalable Approach to Connecting Everything*. New York: Apress.

Dawson, R. (2014). The New Layer of the Economy Enabled by M2M Payments in the Internet of Things. Trends in the Living Networks, September 16, 2014. http://rossdawsonblog.com/weblog/archives/2014/09/new-layer-economy-enabled-m2mpayments-internet-things.html

Ferrara, P. (2013). *Rethinking Money: The Rise of Hayek's Private Competing Currencies*. Forbes, March 1, 2013. http://www.forbes.com/sites/peterferrara/2013/03/01/rethinking-money-the-rise-of-hayeks-private-competing-currencies/

Lee, T.B. (2013). *Bitcoin Needs to Scale by a Factor of 1000 to Compete with Visa. Here's How to Do It*. The Washington Post, November 12, 2013. http://www.washingtonpost.com/blogs/the-switch/wp/2013/11/12/bitcoin-needs-to-scale-by-a-factor-of-1000-to-compete-with-visa-heres-how-to-do-it/.

Swan, M. (2015). *Blockchain: Blueprint for a New Economy*. USA: O'Reilly Media, Inc.

Chapter 9
Response of Islamic Financial Institutions

Introduction

Undoubtedly, fintech growth is unstoppable but understanding the future of fintech requires a re-engineering of how banks operate and in-depth analyses of its customer experience. E-commerce businesses like Amazon, Apple, Facebook, and Google prove that smart data management can create a customer understanding like no other. Across retail, wholesale, and capital markets, banks are keenly aware that the digital-first model based on high-performance data analysis will create a massive advantage. This chapter will discuss the key success determinants to remain competitive in the global market for Islamic financial institutions (IFIs) with the use of fintech. It will also elucidate the challenges, which the Islamic finance industry may face in the adoption and implementation of new tech. Finally, we end with a proposal for a collaborative approach for IFI in order to harmonize strategies and adapt to the rapidly changing landscape of the market.

Important Success Factors in this Era of Digitization

Better Customer Experience with Customer Centricity

Customer centricity has been one of the driving innovations in financial services, and this is also true for the Islamic finance industry. Tech-savvy digital consumers want more personalized services that enhance convenience and improve security. Shifting from product thinking to customer-centric offerings demands speed, agility, and the ability to innovate. Monetizing social media platforms have emerged as opportunities to diversify firms' income by engaging millennial consumers. Digital experience will draw people into continual virtual engagements and online transactions.

Customers are reshaping and redefining their expectations, taking their cues from several industries that provide multichannel access, seamless integration, product simplicity, and "segment-of-one" targeting.[1] In the last few years, it became clear that customers wanted to be able to do *everything* on their mobile phone, including applying for a bank account, or insurance claim. They want personalization, convenience, accessibility, and ease of use. They wanted to feel like their bank was anticipating their needs, not crafting product offerings that made sense only from the banks' bottom-line perspective. They expected no surprises and demanded

---

[1] "Segment-of-One Marketing" is the ability to track and understand individual customer behavior.

transparency in terms of fees. Seventy-five percent of PricewaterhouseCooper's (PwC's) survey respondents from the banking and fintech sector saw an increased focus on the customer as the most important area of impact to their business.

King (2014) forecasted that the future of the bank will have a very different organizational structure. He further argued that the entire customer facing organization and supporting platform needed to change radically. As customer expectations are changing, companies are forced to adapt. It is expected that in 2020, companies must focus on using big data to predict customer decisions and make such intelligence accessible throughout the enterprise. In the future, customers will want to do business with firms and companies that offer a consistent, informed and greater experience across all channels of communication, taking into consideration that customers will have different preferences.

There is fierce competition among banks and financial institutions to provide the most seamless services at the lowest price, to retain loyalty, and win new business. They are aware that providing customers with experience-rich banking and placing them foremost is essential for success. Those who manage and embrace the customer-centric approach will thrive in the market (Dharmesh, 2016).

Agility and Scalability

Agility is one of the most discussed and crucial attributes of successful fintech companies. The point of agility is the ability to adapt and be nimble in the environment of competition, unexpected and unanticipated changes and opportunities. For an organization, agility is needed to thrive and take advantage of changes by quickly assembling its organizational parts: technology, employees and management, in order to take advantage of an opportunity. In this way, any organization can cater to the needs of their customers in a changing and turbulent environment in an effective and deliberate way (Goldman, 1995).

Scalability is the capability of an entity to grow and to expand across markets. It also includes the ability and capacity of the technology to expand or accept expansion to perform the increased workload without compromising efficiency, and effectiveness. It is dealt with through networks, systems, and processes.

In organizational and business perspectives, scalability is most important to meet the demands of the market. It allows companies to reach new markets that would have required them to open a satellite office or a branch in a geographical location whose market they may not be familiar with, along with new employees that are not proven. Scalability allows businesses to expand across boundaries with a single team that can be based at the headquarters, where the company was originally founded, or regionally, if a presence in an area is of value.

Islamic banks need agile product and technology development skills to bring new products and capabilities to the market much quicker than today. This requires continual iteration, real-life pilot testing, and rapid learning from customers.

To foster the fintech or Islamic fintech industry, there is the need to establish an innovation ecology. Stefik and Stefik (2006) explained this term as: "An innovation ecology includes education, research organizations, government funding agencies, technology companies, investors, and consumers." Digital innovation will drive innovative products and services to the end users. It can also make products and services cheaper and more accessible for the unbanked and underbanked population.

The main entities within the innovation ecosystem are the regulators, Islamic fintech companies, IFIs, venture capitalists, government agencies, strategy and technology consultants, media and academia. These entities make up the demand and supply sides of the digital ecosystem. Every crucial component gives support to each other and strengthens each other for the attainment of common and collective objectives. Each party plays its role and uses its resource and capability to provide solutions. Regulators may provide innovation-friendly policies and an environment that gives incentives to Islamic fintech platforms to test and refine their innovative ideas, and IFIs may provide financial services or access to their internal sources and financial expertise. Incubators and regulatory sandboxes allow for the trial of prototypes in a controlled environment, while the media and academia may provide insights into trends and conduct proof-of-concept research to determine viable solutions for the gap in the industry. Managers must ensure their organizations can pivot with market shifts, even dropping or switching partnerships if the going gets too rough. The ability to adapt to new conditions will be a driving factor in maintaining the digital ecosystem, as partners and suppliers change, and customer needs evolve.

Developing partnerships with a range of actors in the Islamic digital ecosystem (see Figure 9.1) adds strength to the community and can be a strategic way for organizations to add value to existing efforts or shore-up their areas of shortcoming and deficiencies. Investments in core and emerging technologies will ultimately define the DNA of the ecosystem. Cloud services, analytics, node architecture and servers, cybersecurity and talent development should be the biggest planned investments in technology.

Cybersecurity Management

Cybersecurity is paramount to rebuilding trust and confidence that previous financial crises have eroded. Successful financial institutions will have invested considerably in this capacity. Recent high-profile security breaches and media commentary surrounding cyberattacks have bred fear and hesitation, further eroding stakeholder

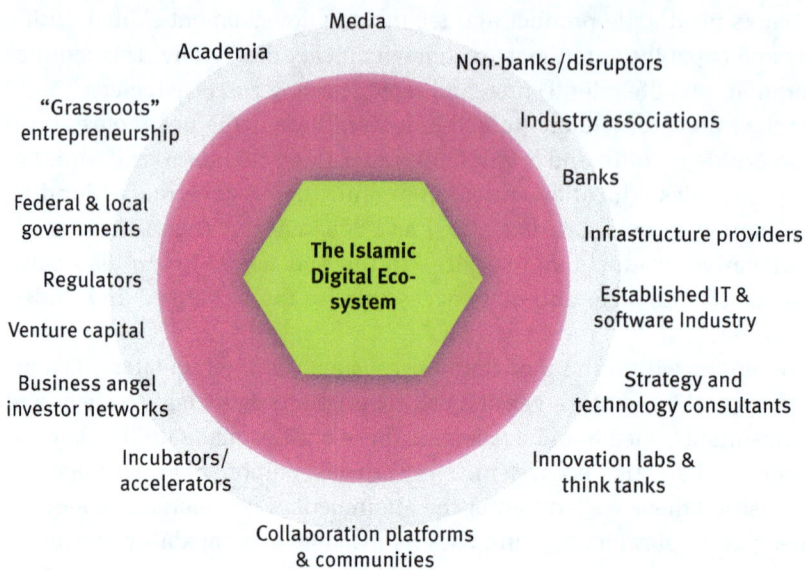

Figure 9.1: The Various Components to the Islamic Digital Ecosystem.

trust. There are now higher expectations about security of information and privacy among clients, employees, suppliers, and regulators. These risks include the internal misuse of social media and organized cybercrime (e.g., mass information theft, or denial-of-service attacks). This makes the fintech industry more vulnerable to cyber threats and attacks. Different reports (CB Insights, 2018; PwC, 2016c) show that cybersecurity management is the top concern of stakeholders of the fintech industry and also the traditional financial industry who are seeking to hire or build in-house fintech outfits or want to collaborate with proven fintech entities. Cybersecurity also attracts regulators to dig deeper into this matter that combines fintech and RegTech (Arner, Barberis, & Buckley, 2016).

The combined use of blockchain, big data, and artificial intelligence (AI) can lead to a better, more sophisticated, and integrated cybersecurity system, which is adaptable and effective. In addition, one of the major challenges from the end users is lack of awareness of cyber or digital risks (Villasenor, 2016) and also their negligence in taking precautionary measures while accessing financial services through digital channels. Awareness programs to educate users are helpful to manage the common cybersecurity risks.

For Islamic banks and institutions, a proactive response is vital. Key priorities include identifying and focusing resources on the business areas most in need of protection. As of 2020, leading banks have developed cybersecurity strategies that are aligned with their business objectives, risk-management protocols, and regulatory requirements. But many existing IFIs still lack the resources to tackle these issues on their own, and, hence, will have to partner with qualified third parties with a full understanding of security requirements, that includes a well-defined Incident Response Plan.

Challenges for Islamic Financial institutions

Regulatory Issues

Due to technological advancements and innovative models, the landscape of the financial industry is changing so spectacularly that it is completely transforming and shifting the world economy (Hayen, 2016). This dynamism in the world economy demands a dynamic and a new set of regulations to foster and regulate the growth of the fintech industry according to fair play, rule of law and best practices. According to International Data Group (IDC), it is estimated that the banks, investment banks and insurance companies globally are investing around US$85 billion just for the provision of regulatory oversight, legislative initiatives, and risk control.

The rule-making process also needs some changes due to its present glacial, unidirectional, and inflexible nature. An agile and results driven process of rule-making is important to set rules and boundaries for the ever-changing environment of finance, in particular, for the Islamic fintech industry (Brummer & Gorfine, 2014).

Regulatory support provides an ecology that helps to foster and promote the new or young entrepreneurs and also other Islamic financial institutions to test their innovative business models. In a few Islamic countries, like Malaysia, its central bank, Bank Negara Malaysia (BNM) is doing well in terms of creating an innovation-friendly regulatory environment, which can be observed from its well-established fintech (including the Islamic) ecosystem.

Likewise, it is advisable that other organizations like international Islamic financial forums and influential entities, like AAOIFI, IsDB, IFSB, ISRA, and IRTI start sharing and discussing new ideas and collaborate with Muslim entrepreneurs to enhance regulations, which can support further growth of Islamic fintech ecosystems worldwide. It is heartening to see that in the second half of 2017 and in 2018, events like the 2nd World Islamic Finance Forum, Blockchain and Waqf have placed fintech as their main themes in their forums. These are indeed encouraging signs that signal awareness and acceptance. Such initiatives provide avenues for regulators and governing authorities to discuss the complex multidimensional issues faced by the Islamic fintech industry and begin engagements with the industry on viable and practical regulations for the industry. Regulators do not want industry players just adhering to rules, or checking boxes but rather, they want them to embrace regulatory intent, and create sound, secure, unbiased businesses, where regulatory compliance and sound conduct is embedded in the processes and values of everyday operations.

Moving forward, the industry could come to a consensus on a set of prudential regulations for Islamic finance (including fintech), which can be applicable in all regions. The formation of consortia and alliances among IFIs, fintech platforms, academia, and regulatory authorities can be a good step forward.

Comfort Zones and Stagnation in Management

The hard regulations and legacy culture in an organization are infused with each other. This impedes the path of an organization to move forward especially when it comes to the path of innovation. This culture of layering and folding of management in decision-making traps an organization in the ropes of stagnation. Risk averse behavior of management becomes more complex when diffused from lower to top management. Fintech provides for quicker, more informed decision making and calculated risk-taking behaviors.

Fintech focuses on access and control of the customers' financial transactions, and Islamic fintech will provide the personalization of finance to the customers by using digital channels and innovative business models within the deployment of big data, AI, and blockchain. The process from inception and opening of an account or executing an investment to the final rewards and other financial transactions can be directly controlled by the end users in fintech solutions.

In a financial organization that is encumbered by layers of management, it is not easily possible to do experimentation for new innovative products and business models. Getting approvals alone will take ages. In addition, experimentation involves failure and the fear of failure results in the lack of support of innovation. It is a fact that without experimentation in this era of digitalization, financial institutions will fail to compete and will not be able to provide the services and products, which the consumers expect.

The Islamic financial industry appears to be slower in the adaptation and experimentation of digitization. There are a number of conventional institutions like CITI bank, Barclays, Bank of England (BOE), and so forth, which have already made innovation labs and incubators to conduct in-house experimental trials by deploying advanced technologies, that is, big data, AI, and blockchain, etc., at different phases. But, IFIs are not showing agility and activeness in this regard. Management of IFIs need to give priority to transforming their organizations because disruptive change is inevitable and it is happening fast. IFIs need to create incentives for innovation and consider how all partners and suppliers contribute to their business development. Partners will drive innovation and growth as the businesses adopt, consume, scale, and leverage innovation for greater market share leadership.

For example, a leading financial services company turned to agile software development to support its goal of organizing around customer experiences rather than products (Olsen et al., 2017). In doing so, it sharpened the focus on raising speed to market and ensuring consistently high customer loyalty scores for sales and service delivery, especially in predominantly digital channels. The company uses agile, cross-functional teams of eight to ten people, aligned to specific customer episodes. Each team brings together the requisite capabilities in business, design, processes, and technology. The company now is taking its experience-led agile approach to scale across the enterprise, through waves of applied learning sessions, and is well on its way to improving productivity by three to four times.

Lack of Talent

Since the beginning of Islamic banking and finance in 1970s, one of the major challenges this industry is facing is lack of skilled talent. Financial Accreditation Agency of Malaysia claimed that in Malaysia, there is the need and demand of approximately 56,000 additional people in the Islamic financial industry by 2020 (WIEF, 2017). Obeidat (2016) also highlighted in his research about human capital in Islamic finance that the sustainability and competitiveness of the Islamic financial industry is highly dependent on the skills and talents of its human capital.

The fintech industry is bringing together information technology (IT) professionals, data scientists, entrepreneurs, programmers, etc., to the financial services industry. This entry of new and diverse skilled people in the circle of the financial services industry makes the fintech industry more diversified and innovative but also somewhat complex. The additional requirement of Shariah expertise and Islamic economics/finance understanding further narrows talent availability. An ideal leader of an IFI would have to be someone adept in business, economics, finance and the Shariah as well as have a technical understanding of new technology.

One way to overcome the dire need of skilled and talented human capital, could be to increase the production of skilled human capital through effective education of intellectual capital in academia and research. The need to bridge academic curricula to the needs of industry is also critical to bring much needed solutions to real problems. Although there are a number of institutions that have already began running courses as part of degree programs in conventional fintech, there are none in Islamic finance programs. There is not a single course on fintech with regards to Islamic finance (ICD &Thomson Reuters, 2017). This is indeed very alarming and requires immediate resolution. When fintech and innovation programs are in place, there should be industrial attachment programs for tertiary students in the form of internships, project collaborations, and exchange programs. For the public or older folks who seek alternative career paths, coding academies need to be developed to skill those interested in coding and programming. It is fairly obvious that as the finance industry gets disrupted, the redundant professionals lose their jobs but the disrupters continue to employ coders, programmers, various IT specialists, and data scientists.

At the university and think tank levels, there should be more collaboration across disciplines, and collaborative cross-training and interdisciplinary research programs to complete the fintech ecosystem to supply quality and knowledgeable talents.

At the bank level, as automation pervades more activities, their workforce must evolve. Thousands of roles are becoming obsolete, including tellers, backoffice processors – even routine call-center agents, as chatbots and robo-advisors take on simple inquiries. Conventional technologies have helped banks to double labor productivity every few years through digitalizing processes and applying more sophisticated industrial methods like capacity planning and lean six sigma. Opimas, a research firm, estimates that by 2025, the rollout of AI technology by financial institutions will reduce employment in the capital markets by 230,000 people, with the largest impact in the asset management industry, where machines will replace around 90,000 people (Olsen et al., 2017). Taiger, for instance, combines machine learning with natural-language processing to automatically identify, extract, cleanse and validate pieces of information from many types of documents. The banking applications include client onboarding, due diligence and combating money laundering. After a large European bank shifted to Taiger's technology for client onboarding, its cost fell 85% and turnaround time shrank from several weeks to seven minutes, with no loss in quality. As AI spreads throughout the industry, bank professionals who previously performed those activities will have to upgrade their expertise to remain relevant.

The greatest talent challenge for IFIs is attracting technical specialists. There is a worldwide shortage of talent in advanced analytics, new technologies such as blockchain and customer experience design. The shortage is worsened by competition from more attractive fintech start-ups and companies that are building interesting solutions. Banks will have to get creative in attracting and nurturing top talent, through incentives such as elevating top performers into key roles with more latitude and flexibility for further innovation, while adapting their respective organizational cultures to manifest this new reality.

Role of Academia and Islamic Fintech Education

In 2018, there were a total of 968 Islamic Finance Education (IFE) providers spread across 77 countries (Refinitiv et al., 2020). There are many types of degrees such as Bachelor's, Diploma, Master and PhD offered in the universities; the bachelor's degree is at the top with a total number of 605, which is based on various subjects such as takaful, Islamic banking, Islamic capital market and Islamic economics. These degrees and program are mainly offered in four countries such as Pakistan, Malaysia, Indonesia, and the UAE. Diplomas in Islamic finance have gained widespread currency; 75 universities in the UAE, the UK, Malaysia, and some other countries are offering 83 basic and advanced diplomas. Out of a total of 968 courses, 445 consists of Islamic finance courses, 371 consist of degree program, and 152 provide basic qualifications. Out of the total, 355 were in Indonesia followed by the UK and Malaysia with 72 and 62 respectively. The coupling of Islamic finance courses with general business studies results in the most common trend. In the UAE alone, the country requires 8,000 more Islamic banking professionals to close the gap of professionals' shortage in its 84 Islamic finance providing institutions such as takaful and Islamic banks.

There has been continuously mushrooming of new private colleges including the bogus ones. Besides, even the public universities of high esteem have diverse curriculums for master's degree, MPhil, and PhD program of Islamic finance. This state of affairs creates confusion not only among students but among staff and practitioners as well. The supervision in IFE for research students is not of a good quality. So, in conclusion, the following points should be noted:

1. The one-way indulgence of IFE with mainstream economics is diverting its curriculum design and structure. It shows the high potential of diverting the IFE to the deviant ideas and terminologies. This trend must be stopped.
2. There is a lot of diversity in courses in IFE offered by different universities. So, some degree of standardization with a measure of flexibility is required. The establishment of accreditation institutions may help to come to grips with the problem.
3. The creation of a proper research environment with sound infrastructure, cooperation between teachers and students, and strong critical thinking skills will be helpful in accelerating the pace and the quality of research development.
4. As the number of students in PhD program is not high. So, for ensuring the quality of research. The doctoral studies should be limited to some universities. It will help in promoting and strengthening excellence. With this cost-effective measure, the output will be more satisfactory and effective
5. The academic staff should be selected based on qualification and merit, rather than connections.
6. The reading material must be prepared by both economists and shariah scholars. This effort will help in the production of professionals, which are both experts in shariah and economy.

Taking the status of IFE into the account, especially in the contemporary digital era, it imperative to produce learned scholars who are both tech savvy and well-versed in the domains of Shariah and finance. Only a comprehensive IFE model can play a substantial role in addressing the challenges faced by this emerging industry.

Muslim scholars need to work on the technological aspects of Islamic finance further, in order to develop and enhance the efficacy of Islamic finance industry. For example, Fintech, Blockchain, Augmented Reality (AR), Virtual Reality (VR) and IoT technologies should attract the attention. The financial technology (Fintech) performs a valuable role in making Islamic finance more accessible customers. At present, we find the leading role of the Fintech industry in financial and banking services. The Islamic finance industry appears highly well-matched that can develop further with Fintech and can accommodate Muslim countries globally to fulfil their desire of using the Shariah-compliant financial system while dealing with different banking and financial transactions. The use of the technology in automating back-office processes is making Islamic finance institutions more beneficial and viable. There is a widely growing network of Islamic Fintech corporations nowadays including Robo-advisory firms like Wahed Invest, and in micro-finance such as Ethis Ventures and Blossom Finance that represent promising partners for Islamic financial institutions (Thomson Reuters & DinarStandard, 2018).

The existing challenges and obstacles in providing quality and result-oriented Islamic finance education and the preparation of competent Shariah scholars and well skilled human capital (as discussed above), require us to frame and develop a comprehensive curriculum that can balance the three significant domains of Shariah, finance and technology in the industry. The need of the hour is the designing of a curriculum that will bridge the gap of knowledge and expertise between the scholars that are trained in Shariah, finance and technology. It should help scholars to use Shariah principles in developing innovative and technology-based, Shariah-compliant products for the industry that are market viable in the modern world. The scholars who are highly equipped with modern technology and at the same time are knowledgeable about in Shariah and finance can provide better alternatives to the financial sector and banking industry. Such scholars can play a significant role in guiding and directing the industry in achieving the objectives of Shariah. The presentation of order, the achievement of benefit, the prevention of harm and the establishment of equality.

Collaboration Models for Islamic Financial Institutions

Interoperability, coordination and collaboration are the essential elements of any developed and successful ecosystem around the globe. This involves different governments, public and private sectors indigenously and outside the region. Public and private sectors can establish safe, secure, reliable, and affordable open and shared platforms for digital payments, banking services and other financial alternatives by converging their offers via omnichannels (offering the customers integrated consistent financial platforms), including decentralized shared ledgers. This will work as the catalyst of financial inclusion and will also enhance the adoption of basic and primary financial services at a larger scale.

This trend of interoperability, coordination and collaboration is pervasive and is prevailing around the world. For example, the Postal Savings Bank of China (PSBC), China's largest lender having a branch network of 40,000 branches, has deepened cooperation with Ant Financial and Tencent in internet and mobile finance. The online banks also aligned with the Chinese government's policy by providing access to financial services to the unbanked Chinese (Duflos, 2015).

Peer-to-peer (P2P) lenders Jimubox, RenRenDai, and Minshengyidai and China Minsheng Bank are helping each other to manage and safeguard funds of investors (Ernst & Young EY, 2016). Dianrong.com and the regional Bank of Suzhou setup a collaboration agreement in 2014 to target small enterprises (Finextra, 2014). More examples exist around the globe.

Interoperability, coordination, and collaboration involve different branches of the government, public and private sectors, indigenously as well as outside the region. Public and private sectors can establish safe, secure, reliable, and affordable shared platforms for digital payments, banking services and other financial alternatives by converging themselves via digital omni channels. This will work as the catalyst of financial inclusion and will also enhance the adoption of basic and primary financial services at a larger scale to those who may not have had access previously.

A comprehensive analysis of different models of collaborations between fintech companies and banks has been done in two reports provided by (EY, 2017; TheCityUK, 2017). Different collaboration models are explained and discussed in these reports. Some of the prominent models are as follows:

– *Hackathons*:
This model is not very formal, and usually is a fun way to invite start-ups and fintech companies to provide a solution on a particular use case or business challenge. Hackathons typically take place in teams and groups of coder-entrepreneurs and programmers. In these events, the organizers set off to test early-stage protypes and ideas in an attempt to solve specific problems and offer solutions. IFIs can get quick and innovative solutions through these kinds of events while fintech companies get to pitch their ideas and take a shot at getting funded or recruited. An example of this model is the LGB innovation lab set by the Lloyds Banking group to test prototypes and find solutions to their operational issues.

– *Start-up Corporate Accelerator Model*:
In this model, fintech companies submit their applications to IFIs to propose solutions or innovation to existing problems in the form of products or services. IFIs then short-list a number of fintech applicants to further develop the proposed innovative services and products. They work together in twelve-week programs where every aspect of the solution is refined and perfected through industry experts' mentorship and internal sources that IFIs are willing to provide. Beyond merely a collaborative arrangement, this model eventually involves equity agreements where IFIs take equity stake in the fintech companies that successfully graduate from their intensive accelerator programs.

– *Enterprise Solutions*:
In this model, IFIs select products or services developed by a fintech vendor and test them in focused groups or preselected group of customers. Upon successful trials, the IFI then scales up the product to its wider market segment. This is a straight-up commercial type of collaboration in which both parties work toward an enterprise solution that can be disseminated throughout the business organization.

– *Model of Corporate Venture Capital* (CVC):
CVC is the investment of corporate funds directly in external start-up companies. This is a simple arrangement in which the IFI takes a minor stake in one or many up-and-coming fintech companies, to secure access to innovative products and services once these fintechs come into the market and start operations. According to the 2017 CB Insights Corporate Venture Capital Report,[2] the number of new CVC firms making first-time investments reached record levels in 2017. One hundred and eighty-six new corporate venture capital (VC) units globally made their first investment in 2017, including stock exchange Nasdaq Ventures, and life insurance provider Northwestern Mutual, among others. Compared to 2016, the number of new corporate VC units making their first investment increased 66%, up from 112.

– *Hybrid Model*:
Hybrid model combines two or more than two models in a manner that IFIs and Islamic fintech platforms will get benefits and share the rewards of collaboration and cooperation. This may include a collaborative agreement based on support and cooperation, and also a commercial agreement that may be based on any other model like CVC, Start-up Corporate Accelerator model. Hackathons also can help IFIs to attract innovative and creative minds who can create much-needed solutions. In a hybrid model all involved parties can reap more benefits and also reduce risks and uncertainty regarding intellectual rights, ownership, costs and profits.

Islamic Fintech Is Opportunity for Islamic Financial Institutions

The report provided by Accenture (2016) shows that banks are now recognizing that fintech companies typically pose more of an opportunity than a threat. The same results are also found in a survey conducted by Finextra and Dove-tail (2017). The majority of the surveys' respondents think that fintech is a great opportunity for the financial industry. In another report (PwC, 2016a) when the respondents were asked a question regarding the main opportunities related to the rise of fintech, majority of the respondents said that fintech reduces costs and improves customer

---

2 https://www.cbinsights.com/research/report/corporate-venture-capital-trends-2017/.

retention. Similarly, in another survey also conducted by PwC (2016c) insurers concluded that the most significant gain from fintech is cost reduction and disintermediation. The report also identified that although people need finance for various reasons like health, education, and setting up small businesses, they cannot be served by Islamic banks with their existing product structures and assessment of customer credit ratings. The paper also highlights the geographical footprint of Islamic banks, which shows that they are primarily operating in big urban cities. Finally, it is argued that most of the Islamic banking debt-based products are close, but relatively expensive, substitutes for conventional banking in terms of financial costs (Shaikh, 2018).

Islamic fintech poses great opportunities for the IFIs. In a recent survey conducted by Council for Islamic Banks and Financial Institutions (CIBAFI), the majority of respondents from the Islamic financial industry agree that Islamic fintech is a great opportunity for IFIs in terms of cutting costs and offering innovative products and eventually reaching the unbanked Muslim population (Vizcaino, 2018). For Southeast Asia, fintech can play the role of change agent toward financial inclusion. According to KPMG,[3] only 27% of the region's 600 million people have a bank account (as of April 2016). This implies that 438 million people do not have access to traditional financial services in this region and in poorer countries like Cambodia, only 5% have bank accounts. This is one of the major reasons for sustained poverty in the region. Notably, Southeast Asia has a higher than global average mobile phone penetration rate. Financial services provided by fintech companies over the mobile phone, such as money transfers at low-cost and short-terms loans, could help to bring people out of poverty in the region. According to the KPMG report, reaching the unbanked population in Association of Southeast Asian Nations (ASEAN) could increase the economic contribution of the region from US$17 billion (2016) to US$52 billion by 2030. Fintech start-ups have the potential to usher in serious social change in the region.

Collaboration Is Better than Competition

It is paramount for traditional IFIs and Islamic fintech to meet the needs of digital transformation and keep on the track of journey of innovation to remain relevant and sustainable.

Traditional IFIs are considered slow in reaction to changes due to many limitations, including additional Shariah regulatory controls and risk averse culture, which do not tend to plague their conventional counterparts. However, IFIs do

---

[3] https://home.kpmg.com/xx/en/home/insights/2016/04/FinTech-opening-the-door-to-the-un-banked-and-underbanked-in-southeast-asia.html.

have some key advantages, if they but recognize them. They have, over a relatively short period of time, built customers' trust, a large network of interested individuals, ethical businesses, and financing resources. To adapt and remain competitive, Islamic banks must overcome old business models, which cannot be modified by implementing new strategies. In short, the fastest way to evolve is for the traditional financial institutions to embrace new partnerships and collaborations with younger and forward-looking start-ups and fintech developers who provide the technological skill-sets to reinvent the future of banking and financial services.

Open Platforms

The traditional approach and model of innovation is called *closed innovation*. This is a model of innovation where organizations use their limited and internal resources, systems, and human power to take initiative and implement their ideas (Fasnacht, 2009). The new paradigm of innovation is called *open innovation*. Open innovation has gained a lot of attention from scholars in the past decade (Mina et al., 2014). The match of open innovation with technological revolution and financial industry's strategy also became the mouthpiece at conferences and seminars, etc. Open innovation authors and scholars mainly focused on the demand and need for the financial organization to surpass their limitations and internal boundaries for accepting and sourcing the paths of knowledge, technology and opportunities (Felin and Zenger, 2014).

For IFIs and also for the Islamic fintech industry, it is noteworthy to give importance and emphasis to open innovation as a central strategy. This brings more efficiency in the operations of an organization throughout the whole process of a customer-centric product development. Also, open innovation is a major element of the collaborative business model, which enables organizations to be flexible and enhance their competitive advantage through leveraging external sources of knowledge, technology, and expertise.

Open Banking or Financial Platforms

The business model of the bank of the future will progress toward an open banking system. Open banking means a platform-based business approach where data, processes, and business functionality are made available to an ecosystem of customers, third-party developers, fintech start-ups, or other strategic partners. The financial services provided may come from banks as well as third parties, like private investors on crowd-funding platforms, HNWIs, venture capitalists or private equity firms. These platforms can be owned by the financial institution or by an enterprising entity (others).

The Financial Institution Owns the Platform

In this platform, the banks develop and own their digital platform where financial products and services from the bank, or not (i.e., from third parties), are offered to the bank's customers. They provide basic offerings and additionally source and/or resell (niche) third-party services, integrating those services in the offer (or redirecting consumers to the third party, that is, a broker business model). This model requires the bank to master the technical integration of the application program interfaces (APIs), as well as processing and analysis of third-party data (as in account aggregation). They will have to manage client relationships, including touchpoints through user interface and user experience (UI/UX), while having the ability to offer "a digital marketplace" where third parties can showcase their products and services to the bank's customers. An example is Royal Bank of Canada teaming up with Wave (a fintech outfit) to integrate accounting, financial and invoicing insights into its online business banking platform. Or Royal Bank of Scotland launching its own automated lending platform in response to the emergence of P2P lending platforms, which was developed by a white-label fintech company called Ezbob.

Other Ownership of the Platform

In this model, the IFI has to develop a niche product expertise area. It must position itself as the leading supplier of a particular product or service (e.g., credit financing) on third-party platforms. This strategy requires them to be narrowly focused yet offering such products or services on multiple other platforms, which require preferred agreement or partnerships with the hosting platforms. An example is Transferwise, which offers international money transfers (multi-currency) in a quicker and cheaper way than traditional banks. Such value will replace money transfer facilities in banks (and elsewhere, like Western Union) as Transferwise gains traction and expands to other platforms. AliPay and AmazonPay are examples that focus on payments, and WeChat on P2P mobile payment.

Fundamental to adapting to the shifts toward the future of financial services and banking, Islamic banks and financial institutions need to:
A. Create the right platform or select the best-fit ones, that is, those that bring the best customer experience or provide the best personalized services (the right service or product at the right time). Those institutions who are able to develop winning platforms through the right use of technology and the right partnerships suited for the products and services will be successful. This can be achieved through deep learning on customers' behaviors through big data analytics and machine learning.

B. Develop adaptive and agile responses to changing business environment. Traditional banks are focused on minimizing risks, while today's customers demand that already, they also expect speed and creative customization to existing products and services. The impact of digital transformation in banking will require Islamic banks to rethink the way the financial ecosystem operates and functions, with a new set of capabilities and closer partnerships with highly agile start-ups and third-party vendors or developers.

Beyond maintaining a strong, independent risk management function that is focused on the core financial risks that banks face, sufficient oversight of operational and reputational risk will be critical.
- Cybersecurity is now at the top of everyone's mind as new technologies, like mobile, expose customer data to greater risks.
- Vendor risk will need to be managed more closely. Islamic banks have many partners, and are responsible and accountable, from all aspects of operations and governance.
- Islamic banks have become information hubs and potential targets as governments ensure the proper payment of taxes, compliance with Shariah and KYC/AML/CTF laws, sanctions, etc.
- Increased regulatory requirements such as stress testing and IFSBs drive greater operational and reputational risk. Islamic banks will need to be able to report detailed information on portfolio metrics, trends, and be able to rapidly model alternative scenarios.
- Risk management will expand and interact more closely with every area of the bank including marketing, product development, business analytics and compensation. This requires a more robust end-to-end view of the business, and an expanded skill set within the risk organization.

Conclusion

Disruptions in banking are pushing all banks (conventional and Islamic) to take more explicit strategy decisions. Many banks have recognized that they need a truly differentiated strategy as the industry's economics have come under pressure from new technology and nontraditional entrants with disruptive business models. Large nonfinance technology firms have also been moving into markets such as payments, raising customers' expectations for better digital tools and simple, convenient service. Ever-stricter capital and liquidity requirements by regulators have reduced banks' own balance sheet leverage. Low interest rates and low economic growth intensify this pressure that weighs on them.

Difficult as strategic choices may be, banks are finding it even more challenging to adapt their operating models quickly to a new strategy – indeed, it is often the biggest obstacle to implementing a distinctive strategy. At present, much effort and money go into operating legacy processes and dealing with regulatory requirements to keep the bank running. Gartner estimates that banks on average spend roughly 60% of their IT budgets to maintain legacy IT systems as compared to just 24% to grow the business and 16% to transform it (Olsen et al., 2017). The global financial crisis, moreover, prompted a greater scrutiny of fiduciary duties, and created mistrust in the banks' legacy talent, systems, and processes, which is being overhauled by the current disruptive revolution.

The promise of blockchain and fintech creates the possibility of coordinating our transactional activities through a multi-strength mechanism of trust and transparency within the now globalized economy. Blockchain is the technology that would operationalize the mechanism of trust as we progress from personal exchange to impersonal exchange without an intermediary. We suspect that the blockchain technological backbone will be commonplace in four to six years' time, through the proliferation of cryptocurrencies, smart contracts, full-reserve lending platforms, multicurrency money transfers, public registries, document consolidation and other processes that are yet to be imagined.

From a broader perspective, fintech will overcome conventional ways of banking/finance/insurance in the coming years and if Islamic economies do not embrace it and develop their own technological ecosystem, they will lose the unprecedented opportunity to level up a 450-year gap in finance that has long suppressed them. The adoption of all forms of financial technology will allow Islamic finance to adapt to the changing landscape of modern economic transactions and carve its own niche in the future digital economy.

References

Accenture. (2016). *FinTech and the Evolving Landscape: Landing Points for the Industry*. https://www.finextra.com/finextra-downloads/newsdocs/accentureFinTech2016.pdf
Arner, D. W., Barberis, J. N., & Buckley, R. P. (2016). FinTech, Regtech and the Reconceptualization of Financial Regulation. *Northwestern Journal of International Law & Business, 37*(3), 1–51.
Bondi, A. B. (2000). Characteristics of Scalability and their Impact on Performance. In *Proceedings of the 2nd International Workshop on Software and Performance* (pp. 195–203). ACM.
Broby, D., & Karkkainen, T. (2016). FINTECH in Scotland: Building a Digital Future for the Financial Sector. Conference paper at the "The Future of Fintech" by International Financial Services District (IFSD), The Technology Innovation Centre, Glasgow. 2 September 2016.
Brummer, C., & Gorfine, D. (2014). FinTech: Building a 21st Century Regulator's Toolkit. *Milken Institute*, 5, 1–15.
CB Insights. (2018). *FinTech Trends to Watch in 2018*. https://research/report/FinTech-trends-2018/
Chishti, S., Barberis, J., & Telfer, J. (2017). *The FINTECH Book: The Financial Technology Handbook for Investors, Entrepreneurs and Visionaries* (Unabridged edition). New York, USA: Audible Studios on Brilliance Audio.

Christensen, C. M. (1997). *The Innovator's Dilemma: When New Technologies Cause Great Firms to Fail (Management of Innovation and Change Series)* (1st ed.). http://gen.lib.rus.ec/book/index.php?md5=84A9DF9C12DFC0314FFFAF2B5BAFE293

Crossan, M. M., & Apaydin, M. (2010). A Multi-Dimensional Framework of Organizational Innovation: A Systematic Review of the Literature. *Journal of Management Studies*, 47(6), 1154–1191.

Dharmesh, M. (2016). Racing from Digital Engagement to Customer Intimacy. https://www.temenos.com/en/market-insight/2016/racing-from-digital-engagement-to-customer-intimacy/

Duflos, E. (2015). New Accounts in China Drive Global Financial Inclusion Figures. Retrieved October 2, 2017, http://blogs.worldbank.org/eastasiapacific/new-accounts-china-drive-global-financial-inclusion-figures. June 18.

Engelen, E., Erturk, I., Froud, J., Leaver, A., & Williams, K. (2010). Reconceptualizing Financial Innovation: Frame, Conjuncture and Bricolage. *Economy and Society*, 39(1), 33–63.

Ernst & Young EY. (2016). *The Rise of FinTech in China* (p. 48). http://www.ey.com/Publication/vwLUAssets/ey-the-rise-of-FinTech-in-china/$FILE/ey-the-rise-of-FinTech-in-china.pdf

EY. (2017). *Unleashing the Potential of FinTechs*. http://www.ey.com/Publication/vwLUAssets/ey-unleashing-the-potential-of-fin-tech-in-banking/$File/ey-unleashing-the-potential-of-fin-tech-in-banking.pdf

Fasnacht, D. (2009). *Open Innovation in the Financial Services Growing Through Openness, Flexibility and Customer Integration*. Springer. http://gen.lib.rus.ec/book/index.php?md5=FB32984EA316E14716C4E0CA8362AF51

Felin, T., & Zenger, T. R. (2014). Closed or Open Innovation? Problem Solving and the Governance Choice. *Research Policy*, 43(5), 914–925. https://doi.org/10.1016/j.respol.2013.09.006

Finextra. (2014, October 13). Bank of Suzhou Collaborates with Dianrong.com on P2P Loans platform. Retrieved October 2, 2017, https://www.finextra.com/pressarticle/57122/bank-of-suzhou-collaborates-with-dianrongcom-on-p2p-loans-platform

Finextra and Dovetail. (2017). *Payments Transformation: Modernising to Stay Relevant in the Digital A*. https://www.finextra.com/surveys/survey.aspx?surveyguid=9d2938cf-345f-43a5-9564-0f28c8398eb8

Finocracy, Alabed. A., & Mirakhor, A. (2017). Accelerating Risk Sharing Finance Via FinTech: Nextgen Islamic Finance. https://journal.wahedinvest.com/nextgen-islamic-finance/

Goldman, S. L. (1995). *Agile Competitors and Virtual Organizations: Strategies for Enriching the Customer*. New York, USA: Van Nostrand Reinhold Company.

Hayen, R. (2016). *FinTech: The Impact and Influence of Financial Technology on Banking and the Finance Industry*. California, USA: Createspace Independent Publishing Platform.

Hitcher, W. (2006). *The Innovation Paradigm*. http://gen.lib.rus.ec/book/index.php?md5=084ADF239859E7609460E88756E70DDF

ICD, and Thomson Reuters. (2017). *ICD-Thomson Reuters Islamic Finance Development Report 2017*. https://www.icd-ps.org/en/common/viewfile?FilePath=~/Uploads/publication/doc/20171205113348810IFDIReport2017.pdf

INCEIF Refinitiv Islamic Finance Knowledge Outlook Report 2020: *Taking Islamic Finance Education to New Heights*.

Irrera, A. (2018, March 6). World Economic Forum Leads Creation of FinTech Cyber Security . . . *Reuters*. https://www.reuters.com/article/us-cyber-FinTech/world-economic-forum-leads-creation-of-FinTech-cybersecurity-consortium-idUSKCN1GI17G

Jagtiani, J., & Lemieux, C. (2017). *FinTech Lending: Financial Inclusion, Risk Pricing, and Alternative Information* (SSRN Scholarly Paper No. ID 3005260). Rochester, NY: Social Science Research Network. https://papers.ssrn.com/abstract=3005260

King, B. (2014). *Breaking Banks: The Innovators, Rogues, and Strategists Rebooting Banking* (1st edition). New York, USA: Wiley.

Koen, P. A., Bertels, H. M., & Elsum, I. R. (2011). The Three Faces of Business Model Innovation: Challenges for Established Firms. *Research-Technology Management, 54*(3), 52–59.

Lacasse, R.-M., Lambert, B., & Khan, N. (2017). Blockchain Technology-Arsenal for a Shariah-Compliant Financial Ecosystem. 5th International Conference of Entrepreneurial Finance, CIFEMA 2017.

Lajis, S. M. (2017). Risk Sharing: Optimising True Potential of Islamic Finance. International Colloquium On Islamic Banking And Islamic Finance Conference, Iran.

Lo, W. K. (1998). Agility, Job Satisfaction and Organizational Excellence–Their Factors and Relationships. *ISO, 9000*, 330–336.

Luke, E. A. (1993). Defining and Measuring Scalability. In *Proceedings of the Scalable Parallel Libraries Conference, 1993* (pp. 183–186). IEEE.

Mina, A., Bascavusoglu-Moreau, E., & Hughes, A. (2014). Open Service Innovation and the Firm's Search for External Knowledge. *Research Policy, 43*(5), 853–866.

Nicoletti, B. (2017). *The Future of FinTech: Integrating Finance and Technology in Financial Services* (1st ed. 2017 edition). Cham: Palgrave Macmillan.

Obeidat, Z. M. (2016). Human Capital Investment and Training in Islamic Banking Industry in Jordan Jordan Islamic Bank for Finance and Investment. *European Scientific Journal, ESJ, 12*(10).

Olsen, T., Judah, M., Fielding, J., Nielsen, N. P., & Phillips, S. (2017). New Bank Strategies Require New Operating Models. Bain & Company's Financial Services. Singapore, Melbourne, New York, Copenhagen and London.

PwC. (2016a). *Catching the FinTech Wave: A Survey on FinTech in Malaysia.* https://www.pwc.com/my/en/publications/catching-the-FinTech-wave.html

PwC. (2016b). *Opportunities Await: How InsurTech Is Reshaping Insurance.* https://www.pwccn.com/en/industries/financial-services/publications/opportunities-await-how-insurtech-is-reshaping-insurance.html

PwC. (2016c). *Turnaround and Transformation in Cybersecurity.* https://www.pwc.com/sg/en/publications/assets/pwc-global-state-of-information-security-survey-2016.pdf

Refinitiv, I., Finance, I., & Outlook, K. (2020). *Taking Islamic Finance Education to New Heights.* UAE.

Sambamurthy, V., Bharadwaj, A., & Grover, V. (2003). Shaping Agility Through Digital Options: Reconceptualizing the Role of Information Technology in Contemporary Firms. *MIS Quarterly, 27*, 237–263.

Sarkis, J. (2001). Benchmarking for Agility. *Benchmarking: An International Journal, 8*(2), 88–107.

Shaikh, S. A. (2018). Role of Islamic Banking in Financial Inclusiveness in Pakistan: Promise, Performance and Prospects. *International Journal of Financial Services Management, 9*(1), 88–102.

Sironi, P. (2016). *FinTech Innovation: From Robo-Advisors to Goal Based Investing and Gamification* (1st ed.). Wiley. http://gen.lib.rus.ec/book/index.php?md5=9c642267bc15cacca438a897623cd022

Skinner, C. (2016). *ValueWeb: How FinTech firms are using bitcoin blockchain and mobile technologies to create the Internet of value.* Singapore: Marshall Cavendish International Asia Pte Ltd.

Slattery, A. (2018, March 6). Cybersecurity Consortium Created to Protect FinTech Industry. Retrieved May 11, 2018, https://www.cbronline.com/news/wef-cybersecurity-FinTech

Stefik, M., & Stefik, B. (2006). *Breakthrough: Stories and Strategies of Radical Innovation* (illustrated edition). The MIT Press. http://gen.lib.rus.ec/book/index. https://php?md5=B1A5F9B3FFE65BF5C53490B52C7B78D6

Tapscott, D., & Tapscott, A. (2016). *Blockchain Revolution: How the Technology Behind Bitcoin Is Changing Money, Business, and the World*. London, United Kingdom: Penguin.

TheCityUK. (2017). *Transformation and Innovation: A Guide to Partnerships Between Financial Services Institutions and FinTechs*. https://www.thecityuk.com/assets/research-report/Transformation-and-innovation-A-guide-to-partnerships-between-financial-services-institutions-and-FinTechs.pdf

Thomson Reuters & Dinar Standard, 2018. *State of the Global Islamic Economy Report 2018/19*, s.l.: Thomson Reuters and Dinar Standard.

Tsai, C., & Peng, K.-J. (2017). *The FinTech Revolution and Financial Regulation: The Case of Online Supply Chain Financing* (SSRN Scholarly Paper No. ID 3035346). Rochester, NY: Social Science Research Network. https://papers.ssrn.com/abstract=3035386

Tufano, P. (2003). Chapter 6 Financial innovation. In George M. Constantinides, M. Harris, & R. M. Stulz (Eds.), Handbook of the Economics of Finance (Vol. 1, Issue SUPPL. PART A, pp. 307–335). Amsterdam, The Netherlands: Elsevier. https://doi.org/10.1016/S1574-0102(03)01010-0

Turner, V., Gantz, J. F., Reinsel, D., & Minton, S. (2014). The Digital Universe of Opportunities: Rich Data and the Increasing Value of the Internet of Things. *IDC Analyze the Future*, 5.

Villasenor, J. (2016). Ensuring Cybersecurity in FinTech: Key Trends and Solutions. Retrieved May 11, 2018, https://www.forbes.com/sites/johnvillasenor/2016/08/25/ensuring-cybersecurity-in-FinTech-key-trends-and-solutions/

Vizcaino, B. (2018, May 2). After Downturn, Islamic Finance Eyes Profits, FinTech: survey. *Reuters*. https://www.reuters.com/article/us-islamic-finance-strategy/after-downturn-islamic-finance-eyes-profits-FinTech-survey-idUSKBN1I30KV

Walker. (2016). *Customers 2020: The Future of B-to-B Customer Experience*. http://www.walkerinfo.com/customers2020/

Waupsh, J. (2016). *Bankruption: How Community Banking Can Survive FinTech* (1st edition). Hoboken, New Jersey: Wiley.

WIEF. (2017, June 16). *Developing Human Capital in Islamic Finance*. Retrieved May 14, 2018, https://infocus.wief.org/developing-human-capital-in-islamic-finance/

Chapter 10
Cash Waqf (Endowments) Management Through the Blockchain

Introduction

Good governance is an essential requirement when managing public funds, especially in the context of strengthening the performance of Islamic social institutions. As public organizations, the performance of Islamic social institutions, like waqf institution, especially in management and service are the yardstick for the growth of public trust. The principles of accountability, duty, justice, and transparency are the foundation of shaping the framework in achieving good governance in all public institutions – Islamic or otherwise. For Muslims, the primary sources of the Shariah (i.e., Quran and Sunnah) and the established Islamic jurisprudence (*fiqh*) provide the framework for Islamic corporate governance to achieve the *maqasid* (objectives) of Shariah (Divine Law).

Latest developments in fintech promises more efficiency and reduced costs causing significant shifts in the financial landscape with the introduction of sophisticated and disruptive technologies like the blockchain. However, in public institutions, the utilization of such technologies is focused on transparency and enforcing accountability rather than cost and efficiency benefits alone. The ability to audit and monitor the movement and transfer of assets to the intended beneficiaries is crucial in dispensing the duty of the authorities, and subsequently establishing trust and improving social capital between citizens and the governing authorities. Providing the public with the appropriate information and the performance of waqf assets are mechanisms where the entrusted authorities can continually improve on to gain support from the public in paying zakat and endowing waqf. The fall of public trust will result in diminishing pools of waqf assets and reduction in its endowment collections, which are critical sources of funds for socioeconomic development of Muslim communities (ummah).

In this chapter, we discuss ways as to how technologies like the blockchain can operationalize the transparency and accountability that is required of important social institutions that govern the dispensation of waqf, and its management and distribution in order to establish equal provision, circulate wealth, enhance small as well as large scale projects for social and economic development, and thus share prosperity for a just social system that enables a more equitable and harmonious society.

The Different Use Cases for Blockchain to Enhance Governance

The technology of blockchain originates from the bitcoin success, which can be used in nonfinancial and financial areas worldwide. The blockchain has caused huge transformation in the digital arena by decentralizing the peer-to-peer (P2P) effects for recording of transactions, such as agreements and contracts that involve third parties. The transactions that take place, which are recorded permanently in public ledger, are affirmed via consensus by the majority of those involved within the system. The blockchain records each transaction with secured storage without involving any additional parties. This "Proof-of-Work" consensus protocol is employed to determine the transaction validity as recoded in blockchain (Davidson et al., 2016). Besides, Kim et al. (2017) suggested the application of blockchain for trade of assets due to its reliability and nonintricate processes. This also ascertains a trading system that reflects prices based on the actual market that cannot be modified or altered. Thus, the technology of blockchain, which follows the success of bitcoin, could be employed for numerous applications, including waqf. The blockchain is deemed to aid in waqf management for it is reflective of charity works and involvement of many parties. As the blockchain can record every transaction and offer transparent report, it will be extremely useful for the benefit of waqifs and beneficiaries, as well as waqf management, which appears to be an essential feature of waqf. Some have also investigated the benefits of blockchain in increasing public services, mainly because it can minimize costs and intricacy, apart from exceptional transaction records. Meanwhile, Ølnes (2016) depicted the advantages of blockchain in its implementation within the online government system, as well as the function of blockchain architecture governance in compliance with the public sphere. Next, Turk and Klinc (2017) proposed the application of blockchain to solve several issues related to managing construction data for decentralization, thus opening research avenue in that path. The blockchain technology incorporates smart contract for automated execution of contract terms in a transparent way (Crosby et al., 2016. On the other hand, Zhang and Wen (2017) asserted the promising potential of blockchain in simplifying the billing system within the P2P energy trade market. Next, Kshetri (2017) claimed that blockchain may prevent forgery and manipulation, thus protecting privacy and enforcing cyber security due to storage of data in cloud. Additionally, Pazaitis et al. (2017) asserted that the blockchain is suitable for commons-based system in support of economy-sharing. Meanwhile, Oh and Shong (2017) claimed that blockchain can diminish third-party involvement within the financial system, which may lead to a shift in the transaction trends among consumers.

Hence, the blockchain technology that follows the success of Bitcoin, may be applied for vast applications, including waqf management. The blockchain can record all transactions and offer a transparent report, which is beneficial for both sellers and buyers as a vital aspect of the e-commerce platform. The impact of e-commerce can be noted in the present lifestyle of many. Hence, smooth transaction needs to be assured by addressing several issues, such as data security, efficient supply chain and systems management, satisfied consumers, and retailers, transactions, and payments, as well as a transparent marketplace. Thus, blockchain technology can solve multiple issues, especially those related to the e-commerce industry.

Some have also investigated the benefits of blockchain in increasing public services, mainly because it can minimize costs and intricacy, apart from exceptional transaction records. Meanwhile, Ølnes et al., (2016) depicted the advantages of blockchain in its implementation within the online government system, as well as the function of blockchain architecture governance in compliance with the public sphere. Next, Turk and Klinc (2017) proposed the application of blockchain to solve several issues related to managing construction data for decentralization, thus opening research avenue in that path. The blockchain technology incorporates smart contract for automated execution of contract terms in a transparent way (Crosby et al., 2016). On the other hand, Zhang (2017) asserted the promising potential of blockchain in simplifying the billing system within the P2P energy trade market. Next, Kshetri (2017) claimed that blockchain may prevent forgery and manipulation, thus protecting privacy and enforcing cyber security due to storage of data in cloud. Additionally, Pazaitis et al., (2017) asserted that the blockchain is suitable for commons-based system in support of economy-sharing. Meanwhile, Oh and Shong (2017) claimed that blockchain can diminish third-party involvement within the financial system, which may lead to a shift in the transaction trends among consumers.

Despite, extensive literatures have studied the use of blockchain in e-commerce but there are limited studies on the Islamic e-commerce mainly related to the blockchain. Much less is found for blockchain applications in waqf management or its administration.

The Essentials to Understanding Waqf

Awqaf (plural of waqf) institutions may comprise "several types and can be aimed at different beneficiaries. They can be either religious or philanthropic. Religious awqaf include mosques, shrines, graveyards, Islamic educational institutions like madrasahs, etc. Philanthropic awqaf include the waqf of a property or asset for a specific philanthropic purpose, like medical aid, general education, inns, etc. Similarly, the beneficiaries of a waqf may be family members (waqf ahli/dhurri), or the general public" (Ahmed, 2004).

The creation of waqf is a way for waqf founders to attain righteousness:

By no means shall ye attain righteousness unless ye give (benevolently) out of that which ye love; and whatever ye give, Allah surely knows it. (Quran 3:92)

The endowment of waqf is one of the known traditions to create unceasing rewards that outlives the founder in his/her short life:

When a man dies his acts come to an end, except three things, recurring charity, or knowledge (by which people benefit), or pious offspring, who pray for him.

(Reported by Abu Hurairah, Sahih Muslim)

The "perpetuity of waqf implies that waqf property needs to be preserved and the benefits can be gained without consuming it" (Kahf, 2003). "When a waqif (a person who waqf his/her assets) surrenders his/her properties as waqf, the properties are no longer his as the ownership of any waqf property belongs to Allah s.w.t. Therefore, an administrator or trustee (mutawalli) has to be appointed to manage the properties in order to ensure perpetuity and that the benefits will be continually disseminated to the beneficiaries."

Waqf property generally cannot be sold or transferred except unless when scholars find it desirable (ISRA, 2018). The process of exchanging the property with another of similar value and religious approval are required to effect asset migration (i.e., istibdal).

Historically, Prophet ﷺ built Masjid Quba and Nabawi in Madinah as waqf for the benefit of Muslims to do their prayers. Prophet ﷺ taught his companions to create awqaf whenever they realized any pressing need in their society. He dedicated his land in Khaybar for the building of a guest house for newly converted Muslims as their numbers grew. The creation of waqf spread to include not only the building of mosques, houses, guest houses, lands, and wells, but almost all goods and social services during the Ummayad and Abbasid times. As years past, the "role of waqf was extended to other socioeconomic welfare of the society such as building and maintaining universities, schools, hospitals, graveyards, orphanages, and others" (Mahamood, 2000). The perpetuity of waqf solidifies it as a truly sustainable development instrument, which is important in poverty alleviation and implementing inclusive finance.

Waqf (plural awqaf) is an endowment established by withholding immovable (Hanafi) and movable (Shafi'e and Hanbali) properties to perpetually spend its revenue on fulfilling public or family needs, depending on the preferences of and conditions set by the founder. In the waqf, the former asset owner relinquishes his ownership rights of the asset to Allah s.w.t. Once the asset is created as waqf, it cannot be given as a gift, inherited, or sold. Only its generated revenue is channeled to the beneficiaries; the main asset remains intact for perpetuity.

Generally, there are three types of waqf based on nature of their beneficiaries:

1. **Waqf khayri (public waqf):** an endowment created by the founder for the general welfare of the poor and the needy in his/her society. This is typically in the form of buildings, such as mosques, guest houses, schools, orphanage houses, hospitals, or in the form of basic infrastructure like bridges and wells, or land for cemeteries.
2. **Waqf dhurri (family waqf):** an endowment created by the founder primarily for his family, that is, children, grandchildren, relatives, or may also be for other persons he specifies. When the beneficiary dies, the waqf asset may be transferred to public welfare purposes.

3. **Waqf al-mushtarak (mixed waqf):** an endowment formed by the founder to support the public needs as well as his family needs.

Waqf can also be classified based on the type of donated asset (ISRA, 2018):
1. **Physical waqf:** this usually involves real estate where either the investment returns are used for social needs or the asset is used directly by the beneficiaries.
2. **Cash waqf:** this involves endowment of monetary assets. This is a more practical and flexible way of raising and applying waqf resources as project returns can be increased while keeping risks lower.
3. **Corporate waqf:** this is accomplished through voluntary acts of endowment of corporate securities for beneficiaries.

The waqf administration structure is typically an independent administration (mutawalli) to ensure proper governance – state-appointed authority (or chief judge) is usually entrusted to supervise all waqf assets to protect from misuse. Founders typically manage their own waqf assets, or this responsibility is given to their respective beneficiaries or appointed persons.

Historical Examples of Waqf Institutions and Their Contributions

Historically, the establishment of Quba mosque is considered as the first waqf property in the Muslim world. This first initiative was taken by the Holy Prophet ﷺ and his teachings were inculcated in the minds of his companions who were motivated for spending in the way of Almighty Allah. The wealthy companions such as Uthman Ibn Affan donated his land for various purposes for the well-being of the Muslim community. Later, waqf became one of the most important economic tools of Islamic states and they used it for the socioeconomic development of the community. A considerable number of humanitarian projects were based on waqf.

The waqf were established for providing food to the hungry and needy; for example: "the waqf Abi Talha who endowed Bairuha gardens and make the profit for the poor and relatives. Also reflected in the well waqf Rumat by Uthman ibn Affan Islamic society so that water needs can be fulfilled" (Rohmaningtyas and Herianingrum, 2017). During the periods of the Umayyad, Abbasid, Mamalik, Ottoman Turks and others, waqf was not only for the poor, but also for the development of educational institutions, libraries, and payment of the salaries of workers and teachers, and even more, for the endowment of scholarships for students.

For example, at the time of the Umayyad dynasty, Tauba Bin Ghar Al-Hadramy strongly supported the development of waqf. He was a judge in Egypt at the time of Hisham bin Abdul Malik. To develop the endowment, Tauba had established waqf institutions under the supervision of a judge and the benefits were distributed to the eligible and needy. In this case, the institution of waqf had a role in eliminating poverty, misery, disease, illiteracy, creating uneven distribution of wealth. The Abbasiyah dynasty had waqf institutions named "Sadr al-Wuqûf," which acted as the caretaker of the waqf assets, managed the staff and administration of the institutions (nadzirs). Thus, the use of endowments had been set up well during this dynasty. As a result, waqf led to the formation of social facilities such as schools and hospitals, and dormitories and hotels for travelers and poor people. In the Ottoman Empire, waqf laws were announced and waqf funds were used widely in social projects such as to build hospitals, educational institutions, and houses for the poor. In the Ottoman period, from the conquest of Constantinople (Istanbul 1453 AD) until the nineteenth century, the number of the schools for higher education built by the waqfs totaled more than 500. One of the examples of the most developed waqf management is that of Al Azhar University, Cairo, Egypt. Being more than a thousand years old, this institution has a huge waqf property. It consists of not only the endowment of land, building and farm but also the endowment of money. Due to this waqf, Al-Azhar University was able to finance the operation of its education over centuries without being dependent on the government's funding and the tuition fees. Furthermore, this university has been able to. over centuries, provide scholarships to more than thousands of students from all over the world. Another remarkable example of waqf is a large and longstanding charitable foundation created by Sultan Salah al-Din al-Ayyubi in 1174. The endowment's income was assigned to the "poor and fuqaha' of Alexandria." Indeed, the endowment appears in the records as "sadir alfuqaha' wa-l-fuqara' fi-l-thaghr al-sakandari," the name of its beneficiaries replacing that of its founder. It is likely that the preference for this title reflects a desire on the part of the local population to bestow an exceptional status on the endowment and make it the focus of special care and attention (Cizakca, 1998; Khan, 2015; Rohmaningtyas and Herianingrum, 2017).

In a nutshell, historically waqf remained an important instrument and has been used for the socioeconomic development of communities and states. Islamic states, dynasties, empires have heavily relied on this instrument and launched a wide array of projects including educational institutions, hospitals, food security programs, orphan care homes, commercial buildings, and welfare projects.

Amid the current COVID situation, the importance of the waqf instrument has increased and countries are realizing its potential. There is a need to use advanced technology such as blockchain and artificial intelligence in developing waqf models to cater to the demands of the technological era.

Waqf Institutions and Modernization

Waqf institutions can be viewed as three sections – waqf procurement section, waqf utilization section, and income distribution section. Hence, waqf institutions should procure highly competent personnel not only in management but also in Islamic finance and investment management. In addition, the waqf institutions should be administered by experienced professionals with deep investment knowledge and skills to keep the assets highly productive and income generating.

The digitization of data constitutes a paradigm shift in transforming workflows and business models of the various sectors of the economy with the increase in the volume of data used in administration for many industries. A "variety of legal technologies has emerged, enabling the digitization and automation of these and other legal-work activities" (Veith et al., 2016). Frequently used contractual agreements can be automated as smart contracts to enable transfer of ownerships and codify preferences and conditions set by waqf founders for future administrative purposes that must be carried out in perpetuity.

The Distinction of Cash Waqf from Other Waqf Models

The creation and development of the Cash Waqf can be traced back to the time of Holy Prophet (PBUH), when Hazrat Hafsah (may Allah be pleased with her), one of the wives of Holy Prophet ﷺ bought a piece of jewelry for 20,000 dirham, and waqf-ed it for the women of al-Khattam family. Though that was jewelry not the cash, the concept of movable waqf can be extracted from this narration. Also, Zufar Ibn al-Huzail, one of the companions of Imam Abu Hanifah, declared cash waqf as a legitimate process. He explained that the process of cash as an asset invested in *mudarabah* (silent partnership) and the profit from that process can be used for waqf if intended that way. The Ottoman Empire approved the practice of cash waqf in the early fifteenth century. The concept of Cash Waqf gained huge popularity among the people of Anatolia and rapidly spread all over its European provinces. The Cash Waqf has some distinguishable features that make it different from general Waqf (Hassan et al., 2019). The following table encapsulates the details of those features.

The most unique and distinguishable feature of the Cash Waqf is that it can be established even through small contributions and people from all classes including lower middle class and lower class; they can participate in helping others in need. Due to the potential benefits of using Cash Waqf, this has become an attractive instrument in Malaysia, Indonesia, Turkey, and Singapore. Various schemes have been launched using Cash Waqf in these countries. The major challenges of traditional waqf systems suffer from poor management of waqf assets and its resulting income (or lack thereof), clumsy or cumbersome processes and mechanisms in place. The sustainability of present models or waqf system demands some updates and relevant innovation in order to adapt to the passage of time and usage. Such changes and innovation keep practical social models alive in every era of time to serve the intended purposes albeit utilizing various tools, including digital technology, for enhancement and efficiency.

The use of blockchain to secure cash movements in the Cash Waqf system is one example where technology can overcome traditional waqf challenges. Table 10.1 explains the development of Cash Waqf model on blockchain.

Table 10.1: The Distinguishing Features of the General Waqf and the Cash Waqf.

Feature	General Waqf	Cash Waqf
Liquid Fund as Corpus	In a standard Waqf, the corpus is usually an immovable, illiquid asset.	In a "Cash Waqf" the main corpus is a "cash capital," which is liquid and able to buy assets or fund services as required.
Immediate Usufruct	An immovable property such as a piece of land may be worth millions but unless it is developed into an income generating project, it is unable to give any consistent benefit.	Even a small amount of Cash Waqf may start generating income through investment right from its inception.
Affordability and Convenience	Not all are able to afford or are privileged to own property, land, or such assets.	With Cash Waqf, it is easy and liquid compared to scarce and immovable assets. This opens waqf opportunities to many Muslims, who wish to contribute to the society through waqf but do not own land or real estate, etc.
Remarkable mobility of Cash Waqf	The traditional forms of Waqf typically have low mobility and a lot more effort is required to achieve the benefits they set out to accomplish.	The core objective of creating a Waqf is more easily achieved via a Cash Waqf due to its flexibility and mobility.
Benefits from Cash	The inflexibility of traditional Waqf can make them suffer from underutilization, or due to seasonal weather conditions not produce regular harvests and/or earn a steady income, etc.	Cash Waqf has the flexibility to *fund* various activities from education to feeding the needy (including refugees and displaced persons), social programs and other religious obligations. When such pliable corpus is invested to grow, a regular usufruct can be earned and spent for almost any welfare purposes.

The Blockchain Cash Waqf Model Development

This model utilizes the concept of Cash Waqf to raise funding directed to the waqf institution and others who have contribution to the services of distribution of Cash Waqf. Cash Waqf usually involve waqf institution, waqif, beneficiaries' investments corporation, and other institution that have cooperation, for example, shops for buying asset.

The blockchain waqf model will illustrate how BC is able to attain the connectivity and transparency of waqf transaction.

Within this concept, funds collected by waqif (donor) are given to nadzir (waqf administrator), who will work with qualified teams to invest the fund in particular sectors, whereby the gains or profits from the investments are channeled to waqf programs.

For waqf, such accountability and proper administration, particularly in its longevity, is required. In order to be a valid and legitimate, a waqf is subject to three key restrictions:
i. **Irrevocability:** once the waqf deed is pronounced in verbal terms or signed in written form, it cannot be revoked.
ii. **Inalienability:** once the deed is performed; the corpus of waqf (principal of the fund) can never be alienated as gift, inheritance, or sale, etc.
iii. **Perpetuity:** it is mandatory upon the trustee to ensure the safeguard of corpus of cash against any loss or reduction, so the benefits of the same may continue forever.

Cash Waqf is a form of waqf (perpetual endowment) where the income generated from the money collected is to be spent, while protecting the principal amount. In a Cash Waqf for charitable purposes (see Figure 10.1):
– Initial cash waqf is used as an investment to generate earnings and reduces the need for further donations.
– The principal amount collected is run like a fund with experienced fund managers to generate the most possible return.
– The returns are what will be spent on charitable causes.

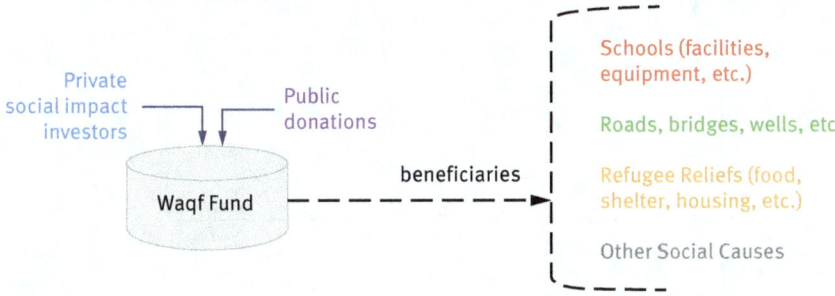

Figure 10.1: Cash Waqf System.

– The Cash Waqf Fund collects its principal capital from socially motivated high net worth individuals (HNWIs) and later the public through donations.
– The principal capital is invested and the profits made will be disbursed to the beneficiaries.

– The Waqf Fund will be run as a professionally managed fund to give the best possible returns.

The Cash Waqf Fund will have independent committees (as shown in Figure 10.2) to ensure proper governance and should be structured as follows:
- **Investment committee:** approves where capital should be invested on recommendation from fund manager
- **Fund manager** (mutawalli)**:** manages the funds and ensures best returns
- **Approval committee:** approves where the proceeds are allocated, that is, which beneficiaries, projects, feasibility, etc.

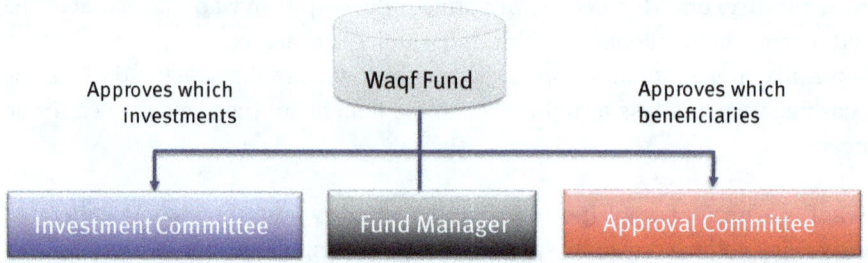

Figure 10.2: Cash Waqf Fund Organizational Structure.

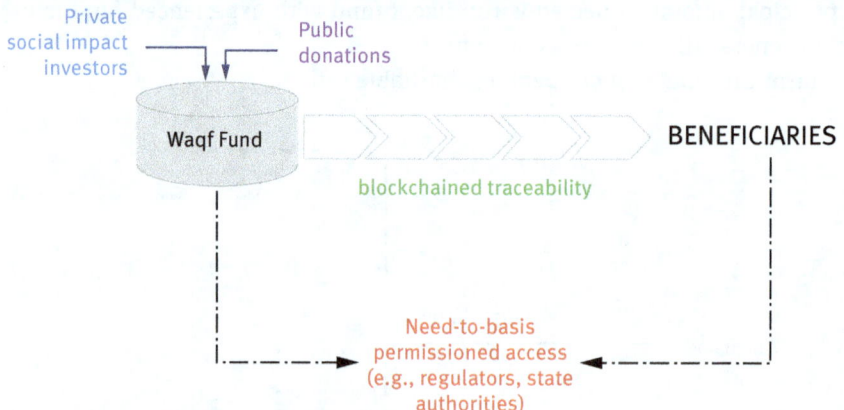

Figure 10.3: Blockchained Cash Waqf Operations.
(Collections, Distribution, Monitoring, and Auditing)

In collecting cash waqf (see Figure 10.3), the waqf center must employ officials who oversee transactions based on requirements to be evaluated by the waqf assessor. Thus, blockchain can be advantageous to preserve transactions made by waqifs in a trustworthy manner. In older methods, the records of transactions cannot be obtained easily, which can be addressed by the blockchain that can keep each transaction record in a secure manner without any data loss or manipulation. Also, for auditing purposes, permissioned access on a need-to basis can be given to the regulators or state authorities to verify the previous ownership of the waqf assets, or the stipulated wishes of the waqf founder, if required for whatever purposes that may arise.

What the Cash Waqf System Seeks to Solve

The cash waqf system is a viable solution for "donor fatigue," which is a recognized problem. It is normal for people to get tired from donating toward the multitude of causes that are brought to their attention. There is also a limited amount that can be set aside for normal working class folks who are financially burdened by their own daily needs and monthly expenses.

Also, there is a lack of accountability surrounding charity today to make it sustainable. Millions are spent on financing charitable causes but there is no visibility on how effective this spending is, or that it is going to the intended beneficiaries mentioned at the fundraising stages. Trusts appears to be a crucial factor in donations and endowments to organizations that have a duty to follow through on their initial intentions and goals.

Furthermore, the performance of such organizations is scantly monitored and rarely assessed due to the belief that there are blessings from good actions, and the assumption is that all proceeds are managed how they are supposed to be. Unfortunately, if any foul play or misappropriation are brought to light, they usually only happen when most, if not all, of the money has been spent.

Benefits of a Blockchainized Waqf System

This proposed blockchained waqf system will make traditional processes of Islamic social systems better and more efficient in their process flows to existing cumbersome processes, which are fraught with moral hazards, agency issues, and leakages. In this manner, a blockchainized transaction is publicly accessible and safeguards sensitive data against hacking and unauthorized alteration. The blockchain verification protocol makes it virtually impossible for any party to modify information on the blockchain secretly. Any form of concealment, fraud, or attempt at misappropriation or misrepresentation violates the principles of justice and fairness in Shariah. A full copy of the blockchain contains every transaction ever executed, making information on the value belonging to every active address (account) accessible at any point in history.

The ability to track and monitor transactions, waqf assets and cash endowment collections physically in the real world with greater transparency builds trust between the waqf center and its donors, the people they serve. This will improve future collections, and their reputation as a credible mediator and regulator.

Automated collections, tracking and processing replaces the laborious auditing and monitoring of fraud and monetary leakages between collection and disbursement, going back-and-forth between claimants, determining rightful ownership in cases of disputes and counterclaims.

The simplicity and speed of execution will increase overall efficiency and usability for authorities put in charge of such religious duties. It also leads to a superior user experience for the users and customers that require such important services.

Since systems are more efficient with automated steps, or less repeating steps done by different parties, resources can be put to better utility for better service value and enhanced support.

Conclusion

The potential of using blockchain as a waqf management system has not been vastly explored. The original aim of this study was to provide conceptual framework of waqf management using blockchain technology. We conclude that blockchain provides solutions to many current problems in waqf management as it can possibly enable transactions, which is easily auditable and costless verification of a transaction. Due primarily to this and other features, blockchain can play a key role in tracking the distribution of funds as well as in handling and dealing many endowment transactions. The moral economy according to the Qur'an is grounded in a framework of equity, where the circulation of wealth pervades through every community so that wealth becomes a tool for equality and enabler for the provision of much-needed infrastructure and services for equal opportunities. It is beyond any doubt that waqf in cash terms offers much liquidity and flexibility in providing such structural requirements and services for its beneficiaries.

References

Ahmed, H. (2004). Role of Zakah and Awqaf in Poverty Alleviation, Jeddah: IRTI, IDB, 2004, 72–73.
Cizakca, M. (1998). Awqaf in History and Its Implications for Modern Islamic Economies. *Islamic Economic Studies*, 6(1), 43–70.
Crosby, Michael, Nachiappan, Pattanayak, Pradhan, Verma, Sanjeev, & Kalyanaraman, Vignesh. (2016). Blockchain Technology: Beyond Bitcoin. *Applied Innovation Review*, 6–19.
Davidson, Sinclair, De Filippi, Primavera, & Potts, Jason. (2016). Disrupting Governance: The New Institutional Economics of Distributed Ledger Technology. SSRN Working Paper.

Hassan, M. K., Karim, M. F., & Karim, M. S. (2019). *Experiences and Lessons of Cash Waqf in Bangladesh and Other Countries. Revitalization of Waqf for Socio-Economic Development, I,* 59–83. https://doi.org/10.1007/978-3-030-18445-2_5

ISRA. (2018). *Islamic Economics: Principles & Analysis*. International Shariah Research Academy for Islamic Finance, Malaysia.

Kahf, M. (2003). The Role of Waqf in Improving the Ummah Welfare. Paper presented at the International Seminar on "Waqf as a Private Legal Body," organized by Islamic University of North Sumatra, Medan, Indonesia.

Khan, M. T. (2015). Historical Role of Islamic Waqf in Poverty Reduction in Muslim Society. *Pakistan Development Review, 54*(4), 979–996.

Kim, N.H., Kang, S.M., Hong, C.S. (2017). Mobile Charger Billing System Using Lightweight Blockchain. In: 19th Asia-Pacific Network Operations and Management Symposium: Managing a World of Things, APNOMS 2017, 374–377.

Kshetri, Nir. (2017). The Economics of the Internet of Things in the Global South. *Third World Quarterly, 38*(2), 311–339.

Mahamood, S. M. (2000). The Administration of Waqf, Pious Endowment in Islam: A Critical Study of the Role of the State Islamic Religious Councils as the Sole Trustees of a Waqf Assets and the Implementation of Istibdal in Malaysia with Special Reference to the Federal Territory of Kuala Lumpur. PhD thesis, Birmingham University.

Oh, J. and Shong, I. (2017), A Case Study on Business Model Innovations using Blockchain: Focusing on Financial Institutions, *Asia Pacific Journal of Innovation and Entrepreneurship, 11*(3), 335–344.

Ølnes, S. (2016). Beyond Bitcoin Enabling Smart Government Using Blockchain Technology. International Conference on Electronic Government and the Information Systems Perspective EGOVIS 2016. Electronic Government, 253–264.

Pazaitis, Alex, De Filippi, Primavera, & Kostakisa, Vasilis. (2017). Blockchain and Value Systems in the Sharing Economy: The Illustrative Case of Backfeed. *Technological Forecasting & Social Change, 125,* 105–115.

Rohmaningtyas, N., & Herianingrum, S. (2017). The Significance of Waqf in Historical and Theoretical Studies. *Journal of Islamic Economics Science, 1*(1), 39–55. https://e-journal.unair.ac.id/JIES/article/viewFile/10628/5996

Turk, Ž., Klinc, R., (2017). Potentials of Blockchain Technology for Construction Management. *Procedia Engineering* 196, 638–645.

Veith, C., Bandlow, M., Harnisch, M., Wenzler, H., Hartung, M., & Hartung, D. (2016). *How Legal Technology Will Change the Business of Law*. Boston, Massachusetts, USA: Boston Consulting Group and Bucerius Law School.

Zhang, Y., Wen, J., (2017). The IoT electric business model: using blockchain technology for the internet of things. *Peer-to-Peer Network Applications 10*(4), 983–994.

Chapter 11
A Unified Islamic Digital Currency – The Digital Dinar

Introduction

This investigation addresses a much-discussed topic at OIC gatherings and among political circles – the unified Islamic currency. The proposal for a Digital Dinar – a unified Islamic currency in digital form – is to achieve the goal of a unified Islamic economy to improve trade between Islamic nations as well as improve the rights and sovereignty of its citizens. In this research, we deliberate on the historical evolution of the forms of money, as well as the advent and the development of digital currencies in recent times. We propose two constructs for the Islamic digital currency (digital dinar) – an Aggregated Sovereign Currencies Construct and the Basket of Commodities Construct.

Why a Unified Currency is Important for the Muslim World

The study of economic and monetary history exhibits that numerous efforts and attempts have been made to introduce a uniform single currency in different periods, empires and regimes. The point worth noting is that the goal of uniform currency has always been supported by political agendas rather than economic agendas. The empires once established, issued a single currency for their conquered territories and through the introduction of a single currency based monetary system, the expansion of political power could be further extended and made complete.

The Roman Empire, one of the largest empires in human history, was established around the Mediterranean region, and during the time of the Qing and Han dynasties in China. The single coinage system was introduced to the Mediterranean region using the silver *denarius*, gold *aureus* and bronze *as*.[1]

China, ruled by a series of dynasties, introduced a new coinage system for its empire after attaining significant political stability. The Chinese empire was also the first empire to introduce paper money as currency,[2] under the Yuan dynasty during the Mongol reign, about a thousand years before paper money was introduced in Europe. This new form of money helped the Chinese emperors to enhance the supply of

---

[1] The as (plural assēs), occasionally assarius (plural assarii, rendered into Greek as ἀσσάριον, assarion) was a bronze, and later copper, coin used during the Roman Republic and Roman Empire.

[2] In Chinese Empire, the Kao-tsung dynasty (650–683) introduced the first paper money. Because of the difficulty of transporting large amounts of bullion over long distances, the bill of exchange was introduced in fourteenth-century Italy to transfer money between cities. Until the nineteenth century, paper currency was only issued in Europe during political or economic emergencies.

money and moved to hoarding bullion (gold and silver) to supplement their treasury resources.

In Islam, the history of money started with the use of the Roman Byzantine gold denarius (dinar) and the Persian silver drahm (or dram). According to economic historians, the Greek adopted it and it became drachma, then the Arabs adopted it and it became dirham. Both were accepted as monetary currency units in the Muslim world, i.e. as money, dinar (gold) and dirham (silver) as currency are mentioned in the Quran, e.g. 3:75 and 12:20. According to Mirakhor (July 2021), verse 19 of chapter 18 of the Qur'an where, in part, money is referred to as "waraq." While it is often interpreted in translation as "silver money," the etymology of the word shows that it refers to very thin layer of a thing like "waraqat al-Shajar" meaning the "leaf of the tree." It also refers to a sheet of paper.[3] The Islamic State itself minted its own dirham as early as 18AH according to prominent Muslim scholars (such as al-Ghazali, Ibn Taymiyyah, Qudama Ibn Jaafar, Ibn Khaldun and al-Maqrizi) who seem to view that the two precious metals are preferred to be used as a medium of exchange and a measure for all things. Gold appears to have played the role of money and means of exchange throughout early Muslim history, although there were some issues with the copper fulus and with fiat money towards the end of the Ottoman empire era (Al-Baz, 1999). The first dated coins in Islamic history were silver dirhams from the Sassanian ruler Yazdegerd III, minted during the rule of Osman Ibn 'Affan, the third rightly guided Caliph of Islam. These coins differed from the original Sassanian ones in that Arabic inscriptions were found in the obverse margins, which read "In the Name of Allah." By the year 75 AH (695 CE) Abdul Malik Ibn Marwan had decided on changes to the coinage system. A scattering of patterned pieces in silver existed from this date, based on Sassanian prototypes, but with the distinctive Arabic verse. These issuances were experimental, but they maintained the Sassanian weight standard of 3.5–4.0 g per coin, and by 79 AH (698 CE) a completely new type of silver coin was created at 14 mints reducing the nominal weight to 2.97 g.

Subsequently, in centuries that followed, there were efforts being made to establish a single monetary currency to unify the Islamic economy. A half century ago, the agenda of forming a currency union was first time initiated by Islamic countries (Bacha, 2008). In 1945, the initiative was discussed among 22 Arab[4] countries from

---

[3] Mirakhor opines that while the verse may be interpreted to refer to a thin sheet of silver, the ayah (verse) itself is silent on the nature of the commodity that constituted it. For example, it could have been paper, gold, silver, copper or other commodities.

[4] The Arab World consists of 22 countries in the Middle East and North Africa: Algeria, Bahrain, the Comoros Islands, Djibouti, Egypt, Iraq, Jordan, Kuwait, Lebanon, Libya, Morocco, Mauritania, Oman, Palestine, Qatar, Saudi Arabia, Somalia, Sudan, Syria, Tunisia, the United Arab Emirates, and Yemen. Arab countries have a rich diversity of ethnic, linguistic, and religious communities. These include Kurds, Armenians, Berbers and others. There are over 300 million Arabs. As a clarification, Iran and Turkey are not Arab countries, and their primary languages are Farsi and Turkish respectively.

the MENA region (the Middle East and North Africa) calling for a common currency, which they specified as "Dinar Arab" (Kamar, 2004). In 2010, the six GCC[5] (Gulf Cooperation Council) countries have come together and announced an expected date to establish a single currency named "Khallegi." This development was followed by another proposal for a monetary union by the Economic Community of West African States (ECOWAS). Even though these plans started with vigor, none of them was eventually implemented.

In the ASEAN region where the three Islamic countries (Malaysia, Indonesia and Brunei Darussalam) make up almost half of the total 600 plus million population, has also mulled over a proposal for a common currency in ASEAN countries. Most recently in December 2019, leaders from a small group of Islamic countries met at the Kuala Lumpur (KL) Summit where Tun Dr. Mahathir Mohamad, the then re-elected Prime Minister of Malaysia spoke again about the need for the unified Islamic currency. According to him, it would reduce their dependence on the U.S. dollar, and help increase the trade between them. A unified currency for the Muslim world will naturally strengthen its economic resilience and standing in the world community, and ultimately help fight poverty and improve the lives of their citizens.

Considerations for a Unified Currency for Islamic Countries

A currency may act as the symbol of a culture that demonstrates the traits of a nation and Islam as a way of life, considers local customs and cultures carefully and treats it with due respect so long as it does not contradict the Shariah. Religion and culture are both indispensable for each other since culture has been a channel for the transformation of religious beliefs among its followers.

Historically, when the caliph Malik ibn Marwan saw the Roman coinage that were common in the Muslim world, his view was that the Muslim empire should have its own coins to demonstrate their culture and religion. Therefore, he introduced a new coinage having presentation of Islam and abolished the use of all other coins. Perhaps, his intention was to emphasize the unity of the ummah rather than their differences.

Politics and worldly power always had and has a critical role in the development of any nation. We have witnessed that those who wields political power writes the historical narrative and rules the world. Ancient Egypt, the Persian Empire, the Roman Empire, the Greek Empire, the Chinese Empire, the Ottoman Empire and the British Empire are examples of historical political powers. Most historical recollections are slightly different from each other. Their power colors their worldviews

---

5 The six countries are Bahrain, Kuwait, Oman, Qatar, Saudi Arabia, and the United Arab Emirates.

over occupied resources and beliefs. One of such belief is that these empires strived to make their currency a unified currency because they viewed that the common currency would translate into economic power and further strengthen their political power. They were of the view that when many territories adopt their currency, trade activities would also increase inevitably.

In the present time, there are a total of 56 Islamic countries and the whole Muslim population is about 2 billion worldwide. In terms of GDP, the contribution of the OIC makes it the second largest economy combined. Among Islamic countries, there is a diverse nature of economic resources, and levels of development where some of them have strong GDP growth such as Qatar and the UAE, while others succumb to poor GDP growth due to various reasons. OIC member countries continue to record significantly higher than average unemployment rates compared to non-OIC countries. Since 2014, the total unemployment rate in OIC countries has been on the rise: 6.7% in 2019 as compared to 5.9% in 2014. The unemployment rate for the youth labour force (14.5% in 2019) is typically higher than the rates for adults in all country groups. Amid the COVID-19 economic slowdown, the ILO expects around a 25 million increase in the number of unemployed people worldwide, which means an additional 6 to 8 million unemployed people in OIC member countries. Moreover, within the group of OIC, 13 countries have poverty rates over 30%. Over the last several years, the OIC member countries witnessed a sharp deterioration in their fiscal balance. High dependence on commodity and primary goods exports makes many OIC countries particularly vulnerable to price fluctuations. There were only ten OIC countries with a fiscal balance surplus in 2018. Intra-OIC export flows have been steadily increasing since 2016 from a level of US$ 254 billion to reach to US$ 331 billion in 2019. Over the last three years, intra-OIC exports increased by more than 30%, which is a significant achievement. Yet, it remains below the total values recorded in 2012. The intra-OIC trade flows have been stuck between 18% and 19% between 2012 to 2019. Despite a drop to 18.1% in 2018, OIC countries have managed to raise the intra-OIC trade flows back to 19% in 2019. However, the sluggish growth in intra-OIC trade flows reduces the prospects for achieving its target of 25%. Furthermore, the total external debt stock of OIC countries continued to increase, which reached US$ 1.68 trillion in 2018. However, in terms of the maturity structure of the external debt, short-term debts accounted for 15.2% of total external debts of OIC countries, as compared to 30.9% of short-term debts of non-OIC developing countries on their total debts. Turkey remained the most indebted OIC member country in 2018 with over US$ 445 billion debt. Although OIC bloc's debt may not be as much as non-OIC countries, we have seen how debt has played a crucial role in the financial stability of nations being the main cause for financial failures and crises both at the corporate as well as at the sovereign levels (Reinhart & Rogoff, 2011).

Among the research done on the OIC, there have been studies on the economic feasibility of a unified currency for different blocs of the OIC. For example, in a study by Razzaghi et al, (2018) where they assessed the feasibility of forming a monetary union among OIC countries by using the Optimum Currency Area (OCA) theory.[6] They concluded that "although most of the regions experience diminishing competitiveness differentials and there is an obvious convergence between economic competitiveness in OIC regions" due to real effective exchange rates being undervalued in almost all of OIC regions within last decade. The key takeaway is that based on econometric models and data, the results show increasing feasibility in forming a single monetary unit for all Islamic countries. In another study by Memet Agustiar (2018), the feasibility of 44 OIC member countries was assessed to form a currency union using the OCA-index. The findings of this study estimate that 63% of pairs of countries in the OIC are ready to form a currency union. The selected OCA's criteria present the best-fit variable in explaining the OCA for the OIC. This paper confirms that economic and geographic heterogeneities are not the main obstacle to forming a currency union. This study provides an important contribution to the theory of OCA primarily in clarifying the application of the OCA conditions in a large observation like the OIC, which comprises many countries and many blocks. This investigation lends evidence that the disparate Islamic countries can form a single currency union, if they want to work together. If there was a counter argument or misinformed belief that there is no feasibility of issuing a unified currency because it may lead to trade imbalance, financial crises and so on, this misperception is not as valid as much as it is being propagated. In fact, the majority of the Islamic countries suffer from inadequate GDP growth due to pervasive corruption, joblessness (particularly youth unemployment), deeply-rooted poverty due to unsound socio-economic policies and behaviors.

The United States remains the preferred reserve currency although its popularity is diminishing in the recent poor leadership term and economic weakness. The global economy seems to be open to alternative currencies in view of rising economic powerhouses like China and the EU. Similarly, the Islamic Economy can be fortified with a unified currency to improve trade among OIC nations as well as other international trade partners. A common currency among trading partners will remove the need for currency hedges, smoothen cross-border settlements for global transactions, and may even prevent illegal financial activities such as money laundering, currency counterfeiting, and other unlawful (*munkar*) transactions.

Evolution of Digital Currencies

With the advent of computer age in 1980s, computers began to take prominent roles both at the workplace as well as in the home. Using computers allowed its users to

---

[6] Optimum currency area theory (OCA) states that specific areas not bounded by national borders would benefit from a common currency. In other words, geographic regions may be better off using the same currency instead of each country within that geographic region using its own currency.

work productively, and as this manner of working gained traction, our work paradigm (including our personal paradigm) shifted significantly to adapt to the digital age. We have no qualms about having our work and personal details encoded digitally to make processes more efficient and quicker. But the trade-offs became evident when hackers started exposing private information in the way it was not supposed to be used. Consequently, cybersecurity evolved, and programmers started working on strengthening and securing electronic transactions and data exchange with the intent to better protect transactions, privacy and digital property. Likewise, a group called the "cypherpunk movement" was conceived with focus on data protection. Within the movement, they conceptualized a type of digital currency with which people had options to send and receive money without the exposure of data and keep themselves untracked. Later on, the discussion was started on the development of a practical digital currency on a larger scale. In 1983, David Chaum, an American cryptographer, published a scientific paper entitled "Blind Signatures for Untraceable Payments" where he outlined the features of an anonymous form of money in a digital format. He turned theory into reality by introducing "DigiCash" which was based on the same Blind Signature technology that ensured privacy and safety of transactions and data between two counterparties. After the emergence of this model, forward-looking businesses started putting pressure on their local banks to integrate their existing payment system with DigiCash because of its ease and agility. This was at the time when the point-of-sale (POS) system was introduced at the major supermarkets. Late in 1997, like-minded people came together and launched the "Cypherpunks distributed remailer (CDR)" with the concept of private communication for marketing offers and discounts, and inadvertently introduced a decentralized email system. Later on, different types of digital money started to emerge, such as "b-money" (a Bitcoin predecessor), but they did not get support from then businesses due to not being integrated with the financial institutions they used. The DigiCash eventually went into bankruptcy because of its low userbase as well as due to some technical issues that went unresolved. In 2002, a computer programmer, Adam Back, enumerated the concept of Hashcash in his paper entitled "Hashcash – A Denial of Service Counter-Measure". In this concept, the proof-of-work system was initially used to limit email spam and denial-of-service attacks, but in recent years became known for its use in bitcoin (and other bitcoin-derived altcoins or PoW-based cryptocurrencies) as part of the mining algorithm. The Hashcash was also considered the most successful digital currency before the advent of the Bitcoin. Since then, Bitcoin has developed to become the most famous digital currency, controversially paving the way for the future of money. Following this, thousands of cryptocurrencies and tokens have been launched to serve the decentralization epoch. As a means of exchange (currency), Bitcoin compared quite favorably to systems like SWIFT, but less favorably to centralized systems like VISA, which could process thousands of transactions per second compared to Bitcoin's three to seven.

But that was never the main proposition. While there are references to lower transaction costs and sizes in the Satoshi whitepaper (in 2008), he presented in the context of a generalized transition to a consensus-driven trust system. There were no explicit references to any given centralized system and certainly no talk of throughput, block size, and the like because in the beginning, that did not really matter. What mattered was an independent peer-to-peer system that established a mechanism for trusted exchange without data leaks and privacy hacks.

The Central Bank-issued Digital Currency (CBDC)

Cryptocurrencies such as bitcoin have foreshadowed a potential digital future for money, though they exist outside the traditional global financial system and are not legal tender like cash issued by governments. It might seem money is already virtual, as credit cards and payment apps such as Apple Pay in the U.S. and WeChat in China eliminate the need for paper currency or coins. But those are just ways to move money electronically. After the emergence of cryptocurrency, countries have started showing interest in a sovereign form of digital currencies where the volatility of cryptos are meted by a stable fiat value. As such, the concept of central bank digital currency (CBDC) was born. While many formats[7] of the CBDC are being evaluated across many sovereign nations, its benefits appear to not only provide more efficient payments but also overcome previous insurmountable barriers, such as the zero lower-bound for monetary policy. The CBDC also allows the government to directly take control over the floated digital currencies in the economy, without having to go through proxies like banks and other financial institutions. Although the CBDC is centralized (i.e. it is issued and regulated by the competent monetary authority of the country), it aims to leverage on the best of both worlds—the convenience and security of digital form like cryptocurrencies, and the regulated, reserved-backed money circulation of the traditional banking system. The respective central banks and/or other competent monetary authority will be solely responsible for its operations and maintenance.

Many central banks, however, have launched pilot programs and research projects aimed at determining a CBDC's viability and usability. The Bank of England (BOE) was the pioneer to initiate the CBDC proposal. Following that, central banks of other nations, like China's People's Bank of China (PBoC), Bank of Canada (BoC), and central banks of Uruguay, Thailand, Venezuela, Sweden, and Singapore, among others, are looking into the possibility of introducing a central bank-issued digital currency.

---

[7] We have an in-depth discussion on the different formats of the CBDC in another book, Beyond Fintech (Mohamed, 2021) Chapter 9. Assessment of each of the four formats covered the attributes and impact of each format on the financial system. Finally, it recommends a solution for minimal disruption to the economy, stronger monetary policy transmission and suggests way forward for adoption of an interest-free monetary system.

Recently, the Chinese government has begun to issue blockchain-powered digital currency to its citizens – the Digital Yuan.[8] The Wall Street Journal reports that 100,000 recipients have been determined by a lottery system and can already spend their digital yuan both in stores and online using a special app. In more recent reports, Beijing said its e-CNY (or digital renminbi) has been tested in more than 70 million transactions worth over $5 billion, as of July 2021. We can expect other countries to follow suit in the near future and in various ways and formats.

Yet, we find Islamic governments lagging in the experimentation of their own CBDC with the exception of Turkey and the UAE. Despite continual criticisms of the conventional interest-based monetary system, little visible effort has been made, apart from outright criticisms rather than taking any real productive actions. We are at a crucial juncture, and it is important to see the vast opportunities which includes a way to establish an interest-free full-reserve financial system that Islamic Finance has been championing for decades. Another critical factor is that most of the Muslim populations are dominated by youths who are naturally tech savvy or tech natives. Technological adoption is ever increasing and there is significant prospect in this trend.

Mirakhor (2017) observed that one of the central problems of major economies is the uncoordinated and mismatched balance sheets of the real, financial, household and government sectors. Ideally, it is presumed that the market would work freely to coordinate the balance sheets and allow for equilibrium to surface. Unfortunately, the current state of economics suffers from a runaway financial sector (now accelerated by stimulus-driven money), which is decoupled from the real sector. This is ever so obvious in the current COVID-19 quarantined economy where businesses are suffering but the stock market record new highs every week. In our current state, we have an economy that apportions only a very small fraction of market trades to capital formation in the real sector resulting in a real sector with corporations overflowing with cash, but not investing. MSMEs become starved for financial resources, and unable to grow and survive, while government sectors amass huge debts to fund their programs, unable to coordinate its balance sheets. The market's inability has spawned a "paper economy" without much connection to the real sector, when in fact, the economy needs a real sector rate of return to replace the mis-pricings of opportunity cost of financial resources from the interest rate system.

When the interest rate mechanism and money-printing austerity measures are no longer available to misallocate financial resources, monetary policy becomes even more effective in inducing private sector portfolio adjustment as it relies on the rate of return to investment in the real sector of the economy (as the true opportunity cost of financial resources) to guide its policy actions. Such systemic change is required for a systemic problem that has gone on for far too long, and it can come in the form of the

---

[8] https://www.wsj.com/articles/china-creates-its-own-digital-currency-a-first-for-major-economy-11617634118.

alternative Islamic financial system through a digitalized currency for more effective policy transmission and monetary control.

For Islamic Finance, the CBDC in a fair and just format will establish a full-reserve system where every deposit is backed by sovereign wealth (i.e. cash, central bank reserves, government securities and assets) that would ensure financial stability which the current fractional-reserve banking system has not been able to address as it is fundamentally-flawed. Preventing private money creation for the sake of financial stability is not a new idea as it was initially proposed in the UK Bank Charter Act of 1844, the US Acts of 1863 and 1864, the Chicago Plan of 1930s and several IMF studies have shown better economic growth rates. We are well aware that there are constant trade-offs in economics, but we cannot trade the stability of our financial future for unrestrained profits through the aggressive expansion of credit.

As we move forward to this proposed system, there are some critical challenges that need to be addressed. One of the major challenges is the collective political will to see this initiative through. The formation of a unified Islamic digital currency will traverse many challenging situations which may drudge up historical wounds and clash present egos. Muslim leaders have to decide what is the cost of their sovereignty, and the price of modern "slavery". The leaders must be cognizant of what "brotherhood" and the concept of the "ummah" really means, instead of empty rhetoric. Overcoming self-driven wants to cater to higher motives beyond national or personal agendas, where pursuing self-interest takes a backseat to uphold the collective interest, is preferred and encouraged. Successful are those who think beyond themselves. There always has been a moral and ethical obligation to human interactions because we are all connected in ways that one may not fathom yet. Globalization has interconnected the world economy in new ways and will continue to do so in yet-to-be discovered avenues. Administering justice and fostering trust by upholding ethical and moral obligations hence reinforces communal solidarity based on shared values, removes fears and suspicion in public and private institutions for a harmonious and profitable existence, by sharing risk in highly uncertain times through reciprocal undertaking.

The second big challenge is to reduce the digital divide in Islamic nations. The success of the unified digital currency relies heavily on the robustness of the technological infrastructure as well as the perspicacity of the technical expertise that supports it. To fully utilize technical capabilities and enhance the Islamic economies through technology innovation, there must be several deep policy and infrastructural changes that we recommend and must take place (see the final section of Chapter 4 – Overcoming the Digital Divide).

Proposed Constructs For The Unified Islamic Digital Currency (DIGITAL DINAR)

The proposed unified Islamic digital currency (or Digital Dinar,[9] Figure 11.1) could be done in either of these two ways – first, in the purist form of currency backed by gold and silver (or any other forms of commodities such as hard commodities and soft commodities with clear price discovery mechanisms). The second way is to aggregate the sovereign currencies of the participating Islamic nations as in the form of a monetary union like the Euro. A common digital currency is also the next logical progression since electronic transactions have begun to dominate global transactions worldwide.[10]

Figure 11.1: Impression of the Digital Dinar.

---

9 The impression of the Digital Dinar is shown in Figure 1. The double 'D's share a single axis (Alif – the singular only God) and the logo can also be seen as an 'S' which depicts Shariah-compliance or halalness.

10 McKinsey Global Payments Report 2020: https://www.mckinsey.com/~/media/mckinsey/industries/financial%20services/our%20insights/accelerating%20winds%20of%20change%20in%20global%20payments/2020-mckinsey-global-payments-report-vf.pdf.

The Aggregated Sovereign Currencies Construct

The Unified Islamic Digital Currency, or Digital Dinar for short, is a cryptographically protected digital currency, pegged to the physical currencies of the 10 largest Islamic economies[11] (in terms of GDP), whose fundamental goal is to help facilitate international and local commerce by becoming the most commonly used exchange medium for trade (Figure 11.2). It operates on a multi-level network, that is both decentralized and distributed, aiming, by design, to provide faster transaction processing than other common cryptocurrencies enabling real-time commercial applications.

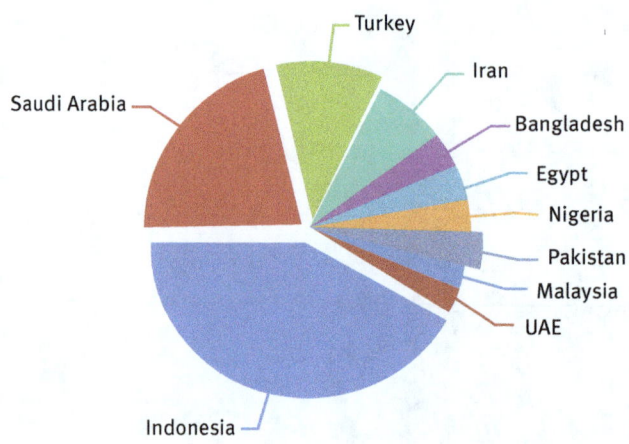

Pegged Distribution of Countries
according to GDP Size

Figure 11.2: The weightage of the Sovereign Currency backing the Digital Dinar is according to the Country's GDP Size.

A unified Islamic central bank (ICB) serves as an initial backbone to deliver an extrinsic value by maintaining sovereign reserves (i.e. cash, central bank reserves, government securities and other assets) equivalent to the monetary volume in circulation and guarantees continuous exchanges. The Digital Dinar is pegged to an aggregation of 10 existing fiat currencies of Islamic nations, chosen for their international importance. Together, they represent about 70% of the total OIC GDP and are representative in the global foreign exchange markets. Each currency proportion is determined by weighting their respective economic importance and international trading volume.

---

[11] As of 2021, the 10 largest Islamic economies are: Indonesia, Saudi Arabia, Turkey, Iran, Bangladesh, Egypt, Nigeria, Pakistan, Malaysia and the UAE.

The Islamic Central Bank (ICB)

The Islamic Central Bank is the governing authority of the Digital Dinar and is owned by the founding countries and shareholders. Its roles comprise acting as a limited central bank: it can print or remove currency from circulation, making it possible to control inflation and guarantees value by keeping monetary reserves equivalent to the total amount in circulation relatively to the pegged fiat currencies. Hence it cannot create currency through interest-rate policies, and adding or removing currency is a transparent process, as it is made with standard transactions registered in the same ledgers, exclusively using the ICB base account, reserved only for these kinds of operations.

Additionally, it is responsible for managing the account windows and leasing them to independent Managing Entities. It has authority over the official account windows, and complete discretion over the allocation of reserved and normal accounts. However, a Managing Entity has total control over its allocated accounts, including the possibility of sub-leasing one or more.

Other functions of the ICB include:
- No trading of pegged fiat currencies with Digital Dinar (majority *fiqh* opines trading of currencies as haram or impermissible) but spot exchange is acceptable;
- Managing the registration of external participants, and attributing them official identification codes;
- Providing its own Signing Node;
- Providing basic network services for users such as but not limited to account attribution, transactions submission, balance viewing;
- Maintaining and updating the source code of the Validating Nodes;
- Providing Validating Nodes in order to ensure the stability of the network;
- Maintaining a Data Tracker, offering unrestricted public access to accounts, transactions, Ledgers, Network Management Blocks, Distributed Automatic Services (DASs), Decentralized Autonomous Organizations (DAOs), exchange rates, et al;
- Resolving disputes over windows allocations and unethical or illegal managing practices, such as but not limited to lies, misrepresentation or disinformation about transactions fees;
- Vetting third-party services and DAOs with the community and help integrate them into the network;
- Provide certification by creating and maintaining the Digital Dinar's Public Key Infrastructure with its own root certificate.

As intended with the network structure, the ICB does not have the permissions to execute, validate or register any transaction without the proper signatures nor, just like any entity managing the various accounts, change public keys linked to activated accounts, which are safeguarded by the Network Management Blockchain. The financing of the ICB will come mainly from the leasing of accounts, reserves income, fees collected from transactions involving accounts from managed windows or donations of investments made to the Digital Dinar.

The functions of a Signing Node are to sign and authorized requests for transactions received from end users or other Signing Nodes, insert the transaction fees data and transmit to the Inbound or Outbound Entity, or directly to a random Validating Node. A Signing Node can also implement an extra layer of security for the network by already making certain verifications about the signatures, balances and duplications.

The Validating Nodes are the currency's workers and form the inner layer of the network. They are responsible for accepting or rejecting transactions, creating the Ledgers, providing access to the third-party services and enabling DAOs to operate. Together with the Signing Nodes, they validate Network Management Entries and create the resulting Network Management Blocks. Though, all decisions are made by reaching a consensus, thus avoiding malicious or faulty operations and allowing not only separation from the rest of the network but also the distribution and decentralization of the currency's core operations. Therefore, a published transaction is already proof of a validated and accepted transaction, leaving the ledgers simply as a tool for overviewing the current state of the network and synchronization between nodes.

Distributed Automatic Services, or DAS for short, are vetted services created by third-parties which become fully integrated by the Validating Nodes such as to autonomously provide them within the network. Those services are vetted by the community and registered into the Network Management Blockchain by the ICB, however they are overviewed by a manager, the company or individual that created the DAS, who defines the service itself, the transaction types and logical processes, and all necessary documentation. A new module is specifically created for each DAS, establishing the implementation of the logical processes and support of the new transactions, to be deployed to all Validating Nodes. Each DAS becomes then usable by the network through any Validating Node running the updated network protocol version. The manager of the service can set how, when and if fees are incurred into the available transactions, these fees are then automatically transferred to the assigned DAS account, which can be from any of the reserved accounts.

Much like with Distributed Automatic Services, Decentralized Autonomous Organizations, or DAOs are vetted and incorporated into the Validating Nodes following the same process. The accounts are reserved, and each is assigned to one of those accounts. Network compensation is reached the same way, from the fees collected, the network's global DAO fee rate is levied and transferred into the base DAO account, to be then redistributed equally into all Validating Nodes. Similarly, the distribution is done DAO-wise, dividing the compensation funds among the Validating Nodes which can operate the DAO and reporting the indivisible surplus.

The Ledgers are the data structures governing the currency. Through them the current state of the currency, balances and transactions, can be easily disseminated, archived and analyzed. They are interlinked, forming a hierarchical chain alike the traditional blockchains, which start with a Genesis Ledger and cannot be altered ulteriorly or deviated from. Each Ledger compensates a fixed period of one hour, regrouping all the validated transactions that were published during that time, meta information about it, all the accounts' balances at its closing and a link to its predecessor Ledger.

The Network Management Blockchain is a secondary blockchain used to complement the currency's Ledgers and allow further transparency, autonomy and greater independence from the Dinar's ICB. As the name portrays, its functionality is to regroup and substantiate all of the diverse information required for the Digital Dinar network and its participants to fully operate. It is composed by Network Management Blocks, created every half hour by both Signing Nodes and Validating Nodes, containing pieces of data, where a single one is called a Network Management Entry, submitted or transmitted by those Nodes. Similar to Ledgers, each Block is identified by a numerical ID and a RIPEMD-160 hash computed by the concatenation of 3 parameters: its ID, the hash of the previous Network Management Block and the Merkle root of the Network Management Entries hashes.

The Basket of Commodities Construct

The Digital Dinar can also be pegged to gold and silver or a "basket" of commodities such as hard commodities and soft commodities with clear price discovery mechanisms. Hard commodities include natural resources that must be mined or extracted—such as gold, rubber, and oil, whereas soft commodities are agricultural products or livestock—such as corn, wheat, coffee, sugar, and soybeans. In this construct, the weightage of the Commodity Reserves backing the Digital Dinar is according to the value of the country's stock of the said commodity or commodities.

Leo Grondona (1890–1982) formulated a system of conditional currency convertibility based on a range of basic, durable and essential commodities. The Grondona system has two basic characteristics; first it handles reserves of each primary commodity separately, and aims only at partial stability in primary commodities prices, thereby limiting the financial liability involved (Figure 11.3). Second, since the system does not involve an open-ended liability, it can be set up by a single issuing entity, and so can use to underlie a currency, which would be pegged to the basket of stable, essential and most common commodities, and thereby help to stabilize the real value of the currency (Grondona, 1975), in this case, the Digital Dinar.

The Grondona commodity convertibility system is based on the original and ancient philosophy of stabilizing commodity prices by accumulating reserves of commodities when prices are falling and releasing the reserves of those commodities when prices are going high (Turnell, 1998). This idea of maintaining reserves of commodities can be traced back to the story of Prophet Yusuf (peace be upon him) in Egypt explained in the Holy Quran; where Prophet Yusuf (peace be upon him) interpreted the dream of the King and warned him of seven years of abundance followed by seven years of famine. He suggested to him to keep some reserves of wheat in granaries during the good years so that there will be some left to consume during the difficult times of the famine when no harvest can be had. Many economists (for example, Keynes, 1938; Graham, 1940; Hart, Kaldor and Tinbergen, 1964; and Lietaer, 2001) incorporated this ancient philosophy of maintaining reserves into their proposals for attaining macroeconomic stability (Turnell, 1998). This idea of currency convertibility not only stabilizes the real value of money but also tends to dampen the sharp fluctuations in the primary commodities market (Collins, 2006).

Commodity Reserve Division (CRD)

The implementation of Grondona system would require establishing a Commodity Reserve Division (CRD) (like any central bank's issue department under the classical gold standard) which stands ready to exchange national currency on demand for each of the selected primary commodities, according to specified price schedules: thereby buying the primary commodities when the prices of primary commodities fall and selling them when prices of those commodities rise (Collins, 1996). The transactions of CRD would be determined by the market participants thereby making its role completely passive (Collins, 2002). And the transactions of CRD would have effect on the country's money supply by an amount equivalent to the value of net sales to and purchases from the CRD. Furthermore, the CRD would publish the price schedule for each individual primary commodity, and the level of reserves of each commodity would also be made public on a regular basis (Collins, 1996).

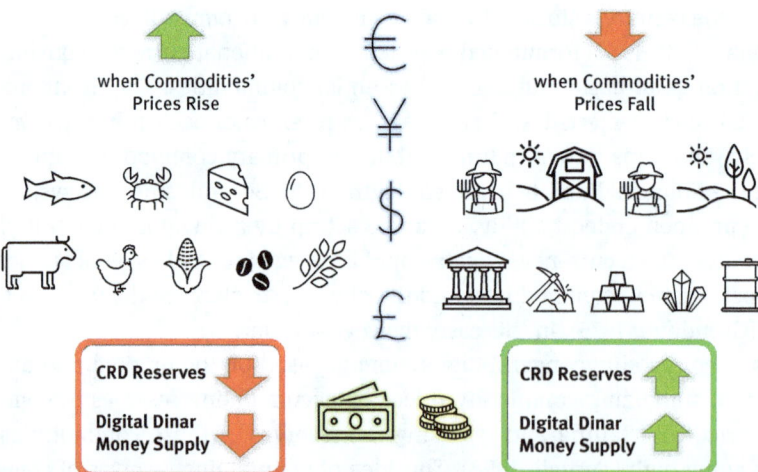

Figure 11.3: The Counter-cyclical Nature of the Grondona System.

The Fixed Price Schedule

The CRD would function under some important rules as formulated by Grondona (1975). Those rules guarantee that the prices at which the CRD stands ready to buy or sell reserves of individual commodities on demand from traders would remain in line with market forces. For that, the CRD maintains a fixed price schedule for each commodity separately. The price schedule would comprise the information about the CRD's buying/selling prices (lower/upper points) of each commodity corresponding to different levels of reserves, and a certain prescribed quantity for each individual commodity, which Grondona called a "block". For simplicity of operations, the CRD deals only in large units of quantity specified separately for each commodity – for example, 10 tons, 20 tons, 30 tons (i.e. on a "wholesale" rather than "retail" scale.) The CRD's buying and selling prices adjust automatically according to that fixed price schedule in the opposite direction to the level of reserves with CRD, in line with market forces. Consequently, the price schedules used by the CRD would not distort commodity market prices. It would rather lessen the large and unexpected fluctuations in commodity market prices (Grondona, 1975; Collins, 1985).

Parameters of the Price Schedule

Grondona (1975) described the parameters of the price schedules for specified commodities which he named the "gearing of the system". These parameters are important in deciding the extent of the system's monetary and economic influence, and the government's financial commitment involved in the resumption of conditional currency convertibility system. These parameters include the range of commodities, initial price levels, size of blocks, width of price-bands and price-steps between successive price-bands. The description of these parameters would provide a detailed explanation of the price schedules used within the system. There are a number of factors that need to be considered in deciding each of these parameters. This would also help determine the optimum scale of the system to have a stabilizing effect on each commodity industry and on the national economy. Further, the level of outlay required during the Grondona system's operation could be determined from the three main parameters of the price schedule that are the size of blocks of each commodity, the width of the price-band between lower and upper points and the size of the price-steps between successive price-bands (Collins, 1985).

Like in the previous construct, this construct will also leverage on a tokenized system to achieve its design and application, utilizing a unified Islamic central bank (ICB) that serves as the backbone to coordinate operations of the group of national CRDs and determines rules for maintaining national reserves equivalent to the monetary volume in circulation in order to guarantee continued exchanges. It operates on a multi-level network, that is both decentralized and distributed, to provide faster transaction processing than other common cryptocurrencies enabling real-time commercial applications.

Benefits to the Digital Dinar Implementation

There are several key advantages for the implementation of the Digital Dinar:
1. Unlike popular mobile payment systems like WeChat and ApplePay, transactions using the Digital Dinar can be done without an internet connection.
2. It need not require a bank account, and hence will be able to serve the unbanked or underbanked, especially in the rural areas. This should be a huge step in financial inclusion and poverty alleviation due to better financial access.
3. The underlying blockchain technology may also help in preventing illegal financial activities such as money laundering, currency counterfeiting and unlawful transactions.
4. It allows real-time records related to money creation and balance sheets so as to advise monetary policies, which can improve economic planning from fast and accurate data.
5. The global use of a common currency reduces time for trade settlements and reduces counter-party risks.
6. It also removes foreign exchange or currency exchange risks since trading transactions using the Digital Dinar need not use different currencies to complete payments.
7. The dependence on traditional cross-border settlement systems like the SWIFT system will be reduced to prevent such systems to be weaponized to impose sanctions on parties deemed as enemies. The Digital Dinar can be an alternative for cross-border payments that prevents unwarranted foreign interference in domestic policies, hence keeping the nation's sovereignty intact.

The Digital Dinar will be an innovative solution for OIC nations to be independent and digitally-ready for the new Islamic economy which integrates AI, big data, blockchain and 5G. The Digital Dinar will also allow Islamic countries to expand its exchange with global trade partners and balance economic governance throughout the world.

Conclusion

Previous efforts to establish a unified Islamic dinar were unsuccessful, primarily because of the absence of unity and collective political will for implementation. The primary view was limited to economic justifications, and limited assessments done on other equally-important factors such as culture, economic progress, acceptance and so on. The impact of a unified Islamic digital dinar on the existing economic system and its institutions needs to be properly assessed and considered before even taking steps towards implementation. Such considerations need to go beyond economic benefits for the countries involved but need to also be driven by the goal of establishing sovereign control over the resources that we are responsible over. The higher purposes (*maqasid*[12]) of the Shariah need to be accomplished (or striven towards), not only in respect of the protection of property (*hifz al-mal*) and the protection of life (*hifz al-nafs*), but also the preservation of our dignity (*'ird*) and security of individual Muslims and the Islamic community worldwide. The current application of technology provides ample opportunity for Islamic countries to achieve this goal through reclaiming our economic prowess via the vast resources under our vicegerency by virtue of establishing a fair and just monetary system that is not based on interest (*riba*) injustice that widens inequality. The issuance of the unified Islamic digital dinar (currency) will help facilitate this intention and foster close economic and trade cooperation, while protecting individual rights and national sovereignty.

In order to achieve this noble agenda, the Muslim world has to first come together and attain the unity that all prophets had come to establish in the time before, through the message of *tauhid*. In doing so, it will enable them[13] to achieve the many goals and desires that have eluded them thus far.

References

Agustiar, M. (2018). The Single Currency for Islamic Nations: Do Heterogeneities Matter? *Journal of Islamic Monetary Economics and Finance*, 4(2), 223–236.

Al-Baz, A. M. (1999). Ahkaam Saref al-Noqood wa al-'Umulaat. Kuwait: Dar al-Nafais.

Alamad, S. (2019). Money, Its Origins, Nature and the Time Value of Money. *Financial and Accounting Principles in Islamic Finance*, 21–47. https://doi.org/10.1007/978-3-030-16299-3_2

Arif, A., & Shabbir, M. S. (2019). Common currency for Islamic countries: is it viable? *Transnational Corporations Review*, 11(3), 222–234. https://doi.org/10.1080/19186444.2019.1657330

Bacha, O. I. (2008). A common currency area for ASEAN? issues and feasibility. *Applied Economics*, 40(4), 515–529. https://doi.org/10.1080/00036840600675653

Brown Randy. (2019). In A U.S.-China Currency War, Who Wins? Forbes.Com. https://www.forbes.com/sites/randybrown/2019/08/15/in-a-us-china-currency-war-who-wins/?sh=b60850a751cb

---

12 The objectives or maqasid of the Shariah had been simplified and summarized by Al-Ghazali into the protection of these five key areas – thought (aql), religion (deen), life (nafs) progeny (nasl) and wealth (mal). In reality, our scholars (as well as our deeper consciousness) urge us to achieve its higher objectives such as equality, trust and social justice through accountability, brotherhood, cooperation and the enforcement of rules and laws to uphold what is right and forbid what is wrong and evil (amr bi-l-ma'rūf wa-n-nahy 'ani-l-munkar). The Caliphate of Islam establishes freedoms (according to the Shariah), enforces justice, ensures prosperity and opportunities for all, and rewards the generous and magnanimous, but chastises the corrupt, opulent and wasteful.

13 As a theological concept, the ummah is meant to transcend national, racial, and class divisions to unite all Muslims.

Collins, P. (1985). Currency Convertibility: The return to sound money. New York: St. Martin's Press.
Collins, P. (1996). "Implications for Japanese Monetary Policy and its Simulation of the Implementation of Conditional Currency Convertibility (the Grondona System)." Tokyo, Japan: Submission to Bank of Japan.
Collins, P. (2002, November). The Grondona System of Conditional Currency Convertiblity: Abasis for Conflict-Free Monetary Cooperation. In Conference on 1st International Conference of the Japan Economic Policy Association (JEPA) Organized by Japan Economic Policy Association, Tokyo.
Collins, P. (2006, Spring). Conditional Currency Convertibility and its Applicability in Japan. Paper presented at Conference on Monetary Economics organized by Japan Society for Monetary Economics, Tokyo.
European Central Bank. (2000). The single currency and European integration. 16 October. https://www.ecb.europa.eu/press/key/date/2000/html/sp001016.en.html
Friedman, R. (1951). Commodity-Reserve Currency. *Journal of Political Economy*, 59, 203–32.
Gautham. (2015). A Brief History of Digital Currency. Newsbtc. http://www.newsbtc.com/2015/11/01/a-brief-history-of-digital-currency/%0Ahttp://andrewdoble.blogspot.co.za/2014/06/a-brief-history-of-digital.html
Graham, F. D. (1940). The Primary Functions of Money and their Consummation in Monetary Policy. The American Economic Review, 30(1), 1–16. http://www.jstor.org/stable/1814476
Graham, B. (1937). Storage and Stability: A Modern Ever-Normal Granary. New York: McGraw-Hill.
Grondona, L.S.C. (1975). Economic Stability is Attainable. London: Hutchinson Benham.
Hart, A.G., Kaldor, N. and Tinbergen, J. (1964). "The Case for an International Commodity Reserve Currency". Geneva: United Nations Conference on Trade and Development.
Hayek, F.A. (1943). A commodity Reserve Currency. *The Economic Journal*, 53 (210/211-Jun-Sep), 176–186.
Ismath Bacha, O. (2008). A common currency area for MENA countries? A VAR analysis of viability. *International Journal of Emerging Markets*, 3(2), 197–215. https://doi.org/10.1108/17468800810862641
Joel, K. (2019). Digital Currency: A Brief History Medium.Com. .https://medium.com/block-journal/digital-currency-a-brief-history-98be6f6f0f10
Kamar, B. (2004). De Facto Exchange Rate Policies in the MENA Region: Toward Deeper Cooperation. Economic Research Forum, Working Papers, 27. http://files/210/Kamar -DE FACTO EXCHANGE RATE POLICIES IN THE MENA REGION.pdf%0A https://www.researchgate.net/publication/46453349_De_Facto_Exchange_Rate_Policies_in_the_MENA_Region_Toward_Deeper_Cooperation
Keynes, J. (1938). The Policy of Government Storage of Foodstuffs and Raw Materials. *Economic Journal*, 48(191), 449–460.
Lietaer, B. (2001). The Future of Money: Creating new wealth, work and a wiser world. London: Century.
Mirakhor, Abbas (2017). Islamic Finance and Financial Repression. https://journal.wahedinvest.com/islamic-finance-and-financial-repression/ Accessed 5th July 2019.
Moessner, R. and Allen, W.A. (2010). Banking Crisis and the International Monetary System in the Great Depression and Now. BIS Working Paper No. 333. December.
Mohamed, H. (2021). Beyond Fintech: Technology Applications for the Digital Economy. World Scientific, Singapore.
OIC. (2020). OIC Economic Outlook 2020. https://www.sesric.org/files/article/735.pdf
Razzaghia, S., B. Salmania, and A. Kazeroonia (2018). Feasibility of a Monetary Union In Islamic Regions of OIC Countries: New Evidence From Competitiveness Differentials. *International Journal of Economics, Management and Accounting*, 26(1), 229–245.
Reinhart, C. M., & Rogoff, K. S. (2011). From financial crash to debt crisis. American Economic Review, 101(5), 1676–1706. https://doi.org/10.1257/aer.101.5.1676
Turnell, S. (1998). The Quest for Commodity Price Stability: Australian Economists and "buffer Stocks". Australia: Macquarie University, Department of Economics.

Index

AAOIFI (Accounting and Auditing Organization for Islamic Financial Institutions) 195
ABA (American Bar Association) 157, 159
Abu Dhabi Global Market. See *ADGM*
Academia 194, 198
Accenture 55, 64, 108, 202, 207
Accidents 144
Accounting and Auditing Organization for Islamic Financial Institutions. See *AAOIFI*
Adaptation 95, 97, 100, 176, 196
ADGM (Abu Dhabi Global Market) 93–94, 104
Adoption 36–37, 142, 160
Advanced technologies 67
Advancements 6, 14, 17, 47, 113, 154, 187, 195
– technological 14, 154, 195
Africa 11, 18, 24–25, 49–50, 73, 78, 105, 112, 123, 144, 225–226
Agility 97, 192, 209
Agility and adaptation 97
Agreements 15, 34, 69, 84, 94, 124–125, 134, 138, 157, 170, 176, 201, 212, 217
Algebra 70
Algorithms 57, 59, 62, 71, 111, 114, 116, 136, 158, 171, 177, 183–184
Alipay 34, 36, 83, 93, 205
Amazon 5, 34, 36, 48, 62, 116, 128, 175, 191
American Bar Association (ABA) 157, 159
AML (anti-money laundering) 39, 53, 55, 61, 122, 126–128, 165–166, 176, 185, 206
Amount 22, 24, 29, 31, 50–52, 91, 100, 111, 113–114, 128, 135, 147, 153, 163–164, 169, 183, 188, 218–219, 221, 235, 238
– total 22, 24, 51
Analytics 6, 12–13, 20–22, 47–48, 53–54, 62, 76, 79, 146, 157–159, 162, 165, 171, 174, 193, 198, 205–206
– predictive 62, 157–158
Antimoney laundering 39, 122, 184
APIs (application program interfaces) 111, 164, 166, 205
Apple 5, 18, 34, 36, 48, 191, 230
Apple pay 18, 34, 36, 230

Application program interfaces (APIs) 205
Applications 7–9, 19, 40, 42, 53, 55–56, 58–59, 62–64, 68, 103, 128, 134–135, 137, 145, 151, 154, 156, 158, 162, 175, 181, 188, 198, 201, 212–213, 223, 234, 240
Apps 7, 18, 34, 54, 116, 128, 131, 175, 230
AR (augmented reality) 31, 98, 199
Arner 14, 16, 19, 44, 194, 207
Artificial intelligence 8–9, 13, 21, 47, 60, 62, 65, 67–68, 94, 110, 113, 157–158, 161–162, 178, 194, 216
ASEAN (Association of Southeast Asian Nations) 8–9, 107, 203, 226, 241
Asia 11, 18–19, 22–25, 36–37, 45, 49–50, 64, 66, 73, 81, 87, 92, 106, 142–144, 151, 186, 203, 209, 223
Asian investments in blockchain fintech 186
Asset management 23, 53, 65, 78, 91, 147, 171, 176, 178, 198
Asset purchase 152
Assets 6, 8, 9, 16–19, 25–27, 40, 42–43, 45, 55, 59–60, 74, 79, 85–86, 108, 117, 124, 129, 148, 151–52, 154, 161, 169, 174–175, 182–183, 188, 211–212, 214–218, 221–223, 232, 234
– real 40
Association of Southeast Asian Nations (ASEAN) 8, 203
Attacks 43, 175, 187, 194, 229
Authenticity 145, 147–148
Automated teller machine (ATMs) 15, 35
Automates 93, 152
Automation 13, 61, 67, 97, 99, 113, 115, 135–136, 156–159, 171, 177, 198, 217

Bahrain 67, 75, 77–79, 105–107, 151, 225–226
Balance sheets 69, 112, 231, 240
Banco Bilbao Vizcaya Argentaria (BBVA) 7
Bank account 123, 173, 191, 203, 240
Bank Indonesia 88
Bank Negara Malaysia (BNM) 30, 44, 75, 82–83, 86, 105, 195
Bank of England (BOE) 21, 70, 196, 230
Bank services 139
Banking 1, 4, 6–8, 11–12, 14–15, 17–18, 21, 23, 27, 33–36, 42, 48, 52, 55, 71, 76–79,

Index

81–82, 86, 89–91, 94–96, 108, 115, 119, 125–127, 134, 138, 148, 150, 170, 174–175, 183, 185–186, 192, 197–198, 200–201, 203–207, 230, 232
– conventional 70, 203
Banking industry 15, 23, 52, 66, 78, 115, 125, 200, 209
Banking sector 21, 91, 94, 127, 186
Banking services 6–7, 52, 55, 82, 90–91, 200–201
Banks 1, 6, 14–15, 17–19, 21, 26, 29–30, 33–34, 42, 50, 52, 55, 59, 61, 67, 69–70, 77–79, 81–83, 85–86, 89, 91–95, 103, 108, 110, 112, 113, 115, 122–123, 125–127, 130, 138–143, 149–151, 164–166, 171, 173–175, 177, 181, 183, 185–187, 190–195, 198–199, 201–207, 229–230
– challenger 52
– conventional 69, 78
– correspondent 122
– investment 115, 195
– large 110, 183
– traditional 19, 89, 205–206
Barberis 14, 44, 194, 207
Benefits 2–4, 55, 68, 101, 103, 110, 117, 119, 137, 141–143, 145, 147, 149–150, 156, 172, 177, 182, 187, 189, 202, 211, 213–214, 217–219, 221, 230, 240–241
– potential 149, 156, 189, 217
BFB 78
Big data 8, 12, 20–22, 47–48, 53–54, 57, 62–63, 68, 79, 91, 113, 158, 161–166, 174, 176–177, 192, 194, 196, 205, 240
Bitcoin 28, 33–35, 39–41, 113, 124–128, 134, 137–138, 172–173, 179–180
Bitcoin blockchain technology 187
BKM 91, 105
Blockchain 8–10, 55–58, 66–70, 111–114, 116–120, 122–134, 138–148, 150–164, 166–180
Block-chain 155
Blockchain
– bitcoin 122, 187, 209
– platform 183
Blockchain application 53, 128, 145, 149, 189, 213
Blockchain business case 146
Blockchain community 133, 185
Blockchain companies 110

Blockchain cryptography works for smart contracts 136
Blockchain economy 187, 189
Blockchain ecosystem 126, 155, 187
Blockchain fintech 186
Blockchain implementation 189
Blockchain industry 8, 186, 189
Blockchain infrastructure 31, 128–129
Blockchain ledgers 122
Blockchain models 182
Blockchain platforms 156, 177
Blockchain protocol software system 122
Blockchain protocols 151
Blockchain revolution 149, 210
Blockchain solutions 146, 184
Blockchain space 8, 110
Blockchain systems 129, 146
– decentralized 189
Blockchain technology 1, 9, 26, 29, 55, 120–121, 126, 148–150, 154, 162, 180–182, 187, 189, 209, 212–213, 222–223, 240
Block-chain technology 2, 156, 170
Blockchain technology
– deployed
– implemented 181
Blockchain technology-arsenal 209
Blockchain technology-how-banks-building-real-time 64
Blockchain-based fintech solution 84
Blockchain-Based Islamic Capital Markets 148–149, 151
Blockchain-based payment, new 154
Blockchain-based smart contracts 137, 141, 156
Blockchain-based technologies 153
Blockchain-based technology, basic 136
Blocks 120, 122, 128–129, 133, 143, 145, 154, 174
Bloomberg terminals 15–16
Blossom 84–85, 108
Blossom finance 152–153, 200
BNM. See *Bank Negara Malaysia*
Bodies 78, 92, 155–156, 158
BOE (Bank of England) 196, 230
Bonds 11, 26, 37–38, 124, 151–152
Borrowers 50, 89–90, 94
Boston consulting group 10, 125, 133, 157, 159–160, 223
Branches 6, 17–18, 93, 162, 200–201
Brands 5, 7–8, 10, 34–36

Index — 245

Brokers 15, 125
Brunei 92, 107
Brunei Darussalam 67, 87, 92–93, 226
BTC 29, 43, 123, 150
Building 9, 35, 75, 78, 101, 153, 182, 207, 214
Building blocks 8, 77, 84, 100, 128–129, 133, 160
Business logic 129–131, 137
– stateful 129, 131
Business models 4, 69, 81, 93, 156, 159, 185, 187, 204, 206, 217
– innovative 6, 52, 67, 71, 83, 90, 195–196
– new 53, 68, 82, 88, 95, 147, 179
Businesses 4–5, 14–16, 21–22, 78–79, 121–122, 167–168, 177–178, 182–183, 187–188
Buyers 18, 36–37, 100, 123, 140, 142, 149, 212

CAGR 22, 24, 34, 49–51, 57, 74
Calculation 70–71, 147
Campaigns 52
Canadian Imperial Bank of Commerce (CIBC) 110
Capabilities 58, 64, 71, 90, 93–94, 99–101, 112, 177, 193, 197, 206, 232
Capacity 9, 53, 117, 125, 134, 177, 192–193, 198
Capital 53, 63, 80, 87, 103, 105, 142–143, 154, 158
– working 142–143
Cases 9–10, 41–43, 73, 75, 114, 116–117, 136–138, 156, 174–175
Cash 17, 39, 85, 88, 126, 145
– digital 21, 122
– waqf 211, 217–221
Catalyst 130, 200–201, 75, 78
CBB (Central Bank of Bahrain) 78, 107
CBDC (Central Bank-issued Digital Currency) 230–232
CC (crypto-conditions) 130
CDD (customer due diligence) 126
Central authorities 2, 20, 183
Central Bank of Bahrain. See CBB
Central banks 26, 30, 42, 49–50, 150, 165, 172, 230
Century 13–14, 17, 70–71, 216–217, 224–225
CFPs 51
Chain 113, 124, 126, 133, 154, 161
Challenges 9, 56, 106–107, 130, 144, 148, 173, 175, 181

Challenges for Islamic financial institutions 195, 197, 199
Channels 5, 8, 37–38, 54, 92, 96, 182
Chatbots 7–8, 157, 170, 198
Choices 2–3, 115, 206
CIBAFI (Council for Islamic Banks and Financial Institutions) 203
Claims 25, 54, 70, 138–139, 145–147, 163
Clients 53, 59–60, 94, 132, 141, 146, 158, 194
Cloud 59, 115–116, 133, 166
Cloud computing 8, 20, 47–48, 56, 65–66, 68, 112, 186–187
Cloud service provider (CSPs) 56
Cloud services 56, 112, 193
Code 129, 135, 139–140, 142–143, 176
CoinGecko 28, 32, 44
Coins 25, 32, 39–42, 91, 121, 129
Collaboration 24, 57, 78, 88, 92–93, 122, 131, 155, 188–193
Collaboration models for Islamic financial institutions 200–201, 203, 205
Combinational 130–131
Committee on Payments and Market Infrastructures (CPMI) 27, 178
Commodities 30, 42, 87, 157
Community 78, 81, 83, 184
Companies 33–34, 42, 57–58, 105–106, 114–115, 143–144, 164, 182–183, 187
Compendious book 71
Competition 6, 100–101, 115, 131, 164–165, 172, 177, 192, 198
Completion 71
Compliance 36, 69, 87, 116, 118, 142, 148, 154, 178
– regulatory 108, 134, 177, 190, 195
Components 113, 120, 124, 134, 186, 194
Computers 61, 64, 66, 123, 125, 129, 136, 142
Computing, decentralized 128–129, 132
Concept 1–2, 4, 13, 28–30, 32, 60, 120, 123, 157–158
Conditions 69, 129, 140–141, 151
Confidence 1, 3, 108, 118, 120, 147, 193
Confirmation 142, 146
Connect 17, 37, 57, 61, 90, 137–138, 157
Connect networks 129, 132–133
Consortium 55, 78, 105, 209
Consumers 10, 14, 17, 35, 37–39, 71, 164, 166, 183
Content 8, 160, 162, 164

Contract management 157, 159
Contract technology, smart 9, 134
Contracts 13, 39, 69, 128–129, 139–143, 153–154, 165
Contractual agreements 124–125, 134, 217
Cooperation 19, 29, 76, 102–103, 151, 156, 191
Coordination 77, 92, 122, 147, 182, 200–201
Corda 183–185
Corporate Venture Capital (CVC) 202
Costs 22, 49, 61, 63, 103–104, 144–145, 157–158, 177–178, 191–192
Council for Islamic Banks and Financial Institutions (CIBAFI) 203
Counterparties 19, 69, 94, 135, 148, 183, 229
Countries 4–5, 32, 34–36, 91–92, 94–95, 98–99, 101, 103–104, 148–150
Courts 137
CPMI (Committee on Payments and Market Infrastructures) 27
Credit 1, 17, 21–22, 38, 60, 91, 116, 143
Cross-border payments 15, 146, 151, 185, 190, 240
Crowdfunding 14–15, 20, 23, 32–33, 49, 52–54, 72, 75, 79–80
Crowdfunding campaigns 33, 75, 90
Crowdfunding including rewards 44, 65
Crowdfunding market, global 51, 66
Crowdfunding platforms 28, 32, 51, 64, 118
Crowdfunding segment 51–52
Crypto assets 79
Crypto-conditions (CC) 130
Cryptocurrencies 28–33, 35–36, 39–42, 44–46, 124, 127, 153, 157, 159
– categorization of 40
Cryptocurrencies and initial coin offerings 25, 27–29, 31, 33, 35, 37, 39
Crypto exchanges 19, 44–45
Cryptography 25, 53, 55, 64, 122, 136, 148, 176, 183
Crypto securities 29, 32, 41
Crypto tokens 42
Crypto world 28
CSPs (cloud service provider) 56
CTF (counter-terrorism financing) 53, 61, 176, 206
Currency 20, 30, 32, 40–42, 125–127, 129, 170
– virtual 27, 33, 183, 185
Customer behavior 6–7, 162, 164, 166, 172, 191
Customer centricity 191

Customer due diligence (CDD) 126
Customer experience 4, 76, 127, 174, 191, 196, 198, 205, 210
Customers 6–8, 17–19, 36–38, 54–58, 131–132, 151, 156–157, 181–183, 186–187
– bank's 205
– new 64, 170
CVC (Corporate Venture Capital) 202
Cyber extortion payments 43
Cyberattacks 33, 43, 124, 172, 180, 183, 193
Cybersecurity 43–45, 47, 112, 165, 167, 174–175, 193–194, 206, 229

DAML (Digital Asset Modeling Language) 183
DARPA (Defense Advanced Research Projects Agency) 61
Data marketplace 130
Data matching 114, 139–140
Databases 111, 123, 128–130, 165–166, 172, 176, 189
Deal activity 22–23, 108
Debit cards 35
Decentralization 96, 124, 161, 169, 180, 182, 189, 212–213, 229, 236
Decisions 3, 49, 64–65
Defense Advanced Research Projects Agency (DARPA) 61
Delays 125–126, 134, 138, 140
Deloitte 24, 44, 55, 59, 65, 96, 105, 110
Development 24–25, 27, 69–70, 72–74, 80, 92–94, 96–98, 102–106, 146–148
Devices 6, 16, 21, 47, 57–58, 62, 121, 146, 175, 180, 182
DFSRG (Digital Financial Services Research Group) 76
Digital asset 21, 42, 126, 128, 172–174
Digital asset holdings 55, 110, 149, 183, 185
Digital Asset Modeling Language (DAML) 183
Digital channels 6, 19, 48, 52, 68–69, 108, 194, 196–197
Digital currencies 15, 30, 41–42, 109, 126, 178
Digital Dinar 224, 233–241
Digital economy 111–112, 114, 116, 118, 120, 122, 124, 126, 128
Digital ecosystem 133, 193–194
Digital Financial Services Research Group (DFSRG) 76
Digital ledger technology. See *DLT*
Digital Malaysia 84–85

Digital payments 15, 25, 37, 51, 68, 101, 189–190
Digital representations 27–28
Digital technologies 12, 14, 77, 99, 146
Digital transformation 4–6, 10–11, 23, 192, 195
Digital transformation and development 3, 5
Digital transformation in financial services 10
Digitalization 3–6, 14, 16, 47, 67, 76–77, 98–99, 196
Digitization 9, 33, 54, 112–113, 153, 156, 191, 193, 196, 217
Disruptions 2, 8, 48, 143, 206
Distributed infrastructure technology 180–181, 188
Distributed ledger technology 28, 55, 110, 152, 171, 183, 222
Distributed ledgers 6, 25, 27, 137, 139, 141–143, 151, 187
Distribution 51, 54–55, 144, 161–162
DLT (distributed ledger technology) 151–152, 183–185
Documents 69, 128, 130, 132, 146, 151, 165–166, 170, 189
Dollars 15, 20, 32, 43, 48, 52, 109, 128, 139, 152, 168
Drive growth of Islamic FinTech 107
DRM (digital rights management) 153, 155
Dubai 45, 75, 78, 84, 93

Earth 2, 15, 119
EBA (European Banking Authority) 27
ECB (European Central Bank) 27, 49–50, 242
Economic transactions 117, 119, 142, 189, 207
Economic value 25, 117
Economy 18, 28, 58–59, 94, 98, 121, 123, 164, 169–171
Ecosystem 56, 90, 98, 119, 176, 183–184, 186, 189, 193
– financial 89, 187, 206, 209
Emergence 9, 16, 19, 21–22, 28, 32, 37, 49, 54
Emergence of Islamic Fintech 67–68, 70, 72, 74, 76, 78, 80, 82, 84, 86, 88, 90, 92, 94, 96, 98, 100, 102, 104, 106
Enablers 9, 101, 134, 141
Endowments 9, 211, 216, 221
Enterprises 20, 56, 70, 98, 100, 130, 134, 201
– medium-sized 7, 50, 80, 138
Entities 32, 38, 42, 55, 126, 145, 149, 152, 181, 193–195, 235

Entrepreneurs 45, 53–54, 78, 93, 166, 188, 197
Entry 47, 152, 157, 164, 197, 237
Environment 3, 75, 93, 106, 175, 182–183
E-payments 33–34, 85
Equality 2, 134, 181–182, 200, 222, 241
Equities 55, 137–138
Era 10, 16, 20–22, 27, 114, 119, 181, 183, 187
Errors 125, 134, 138, 142, 146, 183
ESMA (European Securities and Markets Authority) 27
Essence 69, 132
Estate, real 19, 26, 37, 40–41, 52, 161, 215, 218
Ethereum 34, 43, 134, 136–138, 157, 167
Eureeca 83
Europe 11, 20–21, 25, 36, 49–50, 72–73, 75, 95–96, 104, 151, 224
European fintech market 21–22
European Securities and Markets Authority (ESMA) 27
Events 43, 140–142, 171, 195, 201
Evolution 13, 15, 17, 19, 37, 44–45, 166–167, 169–170, 174–176
Evolution of legal services 156–157
E-wallets 21, 37–40, 98, 179
– adoption of 36–37
Exchanges 30, 35–36, 41, 44, 121–122, 126–128, 137, 169, 171–173
– decentralized 33
– medium of 25–26, 28, 225
Execution 55, 76, 139, 141–142, 145, 173
Expanded use cases of blockchain 134, 136, 138, 140, 142, 144, 146, 148, 150, 152, 154, 156, 158, 160
Experimentation 102, 133, 184, 196, 231
Exploring Islamic FinTech seminar 92
Explosion 108, 113–114

Failure 96, 102, 154, 196
Family 150
FATF (Financial Action Task Force) 26, 28
Fiat currency 27, 32, 40, 42, 150–151
File systems 128, 130
Files 128–129, 157
Finance 6, 17, 19, 45, 49, 70–71, 105–110, 185–188, 198–199
Finance industry 8, 28, 33, 68–69, 71, 92, 96, 152, 191, 197, 199–200, 208
Financial Action Task Force (FATF) 28
Financial crisis 14, 17–18, 24, 95, 207

Financial inclusion 11, 47, 67–69, 76, 81, 88–89, 94, 107, 200–201, 203, 208, 240
Financial industry 2, 4–6, 9, 13, 16, 92, 95, 114, 119
Financial Industry Regulatory Authority (FINRA) 60
Financial innovation 18, 47–51, 53–54, 90, 93, 208, 210
Financial institutions 5–7, 13–14, 20, 72, 87–88, 93, 115–120, 187–188, 194
– international 95
– regulatory 23–25
Financial instruments 1, 57, 115, 124
Financial products 7, 11, 67, 82, 90
Financial products and services 4, 9, 11, 14, 16, 18, 47, 54, 68, 178, 205
Financial regulators 17–18
Financial services 10–11, 13, 16–17, 20–22, 38–39, 72, 138–139, 169–170, 192–194
– primary 200–201
Financial services industry 4–6, 8, 14, 16, 18, 20, 24, 31, 47–48, 55, 57, 63, 67, 143, 160, 197
Financial services industry perspective 47–49, 51, 53
Financial services institutions 56, 210
Financial services investors 110
Financial services providers 15–16, 18, 83
Financial Services Regulatory Authority (FSRA) 92, 104
Financial services sector 11, 77, 82, 93, 110, 177
Financial services technology consortium 12
Financial system 3, 122
Financial technology 11, 15, 44, 71, 75, 82–83, 105–106, 108, 186, 199, 207–208
Financial technology handbook 44, 197, 207
Financial transactions 8, 14, 18, 20, 64, 119, 124, 148, 150, 161, 170, 196, 200
Financing 70, 72, 79, 84, 86, 111, 113, 116, 144–147
Finextra 78, 105, 148, 151, 201–202, 207–208
FINRA (Financial Industry Regulatory Authority) 60
Fintech 8–10, 13–28, 44–47, 56–70, 91–93, 95–96, 105–108, 185–186, 196–199
– conventional 67–68, 71, 74, 97, 197
– Fintech accelerators 19
– Fintech adoption 67, 80

– FinTech book 44, 207
Fintech companies 20, 22, 24, 26–27, 55, 57, 101–102, 156, 190–192
– new 17, 24
Fintech developments 18, 71, 73
Fintech ecosystem 70, 99, 105, 188
– designed 12
– robust 77
– sustain Bahrain's 78
– vibrant 80, 82
Fintech evolution 13–14
FinTech firms 20, 107, 209
Fintech funding 22–23, 186
FinTech futures 78, 81, 105
Fintech hub 23–24, 44, 78, 80–81, 91, 94, 105
Fintech industry 46, 49, 83, 90, 97, 193–195, 197, 200, 204, 209
Fintech innovations 15
Fintech innovators 24
Fintech investment in Asia-Pacific 23
Fintech investments 11, 22, 25, 78, 87, 91
Fintech investments in Turkey 91
FinTech Istanbul 91
FinTech Istanbul & BKM 91, 105
FinTech Malaysia 83–84, 105
Fintech market 24–27, 99, 102
Fintech participants 93–94
Fintech platforms 6, 11, 68, 78–79, 81, 97, 193, 196, 202
– conventional 97
– new Islamic 71
Fintech products 11–12
Fintech revolution 48, 53, 67, 71, 82, 178
Fintech sector 48, 75, 78, 80, 85, 87–88, 91–92, 96, 192
Fintech segments 91
Fintech startups 7, 21, 44, 75, 78, 82, 95, 105–106
Fintech start-ups 19, 34, 55, 92, 95, 105, 108, 198, 203–204
FinTech Switzerland 18, 44
Fintech transaction value 49
FinTech trends 21, 44, 207
Fintech vendor 11, 202
Firms 17, 20, 23, 55, 58, 62, 106, 113, 155
Focus 26, 79, 84, 90, 137–138, 143, 146, 173, 176–177
Forbes rankings 5
Foreign banks 1, 95

Index

Foundation 2, 8, 14, 34, 77, 118, 120, 134, 151, 168, 211, 216
Framework 82, 96, 103, 108, 119
Fraud 2–3, 59–60, 129–131, 134, 139, 144, 146–147, 152, 154
Frontier, next 65
FSRA (Financial Services Regulatory Authority) 93, 104
Functions 29, 35, 53, 61, 75, 86, 110, 115, 141–142, 147, 206, 235–236, 242
Funding 26, 33, 53, 55, 72, 77, 81, 144, 148
Funds 33–35, 53, 75–76, 78, 81, 86, 93, 95, 146–148
– public-private fintech investment 95
– raising 28–29, 32, 74, 86

GCC (Gulf Cooperation Council) 8–9, 73, 75, 78–9, 143–144, 226
GDP (gross domestic product) 4, 10, 76–77, 80, 227–228, 234
Gen.lib.rus.ec/book/index 10, 208–209
Global landscape 8, 11–12, 14, 16, 18, 20–24, 26, 28, 30, 32, 34, 36, 38, 40, 42, 44, 46, 67, 71
Globe 14, 16, 23, 32, 34, 36, 43, 61, 71, 73, 98, 120, 200–201
Gold 29–30, 41–42, 157
Gold label fintech products 12
Goods 17, 29, 39, 41, 61, 145–147, 151, 170
Google 5, 18, 34, 45, 48, 62, 111, 191
Governments 1, 4, 42, 74–75, 99, 102–103, 137, 143, 152, 181, 186, 190, 194, 200, 206, 230–231
Grondona 237–239
Gross domestic product. See *GDP*
Groups 11, 61, 122, 201–202, 227
Growth 5, 21, 24, 26–27, 101, 104, 111, 149–150, 185–187
Growth rate 22, 24, 51, 58, 87, 143, 232
Gulf Cooperation Council. See *GCC*

Hackathons 201–202
High-performance compute (HPC) 130
History 13–14, 16, 18, 20, 22, 24, 26, 28, 72–73
HPC (high-performance compute) 130–131
Human advisors 19, 60
Human beings 2–3, 62, 119, 178
Humans 61, 168, 180

IAP (Investment Account Platform) 75, 208
IBM (International Business Machines) 15, 59, 64, 81, 185
ICOs (initial coin offerings) XIII, 25–26, 28–29, 31–32, 37–41, 96
ICTs (information communication technologies) 4, 77–78, 80, 83–85, 97–99
IDC (International Data Corp) 56–57, 195
IETF (Internet Engineering Task Force) 130
IFIs (Islamic financial institutions) 75, 191, 193–194, 196–198, 201–205
IFSB (Islamic Financial Services Board) 143, 195, 206
IFSI (Islamic Financial Services Industry) 143–144
ILP 130, 132
IMF (International Monetary Fund) 9, 26–27, 172, 232
Implementation 8, 25, 69, 85, 93, 100, 104, 114, 129–130, 167, 170, 183–185, 188–189, 191, 212–213, 236, 238, 240–241
Importance of Fintech 47
IMS (Innovation Market Solutions) 15–16
India 23, 35–36, 81, 93–94, 108
Individuals 1, 42, 50–51, 60, 70, 118, 120, 127, 135, 189, 204, 219
Indonesian Fintech investments 87
Industrial revolution 13, 24, 161
Industries 4–7, 52, 96–97, 104, 129, 156, 161, 177, 180, 182, 191, 217
Industry participants 12, 16, 149, 187
Inequality 9, 118, 241
Information 4, 11, 13, 16–17, 25, 35, 47, 53, 55–57, 59, 62–63, 69, 76–77, 91, 97, 102, 111–113, 120–121, 123, 125–127, 139–140, 143, 146–148, 153–154, 157–158, 161, 163–167, 170–172, 174–176, 180–181, 184–185, 189, 194, 197–198, 206, 211, 221, 229, 237, 239
Information communication technologies. See *ICTs*
Information technology 11–12, 56, 76, 125, 143, 185, 197
Information Technology University (ITU) 76
Infrastructure 12, 14, 20, 31, 33, 55–57, 72, 76–78, 95, 98–99, 101–103, 111–112, 114, 116–117, 129–130, 136, 137–138, 141–142, 152–153, 164, 170–172, 180–181, 186, 188, 190, 194, 199, 215, 222, 232, 235

– blockchain-based payments 146
Initial coin offerings. See *ICOs*
Initial coin offerings 25, 28
Initiatives 8, 23, 64, 75, 79–80, 85, 89, 92–93, 95–96, 100, 102–104, 195
Innovation 4–5, 8–9, 12, 14–15, 18, 22, 47–48, 50, 71, 76, 78, 80, 88–90, 93, 95–97, 99–104, 108, 119–120, 124, 133, 152, 156, 170, 191, 193–198, 201, 203, 217, 232
– open 204
Innovation ecology 193
Innovation Market Solutions (IMS) 15–16
Innovational funding 51
Innovative products 18, 95, 193, 196, 202–203
Instant payment infrastructures 141–142, 170
Institutional investors 115, 152
Institutions 7, 17–18, 32, 63, 67–70, 82, 95–98, 111–116, 118–119, 125–128, 149–152, 165, 185, 191, 195, 196, 205, 211, 215–217
– microfinance 77
Insurance companies 53–54, 195
Insurance market, global 143
Insurance sector 23, 143
Insurers 54, 127, 139, 145–147, 164–165, 177, 203
InsurTech 13, 20, 53–54, 75, 79, 85, 89, 94
Integration 52–53, 67, 96, 100, 111, 140, 161, 167, 170, 185, 186, 191, 205
Intellectual property (IP) 9, 102, 153, 158
Interfaces, application programming 21, 111, 163
Intermediaries 19, 27, 39, 120, 125, 134, 137, 148, 150, 155, 180, 187
International Business Machines (IBM) 15, 59, 64, 81
International Data Corp. See *IDC*
International Financial Services District (IFSD) 197
International Monetary Fund (IMF) 9, 26–27, 172, 232
International supplier payments 123
Internet 4, 6, 8–9, 12, 15, 17, 27–28, 33–34, 36, 47, 51–52, 56–58, 60, 68, 80–81, 87, 89–90, 94–95, 98–99, 110–112, 130, 132, 139, 146, 180, 201, 240
Internet Engineering Task Force (IETF) 130
Internet of things. See *IoT*

Interoperability 77, 89, 92, 125, 134, 139–140, 156, 172, 187, 200–201
Investment Account Platform (IAP) 75
Investment management 17, 59, 217
Investors 23–24, 37–39, 75, 78, 94, 108, 115, 147, 153, 204, 219–220
Invoices, international supplier 123, 140
IoT (internet of things) 8, 12, 20, 47, 54, 57–58, 68, 70, 98, 130, 146, 163–164, 180–183, 199
IP. See *intellectual property*
IPFS 128, 130–131, 133
Iran 144, 234
Islam 2, 70, 92, 97, 119, 226
Islamic banking 78, 90, 198–199, 203
Islamic banking and finance 68–71, 197
Islamic banks 69–70, 77–78, 193, 203–204, 206
Islamic banks and financial institutions 203, 205
Islamic capital markets 148, 151
Islamic central bank 235–237, 239
Islamic crowdfunding 67
Islamic digital ecosystem 193
Islamic economies 99–100, 137, 143, 207, 232
Islamic finance 8, 67–72, 75, 82, 90, 92, 95–96, 119, 139, 151, 161, 196–200, 207, 231
Islamic finance industry 96, 200
Islamic financial hubs 75
Islamic financial industry 77, 196–197, 203
Islamic financial institutions 69, 151, 178, 191, 195
Islamic financial services 68, 83
Islamic Financial Services Board. See *IFSB*
Islamic Financial Services Industry (IFSI) 143–144
Islamic financial technologies 75, 92
Islamic Fintech 8, 67–75, 78, 85, 92, 96–97, 196, 197, 200, 202–203
Islamic fintech companies 70, 74
Islamic Fintech developments 71
Islamic fintech ecosystems 195
Islamic fintech fraternity 8
Islamic fintech industry 97, 193, 195, 204
Islamic Fintech landscape 71–72, 74
Islamic fintech platforms 68, 71, 97, 193, 202
Islamic fintech players 71
Islamic insurance 143

Islamic transactions 134
Islamic world 28, 97
ITU (Information Technology University) 76

Jurisdictions 17, 23, 26, 32, 39, 52, 137, 139, 142, 144, 152, 177, 181

Kenya 24, 123
Key 54–55, 101, 103, 122, 124, 136, 148, 188
– private 33, 122, 136
Khalifah 2, 119
Kickstarter 51–52
Kingdom 78–81
Know-your-client. See *KYC*
KPMG 13, 59, 186, 203
KYC (know-your-client) 53, 55, 85, 12–127, 146, 165–166, 176, 206
KYC information, customer's 127

Lack 9, 18, 23, 36, 43, 140, 169
Lahore, first FinTech Center in 76
LaunchGood 81
Law 4, 32, 57, 125, 134, 137, 156–157, 159, 195
Learning 61–62, 70, 171, 193, 197–198, 205
Ledgers 122–123, 125–126, 141, 147, 149, 235, 236, 237
Legal business model 157, 159
Legal prose 137
Legal services 156–158
Legal technology 159
LegalTech 156–159
Lending 7–8, 13, 17–18, 20–22, 24, 50, 74, 81, 85, 88–89, 94–95, 118, 181, 205, 207
License 35, 79, 83
Limitations 34, 96, 181, 185–186, 189, 204
List of Indonesian Fintech investments 87
Loans 50, 124, 138, 151, 203
Local currency 123, 152
Logic 62, 130–131, 137
London 15, 75, 95–96
Long-Term Capital Management. See *LTCM*
LTCM (Long-Term Capital Management) 17

Machine learning 5, 8–9, 12, 61, 131, 158, 170–171, 177, 205
Machines 61, 99, 131, 198
Malaysia 36, 72, 75, 82–87, 144, 152, 186, 195, 197, 199, 226

Management 9, 15, 23, 53, 57, 78, 100, 112, 147, 157–158, 162, 165, 177, 196, 211
– wealth 53, 74, 94
Market participants 114, 149, 153, 238
Markets 16, 18, 68, 90, 98, 111, 118, 137, 142, 144, 151, 182, 192, 206
– capital 74, 138, 149, 151, 183, 198
– emerging 76
McConaghy 131
MDeC (Multimedia Development Corporation) 83
Media Rights 9, 153
Mega 23, 156
Merchants 14, 15 18, 34–36
Micropayments 153–155
– blockchain-enabled 154
Middle East (MEA) 24, 78, 98, 108, 151, 226
Migration 4, 112–113, 139, 214
Miners 122, 126, 183
Mobile 7, 12, 16, 18, 24, 34, 47–48, 76, 81, 111, 201, 203
Mobile subscriptions 58, 80
Models 58, 61–62, 71, 96, 136, 163, 170, 189, 200–202, 217
– hybrid 203
Modified 204, 212
Money 17–18, 77, 102, 121, 216, 224–225, 229–232
Money transfers 49, 55, 121, 150, 172, 203, 205, 207
M-PESA 24, 35, 123
MSC Malaysia 84–85
MSMEs 7, 89, 128, 152, 231
Multimedia Development Corporation (MDeC) 83–85
Muslim community 98
Muslims 3, 9, 70–71, 134, 211, 214, 241

Nasdaq 15, 54, 90, 126, 202
National Institute of Standards and Technology (NIST) 56
Neo-banking 52, 69
Neo-banks 52, 94
Network 25, 77, 90, 115, 121, 125, 129, 132, 142, 154, 175, 183, 187, 235–237
– connecting 132
Neural networks 62
New entrants 14, 17, 24–25, 34, 48, 78, 81, 88, 90, 93, 95

NIST (National Institute of Standards and Technology) 59
Nodes 2, 43, 120–121, 183, 189, 237
Noncash transactions 48
North America 4, 22–23
Number 4–5, 20, 22–23, 31, 58, 74, 110, 150, 169

Objects 58, 63, 180
Obsolete 154, 156, 198
OIC (Organization of Islamic Countries) 28
Online platforms 60
Opaqueness of blockchain platforms and standards 156
Open API 111
Organization of Islamic Countries (OIC) 32
Organizations 9, 51, 57, 91, 97, 108, 119, 126–127, 181–182, 193, 204, 221, 235–236
OTC market space 152

Pakistan 76–77, 99, 144, 198
Pakistan and fintech and blockchain 77
Pakistan Telecommunication Authority (PTA) 76
Parameters 137–138, 168, 237, 239
Participants 12, 16, 40, 93–94, 112, 114, 116, 143, 149, 153–154, 235, 237–238
Parties 29, 69, 94, 122–125, 136, 140, 148, 205, 212
Partners 157, 187, 193, 196, 200, 228, 240
Partnerships 78, 80, 89, 91, 102, 147, 193, 204–206
Path 71, 112, 196
Payment credentials 35
Payment infrastructure 33–34, 172
Payment instruments 35
Payment methods 32–36
Payment platforms 34, 90, 116, 122
Payment service providers (PSPs) 34
Payment transactions 91, 154, 156
Payments 15, 18, 23, 33–34, 48, 55, 89, 93, 122–123, 146, 150–151, 172, 182
– mobile 48
Payments industry 34–35, 48, 55, 150
Payments sector 22, 83
Payments systems 126, 172
PayPal 17–18, 34, 36, 48, 122
PBFT (Practical Byzantine Fault Tolerance) 184

Platforms 19, 24, 34, 43, 51, 83, 89, 97, 111, 156, 176–177, 183, 205
– blockchain-based 176
– mobile 112
– shared 127, 200–201
Population 4, 6, 51, 68–69, 76, 87, 89–90, 144, 231
Potential users 22
Practical Byzantine Fault Tolerance (PBFT) 183
Predictions 5, 61–62, 64, 170–171
Prices 17, 39, 120, 168, 212, 237–239
Processing 54, 61, 70, 113, 121, 129–131, 138–140, 158, 169, 174
Productivity 125, 134, 147, 161, 197–198
Products 4, 7, 11–12, 15, 47, 68, 88, 95, 113, 139, 178, 193, 205
– new 95, 139, 193
Programmers 128, 131, 197, 201, 229
Projects 31, 61, 85, 90, 104, 183, 211, 215–216
Property, intellectual 102, 153, 158
Providers, global blockchain payments solution 81
PSPs (payment service providers) 34
PTA (Pakistan Telecommunication Authority) 76
Public blockchain 123, 168, 184, 186
Public Investment Fund (PIF) 80
Purchase 8, 35–36, 111, 145, 152, 163
PwC 6, 31, 53, 203

Qatar 144, 225–227
Quality 20, 83, 102, 113–114, 146, 153, 166–167, 198–200
Quarter 22–23, 31, 50, 95, 108, 186

Reciprocity 118–119
Region 22–25, 36, 77–81, 87, 90, 99, 108, 123, 144, 176, 200, 203, 224, 226
Register 31, 60, 124, 131, 235
RegLab 93
Regtech 23–24, 75, 165, 194
Regulations 12, 20, 31–32, 53, 60, 94–95, 113–115, 161, 184–185, 195–196
– new 88, 91, 95, 114
Regulators 12, 18–19, 38, 67, 81, 95–96, 114, 126, 135, 146, 149, 185–186, 189, 193–196, 221
Regulatory authorities 4, 32, 41, 83, 87, 196
Regulatory sand-boxes 186, 193
Reinsurers 139, 146–147

Research 14, 51, 56–57, 59–61, 79, 98, 100, 157–158, 193, 197–199, 212–213, 227
Resources 8, 14, 56–57, 96, 115, 118, 128, 139–140, 194, 222, 227, 231, 237, 241
Respondents 6, 53, 59, 192, 202–203
Response of Islamic financial institutions 191
Retail 17, 21, 57, 138, 152, 181
Revenues 12, 154–156
Revolution, technological 71, 204
Rewards 29, 102, 196, 202, 213
Ripple 121, 142, 150–151
Ripple's blockchain banks 150
Risks 1, 16–17, 50, 94, 118, 140, 146, 162, 165, 167–169, 171–172, 174–176, 194, 202, 206, 215, 240
– oracle 168
– protocol governance 168
– reputational 57, 206
– scaling 169
– smart-contract 168
Robo-advisors 19, 59–60, 170, 198
Royalty payments 155
Rules 19, 32, 41, 67–68, 94, 161, 184–185, 190, 226, 239

Sales 7, 98, 143, 197, 238
SAMA (Saudi Arabian Monetary Agency) 81
Samsung pay 18
Sandbox 84, 90, 93, 186
Saudi Arabia 73, 80, 143–144, 234
Saudi Arabian Monetary Agency (SAMA) 80
Scalability 9, 61, 135, 142, 169, 184, 192
Scholars 39, 41, 70, 97, 134, 177, 199–200, 204, 214, 225
SEB 61
Sectors 13, 57, 80, 94, 98, 157, 162, 217, 231
– financial 8, 67, 93, 119, 200, 231
– private 200–201
– takaful 134
Securities 15, 17, 26, 32, 38, 41, 55, 61, 115, 125, 129, 137, 139–140, 166, 184–185, 215, 232, 234
Securities commission Malaysia 83, 152
Securities Investor Protection Corporation (SIPC) 60
Securities transactions, clearing and settlement of 125
Security token 37–38, 40
Segments 12, 20, 53, 67, 71, 91, 153

Sellers 123, 142, 149, 212
Services 6, 17, 24, 26, 31, 47–48, 50, 52, 56, 59, 68, 71, 76, 89, 97, 139, 157, 166, 186, 191, 193, 202–205, 222
– cloud computing 56
– consumer-ready blockchain 111
– customer 61, 164
– customer-centric 6, 11
– retail customer 57
Settlement 55, 110, 124–125, 134, 140, 148–151, 189
SFC (Singapore FinTech Consortium) 78
Shariah 9, 38, 41, 67, 69, 83, 134, 151, 177, 197, 199–200, 203, 206, 211, 240
Shariah compliance 97, 165, 177
Shariah-compliant 40, 68, 71, 78, 151–152, 200
Shariah-compliant financial products 68
Sharing 37, 58, 117, 127, 150–152, 189, 195, 233
Sharing economy 8, 25, 53, 117–118, 145
– new 19, 119
Sharing model 38, 69
Shariyah Review Bureau (SRB) 151
Singapore 19, 21, 23, 31, 90, 92, 163, 217, 230
Singapore FinTech Consortium (SFC) 78
SIPC (Securities Investor Protection Corporation) 61
Skills 24, 92, 100, 101, 103–104, 182, 193, 197, 199, 217
Smart contract applications 142
Smart contracts 54, 68, 124–125, 131, 134–139, 141–142, 145, 147, 170, 185, 217
Smart Contracts in Islamic Transactions 134
Smart Contracts on Blockchain 125
Smartphones 6, 25, 34, 36, 47, 63, 94
SMEs 50, 83, 139
Social networks 22, 182
Software 29, 48, 59, 61, 111, 120–122, 125, 134, 137–138, 157–158, 168–169, 182, 187, 196
Solutions 7, 12, 17, 21, 42, 48, 53, 61, 63, 83, 89–90, 102, 108, 111, 114, 134, 139–140, 145, 147, 149, 157, 165, 172, 175–176, 183–184, 186–187, 193, 196–198, 201–202, 222
Source 3, 17, 97, 118, 127, 174, 180, 205, 235
Southeast Asia 92, 151, 203
Space 21–22, 78, 83, 88, 111, 113, 153
Spending 12, 56–57, 171, 215, 221
SQL 129

SRB (Shariyah Review Bureau) 151
Standards 11, 83, 85, 101, 154, 156
Start-ups 11, 19–20, 24, 34, 54–55, 64, 67, 82–83, 91–92, 95, 103–104, 109, 110, 138, 157, 161, 185–186, 198, 201, 203–204, 206
State 32–33, 48, 118, 120, 129–133, 135, 137, 143, 199, 221, 231, 236
Stateless 129–130
Statista 21–22, 24, 48, 51–52
Stefik 193
Stellar 130, 141, 151
Storage 9, 39, 55–56, 128–129, 131–132, 154, 164, 174, 212–213
Students 7, 94, 197, 199, 215–216
Subsets 130, 149
Success 7, 38, 51–52, 61, 104, 109, 114, 132, 164, 185, 188, 191, 212, 232
Success rates 52
Sukuk 151–153
Supply chain 70, 139–142, 181, 213
Survey 6, 53, 59, 76, 156, 166, 192, 202–203
Swan 180
SWIFT 15, 122, 127, 131–132, 150, 229, 240
Systems 3, 12, 16–17, 28, 34, 42, 61, 111, 116, 125, 129–131, 146, 167, 171–172, 190, 222, 229, 240
– open 111, 168

Table 5, 13, 14, 25, 26–28, 33, 35, 38, 39, 50–52, 75, 82, 87, 155, 218
Tablets 58
TCP/IP 132
Technological Perspective 47, 54–57, 59, 61, 63
Technologies fintech companies 12
Technology 1–5, 7, 9, 14–18, 48, 55, 63, 71, 76, 82, 95, 114, 119, 120, 134, 157, 165, 167, 171, 176–177
– emerging 183–184
– new 4, 93, 97, 114, 185, 206
– revolutionary 55
Technology companies 14, 180, 193
Test 67, 81, 83, 88, 90, 93, 186, 193, 195, 201–202
Third parties 131, 139, 146, 195, 205
Threat 53, 115, 148, 156, 168, 175
Token storage 129

Tokens 19, 25–26, 29, 32, 37, 39, 40–42, 129, 150, 168–169, 229
– digital 86, 148
Total addressable market (TAM) 159
Traction 21, 38, 143–144, 205
Trade 32, 69, 99, 113, 116, 125–126, 134, 138–142, 153, 187, 212, 227–228, 232, 234, 241
– international 123, 228
Trade cryptocurrencies 32
Trade finance 55, 138–142, 170, 181
– blockchain-based 140, 142
Trade transactions 139, 142, 148
Trademark Protection 9, 153
Traders 32, 116, 134, 239
Trading 12, 16–18, 32, 54, 64, 113, 125, 137, 139, 148, 151, 184, 188, 212, 228, 234–235, 240
– open account 139–140
Trading platform 148
Trading securities 55, 115, 137
Transaction confidentiality, maintaining 152–153
Transaction costs 82, 117–118, 229
Transaction data 183
Transaction value 21–22, 24, 48, 49, 51
Transactions 33, 43, 47, 97, 113, 120, 122, 136, 154, 156, 168, 172, 177, 183, 187, 212, 220, 229, 235–238, 240
Transfers 12, 15, 54, 121, 137, 151, 171–172, 203, 205
Transformation 3–6, 20, 69, 80, 93, 111, 145, 161, 165, 212, 226
Transnational 9, 181–181
Transnational organizations 181–182
Transparency 59, 70, 111, 113, 134, 137, 140–141, 143, 152, 170, 181, 192, 207, 211, 219, 222
Trust 1–3, 18, 94, 116–120, 122, 137, 146, 154, 165, 169, 182, 188, 193, 207, 211, 222, 230, 232
– extending 118
public 1, 211
Turkey 90–92, 227, 231
Turkish Fintech ecosystem 91
Turkish government 92
Types 12, 15, 25–26, 32, 35, 39, 48, 101, 126, 136–137, 144, 174, 198, 214, 230, 236

UAE 24, 72, 94, 144, 199
UK 21, 32, 72, 95–96, 186, 199
United States 1, 16–17, 22–23, 32, 36, 48, 91, 95, 108, 228
University 43, 76–77, 198, 216
Usage 13, 36, 40–41, 70, 111–112, 116, 152, 155, 181, 188
Users 22, 24, 32, 54, 81, 94, 116–117, 164, 168, 194, 222, 235–236
UX 116

Value 3–5, 22, 26, 37, 39, 48–49, 91, 117, 121, 124, 129, 132, 148, 163, 185, 192, 214, 221–222, 230, 234, 237
Value blockchain transactions, high 189
Value chain 7, 93, 121, 154, 187
VC-backed fintech companies in Asia 23

Vendors 51, 56, 111–112, 115–116, 206
Verification 53, 114, 126–127, 146–147, 162, 221–222
Visibility, real-time 140–141

Wahed Invest 78, 200
Wallets 35, 77, 171
Workflow 137, 140, 149
World 6, 8, 16, 28, 58, 63, 75, 91, 95, 97–99, 112, 128, 142, 168, 184, 232
World Bank 9, 26, 28, 75
World Trade Organization (WTO) 181
Worldpay 37
Worldwide big data technology and services forecast 65
WTO (World Trade Organization) 181
www.statista.com 46, 66

www.ingramcontent.com/pod-product-compliance
Lightning Source LLC
Chambersburg PA
CBHW081825230426
43668CB00017B/2380